ROUTLEDGE LIBRARY EDITIONS:
THE LABOUR MOVEMENT

Volume 19

EMPLOYERS AND LABOUR IN
THE ENGLISH TEXTILE
INDUSTRIES, 1850–1939

EMPLOYERS AND LABOUR IN THE ENGLISH TEXTILE INDUSTRIES, 1850–1939

Edited by
J. A. JOWITT AND A. J. MCIVOR

LONDON AND NEW YORK

First published in 1988 by Routledge

This edition first published in 2019
by Routledge
2 Park Square, Milton Park, Abingdon, Oxon OX14 4RN

and by Routledge
711 Third Avenue, New York, NY 10017

Routledge is an imprint of the Taylor & Francis Group, an informa business

© 1988 J. A. Jowitt and A. J. McIvor

All rights reserved. No part of this book may be reprinted or reproduced or utilised in any form or by any electronic, mechanical, or other means, now known or hereafter invented, including photocopying and recording, or in any information storage or retrieval system, without permission in writing from the publishers.

Trademark notice: Product or corporate names may be trademarks or registered trademarks, and are used only for identification and explanation without intent to infringe.

British Library Cataloguing in Publication Data
A catalogue record for this book is available from the British Library

ISBN: 978-1-138-32435-0 (Set)
ISBN: 978-0-429-43443-3 (Set) (ebk)
ISBN: 978-1-138-32838-9 (Volume 19) (hbk)
ISBN: 978-1-138-32840-2 (Volume 19) (pbk)
ISBN: 978-0-429-44868-3 (Volume 19) (ebk)

Publisher's Note
The publisher has gone to great lengths to ensure the quality of this reprint but points out that some imperfections in the original copies may be apparent.

Disclaimer
The publisher has made every effort to trace copyright holders and would welcome correspondence from those they have been unable to trace.

Employers and Labour in the English Textile Industries, 1850-1939

Edited by
J.A. JOWITT and A.J. McIVOR

ROUTLEDGE
London and New York

First published in 1988 by
Routledge
a division of Routledge, Chapman and Hall
11 New Fetter Lane, London EC4P 4EE

Published in the USA by
Routledge
a division of Routledge, Chapman and Hall, Inc.
29 West 35th Street, New York NY 10001

© 1988 J.A. Jowitt and A.J. McIvor

Printed and bound in Great Britain by
Biddles Ltd, Guildford and King's Lynn

All rights reserved. No part of this book may be reprinted or reproduced or utilized in any form or by any electronic, mechanical, or other means, now known or hereafter invented, including photocopying and recording, or in any information storage or retrieval system, without permission in writing from the publishers.

British Library Cataloguing in Publication Data

Employers and labour in the English
  textile industries 1850–1939.
  1. England. Textile industries.
  Industrial relations, 1850–1939
  I. Jowitt, J.A. II. McIvor, Arthur
  331.0477'0942
  ISBN 0-415-00354-7

Library of Congress Cataloging-in-Publication Data

ISBN 0-415-00354-7

DEDICATED TO THE MEMORY OF
JILL NORRIS AND STEVE JONES

CONTENTS

List of Tables   iii
Acknowledgements   v
Introduction   vii

Section I. Employers and Employers' Organisations

1. COTTON EMPLOYERS' ORGANISATIONS AND LABOUR RELATIONS, 1890-1939   1
   Arthur McIvor

2. PRAGMATISM vs. PRINCIPLE: COTTON EMPLOYERS AND THE ORIGINS OF AN INDUSTRIAL RELATIONS SYSTEM   27
   Andrew Bullen

3. PROTECTING THE INTERESTS OF THE TRADE: WOOL TEXTILE EMPLOYERS' ORGANISATIONS IN THE 1920s   44
   Irene Magrath

4. COTTON EMPLOYERS AND INDUSTRIAL WELFARE BETWEEN THE WARS   64
   Steve Jones

Section II. Trade Unions and Labour

5. THE RETARDATION OF TRADE UNIONISM IN THE YORKSHIRE WORSTED TEXTILE INDUSTRY   84
   Tony Jowitt

Contents

6. LANCASHIRE COTTON TRADE UNIONISM   107
   IN THE INTER-WAR YEARS
   Alan Fowler

7. WORK, WAGES AND INDUSTRIAL RELATIONS   127
   IN COTTON FINISHING, 1880-1914
   Arthur McIvor

Section III. **Women in Textiles**

8. SKILL AND THE SEXUAL DIVISION OF   153
   LABOUR IN THE WEST RIDING TEXTILE
   INDUSTRY, 1850-1914
   Deirdre Busfield

9. WOMEN AND INDUSTRIAL MILITANCY: THE   171
   1875 HEAVY WOOLLEN DISPUTE
   Maria Bottomley

10. "WELL FITTED FOR FEMALES." WOMEN   187
    IN THE MACCLESFIELD SILK INDUSTRY
    Jill Norris

11. WOMEN AND WORK IN THE LANCASHIRE   203
    COTTON INDUSTRY, 1890-1939
    Michael Savage

Select Bibliography   224
Notes on Contributors   228
Index   230

TABLES

1.1	N. and N.E. Lancashire Cotton Spinners' and Manufacturers' Association: Proportion of Machine Capacity (loomage) Organised, 1890-1939	3
1.2	Federation of Master Cotton Spinners' Associations: Proportion of Lancashire Machine Capacity (spindleage) Organised, 1892-1939	5
1.3	Lancashire Master Cotton Spinners' Associations: Size of Firms in Membership, 1899-1939	8
1.4	Local Master Cotton Spinners' Associations: Differences in Representation, 1914-1935	16
3.1	Employers' Organisations in the Wool Industry, 1931	49
3.2	Woollens and Worsteds - World Exports, 1920s	56
5.1	Percentage Composition of the Textile Labour Force in Bradford in 1911	87
5.2	The Formation of Worsted Trade Unions in the Nineteenth Century	88
5.3	Trade Unions Formed in the Yorkshire Wool Textile Industry with the Dates of Formation and Membership in 1910	88
5.4	Composition of the Labour Force at Whetley Mills, Bradford, January 1873	92
5.5	Exports of Worsted Stuffs, Yarns, Tops and Alpaca and Mohair Yarns, 1866-1905	95
6.1	Trade Union Membership in the Cotton Industry, 1900-1938	110
6.2	The Cotton Industry in the Inter-War Years	111
6.3	Cotton Trade Union Membership in Blackburn, Bolton, Nelson and Oldham, 1900-1937	117

Tables

7.1	Numbers Employed (Cotton Calico Printers, Dyers and Bleachers), 1881 and 1891	129
7.2	Numbers Employed in Textile Finishing in Lancashire, 1901 and 1911	130
7.3	Trade Unions Recruiting Cotton Finishers, 1890s	137
7.4	The Textile Workforce by Gender, 1891	143
7.5	Female Membership of Trade Unions in Textiles, 1899 and 1913	144
10.1	Occupations in Macclesfield, 1921	190
10.2	Silk and Clothing Workers in Macclesfield, 1921	192
11.1	Spinning and Weaving Employment in Lancashire, 1901	207
11.2	Age Profile of Female Cotton Workers, 1911	209
11.3	Union Density in Cotton Weaving Towns, 1891	212
11.4	Wage Changes in Cotton Weaving, 1886-1906	214
11.5	Male and Female Unemployment in Lancashire Cotton, 1931	217

ACKNOWLEDGEMENTS

This book could not have been produced without the assistance of a large number of individuals and institutions. A collection of essays is, in essence, a product of teamwork and our first and most significant debt is to the individual contributors. As editors, we have benefited greatly from conversations and discussions with contributors about the nature of industrial relations in textiles and must sincerely thank them for consistently responding with good humour and rapidity to our requests for modifications and revisions. Editing a collection of essays imposes particular problems, but at the same time we are indebted to all those concerned for helping to make it an interesting and enjoyable experience.

For financial and secretarial help and support we would like to record our thanks to the Department of Adult and Continuing Education of the University of Leeds and the Department of History of the University of Strathclyde. Three chapters in this collection (Chapters 1, 2 and 7) are based on research funded by the Economic and Social Research Council (E.S.R.C.) reference number F00232204. For assistance in the form of research grants linked with other chapters, thanks are due to the British Academy and the Pasold Research Fund.

Without the numerous collections of textile documents to be found in libraries, public record offices, trade union, employers' association and private archives throughout the north of England this book could not have been produced. All the contributors would like to express a very real debt to the custodians of those records for allowing access and for their help, dedication and efficiency in locating pertinent material and making it available for consultation. We would also like to thank Drummond Group PLC for permission to reproduce on the front cover one of their collection of mill photographs.

Special thanks are due to Irene Scouller who typed the manuscript, transformed rough drafts into superb copy, and solved a whole range of tricky presentation problems, thus making our job

Acknowledgements

all the easier. Few authors or editors can have been blessed with such a fast, accurate and perceptive typist. Particular thanks also to Richard Taylor and Jill Liddington who read and commented on all or part of the manuscript and to John Butt, Hamish Fraser, Jim Treble and Eleanor Gordon for comments, encouragement and support. We would also like to openly acknowledge our huge debt to the many teachers, colleagues and students who have, over the years, moulded and stimulated our interest in the social history of the textile industry.

Inevitably, a considerable burden has fallen on our families whilst we have been preoccupied with this volume and we would like to gratefully acknowledge the active encouragement, criticism and co-operation of Nancy Jowitt and Brenda McIvor and the forbearance of our children, Kieran and Tom McIvor, Paul and Laura Jowitt.

Finally, we would like to dedicate this book to two of the contributors, JILL NORRIS and STEVE JONES, both of whom were tragically killed in separate accidents quite recently. Their chapters reflect their outstanding work in the areas of industrial relations, textile, labour and feminist history. Both are deeply and sadly missed and we hope that this book, in a very small way, will act as a memorial to Jill and Steve.

INTRODUCTION

Tony Jowitt and Arthur McIvor

This contribution to the social history of the textile industry has its origins in a textile history conference organised at Bradford by the Department of Adult and Continuing Education of Leeds University in the Autumn of 1984. Many of the contributors to this collection gave papers at the conference, whilst at a later date, others were asked to contribute to the collection in order to broaden its content. The book examines aspects of labour and industrial relations history in the textiles sector of Northern England before World War Two, with contributions on wool, worsted, silk, cotton spinning, weaving and finishing. Our main aim has been to supplement existing literature by providing a collection of essays which incorporates some of the recent research on particularly neglected areas, most notably (though not solely) on women and employers in the industry. The collection also reflects a desire to synthesise the approaches (which have often been assumed to be mutually conflicting) of labour historians, researchers interested in employers' and labour management strategies, and the emerging women's studies specialists. Our underlying rationale is that industrial relations can only be understood if viewed within a much wider framework which encapsulates, as far as possible, the experience of all involved groups.

Since the 1960s there has been a plethora of published work in the fields of industrial relations and labour history. Through this expansion in research activity it has become increasingly evident that the pattern of working class experience and industrial relations is extremely complex and diversified. The character and flavour of labour relations was determined to a greater or lesser extent by differences between industries, regions, product specialisms, skills, occupations, gender, communities, local labour markets and particular product market trends, amongst other things. This was most noticeably so in the pre-1914 period, as E.H. Hunt in British Labour History, 1815-1914, (London, 1981) and C.J. Wrigley in A History of British Industrial Relations, 1870-1914, Brighton, 1982) have recently

Introduction

affirmed. In consequence, there is a pressing need to re-examine current generalisations, complement text-book syntheses and reconstruct labour and industrial relations history through a multiplication of in-depth industry case studies. This volume is an attempt to go some way along this route.

The landscape of the Yorkshire and Lancashire mill districts has been fundamentally transformed during the last thirty years. That most distinctive feature of the Victorian textile sky-line, the mill chimney, has now almost completely disappeared, and with it has declined an industry which, for more than a century, dominated those towns and villages and the lives of their inhabitants. The textile districts of Yorkshire and Lancashire were the cradle of the industrial revolution - the laboratory where a new urban-industrial society was brought into being. Towns like Bradford and Oldham, Blackburn and Halifax, were transformed in little more than a generation from overgrown villages and small market towns into large urban industrial centres. Between 1800 and 1850 Bradford grew from a small town of 13,000 inhabitants into the seventh largest town in the United Kingdom with a population of more than 100,000. That colossal growth, which was paralleled in many other places across the northern textile districts, and which so astonished and enthralled contemporary commentators, was built on a massive and sustained industrial growth. In Bradford in 1800 there was one small spinning mill. By 1850 there were 129 mills in the district. (1) On the other side of the Pennines, Oldham experienced a similar growth for it expanded from a community of some 10,000 inhabitants with 12 mills in 1794 to a large industrial town of around 80,000 by 1866, with more than 120 cotton spinning mills alone. (2)

It was here that the new capitalist order of society came into active operation. First in the domestic system and then in mechanised factory production the early entrepreneurs felt their way towards industrial organisation and production, and in doing so created a distinctive pattern of life. The texture of mill life was deeply embedded in these communities. From the small single mill factory village to the mill districts of the large towns and cities, the mills physically dominated the streets of domestic housing that usually surrounded them, the mill hooter providing the time discipline. The characteristics of employment, with large proportions of female and adolescent workers, produced a distinctive effect on family life, so that from an early age youngsters were socialised into the textile pattern of life.

By 1850 the cotton, woollen, worsted and silk industries were already mature or were approaching maturity. In the cotton and the worsted industries a completely mechanised factory base was either present or was to be so within the next decade. Only in woollen cloth production did mechanisation lag slightly behind. In the middle of the nineteenth century over half a million workers were employed in the cotton, wool and worsted textiles sector in Britain, around 330,000 in cotton and 154,000 in wool and worsted factories. (3) Around 75 per cent of these workers

Introduction

were located in the north of England. The silk industry was also at its ascendancy in the mid-nineteenth century, employing over 100,000. This figure dwindled to 32,200 in 1907 (around 70 per cent of which was female) largely due to foreign competition which forced rapid contraction of this sector and geographical concentration around the Macclesfield area. (4)

In the decade 1910-20 the English cotton, woollen and worsted industries reached their historic peak in terms of output, numbers employed and machine capacity. The annual consumption of raw cotton and wool multiplied almost four times between 1850 and 1912-13, and over the same period production of woven cotton piece goods multiplied sixfold, 80 per cent being exported. Indeed, almost a third of the income generated by all U.K. exports derived from the textile sector on the eve of the First World War. The 1907 Census of Production reported a total of 1.25 million workers in the British textile industry - 572,000 in cotton and 264,000 in wool and worsted. Numbers employed in textiles continued to rise to a peak of around 1.5 million in 1914, the cotton sector alone accounting for around 650,000 in more than 2,000 mills. (5)

During this mature phase the North England textile industry was characterised by diversity and heterogeneity in structure and location. Whilst there was a trend towards increased scale in company size with the limited liability movement from the 1860s (especially in south-east Lancashire), private, family owned firms remained important, in some areas pre-eminent, up to the First World War. There were quite marked geographical divisions, for the textile industry was characterised by spatial fragmentation. Cotton was concentrated within Lancashire; wool and worsted in the West Riding of Yorkshire and silk in Cheshire, increasingly in the Macclesfield district. There was also a tendency towards process and product specialisation within these districts. In worsteds and cotton the former development was indicated by the combined process firm being superseded, albeit slowly and fitfully, by the specialised, single process, horizontally organised company. Whilst the American textile industry was experiencing a transition towards an oligopolistic situation, with the integration of marketing and manufacturing and the development of large vertically integrated mills, the British textile industry, with some notable exceptions, remained fragmented, specialised and relatively small in plant scale. Only in the woollen sector did the vertically integrated mill remain the norm, however, although woollen mills remained vertically integrated they also remained very small in plant size, certainly much smaller than was the norm in the worsted and cotton sectors.

Product specialisation was never complete and there were often overlaps and clashes of interest. Yet within Lancashire, cotton spinning was concentrated in the south-east of the county, while weaving was largely restricted to the north and north-east. Bolton and Manchester were the centres for fine spun yarns (used for spool cotton, lace, etc.) using mainly Egyptian raw cotton. Oldham and south-east Lancashire firms mostly spun medium and

Introduction

coarse quality yarns from American cotton for weaving. Preston and Chorley wove light, medium and heavyweight fancy, high quality goods, largely for home consumption. The Blackburn district was the centre for dhooties and shirtings, made largely for export to India, whilst Colne and Nelson specialised in coloured goods.

Product specialisation was also well developed in the West Riding. There was a basic division between the woollen and worsted areas, the latter based on the centres of Bradford, Halifax and Keighley and the area to the north west of these urban centres. The woollen trade was centred on Huddersfield, the Heavy Woollen district around Cleckheaton, Heckmondwike, Dewsbury, Batley, Ossett and Morley, and stretched as far as Leeds. In addition to this basic division there was a complex pattern of product specialisation which meant that Bradford was the centre of the cheap mass production of worsted cloth, of mohair and alpaca spinning, of specialised woolcombing and the merchanting centre. Dewsbury and Batley were the centres of the shoddy and mungo trades, with their own specialised labour force, producing cheap woollens, in items like blankets. Huddersfield was the centre of the better quality woollen production and latterly of fine worsteds. The Colne Valley, in centres like Milnsbridge, Slaithwaite and Marsden, produced cheap woollen cloth. Halifax, as well as being a worsted centre, specialised in the production of carpets, whilst further up the Calder Valley there was some linkage with the Lancashire cotton industry and also the production of low quality fustians. Finally, Keighley produced worsted yarns and was an important textile machine making centre. (6)

As the textile industry was the pacesetter in the process of industrialisation, so in the twentieth century it has also been in the forefront of the process of de-industrialisation. Since the First World War the industry has gone from a position where it was one of the leading sectors in the British economy to one of increasing marginality in terms of overall British industrial production. The drop in world demand for cloth and the generally depressed trading conditions of the inter-war years hit textiles particularly hard. Cotton was more severely affected than wool because of its much heavier export orientation. In wool and worsted, the production of tops and yarn held up relatively well, though the production of tissues declined by almost 25 per cent between 1912 and 1939 and exports of tissues by nearly half. (7) Even during the pre-1914 period, whilst there was an expansion in absolute terms, Britain's proportion of the world's cotton output was declining. (8) Absolute decline for cotton was the scenario of the 1920s and 1930s. Output levels had declined by 1938-9 to under 40 per cent of 1913 figures; machine capacity was reduced by scrapping 38 per cent of installed spindleage and 43 per cent of looms; cotton cloth exports in 1938 stood at between a quarter and a fifth of 1913 levels. (9) The human dimension of this contraction included multiplying bankruptcies, endemic unemployment and under-employment, poor earnings, deprivation and

Introduction

poverty, an ageing workforce, increased workloads, and an undermining of workers' bargaining power, customary work patterns, rhythms and relationships. Official unemployment figures at the worst phase of the recession, 1930-2, topped 35 per cent for wool and 45 per cent for cotton. (10) Total employment in the British textile industry declined by almost half a million between 1913 and 1939. In 1938, the wool and worsted industry employed 216,000 workers and cotton provided jobs for 393,000. (11)

Moreover, after the brief post World War Two 'boom' period for textiles, retrenchment and contraction again set in from the early 1950s. As a result, the role of the industry within the local and regional economy of northern England has become increasingly marginal. Only the barest rump of an industry remains. In the mid-1980s, for example, less than 40,000 workers found employment in the 203 remaining cotton spinning, doubling and weaving mills. (12) Production of cotton cloth just topped 500 million linear metres, around a mere fifteenth of output levels 70 years earlier. Wool textile production held up somewhat better. In Huddersfield 30 per cent of the labour force was still employed in the textile sector in 1965, and in Bradford 34 per cent was similarly employed in 1961. However, since that time there has been a massive contraction in terms of plant, machinery and employment. Bradford, in the nineteenth century known throughout the textile world as 'worstedopolis', only employed some 27,461 textile workers in 1978, 14.7 per cent of the labour force. (13) Thus the textiles sector provides a classic example of a declining industry in a post-industrial society.

Over the last fifteen years there has been a resurgence of interest in the textile industries and the communities that supported them. The interest in and value of L.S. Lowry's paintings has increased almost proportionately as the mills and the streets that he painted have been demolished. There has been a growth in textile and industrial museums and a remarkable interest in recording the oral testimony of textile workers. This interest has also been reflected in the field of historical scholarship where textile production has provided the basis for a number of stimulating studies. Both in Britain and the U.S.A. historians have utilised different aspects of the historical study of the textile industry to pioneer a number of new approaches to understanding the past. Alan Dawley has said of this phenomenon: "everywhere dead mill towns are being reborn in late twentieth century minds". (14)

In the U.S.A. this has been seen most clearly in a number of works, including Anthony Wallace's, Rockdale: The Growth of an American Village in the Early Industrial Revolution, (New York, 1978) which utilised the approach and techniques of anthropology to delineate the formation and the workings of an early mill community; Tamara Hareven's Family Time and Industrial Time, (Cambridge, 1982) which incorporated the developments made in the field of demographic and family history, and allied this with an extensive oral history project to analyse the world of work and

Introduction

home of the factory workers of the giant Amoskeag Mills in Manchester, New Hampshire; John Cumbler in Working Class Community in Industrial America: Work, Leisure and Struggle in Two Industrial Cities, 1880-1930, (Westport, 1979) used techniques first developed in community studies to recreate in detail the structures of life in the cotton manufacturing city of Fall River. More recently Philip Scranton in Proprietary Capitalism: The Textile Manufacture at Philadelphia, (Cambridge, 1984) has utilised the techniques developed by social historians to study an elite group - the Philadelphia textile capitalists - who developed a pattern of production which contrasted sharply with the classic corporate pattern of the New England system in Lawrence and Lowell and was much closer to English practice.

In Britain there has been a corresponding interest amongst historians reflected in the recent publication of two scholarly general surveys of the cotton and woollen and worsted industries, in D.A. Farnie's, The English Cotton Industry and the World Market 1815-1896, (Oxford, 1979) and D.T. Jenkins and K.G. Ponting, The British Wool Textile Industry 1770-1914, (London, 1982). In addition to these general surveys which have incorporated the fruits of recent research there has been a number of exciting and stimulating studies. Amongst these are Pat Hudson's 'Proto-industrialisation: the case of the West Riding' in History Workshop, 12, 1981, where she attempted to apply the conceptual techniques associated with proto-industrialisation to the domestic woollen industry of the West Riding. A Marxist historian, John Foster in Class Struggle and the Industrial Revolution, (London, 1974) has examined the onset of industrial society on the cotton town of Oldham, the development of a class conscious proletariat which opposed the new capitalist structure, but which in turn was successfully accommodated within the system, largely through the breakdown of class solidarity linked with the development of a labour aristocracy. Patrick Joyce in his stimulating and pioneering book, Work, Society and Politics: The Culture of the Factory in Later Victorian England, (London, 1980) has analysed the success of the factory communities in adopting modern factory production and a factory proletariat without accompanying radical or revolutionary developments. In the northern textile districts, employers were strikingly successful in imposing hegemony, largely through paternalistic modes, which, "entered into work people's lives to a degree that made their acceptance of the social regime of capitalist industry a matter of inward emotion as of outward calculation". (15) To be sure, Joyce's work has been the subject of much contentious debate amongst historians, with reservations in particular being voiced over his denial of the importance of a labour aristocracy in the factory communities and his understatement of raw industrial conflict, which occasionally, as in Lancashire in 1878, assumed extremely violent forms. (16) Two other recently published works, concentrating on the relationship between society and politics in the textile mill communities, merit attention. A. Howe's, The Cotton Masters, 1830-

Introduction

60, (Oxford, 1984), provides a detailed examination of the sociopolitical role of this elite group within the middle class of Victorian Lancashire, whilst in contrast, J. Liddington and J. Norris in One Hand Tied Behind Us, (London, 1978), give a fascinating account of the contribution of Lancashire women to the suffrage movement.

Work on the Scottish textile industry has tended to focus on the pre-eminence of cotton within the early nineteenth century Scottish economy. The early collective organisation and militancy of the pivotal cotton mule spinners and the handloom weavers has attracted attention in the work of W. Hamish Fraser and N. Murray, whilst J. Butt and others have analysed the history of the utopian model mill community established by Robert Owen at New Lanark. (17) The only other major area of research into the social history of Scottish textiles has been into the Dundee jute industry, most notably by W. Walker, in Juteopolis, (Edinburgh, 1979) and, more recently, by Eleanor Gordon. Gordon has investigated the experience of women in jute and their role in collective organisation and militant action prior to World War One, arguing persuasively that the myth of female acquiescence should be rejected. (18)

Trade union and labour relations history in textiles has also been the focus of a number of recently published works, including H.I. Dutton and J.E. King, Ten Per Cent and No Surrender, (Cambridge, 1981), J.L. White, The Limits of Trade Union Militancy, (Westport, 1978) and the recent histories of the Amalgamated Weavers' Association, the Nelson Weavers, the Cotton Spinners and the Cardroom Amalgamation. (19) This research has gone some way to revise hypotheses and illuminate some of the limitations of the pioneering history of the cotton unions, now over twenty-five years old, by H.A. Turner, Trade Union Growth, Structure and Policy: A Comparative History of the Cotton Unions, (London, 1962).

All of these developments have made the field of textile history an exciting and stimulating area of research. However, there remain obvious and quite serious gaps in the literature, with the inter-war years in particular being thinly researched. Moreover, a number of topics remain grossly neglected including the experience of women, the role of employers and their organisations in textiles, labour management and supervision, the work process, and trade unionism outside the cotton sector.

Many people can still recite the litany of inventors and entrepreneurs who transformed the textile industry in the late eighteenth century and early nineteenth century - Hargreaves, Arkwright, Crompton, Roberts, Lister, Noble. However, employers as a subject of study have been curiously neglected in British historical scholarship. (20) Recently there has been increased interest in this field, partially motivated by the continuing debate about the role of the entrepreneur in adapting to changing economic conditions towards the end of the nineteenth century and his role in regenerating British industrial performance. (21) Nevertheless, the policies which employers have used to control

Introduction

and manage labour have attracted little attention. This is the theme of the first section of our book. In Chapter 1 Arthur McIvor presents a survey of employers' organisations in cotton textiles taking the analysis beyond Joyce to focus on the evolution of institutionalised, bureaucratic, collectively initiated forms of labour management up to the 1930s. The chapter outlines the variables encouraging collective organisation amongst employers, discusses the labour relations strategies of employers' associations, and analyses the role they played in the maturation of an industrial relations system before 1914. It goes on to assess the employers' offensive in the inter-war years when they attempted to re-impose managerial prerogatives and slash production costs, which ultimately came to undermine completely the formal collective bargaining system in cotton.

In Chapter 2 Andrew Bullen analyses the genesis of employers' collective organisations in the cotton weaving sector in the 1850s and the relationship between trade unionism and employers' associations. Bullen argues that it is necessary to recognise the varied responses of employers to trade unionism and relate employers' labour relations strategies in this period to product market specialisms and to local labour market characteristics. Irene Magrath investigates in Chapter 3 the fortunes of the wool textile employers' organisations in the difficult trading conditions of the 1920s. The chapter focuses on the contradiction between apparent organisational and structural unity amongst wool employers and the reality of sectional interests and severe fragmentation in labour relations policy. The consequence of the adverse market conditions of the 1920s was a collapse of consensus and cohesion amongst employers who found it increasingly hard to forge uniform strategies to deal with widely disparate trading experiences.

During the nineteenth century, and in particular during the mid-Victorian period, textile employers developed a paternalistic ethic in order to integrate or incorporate the new factory labour force. Throughout the northern textile districts a prime example of this process was the creation of model industrial villages, most notably those of Titus Salt at Saltaire, Edward Akroyd and the Crossley family in Halifax, Hugh Mason in Ashton-under-Lyne and the Gregs at Styal, Cheshire. Many manufacturers, as Patrick Joyce has so eloquently described, were attempting to ensure the support and loyalty of their workforces through the introduction of features such as works trips, the patronage of adult education, and the development of works cricket teams and brass bands. Steve Jones in Chapter 4 examines the continuation of employer welfarism in the form of support for leisure and recreational facilities in the inter-war period, showing that it still constituted an important element in employers' labour management policies, particularly in so far as industrial welfare created a more efficient, better controlled and loyal workforce.

The second overall theme of the book is that of labour, in particular how textile workers developed forms of industrial

Introduction

organisation and how this trade unionism operated. Standing at the heart of this section is the problem of why Lancashire cotton workers were highly organised and militant, whilst woollen and worsted workers remained pitifully weak and relatively unorganised until the First World War; why formalised collective bargaining was the norm in Lancashire by the end of the nineteenth century and yet was only introduced into the woollen and worsted industries of the West Riding by the actions of the state during the First World War. In Chapter 5, Tony Jowitt examines the reasons for the retardation of trade unionism in the worsted industry of the West Riding, drawing attention to a number of interrelated factors, which include the role of women workers as scapegoats, the high numbers of adolescent workers, the sectionalism of the trade, the disunity of the worsted employers and the problems that international competition and changed trading conditions in the last quarter of the nineteenth century imposed on the industry. Alan Fowler examines Lancashire cotton trade unionism in the inter-war period in Chapter 6, challenging conventional interpretations of the docility of British labour after the General Strike in 1926, looking at the activities of the spinners, the cardroom operatives and the weavers, and their militant reactions to the problems that beset the industry during the period. In Chapter 7, Arthur McIvor explores the nature of work, the emergence of trade unionism and industrial relations in a neglected sector, cotton finishing, over 1880-1914. It is argued that there was a marked heterogeneity in the experience of the elite craft artisans, the overworked and underpaid bleachers and dyers and the degraded, undervalued minority of female finishing workers. This was the result not only of traditional differences in skill, labour market scarcity, status and earnings, but also the consequence of stark divergencies in employer labour management strategies and attitudes, and the decentralised and relatively poorly developed formal industrial relations system in the industry before World War One.

Up until very recently and the introduction of Asian labour, the textile industry employed a larger proportion of women than men. Our final section examines different aspects of the nature of female employment and the dimensions of patriarchal dominance before World War Two. Together, these chapters clearly indicate that work was important to women and that it is a gross oversimplification to typecast female workers as unskilled, apathetic and quiescent in the workplace and in their relationships with management and employers. In Chapter 8, Deirdre Busfield outlines the process whereby patriarchal authority was reproduced in the workplace in the Yorkshire textile industry before 1914. Women workers were disadvantaged by being refused trade union membership and, in most cases, being denied access to occupations involving a high degree of genuine skill. Nevertheless, many female tasks were, in fact, intrinsically as skilled as many male occupations, however, male jobs were invariably 'labelled' as skilled, and recognised and remunerated as such, whilst equivalent

Introduction

female occupations were downgraded and poorly paid. This was a process, Busfield argues, in which both trade unions and employers in the West Riding colluded.

Maria Bottomley, in Chapter 9, has analysed the role of women workers during the 1875 dispute in the heavy woollen district of Dewsbury and Batley. She challenges the myth of female acquiescence in industrial relations by showing how the strike was initiated and organised by women workers, and how the conflict led to the formation of a trade union dominated by women. Interestingly, Bottomley goes on to note how social pressures and patriarchal attitudes and values in the immediate post-strike period worked to marginalise women from their union, which gradually became controlled by male weavers and which ultimately lost its separate identity in a merger in 1883.

In Chapter 10, the late Jill Norris assesses the work experience of women in the Macclesfield silk industry and contrasts the popular image of cleanliness, gentility and elevated status associated with silk manufacture, with the harsh reality of female workers' lives. Most women were grossly overworked through having to bear the double burden of paid work and unpaid labour in the home. Moreover, work for women in silk was poorly paid and usually monotonous, and female skills undervalued, a development which Norris terms 'social destruction of skill' in juxtaposition to H.A. Turner's hypothesis of 'social construction' of skills, achieved most notably by the male cotton spinners.

Finally, in Chapter 11, Michael Savage has analysed the diverse and changing experience of women workers in the cotton industry between 1890 and 1939, drawing out comparisons between cardroom workers and weavers, and arguing that crucial differences existed in women's work, role and political consciousness between regions and towns, depending partly on product specialism, local labour market characteristics and modes of skill transmission. Fundamentally, however, women remained in a subordinate position in the cotton workforce before 1914. Savage identifies two parallel developments after World War One. Firstly, state intervention in recruitment via the labour exchanges eroded the dominant role of the overlooker and this provided women with more independence and autonomy in the workplace, which in turn fuelled worker solidarity and industrial action. On the other hand, however, women workers continued to face discrimination on a number of counts during the slump; finding it difficult to break the male monopoly of union leadership and executive committee membership; finding work rationalisation schemes like the more looms system directed primarily against married women's employment, and experiencing higher levels of unemployment compared to male cotton textile workers.

Inevitably with such a collection of essays there are gaps, and deficiencies and those that immediately spring to mind (there are undoubtedly many others) ought to be made explicit. Our book focuses on the textile sector in the North of England and the reader will find nothing in it (except perhaps a passing

Introduction

reference) on textile manufacture in other regions of Britain, nor anything of substance on most of the smaller sections of the trade, including jute, lace, hosiery, linen or artificial fibre manufacture (rayon). The constraints of existing known research, combined with a conscious desire to avoid simply repeating work published elsewhere, and our own limitations and interests determine the overall coverage of the book. We would have welcomed, in particular, more in this volume on the relations between capital and labour in wool and worsted up to World War One. This, we regret, has not proved possible and in our defence we can only fall back on the old adage that it is sincerely hoped that this collection of essays will interest readers enough to stimulate further research to plug obvious gaps and to extend the discussion, and that it may encourage more industry case studies on labour and industrial relations history.

NOTES

1. For the growth of population in Bradford see C. Richardson, A Geography of Bradford, (Bradford, 1976), pp. 91-102, and for the expansion in the worsted textile industry, G. Firth, 'The Bradford Trade in the Nineteenth Century', in D.G. Wright and J.A. Jowitt, Victorian Bradford, (Bradford, 1982), pp. 7-33.
2. J. Longworth, The Oldham Master Cotton Spinners Association Limited, 1866-1966, (Oldham, 1966), p. 9.
3. A.E. Musson, The Growth of British Industry, (London, 1978), pp. 202, 207. C.H. Lee, 'The Cotton Textile Industry' in R. Church (ed.), The Dynamics of Victorian Business, (London, 1980), p. 161.
4. A.E Musson, op. cit., p. 211.
5. B.R. Mitchell and P. Deane, Abstract of British Historical Statistics, (London, 1962), pp. 60, 179, 182; H.A. Turner, Trade Union Growth, Structure and Policy, (London, 1962), pp. 20-2; J.L. White, 'Lancashire Cotton Textiles', in C.J. Wrigley (ed.), A History of British Industrial Relations 1870-1914, (London, 1982), p. 210.
6. For product and process specialisation in Lancashire and West Yorkshire see D.A. Farnie, The English Cotton Industry and the World Market, 1815-1896, (Oxford, 1979); D.T. Jenkins and K.G. Ponting, The British Wool Textile Industry, 1770-1914, (London, 1982); N. Smith, 'Trends in the Geographical Distribution of the Lancashire Cotton Industry', Geography, XXVI, 1941, pp. 7-17; J.H. Clapham, 'Industrial Organisation in the Woollen and Worsted Industries of Yorkshire', Economic Journal, XVI, 1910.
7. J.H. Porter, 'Cotton and Wool Textiles', in N.K. Buxton and D.H. Aldcroft, British Industry Between the Wars, (London, 1979), pp. 26-7.
8. J.L. White, in C.J. Wrigley, op. cit., pp. 209-210.
9. J.H. Porter, op. cit., pp. 29, 44. See also M.W. Kirby, 'The Lancashire Cotton Industry in the Inter-War Years', Business History, XVI, no. 2, 1974, pp. 145-59.

Introduction

10. J.H. Porter, op. cit., p. 28; see also Board of Trade, An Industrial Survey of the Lancashire Area, (HMSO, London, 1932), pp. 94-129.
11. A.E. Musson, op. cit., pp. 318, 322.
12. Figures courtesy of Bob Stott of the Textiles Statistics Bureau, Royal Exchange, Manchester. For more detail see the Bureau's Quarterly Statistical Review. On the contraction of cotton after 1950 see J. Singleton, 'Lancashire's Last Stand: Declining Employment in the British Cotton Industry, 1950-1970', Economic History Review, 39, 1986.
13. Bradford Metropolitan Council, Bradford in Figures, (Bradford, 1984), p. 36.
14. A. Dawley, 'Death and Rebirth of the American Mill Town', Labour, Le Travailleur, vol. 8/9, autumn, spring 1981/2, p. 137.
15. P. Joyce, Work, Society and Politics (London, 1980), pp. xiii-xiv.
16. See for example the critical reviews of Joyce by K. McClelland, in History Workshop Journal, 11, 1981, pp. 169-73 and by N. Kirk in The Bulletin of the Society for the Study of Labour History, 42, Spring 1981, pp. 41-43.
17. W. Hamish Fraser, 'The Glasgow Cotton Spinners, 1837' in J. Butt and J.T. Ward (eds.), Scottish Themes (Edinburgh, 1976); W. Hamish Fraser, Conflict and Class: Scottish Workers, 1700-1838 (Edinburgh, 1987); N. Murray, The Scottish Handloom Weavers, 1790-1850 (Edinburgh, 1978); J. Butt, ed., Robert Owen, Prince of Cotton Spinners (Newton Abbot, 1971). See also J. Butt and K. Ponting, eds., Scottish Textile History (Aberdeen, 1987), which incorporates two chapters on early textile trade unionism, and A.J. Robertson, 'The Decline of the Scottish Cotton Industry, 1860-1914', Business History, 12, 1970.
18. E. Gordon, 'Women and the Labour Movement in Scotland, 1850-1914' (Ph.D. thesis, Glasgow University, 1985); 'Women, Work and Collective Action: Dundee Jute Workers 1870-1906', Journal of Social History (Fall, 1987); 'Women, Trade Unionism and Industrial Militancy, 1850-1890', in Glasgow Women's Studies Collective, Uncharted Lives (Glasgow, 1983).
19. A. Bullen, The Lancashire Weavers' Union, (Rochdale, 1984); A. and L. Fowler, The History of the Nelson Weavers' Association, (Nelson, 1984); A. Fowler, et. al., Barefooted Aristocrats (Littleborough, 1987); A. Bullen and A. Fowler, The Cardroom Workers Amalgamation (Rochdale, 1986).
20. For example, V.F. Gilbert's Labour and Social History Theses, 1900-1978, (London, 1982) includes 115 entries on trade unions and only 5 on employers and employers' organisations. None of these works refers directly to the textile industry.
21. See for example L.G. Sandberg, Lancashire in Decline (Columbus, Ohio, 1974) and a number of essays by W. Lazonick, most specifically, 'Industrial Organisation and Technical Change: The Decline of the British Cotton Industry', Business History Review, 57, 1983.

Section I.

EMPLOYERS' AND EMPLOYERS' ORGANISATIONS

Chapter 1

COTTON EMPLOYERS' ORGANISATIONS AND
LABOUR RELATIONS, 1890-1939

Arthur McIvor

The history of employers' organisations and capitalist labour relations policies is a woefully neglected area of study, and despite the efforts of a few recent researchers to fill this void, a very serious gap still remains. (1) The conventional histories of the cotton trade have little to say about employers' organisation or multi-employer labour relations strategy, and yield only a brief, non-analytical narrative of the institutional history of the combinations of masters in the industry. The result is that, without a serious assessment of the role and strategies of employers and their associations, existing industrial relations history remains largely one-sided and lacking in balance. This chapter provides a case study of an industry which has a long tradition of strong organisation amongst masters and men. (2) The first section investigates the emergence of cotton employers' associations, outlining some of the divisions within cotton employers' ranks and offering an explanation for the relatively high levels of employer solidarity in the industry. The second section analyses the development of multi-employer labour relations strategies and tactics in cotton up to World War One, focusing on the causation, dimensions and implications of the trend towards a formal, sophisticated industrial relations system. The final section discusses the impact of the inter-war economic slump, which witnessed, it is argued, an employers' efficiency offensive against labour and a serious decline in employers' collective organisation, with the initiative in industrial relations policy-making shifting increasingly away from the employers' associations and back to the individual firms in the cotton trade.

I. Genesis, Structure and Development

Broadly speaking, employers' associations can be defined as a group of employers who combine together with the object of protecting and promoting their business interests. Their activities often encompass trade regulation, pressure group action relating to legislation, and labour relations. As far as the latter is concerned, employers' associations have played an important role in collectively defending the employers' prerogative to manage and control work, in maximising profit margins and in regularising industrial relations in the trade. These initiatives have been obscured, however, by an emphasis in industrial relations history on the single entrepreneur/employer and the achievements of trade unionism. Increasingly as the nineteenth century progressed, individualistic and paternalistic employers broke with the tenets of popular anti-combination ideology and came to rely on the masters' association for protection and guidance.

In cotton, the first known example of an employers' combination is in 1745; and firm evidence has been found of formal employers' associations dealing with labour matters in the period when they were illegal under the Combination laws over 1799-1824 in the coal, shipbuilding, paper and printing trades, as well as cotton. (3) This is not the place for a detailed examination of the origins of cotton employers' associations, which has been dealt with elsewhere. (4) Suffice to say that permanent, formal, local cotton masters' associations emerged around the middle of the nineteenth century, partly, though not wholly, stimulated into existence by labour militancy and the influential success (especially in Lancashire) of the organised engineering employers in the 1852 lock-out. (5) An important characteristic of these associations was that they tended to be sectionally specific, mirroring the marked geographic and product specialisation divisions which emerged within the nineteenth century cotton trade in Lancashire. Within the weaving sector, solidarity amongst employers was enhanced considerably in 1866 when Blackburn, the largest weaving district in Lancashire, was persuaded to abandon its isolationist tendencies to join forces with the associated Preston and Burnley employers in the North and N.E. Lancashire Cotton Spinners' and Manufacturers' Association (N.C.S.M.A.) This organisation encompassed around 60 per cent of the machine capacity in the three major weaving towns in 1891. There remained, however, considerable differences in levels of local organisation and administration. Moreover, local associations retained a large degree of autonomy and conflicts of interest periodically erupted which crucially weakened the employers' united front. <u>Textile Mercury</u>, the employers' trade and technical journal and relentless proponent of tighter employer solidarity, exposed the poor state of employers' organisation in North Lancashire in 1896:

> There are as yet too many loosely-compacted local associations, deficient in all the principal elements of a strong organisation. These, again, have only slight connection with any federation of employers' associations. They are quite as apt, and rather more so, to go their own way, if they can see the shadow of a local advantage by so

doing...Too often there is no chairman; sometimes no secretary, or one secretary for several associations. To how many of the local associations of Lancashire employers do these remarks apply? We hardly care to make an estimate, but the number is considerable. (6)

Much reorganisation and rationalisation occurred in the later 1890s, not least with the disbandment of a rival weaving employers' federation, the United Cotton Manufacturers' Association (established 1890), and the strengthening and consolidation of the N.C.S.M.A. By the turn of the century the geographical basis of the latter federation had been widened significantly and twelve local associations were affiliated, representing all the major cotton weaving towns in Lancashire. Solidarity continued to improve and, as Table 1.1 illustrates, the density of organisation peaked in the early 1920s with almost 66 per cent of the Lancashire trade represented in the N.C.S.M.A. Sectional conficts of interest remained, however, and were to re-emerge strongly during the harsher economic climate of the inter-war recession and to result in a serious undermining of the collective strength of capital in the industry.

Table 1.1: N. and N.E. Lancashire Cotton Spinners' and Manufacturers' Association: Proportion of Machine Capacity (loomage) Organised, 1890-1939

Year	Percentage Organised
1890	24.6
1892	33.0
1900	44.0
1914	61.0
1920	65.5
1925	63.6
1930	58.8
1932	52.9
1935	58.0
1939	61.4

Sources: Percentage derived from comparing data on N.C.S.M.A. membership in their Minutes before 1912, and their Levy Book, 1912-47, with statistics on the entire Lancashire trade from Worrall's Cotton Spinners' and Manufacturers' Directories, 1890-1939.

Spatial segregation and product specialisation played an important part in limiting solidarity and organisation amongst masters in the spinning section of the cotton industry. Local associations of employers were in existence in the third quarter of the nineteenth century in most of the large spinning towns, including Oldham, Bolton and Ashton. However, there is little evidence of any effective inter-association collusion as far as labour relations strategy was concerned, until the early 1890s. A federal body called the Cotton Spinners' Association (C.S.A.) had been created in 1866 and by the late 1880s this organisation was a fairly representative body, amalgamating spinning interests in the South-East Lancashire coarse spinning district, the Bolton fine spinning area and the North Lancashire mixed areas. In 1888, 266 firms owning something like 45 per cent of the total spinning capacity in Lancashire affiliated to the C.S.A. (7) However, this organisation was strictly a trade regulatory body and did not formally discuss industrial relations matters. Only in the late 1880s was it proposed to include labour matters within the purview of the C.S.A. In the event, the Oldham masters preferred to establish a new federation of employers to manage the labour relations strategy of the trade.

The labour relations policy of the cotton spinning masters was thus kept localised until 1891, when nine local associations got together, under the auspices of the Oldham association, to establish the Federation of Master Cotton Spinners' Associations (F.M.C.S.A.). Previously, a pattern had emerged whereby the Oldham masters were left to fight the major industrial relations conflicts of the trade alone, with the neighbouring local associations having explicit or implicit agreements with their operatives to follow settlements in Oldham one week or so later. (8) The creation of the F.M.C.S.A. in 1891 potentially almost doubled the number of workers who might be thrown out of work in the case of a general lock-out. However, the South-East Lancashire masters failed in their original objective of creating a single federation incorporating the whole of the cotton trade. The North Lancashire masters held aloof and, more significantly, the Bolton fine spinners refused to affiliate, primarily because they preferred independence and feared being drawn into the kind of intense conflict which characterised industrial relations in the Oldham district over the 1870s and 1880s. Moreover, the limited liability companies which dominated the F.M.C.S.A. were seen as a threat to the business of the older Bolton and North Lancashire private firms. These divisions and antagonisms hindered the development of a fully representative spinning employers' federation, at least prior to the turn of the nineteenth century. (9)

Consequently, as Table 1.2 shows, the F.M.C.S.A. organised less than 40 per cent of the trade in the 1890s. This relative weakness in organisation and solidarity not only prejudiced the position of the spinning employers in the two industry-wide lock-outs over 1891-3, but was an important factor in the federation's conciliatory strategy over 1893-1905 (of which more will be said later). In 1905, the Bolton association, feeling threatened by more militant union tactics, was induced to affiliate to the F.M.C.S.A. and this raised the proportion of the spinning trade federated to 60 per cent. Solidarity continued to increase and, as with the master weavers, the density organised in the F.M.C.S.A. peaked over the early 1920s, at around 80 per cent, and declined thereafter.

Table 1.2: The Federation of Master Cotton Spinners' Associations: Proportion of Lancashire Machine Capacity (spindleage) Organised, 1892-1939

Year	Percentage Organised
1892	39.2
1897	37.1
1903	42.8
1914	64.3
1920	76.2
1922	80.3
1930	71.3
1933	65.9
1939	70.9

Sources: Percentage derived from comparing data on F.M.C.S.A. membership (excluding the Yorkshire association) from their Yearbooks and Annual Reports, 1892-1939, with statistics on the entire Lancashire trade from Worrall's Cotton Spinners' and Manufacturers' Directories, 1892-1939.

The cotton spinning and weaving employers' organisations remained distinct from each other and largely autonomous in their labour relations strategy prior to World War One. The N.C.S.M.A. rejected the approach of the Oldham master spinners and the F.M.C.S.A. leaders, Charles Macara and John Tattersall (10), to establish one industry-wide federation in the 1890s and there was very little formal co-operation or display of solidarity by the master weavers in the spinning lock-out of 1911-12. Short time was usually resorted to by the section which was not immediately affected by the dispute, but only out of expediency, rather than sympathy, due to the lack of demand for yarn or lack of raw material resulting from the stoppage. No evidence has been found of either organisation contributing to the other's strike funds. In 1899, a measure of co-operation was agreed to by all the major cotton employers' associations in Lancashire with the creation of the Cotton Employers' Parliamentary Association (C.E.P.A.). However, as its name implies, this body performed the role of a parliamentary pressure group for the cotton industry, co-ordinating the strategy of the cotton masters on legislative matters, taxation, factory reform, rating proposals, machinery, tariffs etc. It was not until the First World War, with the establishment of the Cotton Control Board, that the two sections of masters in the trade integrated their labour relations strategy and co-ordinated wage movements in the industry.

Despite divisions within their ranks, the local cotton employers' associations were amongst the best organised groups of employers in British industry, the largest associations having over 70 per cent of local firms in membership as early as the 1890s. How can the extent of employers' solidarity in the cotton trade be explained? The accepted view is to stress the power of trade unionism in the industry and to argue that formal employers' associations were a defensive response to the organisation of labour, and that organisations were developed on a permanent basis when individual employers felt their managerial prerogatives threatened within their own firms by the collective organisation of their operatives. (11) There is much sense in this hypothesis, and a volume of evidence from a number of industries does indicate that employers did often react vigorously to accelerating labour militancy. The F.M.C.S.A. was formed in 1891, we are informed, "to counter the threats and violent actions recently undertaken by the operatives and their unions". (12) The Royal Commissions in 1868-9 and 1892 both recognised the catalytic effect of unionisation on employers' organisation. (13) Once established, improvements in trade union organisation prompted reorganisation or a membership drive amongst employers, and vice versa, to retain the balance of power. Until World War One, for example, the membership fluctuations of the Oldham Master Cotton Spinners' Association and the Oldham Operative Spinners' Association correlated almost exactly. Moreover, both sides came to realise the advantages to each other of collective organisation. An indication of the deep faith which built up with regard to regularised industrial relations is this statement by the Bolton Operative Spinners, made, significantly, shortly after the long Brooklands lock-out:

> Experience has taught us that our greatest source of trouble is the employer who acknowledges no authority, who declines to unite with his fellows, and who, to use his own words, plays for his own hand. We prefer to deal with the employers as a body, through expert representatives, and the action of the employers' federation since it came into existence notwithstanding, we still have explicit faith in the mutual advantages to be derived from the well-knit combinations of both employers and workmen. (14)

By the mid-1890s most of the organised employers would have agreed with the sentiment behind this statement.

Clearly, trade unions and employers' associations were inextricably interrelated in their development, but the 'responsive' hypothesis alone is too simplistic and does not adequately explain the high level of employer solidarity and organisation in cotton. Whilst protection against trade unions and their snowballing strike tactics might be the raison d'etre of an employers' association, there was another important inducement prompting employers to organise collectively: the advantage of collective organisation in controlling competition - on product price and for labour - between firms in the industry. Here lies the explanation for the F.M.C.S.A.'s organised short-time movements and for the employers' willingness, and in some cases enthusiasm, to negotiate standardised local and district wage lists which implicitly (and sometimes explicitly, as in 1866 in Oldham) conceded a degree of union recognition. Quite simply, in an industry where labour costs were a high proportion of total costs (especially in the weaving sector), this ensured that competition between firms was 'fair'. Indeed, the local associations and employer federations in the cotton industry came to resent those unorganised employers and districts which undercut local and, later, Uniform Lists of wages; and it became part of a conscious policy to promote trade union attempts to organise such 'outlying' areas and impose the accepted rate for the job. (15) Furthermore, it might be argued that the degree of competition on price was most intense in an industry like cotton (and coal), where, despite marked geographical and specialisation divisions, the product was relatively standardised (compare, for example, engineering). Thus, the inducement of competition control may perhaps help to explain events which cannot be manipulated to fit the 'responsive' hypothesis; such as the fact that the first evidence of employers' association in cotton precedes that of a trade union, and that the creation of the powerful N.C.S.M.A. in 1866 actually predated the existence of an effective central union of operatives which combined the three major areas of Blackburn, Preston and Burnley by many years.

The relatively high level of organisation and solidarity amongst the Lancashire cotton employers was due to a conjunction of factors: the long tradition of trade unionism; the incentive offered to control competition on price and for labour; and geographical concentration of the trade. Solidarity was further influenced by other contributory factors, including government legislation and policy in the 1870s (legitimising the trade union's legal position) and the 1890s (encouraging voluntary conciliation) and changes in the structure of business organisation. It appears that concentration and the growth of joint stock companies stimulated a shift from paternalist forms of labour management towards more delegated, institutionalised structures and more bureaucratic forms of labour control strategies through collective organisation. (16)

Nevertheless, even in cotton a proportion of employers still preferred to go it alone, rejecting association membership and ignoring agreements and restraints. Evidence in Table 1.3 suggests, however, that by the late 1890s the majority of these tended to be the smallest firms. They were also often the most poorly unionised in more remote country districts which competed 'unfairly', according to the organised masters, by undercutting standard wages and prices. (17) A desire for independence, the ability to establish their own viable personnel departments and disagreement with some of the attitudes and policies of the multi-employer combinations, also kept a handful of the largest firms from membership. Such firms were always a more acute embarrassment to the employers' associations than the myriad of smaller 'undercutting' masters. The Textile Mercury contemptuously commented in 1896: "When a man has become purse-proud - too proud to join his fellows in the trade to protect its interests - it is quite time he retired from it. He has become a source of weakness to it and a danger to its welfare." (18)

Table 1.3: Lancashire Master Cotton Spinners' Associations: Size of Firms in Membership, 1899-1939

Size of firms (by no. of spindles)	Percentage of the total number of firms in each size category who were organised in local cotton spinning associations.		
	1899	1920	1939
Up to 29,999	23.0	35.1	40.6
30,000 - 99,999	74.7	82.9	82.2
100,000 - 149,999	71.4	84.3	90.8
Over 150,000	81.5	87.7	81.0

Sources: Percentages are derived from comparing the Membership Lists in the F.M.C.S.A., Annual Reports, 1899, 1920 and 1939, with Worrall's Cotton Spinners' and Manufacturers' Directories, 1899, 1920 and 1939.

II. Labour Relations Strategies:
   The Formalisation of Industrial Relations

The creation of an employers' organisation often had a paradoxical effect on industrial relations. Organisation strengthened the employers' arsenal of coercive anti-trade unionist and strikebreaking tactics - the lock-out; victimisation; blackleg importation; legal action - enabling unions to be autocratically suppressed. The Shipping Federation, established in 1890, is one such example of an exclusionist, vehemently anti-union employers' organisation. (19) The early cotton employers' associations, including those organised against John Doherty's spinners in the 1820s and the Oldham and Preston operatives in the 1830s, were also of this type. (20) However, the development of a network of permanent employers' associations was also an essential precondition for collective bargaining with organised labour. For this to become reality, a change in attitude had to occur, and one historian has argued that the late 1850s and early

Cotton Employers' Organisations

1860s witnessed the crucial shift from coercion and exclusion to recognition of unions and a more conciliatory labour relations strategy in Lancashire. (21) It was, however, no overnight development. Recognition spread by degrees, sporadically and experimentally throughout the second half of the nineteenth century.

Substantive agreements in cotton usually came first, sometimes linked with or followed by procedural disputes arrangements. Uniform piecework wage lists were negotiated by the employers' and operatives' associations in the 1850s, 60s and 70s, and many of these incorporated rudimentary disputes conciliation procedures, whereby grievances were to be discussed by the secretaries of the respective organisations prior to any stoppage of work. (22) The trend was towards uniformity in the piecework wage basis. In weaving, the Uniform Wage List of 1892 amalgamated the Blackburn, Preston and Burnley lists, whilst in spinning, the majority of operatives in Lancashire by the 1890s were paid by either the Oldham (coarse) or Bolton (fine) lists. (23) Recognition of cardroom workers and female ring spinners came later, with wage lists and rudimentary conciliation procedures being conceded in Oldham in 1891, Universal Lists negotiated over 1903-7 and a Ring Spinning List in 1913. (24) The local disputes procedures were further extended in 1881 in weaving and in 1893 in spinning (Brooklands) when machinery was established allowing for formal joint domestic, local and national meetings to take place, prior to any strike or lock-out. Though procedure was tightened up on several occasions prior to 1914, a scheme proposed by Charles Macara, the F.M.C.S.A. president, for a sliding scale to regulate automatically wage movements (as in coal mining) had to be abandoned, the federation and the unions disagreeing on points of detail. (25)

Why did employers accept the switch from anti-unionism to an incorporative, procedural labour management strategy? Undoubtedly, the increase in competition in product markets from the 1870s (prompting a 'speed-up' movement in the mills) encouraged employers to seek solace by controlling competition on labour costs through the Uniform Wage Lists. However, the desire to contain and neutralise the growing power of the trade unions was a paramount consideration influencing employers to develop and commit themselves to collective bargaining. Coercive control - via trials of strength - proved increasingly provocative and costly. Significantly, the main developments in collective bargaining in cotton came after the experience of extended and very damaging periods of industrial conflict when labour had illustrated its power to resist. The 1881 weaving disputes procedure following the violent 1878 weavers' dispute (after a respectable 'cooling off' period allowing the legacy of intense bitterness to dissipate) and the 1893 spinning conciliation machinery after the 1891 Stalybridge and 1892-3 Brooklands lockouts. Moreover, fear of a resurgence of large-scale union retaliation, combined with an awareness of their own organisational weaknesses, resulted in the F.M.C.S.A. letting slip opportunities to push for further wage reductions over 1893-8. Over the same period, however, full recognition was being refused to the relatively poorly organised cardroom operatives, female ring spinners, clothlookers and warehousemen. Clearly, employers' labour relations strategy was crucially affected by the bargaining power of particular groups of operatives.

Collective bargaining had important consequences for both capital and labour in cotton. Recognition encouraged wage rationalisation, increased union involvement in decision making and raised union prestige and authority. Disputes procedures and agreements reduced industrial conflict, acting as a buffer against drastic movements in wages and conditions in periods of either extreme recession or trade 'boom'. The ideology of common interests and interdependency replaced that of open antagonism between masters and men. R.F. Dyson has also argued that procedure in cotton worked to restrict technological advance by forestalling arbitrary managerial changes in work practices and processes, notably in the cardroom in the 1900-14 period. (26) Certainly, collective bargaining further encouraged unionisation and employers' organisation in order to meet the complicated administrative and mathematical requirements of joint negotiation in cotton. Public relations statements stressed, moreover, that collective bargaining meant a dispassionate and unbiased consideration of the merits of each case, thus providing just settlements acceptable to both sides without loss of production or wages.

The reality of the situation was, however, somewhat different. Doubts have been expressed as to whether the benefits of pre-1914 collective bargaining procedures were equitably distributed between both sides, and the evidence on the employers' side does indicate that they gained disproportionately from the transition to a more conciliatory labour relations strategy. The fall in time lost through industrial disputes after 1893 indicates that the formalised procedure did succeed for many years in the primary objective of reducing the damaging effects of industrial conflict. (27) Moreover, it has been persuasively argued by J.H. Porter that wage rates may have become considerably less flexible in an upward direction as a result of the five per cent restriction clause of the Brooklands Agreement. (28) The procedure was very largely established on the employers' terms, with the 'state of trade' and wage rates paid by neighbouring competitors as the only criteria accepted by the employers in negotiating a wage change. This made procedure particularly restrictive to labour in the pre-1914 period of rising living costs. In joint bargaining, emphasis was also laid on carefully collected and well documented evidence, and here the employers had the considerable advantages of greater organisational and secretarial services to back up their cases.

Therefore, whilst the unions may well have taken the initiative in demanding collective bargaining with the employers, it was the employers' organisations which invariably exploited the opportunity provided by conciliation to impose a new form of procedural control over labour. Some far-sighted and shrewd employers - like Charles Macara - realised the potential advantages very early. Despite some initial criticism of the degree of 'class collaboration', most of the other employers in the trade became committed to conciliation through experience. (29) Employers benefited because disappointing decisions of conciliation boards were endorsed by the workers' own officials, who were given the responsibility of policing collective agreements. Rank and file labour militancy could be contained and work stoppages forestalled whilst a lengthy period of negotiation occurred. Whilst negative evidence indicates that collective bargaining may well have worked somewhat more equitably in weaving than spinning, it appears nevertheless that the switch to a procedural mode of control over labour in cotton paid dividends for employers. Confirmation of this is provided by the fact that the F.M.C.S.A. remained firmly committed to working within the established collective bargaining procedures from 1893, whilst on the union side periodic complaints as to the unjust working of the procedure accrued from the mid-1890s, culminating in the eventual abrogation of the Brooklands Agreement by the Spinners' Amalgamation in January 1913.

From the early 1890s, the commitment to procedural control as a strategy by employers in cotton was deep-rooted. Nevertheless, coercive tactics, such as lock-outs, victimisation, labour replacement and legal action, continued to be used as a second line of defence by the organised employers, usually brought into action only when collective bargaining machinery was exhausted or ignored by the trade unions or work group. The role of employers' associations in the breaking of strikes has been discussed in detail elsewhere. (30) The cotton associations organised the importation of blackleg labour, arranged protection, and paid travelling expenses in a number of disputes, including the 1891 Stalybridge mill strike. (31) They also co-ordinated a number of lock-outs and elaborated various methods of victimising strikers to prevent them getting work elsewhere, including the retention, illegally, of operatives' birth certificates. (32) The evidence suggests, however, a far more limited use of such provocative tactics in cotton than was common over 1890-1914 in, for example, the shipping and engineering trades.

The cotton employers' organisations, however, particularly favoured two tactics: use of the law courts, and sophisticated strike indemnity schemes. The courts were used to establish important legal precedents - as in the 1901-2 Banister and Moore picketing case - and to impose fines on strikers who left work without notice in breach of contract. By the 1890s it was an understood rule that the cotton employers' associations would defray a member firm's bill for legal expenses incurred in this way. (33) The law courts were thus used to enhance managerial discipline and authority and particularly to reduce the incidence and effects of wildcat strikes, especially of piecers and tenters. Financial support was also given to member firms by the cotton employers' associations in the event of a strike, to induce individual employers not to give way to sectional trade union attack and thus compromise managerial rights and prerogatives, or prompt a wage escalation spiral. Both the master weavers and spinners had a high subscription, high benefit policy, and regular strike indemnity pay-outs were designed to cover generously fixed charges, salaries payable and expenses in stopping and re-opening the works. The size of payments was kept flexible and when trade was particularly buoyant, as over 1912-14, the organisation resorted to paying relatively high individual strike compensation as its primary tactic in neutralising sectional trade union offensives. (34)

The particular mix of conciliatory and coercive tactics adopted by the cotton employers' associations depended to a large extent on the strategies formulated by the trade unions, relative organisational strengths and weaknesses, and the state of product markets. The labour relations policy of the spinning employers remained highly sensitive to short-term fluctuations in the trade cycle with significant 'offensives' against labour occurring over 1891-3 and 1908-10, corresponding to the worst troughs in trade. In contrast, in weaving no centrally organised wage reduction movement or lock-out was called by the masters' associations, despite periodic short recessions, from the mid-1880s to 1911. This could have been an indirect response to the violent confrontation of 1878, and may well reflect a deep-rooted satisfaction with conciliation procedures and wage rationalisation under the Uniform List. (35) A strident employers' strategy may also have been undermined by relative organisational weaknesses. This long period of comparative quiescence in weaving still remains inadequately explained and under-researched.

In spinning, however, the labour relations strategy of the S.E. Lancashire masters over the early 1890s was initially hostile and coercive (though not distinctly anti-unionist) with the new organisation, the F.M.C.S.A., eager to reassert eroded managerial prerogatives. (36) The depressed state of product markets provided the opportunity. The details of the 1891-3 'backlash', incorporating two industry-wide lock-outs are well known. (37) However, it needs to be stressed that the failure of the employers to get more than a 2.9 per cent wage reduction reflects not only the tenacity and strength of the operatives' unions, but also the lack of cohesion amongst cotton employers. Organisational weakness induced the F.M.C.S.A. to take no further initiatives until the fine spinning masters of Bolton, Manchester and Chorley joined the organisation over 1905-8. Consequently, increased solidarity provided the confidence to embark again on a concerted offensive in the 1908-10 recession, locking-out on two occasions to reduce wages and protect managerial prerogatives, and imposing a five year wage 'freeze', covering 1910-15.

How did cotton employers react to the upsurge in worker militancy over 1911-14, when product markets in cotton were at their most buoyant for many years? Uncharacteristically, the master weavers embarked on a two week lock-out of the trade in January 1912 as a defensive measure against union attempts to enforce a closed shop. This action is a clear indication that issues and management prerogatives could, on occasions, transcend product market pressures, for trade over 1911-12 was generally very brisk. It was, in short, an inopportune time for an industry-wide lock-out. Fierce employer opposition to the closed shop in 1911-12 also clearly illustrates the limits of employers' incorporative policies in the pre-war period.

However, in the two year period directly preceding the war, when consumption of cotton and exports of finished goods reached a statistical peak, cotton employers' strategies did respond to market pressures by remaining particularly conciliatory, being designed specifically to localise and de-escalate industrial conflict. Joseph White has recently charted the breadth of cotton union militancy over 1910-14. (38) In 1913 in particular, the unions were laying down a challenge to the employers by reviving the closed shop issue, simultaneously striking 15 mills alleging 'bad spinning' and withdrawing from the Brooklands disputes procedure. Mill strikes escalated, yet in face of what amounted to the most widespread sectional attack in its history, the spinning employers did not retaliate and escalate the conflict by resort to a lock-out. The N.C.S.M.A. responded in a similar way in 1913 when sectional strikes re-occurred on the non-unionist issue. The organisation reneged on a previous undertaking to take a hard line, quietly dropped proposals to take out summonses and blacklist strikers, and left two member firms in Nelson to fight the strikes alone. (39) Historians have tended to neglect industrial relations in the trade sectors where labour militancy was not particularly marked over 1911-14. In cotton, at least, evidence suggests that the de-escalation policies of the employers helped to limit the scale and determine the character of industrial conflict in this period.

Moreover, the peculiar circumstances of the First World War period and the brief post-war replacement boom, 1919-20, worked to soften further employers' labour relations strategies in cotton textiles. Employers' power and independence were eroded by drastic labour shortages, government intervention and a wartime public relations exercise which stressed co-operation and the concession of full collective bargaining and consultation rights to labour. Spiralling inflation in labour costs continued until the winter of 1920-1, and the position of employers' organisations was further compromised by individual firms making unilateral agreements and conceding extra inducements above list wages to attract scarce labour. (40) Loyalty to federation rules and customs rapidly deteriorated, with the customary use of the 'enquiry note' and the non-employment of strikers being widely ignored, particularly over 1919-20. Evidence also suggests that the employers' associations in cotton continued to isolate domestic mill strikes and sectional attacks over the war period, and to reject the lock-out option. In Oldham alone from 1914 to 1919 there were at least six mill strikes of over three months' duration which the federation allowed to run on without interference. For almost the whole of a decade, over 1911-20, the cotton employers were forced on to the defensive.

Cotton Employers' Organisations

III. The Employers' Inter-War Offensive

Pre-war and wartime co-operation and incorporation strategies proved to be transitory with the onset of the 1920s recession in cotton and many other industries. They gave way to the free play of economic forces and a more self-interested and coercive strategy amongst many employers. (41) The collapse of the cotton trade in the 1920s and 1930s had two main effects on employers' organisation and strategy. Firstly, employers' policies hardened and evidence suggests a dual offensive to re-impose managerial prerogatives and authority, and to reduce drastically production costs. Secondly, the intensified competitive environment led to a marked decline in solidarity amongst employers, a growing inability of the industry-wide federations to follow any sort of consensus strategy, and a tendency for the initiative in wage determination and industrial relations to pass back to the individual firm.

The initial reaction of the spinning employers to the slump was to organise short-time working. Only after this failed to improve profit margins did the spinning and weaving federations combine to enforce wage reductions in 1921 and 1922. The costs reduction drive continued on a domestic, local and national level up to the mid-1930s, further industry-wide wage reductions being imposed in 1929 and 1932, and in weaving in 1935. Some employers pressed further, eager to exploit their enhanced bargaining power resulting from the recession. Savage has indicated how a more strident, direct form of management control emerged in the 1920s and '30s which curtailed the traditional craft controls, independence and authority of cotton overlookers in the workplace. (42) A successful attack was also made to reduce the guaranteed minimum wage of the tapers and overlookers, and in Blackburn the tapers' guaranteed week was abolished completely in 1936. (43) Wage inducements above Uniform Lists, common over 1915-20, disappeared and the trend reversed to one of wage cribbing and unofficial undercutting, usually on the grounds of competitiveness. (44) Work was increasingly intensified and speeded-up. The spinners' cleaning time agreement of 1919 was abrogated by the F.M.C.S.A. in 1929, thus pressing the division of labour further and forcing operatives to spin for a fully productive 48-hour week. Individual workloads were increased and manning levels reduced, primarily by changing the type of cloth or yarn produced, using inferior material and increasing the number of looms tended by weavers and supervised by overlookers. (45) Demarcation privileges were eroded, and the replacement of expensive skilled labour with cheaper, less skilled workers continued. Jobbers, for example, took over a number of traditional duties of overlookers with the abrogation of the gaiting-up agreement by the employers in 1931. (46)

Many employers intensified supervision on the shop floor, imposed stricter quality control and attempted to reimpose their authority over the labour process. The Blackburn masters reasserted their fundamental managerial prerogatives: "We claim the right as employers to employ whom we think fit, and also the right to make a change without being compelled to give a reason". (47) Complaints of 'driving' and 'tyranny' multiplied, dismissal cases clogged up the disputes procedure and the fining of operatives for sub-standard work was revived, the employers establishing the legality of imposing fines in two legal cases in the late 1920s. (48) Increased pressure of work exacerbated industrial fatigue and resulted in deteriorating general standards of health at work in cotton textile factories outside the thin paternalist strand of employers between 1921 and the passing of the Factory Act of 1937. (49) Lock-out propensity and victimisation also revived as tactics utilised by employers' associations to discipline the labour force. In a phase of direct brinkmanship in the 1920s, the F.M.C.S.A. threatened a general industry-wide lock-out on five separate occasions in response to individual mill disputes. On each occasion the operatives were forced to back down. Evidence also suggests that labour replacement during disputes was revived as an employers' weapon, especially over the period of intense industrial conflict and mass unemployment, 1929-32. The cotton unions claimed that in 1932 around 5,000 of their members had been victimised by replacement. (50) Moreover, in the Midland Hotel Agreement which settled the 1932 disputes, the employers refused to forgo their privilege to victimise strikers selectively. Other cotton employers victimised workers for their militancy and their left-wing political affiliations and activities, making use of the central anti-labour propaganda, blacklisting and monitoring agency established in 1919, the Economic League, to obtain information on employees and job applicants. (51) In total, around 32 million working days were lost from disputes in the textile sector over 1921-32. (52) The vast majority of these were the result of a return to a strident policy of cost reductions and the re-imposition of managerial authority by the cotton employers.

Paradoxically perhaps, the employers were also weakened by the inter-war slump. The collapse in union membership in this period significantly reduced the pressures for strong employers' combination. Solidarity amongst employers was further eroded as competition between firms degenerated into an undercutting wage and price war. Moreover, the consensus view disintegrated dramatically because the impact of the recession was patchy in the 1920s. Manufacturing firms producing coarse and plain cotton goods and dependent on the Indian and Chinese trade were particularly hard hit, whereas other markets, including Scandinavia, Australasia and to some extent South America and Africa, held up relatively well. (53) In the spinning sector, the markets for fine quality cotton yarn remained relatively buoyant in the 1920s, whereas the bulk trade in American grade yarn collapsed, due to the loss of Indian and Chinese trade and growing Japanese competition. (54) Finally, firms which extensively reorganised over 1919-20 often found themselves in a desperately poor competitive position in the 1920s because of high interest rates and depreciation charges on loan capital. (55) Many of the worst hit firms gravitated towards membership of the Provisional Emergency Cotton Committee - a breakaway group of employers, headed by Charles Macara, which was severely critical of the strategy of the employers' federations during the recession. (56)

There developed a widening divergence of views within the cotton industry on how to tackle its problems. There was a growing polarisation between employers who favoured the incorporationist and conciliatory labour relations strategy, and those who were opposed to collective bargaining and favoured confrontation. In trade policy, there was a clash of interests between those employers who subscribed to a continuation of free and open competition, and those who supported a crisis recovery package based around some form of central control of the industry and legalised price fixing arrangements. These divisions were epitomised by the clash between the conservative Bolton fine spinning employers, led by their president William Howarth, and the Provisional Emergency Cotton Committee, which supported a programme of radical change. (57) Significantly, relative buoyancy in the Bolton trade made the employers considerably less vigorous in the campaign to revive the industry, reduce production costs and reassert managerial authority on the shop floor. For this apathy they were severely admonished by the F.M.C.S.A. in 1931. (58)

Table 1.4: Local Master Cotton Spinners' Associations: Differences in Representation, 1914-1935

District	Percentage of total spindleage organised in local cotton spinning employers' associations		
	1914	1920	1935
Ashton	78.8	82.5	60.2
Bolton	80.3	87.2	84.1
Bury	57.6	69.4	66.6
Chorley	36.8	67.5	96.9
Farnworth	65.1	68.7	99.3
Heywood	77.4	83.3	56.1
Manchester	80.0	92.1	84.4
Oldham	82.6	91.5	75.0
Rochdale	76.8	80.6	60.7
Stockport	32.6	68.1	61.4

Sources: Percentages are derived from comparing the total number of spindles in all the firms in these districts as ascertained from Worrall's Cotton Spinners' and Manufacturers' Directories for 1914, 1920 and 1935 with the spindleage of member firms of the local master cotton spinners' associations, from the F.M.C.S.A. Membership Lists in the Annual Reports for 1914, 1920 and 1935.

Cotton Employers' Organisations

In such an environment, it became increasingly hard for the employers' federations in the industry to formulate any kind of common strategy. Inability to decide on policy direction resulted in inaction. Consequently, many firms left their local associations to go their own way, and, as Table 1.4 indicates, solidarity waned to a significantly larger degree in the medium and coarser sectors of the spinning trade hardest hit by the slump, particularly in Oldham, Ashton, Rochdale and Heywood.

From a peak of over 65 per cent of the trade, N.C.S.M.A. membership slumped to 53 per cent by 1932-3. Similarly, F.M.C.S.A. membership fell from representing 80 per cent of the trade to 65-7 per cent over 1931-5. (59) (See Tables 1.1 and 1.2.) Attendance at general meetings, another indicator of employers' solidarity, also declined in a number of local associations in the 1920s and early 1930s. Moreover, many firms - including many members of the Provisional Emergency Cotton Committee - retained their membership of employers' associations, but increasingly ignored federation agreements and collective bargaining restraints, and repeatedly undercut wage lists. (60) Disloyalty grew to serious proportions and clearly the initiative in industrial relations and wage determination was passing from employers' organisations back to individual firms.

Industrial conflict in cotton culminated over 1930-2 in the long stoppages of production caused by the more looms issue and the employers' suspension of collective bargaining agreements and restraints. The details of these events are well known, through the research of Bullen, Fowler, Riley, Hopwood and Turner. (61) Essential in understanding the crisis of 1930-2 is an awareness of the background of an intensifying employers' offensive and the serious erosion of employers' solidarity and cohesion in Lancashire. The attempt to get weavers to work more looms was a constituent part of the costs reduction offensive, interpreted by the employers as an issue of managerial prerogative: "The question has resolved itself into whether or not an employer should be allowed to use his machinery in the manner in which he thinks best, or whether he must be governed by the operatives' association". (62) The failure to win the more looms lock-out in the winter of 1930-1 was due, however, not only to powerful union and work group opposition, but also to lack of commitment on the part of the employers. The employers were divided, with Burnley being most vocal in support of the new system, whilst many other employers - including a large proportion in Blackburn, Colne and Preston - doubted whether it would benefit them on the particular classes of work they were producing, and raised serious misgivings about the lack of consultation of rank and file employers prior to the calling of the lock-out. (63) The N.C.S.M.A. Executive called off the lock-out unconditionally after seven weeks, significantly because they sensed that the employers lacked 'the will to win'. (64)

The period 1930-2 also witnessed a breakdown of the formal collective bargaining system in cotton. Disaffection amongst employers at the inaction and inconclusive policies of their associations, and frustration over the more looms failure resulted in more and more firms ignoring agreements made centrally, and unilaterally imposing wage rates below list, working longer hours and adjusting manning levels and workloads as they saw fit. (65) Indeed, the pressure of this rank and file employers' movement was so strong that the employers' federations were forced in 1932 to suspend all collective agreements, leaving their members free to exploit the situation fully. (66) There followed a chaotic period of cut-throat unregulated competition between employers and practically unrestricted class warfare in the spring and summer of 1932. Relations between management and men were at their worst since the bitter conflict of 1878.

In the event, the Ministry of Labour intervened after several months to restabilise industrial relations in the industry. Abrogated agreeements were restored, collective bargaining accepted explicitly by both sides and the established disputes procedure extended to include a Conciliation Committee as a final body of appeal, incorporating voluntary independent arbitration. There are significant similarities between the Brooklands Agreement of 1893 and the Midland Hotel Agreement of 1932. Both marked a watershed in their respective periods between industrial militancy and relative peace. This was true of the 1932 agreement despite subsequent recurrent problems on the 'more looms' question and the undercutting of wage lists.

In the final analysis it should be stressed that the militancy of the cotton employers in the inter-war years had its limitations, particularly at the point of production. Failure to modernise or introduce methods of scientific labour management on a large scale underlay such limitations. (67) The spinning employers proved to be unwilling to press for fundamental reforms in work processes, manning levels and the division of labour, made no great effort to promote shift working or more mule working, nor did they openly encourage the more rapid diffusion of the ring frame. By 1939, less than 30 per cent of total spindles in Lancashire were ring. Apart from the constraints of capital availability, this may have been partially due to a factor which Deirdre Busfield has highlighted in her paper, the collusion of employers in the traditional sexual division of labour, for the ring frames were operated by women. (68) The attack on the spinning work team division of labour (one minder and two piecers) by the system of joiner-minding (two low status spinners), also developed tardily, and by 1930 it has been estimated that only around 12 per cent of the spinners in Lancashire were joiner-minders. (69) Similarly, high draft winding in the cardroom and the new vacuum stripping apparatus - technology which the employers felt could be manned by females and would halve the numbers of strippers and grinders needed - developed only very slowly. (70) Moreover, no concerted attempt to make a direct attack on trade unionism using the employers' organisations as the vanguard of the offensive was ever carried out, though this was threatened in 1931-2. (71) Fundamentally, trade unions remained an accepted part of the fabric of industrial relations in cotton with a crucially important policing role to play.

The offensive on the more looms issue and the encouragement of the use of automatic looms by the weaving employers' federation is indicative that such conservatism in labour management was less evident amongst the cotton manufacturers. Arguably, this could have been because labour costs in relation to total costs were much higher in weaving than in spinning. However, the final settlement of the 'more looms' question in the agreements of 1932 and 1935 was severely restrictive on the employers and the conditions and wage basis established was so high in relation to the competing four looms list that the incentive to go over to more loom working was minimised. Indeed, this was the very objective of traditional four loom working areas like Blackburn, where the competitive edge of the six looms per weaver firms had been resented. (72) Consequently, by 1939 only around 20 per cent of Lancashire weavers were operating either automatic looms or more than the traditional complement of four looms. (73) This was all in direct contrast to the U.S.A., where modern technology, output standardisation, scientific management and the continuous operation of the plant, led to major innovations in manning levels and the division of labour, with a commensurate increase in productivity.

A new pattern of industrial relations emerged in the cotton industry after 1932. Government intervention, firm trade union opposition and some stabilisation in the trade in the later 1930s promoted a revived commitment to a co-operative and incorporationist employers' strategy. As Tables 1.1 and 1.2 show, this was paralleled by some revival in employers' solidarity. The creation of the Conciliation Committee in 1932, the legalisation of the Uniform Wage List in 1935, the 'recommendation' of the F.M.C.S.A. in 1935 that they preferred their operatives to be members of a trade union, the growing power of the Joint Committee of Cotton Trade Organisations (established 1928), joint action to tackle the redundant machinery problem (by the 1936 Spindles Act) and the elimination of lock-out action and threats after 1932, are all indicative of a softening of employers' policies towards fuller incorporation and co-operation with organised labour in the later 1930s.

IV. Conclusions

This chapter has investigated labour relations from the employers' perspective, concentrating in particular on the development of multi-employer organisations and the role such associations played in the industrial relations system in cotton. Such an approach is justified by a belief that in order fully to understand industrial relations history it is necessary to analyse the organisational forms and collective strategies adopted by capital, as well as labour. The conclusions are tentative and provisional. Perhaps inevitably so, for there has been very little research undertaken in this area and consequently there exists a minimal amount of theory to draw comparisons with and test hypotheses against. To this end, more case studies and comparative investigations are needed.

Employers' organisations in cotton were formed with two primary objectives: to protect and maximise profit margins, and to defend and promote employers' prerogatives to manage and control work as they thought fit. The 'responsive' hypothesis, which explains the development of employers' organisations solely as a defensive response to labour has, however, been found wanting. Clearly, trade union and employers' association development in cotton was closely interrelated and the threat to an individual employer of the collective organisation of his workforce did provide a powerful incentive to organise. However, possibly an equally important inducement to organise in cotton came from the advantage which association offered to control competition in the industry. These factors - together with contributory variables, including government legislation and policy, changes in the structure of business organisation and geographical concentration - help to explain the relatively early experience of employer combination and the statistically very high levels of solidarity, via association membership, exhibited amongst the Lancashire cotton employers, especially from the 1890s on. However, such aggregate statistics hide very significant divisions of interest and strategy amongst the largely autonomous local associations, based on sectional specialisms, distinct product markets and, to some degree, type of firm. These divisions came to have a crucial impact on both the form and effectiveness of employers' labour relations strategies.

The creation of employers' associations had a paradoxical effect on industrial relations. On the one hand, it could significantly strengthen the employers' arsenal of coercive anti-unionist tactics. On the other hand, it was an essential precondition for orderly collective bargaining. Recognition and collective bargaining spread by degrees in cotton in the second half of the nineteenth century and by the 1900s the labour relations strategy of the organised employers was firmly committed to conciliation and a formal industrial relations bargaining system, with coercive strikebreaking tactics held in reserve, as a second line of defence, should procedure be ignored or break down. It has been argued that employers made the switch to a procedural mode of control over labour to contain trade union power and militancy, and that up to 1914 the cotton employers gained disproportionately from this transition to a more formalised and bureaucratic industrial relations system. After 1920, however, collective bargaining agreements may well have acted as a buffer restricting the erosion of labour costs and hence workers' living standards, and, in this sense, working disproportionately against capital - that is prior to their breakdown over 1930-2.

The form, effectiveness and particular mix of conciliatory and coercive tactics on the part of employers at any one time depended partly on relative organisational strengths and weaknesses, partly on how far the issue encroached into predetermined managerial rights and prerogatives, and partly on the state of product markets. The evidence suggests that sustained periods of market buoyancy, as over 1911-14, did prompt the organised cotton employers to adopt particularly defensive tactics, designed to de-escalate and localise conflict, and that this successfully contained the extent of labour militancy in cotton over the immediate pre-war years. Likewise, the inter-war economic slump provided the preconditions for an unparalleled employers' offensive which eroded the very concept of union recognition and collective bargaining over the worst years of 1930-2. However, the impact of short-term fluctuations in the trade cycle is more ambiguous. Evidence indicates that the labour relations strategy of the organised master weavers, in particular, was very insensitive to relatively short recessions and booms before World War One.

It has been argued that during the inter-war depression, cotton employers' strategies hardened and that they embarked on a dual offensive to reimpose managerial prerogatives and authority in the workplace, and to slash production costs. This efficiency offensive was limited, however, to within the parameters of the existing technology as an alternative strategy to the more costly process of re-equipment and structural reorganisation. The depression years also witnessed a severe erosion of employers' solidarity, which was undermined by the collapse in trade union membership, the intensified, cut-throat, competitive environment and, most significantly, by the patchy impact of the recession on specialised product markets. Divisions within the cotton employers' federations reached such proportions that a consensus labour relations strategy proved increasingly difficult to formulate. Central indecision, inactivity and weakness led to breakaways, disloyalty and, especially over 1929-32, the initiative in industrial relations policy making returning to the level of the individual firm. The evidence for cotton thus provides some verification of the Donovan hypothesis that employers' associations after World War One were losing their innovatory role and abdicating the initiative in structuring the industrial relations systems of their industries. (74)

NOTES

I am pleased to acknowledge my thanks to A. Bullen, A.E. Musson, H. Gospel, D.A. Farnie and S. Jones for helpful comments on earlier drafts, and to the various employers' organisations in Lancashire who have allowed access to their records. This chapter is based on research funded by the Economic and Social Research Council (E.S.R.C.) reference number FOO232204.

Abbreviations:
F.M.C.S.A.   Federation of Master Cotton Spinners' Associations

Cotton Employers' Organisations

M.C.S.A.   Master Cotton Spinners' Association
N.C.S.M.A. North and N.E. Lancashire Cotton Spinners' and Manufacturers' Association
C.S.M.A.   Cotton Spinners' and Manufacturers' Association

1. On cotton textiles, see in particular, A. Bullen, The Cotton Spinners' and Manufacturers' Assocation and the Breakdown of the Collective Bargaining System in the Cotton Manufacturing Industry, 1928-35, (1980, M.A. thesis, Warwick University); R.F. Dyson, The Development of Collective Bargaining in the Cotton Spinning Industry, 1893-1914, (1971, Ph.D. thesis, Leeds University); R. Smith, A History of the Lancashire Cotton Industry, 1873-96, (1954, Ph.D. thesis, Birmingham University); and A. Howe, The Cotton Masters, 1830-1860, (Oxford, 1984). See also, A. Yarmie, 'Employers' Organisations in Mid-Victorian England', International Review of Social History, XXV, 1980, Part Two; W.R. Garside and H. Gospel, 'Employers and Managers' in C.J. Wrigley, (editor), A History of British Industrial Relations, 1870-1914, (Brighton, 1982); H. Gospel, Employers' Organisations: Their Growth and Function in the British System of Industrial Relations in the Period 1918-1939, (1974, Ph.D. thesis, London School of Economics); H. Gospel, 'Employers and Managers: Organisation and Strategy, 1914-39', Ch. 4 in C.J. Wrigley (ed.), A History of British Industrial Relations, Vol. 2, 1914-39 (Brighton, 1986).

2. For a more detailed account see A.J. McIvor, Employers' Organisations and Industrial Relations in Lancashire, 1890-1939, (1983, Ph.D. thesis, Manchester University).

3. H.A. Turner, Trade Union Growth, Structure and Policy, (London, 1962), pp. 370-1; A. Yarmie, op. cit., p. 211; A.E. Musson, Trade Union and Social History, (Harmondsworth, 1974), pp. 137-155; D.C. Coleman, 'Combinations of Capital and Labour in the English Paper Industry, 1789-1825', Economica, Feb. 1954, pp. 32-53; E.P. Thompson, The Making of the English Working Class, (Harmondsworth, 1963), p. 219.

4. For the crucial developments of the 1850s see A. Bullen, ch. 2.

5. H.I. Dutton and J.E. King, Ten Per Cent and No Surrender, (Cambridge, 1981), pp. 34, 88-9.

6. Textile Mercury, 22 Feb. 1896, p. 144. See also Textile Mercury, 13 Jan. 1894; 25 Aug. 1894. This weekly journal was fiercely anti-unionist and, significantly, sponsored financially by the cotton employers' federations. See N.C.S.M.A., Minutes, 13 Nov. 1896; Oldham M.C.S.A., Committee Minutes, 21 Apr. 1896.

7. Membership derived from comparing the membership list of the Cotton Spinners' Association in their Annual Report, 4 Sept. 1888, with Worrall's Cotton Spinners' and Manufacturers' Directory for 1888. A similar percentage of the trade was not organised in the F.M.C.S.A. until 1901.

8. Ashton M.C.S.A., Minutes (General Meeting), 3 March 1892; F.M.C.S.A., Annual Report, 1891-2.

9. Bolton M.C.S.A., Minutes, 14 Nov. 1892, and see R.F.

Dyson, op. cit., pp. 113-15.

10. For the short biographies of these employers' leaders see A.J. McIvor, 'Charles Macara' and 'John B. Tattersall' in the Dictionary of Business Biography, Vol. IV, (London, 1985), pp. 7-14; Vol. V (London, 1986), pp. 444-54.

11. A. Yarmie, op. cit., pp. 209-15; E. Wigham, The Power to Manage (London, 1973), pp. 1-2; K. Burgess, The Origins of British Industrial Relations, (London, 1975), pp. vii-viii.

12. R. Smith, op. cit., p. 273.

13. R.C. on Trade Unions, Eleventh and Final Report, 1868-9, XXXI, Majority Report, Q. 41; R.C. on Labour, Final Report, Pt. 1, 1894, p. 31.

14. Bolton Operative Spinners' Association, Annual Report, 1892, p. 4. See also R. Smith, op. cit., pp. 262-3.

15. N.C.S.M.A., Minutes, 12 Jan. 1897; 20 Aug. 1897; 31 May 1910; 9 Sept. 1910. See also A. Bullen, ch. 2.

16. A. Yarmie, op. cit., pp. 212-13.

17. R.C. on Labour, Final Report, Part 1, 1894, p. 32; Bolton M.C.S.A., Minutes, 3 June 1892; Bolton M.C.S.A., Survey of Non-Members, 1908-9.

18. Textile Mercury, 22 Feb. 1896, p. 145.

19. See A.J. McIvor, 'Employers' Organisation and Strike-breaking in Britain, 1880-1914', International Review of Social History, XXIX (1984), Part 1, pp. 7-8. See also L.H. Powell, The Shipping Federation, (London, 1950), passim.

20. R. Kirby & A.E. Musson, The Voice of the People: John Doherty, 1798-1854, (Manchester,1975), pp. 128-32.

21. A. Howe (1984), op. cit., pp. 177-8.

22. E. Hopwood, The Lancashire Weavers Story, (Manchester, 1969), pp. 33-6; H.A. Turner, op. cit., pp. 388-90; S.W. Webb., A History of British Trade Unionism, (London, 1920), pp. 485-7.

23. J.H. Porter, 'Industrial Peace in the Cotton Trade, 1875-1913', Yorkshire Bulletin of Economic and Social Research, 19, 1967, pp. 49-50.

24. On the rather neglected cardroom workers see A. Bullen & A. Fowler, The Cardroom Workers' Union (Rochdale, 1986).

25. F.M.C.S.A., Annual Reports, 1899 and 1906; Oldham M.C.S.A., Annual Reports, 1906, pp. 6-7; 1911, p.6; N.C.S.M.A., Joint Minutes, 1 December 1909.

26. R.F. Dyson, op. cit., pp. 534-8. See also Textile Mercury, 1 Aug. 1896, p. 86; Manchester Guardian, 14 February, 1901.

27. See B.R. Mitchell & P. Deane, Abstract of British Historical Statistics, (Cambridge, 1962), p. 72.

28. J.H. Porter (1967), op. cit., pp. 58-9.

29. R. Smith, op. cit., pp. 308-9.

30. See footnote 19. On strikebreaking in cotton finishing, see ch. 7, section III.

31. See Board of Trade (Labour Department), Annual Report on Strikes and Lock-Outs, 1891, 'Employers' Reports', Case 746, p. 314. Also, Textile Mercury, 1 Sept. 1894, p. 176, 17 Nov. 1894, p. 384, 1 Dec. 1894, p. 436.

32. See Hesketh Booth, Solicitors, Legal Opinion No. 34, March 1909, to the Oldham M.C.S.A.; Textile Mercury, 30 June 1894, p. 522; 3 Nov. 1894, p. 353; Daily Dispatch, 14 May 1913.
33. Oldham M.C.S.A., Committee Minutes, 15 June 1894; 29 Jan. 1897; Cotton Employers' Parliamentary Association, Minutes, 7 March 1902; Blackburn C.S.M.A. Minutes, 5 Dec. 1901.
34. See the Board of Trade, Annual Reports on Strikes and Lock-Outs, section on employers' strike compensation payments, and R. Smith, op. cit., p. 303. The Ashton association were on occasions paid enough to allow dividends to shareholders. See, for example, Ashton M.C.S.A., Minutes, 29 December 1891 and 3 March 1892. Some local associations also arranged to execute a firm's orders during a strike. See N.C.S.M.A., Minutes, 4 May 1900.
35. See the evidence of J. Rawlinson, Secretary, N.C.S.M.A., in the R.C. on Labour, Digest of Evidence, C, Vol. 1, 1892, Cmd. 6708, pp. 13-15.
36. Textile Mercury, 27 January 1894, p. 76.
37. H.A. Clegg, A. Fox and A.F. Thompson, A History of British Trade Unionism, Vol. 1, 1889-1911 (Oxford, 1964), pp. 112-17; K. Burgess, op. cit., pp. 280-6; R.F. Dyson, op. cit., pp. 288-316; A. McIvor, thesis, pp. 121-36.
38. J.L. White, The Limits of Trade Union Militancy, (Westport, Connecticut, 1978).
39. N.C.S.M.A., Minutes, 2 February 1912 and 21 February 1913; Nelson C.S.M.A., Minutes, 18 November 1912 to 28 August 1913.
40. General Union of Associations of Loom Overlookers, Jubilee History, (1935), pp. 42-3; N.C.S.M.A., Joint Minutes, 14 August 1917.
41. W.R. Garside, 'Management and Men' in B. Supple (ed.), Essays in British Business History, (Oxford, 1977), pp. 259-62; K. Middlemas, Politics in Industrial Society, (London, 1979), p. 128; R.A. Leeson, Strike: A Live History, 1887-1971, (London, 1973), pp. 52, 78-9, 143. See also H. Gospel, ch. 4 in C.J. Wrigley, ed. op. cit., 1986.
42. M. Savage, 'Capitalist and Patriarchal Relations at Work: Preston Cotton Weaving, 1890-1940', ch. 10 in L. Murgatroyd et al, editors, Localities, Class and Gender, (London, 1985), pp. 188-93.
43. For the struggles against the tapers see the Blackburn C.S.M.A., Minutes, 17 February to 28 June 1921; the Tapers' Agreement of Sept. 1930 and Minutes, 29 June 1936. For the conflicts with the overlookers refer to the N.C.S.M.A., Minutes, 21 Jan. 1921 and Joint Minutes, 5 August 1921. See also the General Union of Associations of Loom Overlookers, op. cit., p. 44.
44. Oldham M.C.S.A., Annual Report, 1920, pp. 10-12.
45. Blackburn C.S.M.A., Minutes, 18 March 1932.
46. Ibid., 12 October 1931. For examples of overlookers being replaced by cheaper labour see the same Minutes, 12 January, 1926; 30 November 1926; 29 August 1927; 6 January 1928.
47. Ibid., 17 January 1927.
48. N.C.S.M.A., Minutes, 26 April 1927; 22 October 1929; 12

December 1930.
49. See A.J. McIvor, 'Manual Work, Technology and Industrial Health, 1918-39', Medical History, Vol. 31, April 1987, pp. 160-89.
50. N.C.S.M.A., Joint Minutes, 9 August 1932 and Blackburn C.S.M.A., Minutes, 28 October 1932 and 25 November, 1932.
51. See A.J. McIvor, ' "A Crusade for Capitalism." The Economic League, 1919-39', in Journal of Contemporary History, Oct. 1988.
52. B.R. Mitchell and P. Deane, op. cit., p. 72. For a detailed analysis of cotton trade union responses to the employer counter attack in the inter-war years see A. Fowler, ch. 6.
53. Exports of cloth in 1938 to India had dwindled to around twenty per cent of their 1925 size and to China to just over one twentieth. See the Oldham M.C.S.A., Annual Report, 1939, pp. 6-7.
54. B. Vitkovitch, 'The United Kingdom Cotton Industry, 1937-54', Journal of Industrial Economics, July 1955, pp. 252-5; M.W. Kirby, 'The Lancashire Cotton Industry in the Inter-War Years: A Study in Organisational Change', Business History, Vol. XVI, No. 2, 1974, pp. 147 and 152.
55. Z. Hutchinson, 'The Trusts Grip Cotton', Independent Labour Party Pamphlets, New Series, No. 28, 1920.
56. The Provisional Emergency Cotton Committee, Reports, 1922-5, published by Sherratt & Hughes, Manchester.
57. Ibid., and see the Bolton M.C.S.A., Minutes, 24 July 1923; 11 November 1924; 27 July 1925; 16 March 1926; and the Bolton Evening News, 24-5 July 1925.
58. Bolton M.C.S.A., Minutes, 1 Sept. 1931.
59. Much of the decline in the membership density of the F.M.C.S.A. can be explained by the refusal of the Lancashire Cotton Corporation to affiliate from its creation in 1929. See the Daily Express, 1 April; the Corporation File in the Oldham M.C.S.A. archives; Preston C.S.M.A., Minutes, 4 February 1931.
60. The Livingstone Mill Company, Oldham, for example, was expelled from the master spinners' federation in 1928 after increasing working hours from 48 to $55\frac{1}{2}$ and running double shifts. Bolton Operative Spinners', Annual Report, 1928, p. 5.
61. See, in particular, A. Bullen, The Lancashire Weavers' Union, (Rochdale, 1984), pp. 50-63, and J.H. Riley, 'The More Looms System', Manchester University, M.A. thesis, 1981. See also A. and L. Fowler, The History of the Nelson Weavers Association, (Nelson, 1984), chs. 4-6; H.A. Turner, op. cit., pp. 327-31; E. Hopwood, op. cit., pp. 95-8; 108-12; and the Board of Trade, Industrial Survey of Lancashire, (H.M.S.O., London, 1932), pp. 137-47.
62. J.H. Grey, president of the N.C.S.M.A., in the Burnley C.S.M.A., Minutes, 7 January 1931.
63. Blackburn C.S.M.A., Minutes, 20 October 1930 to 11 February 1931. Preston C.S.M.A., Minutes, 27 April 1931.
64. N.C.S.M.A., Minutes, 28 January 1931; 6 and 13 February 1931.

Cotton Employers' Organisations

65. Factory Inspectors Reports, for 1933, p. 81; for 1934, p. 91. One result was a considerable increase in legal breaches of the Piecework Particulars Clause of the 1901 Factory Act.

66. Blackburn C.S.M.A., Minutes, 29 April 1932 and 2 May 1932. A similar process of growing employer disunity and erosion of collective bargaining occurred in wool; see I. Magrath, ch. 3, section II.

67. Board of Trade, Industrial Survey of Lancashire, (1932), pp. 15-19; 131-47.

68. See ch. 8, D. Busfield, 'Skill and the Sexual Division of Labour in the West Riding Textile Industry, c. 1850-1914'.

69. W. Lazonick, 'Industrial Relations and Technical Change: The Case of the Self-Acting Mule', Cambridge Journal of Economics, No. 3, 1979, pp. 248-9.

70. Bolton M.C.S.A., Special Committee Minute Book, 6 May 1931; 11 August 1931; and for the agreement, 19 August 1931. However, there is very little hard evidence of determined union opposition to the newer ring spinning, high draft winding and automatic loom technology, which makes the employers' lack of initiative even more surprising. See W. Lazonick, op. cit., pp. 255-7 and A. Fowler, 'Trade Unions and Technical Change: The Automatic Loom Strike, 1908', North West Labour History Society Bulletin, 1979-80, pp. 43-55.

71. The Bolton spinners perceived that firms were being given a mandate to 'have a go' at the unions in an intensified cost-reduction drive over 1930-2, which included a challenge to "practically the whole of the concessions gained during the last fifty years of strenuous trade union effort". Bolton Operative Spinners' Association, Annual Report, 1931, p. 4.

72. Blackburn C.S.M.A., Minutes, 4 July 1933; 4 September 1933; 1 November 1933.

73. N.C.S.M.A., Wage Censuses File, Table 3, 'Systems of Weaving'.

74. Royal Commission on Trade Unions and Employers' Association, Final Report, (H.M.S.O., London, 1968), pp. 20-1.; V.G. Munns and W.E.J. McCarthy, Employers' Associations, (Donovan Commission Research Paper 7, H.M.S.O., London, 1967), p. 1. For a stimulating general discussion which emphasises the inherent weakness of employers' organisations in Britain see J. Zeitlin, 'From Labour History to the History of Industrial Relations', Economic History Review, XL, 2, 1987, pp. 173-6.

Chapter 2

PRAGMATISM vs. PRINCIPLE: COTTON EMPLOYERS
AND THE ORIGINS OF AN INDUSTRIAL RELATIONS
SYSTEM

Andrew Bullen

The 1850s have long been recognised as a turning point in industrial relations, particularly in the cotton industry. Whereas in the 1840s considerable violence attended disputes between masters and operatives, the conflicts of the following decade were characterised by order and discipline. Union leaders were less likely to be arrested, the police replaced the army in picketing control and with knobsticks being little used the antagonism and bitterness that previous years had witnessed were considerably diminished. 'New model employers', while not dominant in the cotton industry, considerably extended the practices of paternalism and welfare capitalism. By 1861, union recognition, almost non-existent in 1850, had gained a tentative foothold in the north-east of Lancashire and there was growing evidence of a new accommodation between capital and labour. Such progress towards a better relationship, however, was not universal. While employers in some Lancashire towns agreed to and promoted joint regulation, others became increasingly anti-union. Furthermore, the period was marked by more major disputes and conflicts rather than fewer, especially as the new decade of the 1860s began. This chapter attempts to explain these trends and contradictory developments and the reasons why some employers over this period moved towards accommodation while others took an opposite direction towards coercive, anti-labour strategies.

I. Industrial Relations in the 1850s

> ...when the historian writes the history of the labouring classes, he will be guided by the Landmarks of Battles distinct as Waterloo and Inkerman, amongst them will be found the Preston Lockout, the Harwood and Padiham strikes and the Colne Struggle. (1)

Between 1853 and 1861 cotton workers were involved in three major wage movements, 1853-4, 1859-60 and 1861. The first of

Pragmatism vs. Principle

these, for an advance of ten per cent, coincided with a general claim amongst workers in many industries, including transport, coal, iron, building and the police. (2) Strikes in a number of Lancashire towns by all grades of cotton operatives culminated in a town stoppage at Stockport, where the object was achieved, followed by the famous Preston Lockout lasting some eight months which ended in the workers' defeat. (3) On the operatives' side control of the campaign was vested in an ad hoc committee covering the whole county, while the employers created the less comprehensive Lancashire Masters' Defence Association (L.M.D.A.) which organised a sympathetic lockout at Burnley, Padiham, Bacup and Wigan. The end of the lockout meant that most of the operatives who had been successful initially in gaining the ten per cent elsewhere, lost the rise with Preston's defeat. (4) The second wage movement began in 1859, with all branches of the industry again asking for a ten per cent rise. Spinners gained a five per cent concession, but early in the new year without the resurrection of the operatives' co-ordinating committees or very much resistance by the employers, a general wage advance of a similar amount was granted to all operatives in the mills. (5) The third and final movement came in 1861, again coinciding with demands in other industries for advances, but this time for the cotton workers a reduction equivalent to the last rise. Piecemeal resistance met with strong reactions from employers, including in the north-east of the county simultaneous lockouts resulting in the local operatives' defeat and in south Lancashire the total collapse of the weavers' union. (6) Against the backcloth of these general wage movements were a number of important town strikes by weavers, of which that of Great Harwood in 1858, lasting thirteen weeks, Padiham, 1859, lasting twenty-six weeks, and Colne, 1860-1, lasting some fifty-two weeks, are the most important. (7) All were fought either to maintain or achieve parity with the Blackburn Standard Wage List.

It was primarily due to these disputes that both masters and men reached new levels of permanent organisation. The Blackburn Weavers' Association which was formed immediately after the Preston Lockout, had reached some 10,000 members by 1858 covering the town and surrounding so called 'out-districts'. (8) As Great Harwood was one of these 'out-districts', the Blackburn Association, under its Secretary Edward (Ned) Whittle, took responsibility for the 1858 dispute and ultimately blame for the unsatisfactory settlement. (9) As a result the 'out-districts' broke away to form the North-East Lancashire Power-loom Weavers' Association (The First Amalgamation), and after incorporating other existing District unions and establishing new ones, raised their membership to 12,000 and set out to bring Padiham up to the 'Standard'. (10) The Burnley employers, seeing their neighbours in difficulties, recreated the L.M.D.A. during the Padiham strike and as at Preston paid financial compensation equivalent to normal profits as an incentive to the millowners directly involved to resist. (11) Essentially the L.M.D.A. represented the leading antagonists of 1853-4, the mill owners of Burnley, Preston and

Pragmatism vs. Principle

Stockport. Blackburn Masters remained aloof, as did most of the employers in the area covered by the South-East Lancashire Powerloom Weavers' Association and the other southern based United Factory Operatives Association (12), both formed in the late 1850s, the latter body being exceptional in organising all types of cotton workers.

Part of the explanation for the pattern of these events lies in the prevailing state of trade. The number of people engaged in the cotton industry rose between 1851 and 1861 from 287,076 to 356,191. The number of cotton factories increased by 60 per cent, spindles rising from 14 million to 21.5 million and power looms from 170,000 to 360,000 over the same years. (13) Yet within what is generally regarded as a boom period there was considerable fluctuation in trade. Markets that were buoyant by 1852 were replaced by poor or indifferent trade by the end of 1853. Late 1855 and early 1856 saw another crisis resulting in short time and in the second half of 1857 mills closed for part of each week. Some recovery occurred in 1858, and 1859 began with better prices until September when a brief period of uncertainty gave way in 1860 to the best trade many could remember. The beginning of 1861 was marked by a complete reversal with over-production and the anticipation of the coming American Civil War initiating another crisis. Such trends were particularly important for the outcome of long disputes and strikes begun in good trade frequently ended in bad. Indeed, the success or failure of industrial action during the 1850s can be explained in large part simply by these fluctuations in trade. The Preston Lockout began when profits were still being made, but ended when employers had little incentive to come to terms, a situation repeated at Colne. Employers compromised in the better trade of 1858 and early 1859 at Great Harwood and Padiham and gave way completely in the boom of 1860. While explaining something of bargaining strength at any one time, the state of trade cannot be seen as the key to the different responses of employers to trade unions. Recognition was not determined solely by the prevailing general economic climate, although good trade may be seen as having a significant effect on union objectives, which in turn engendered employer willingness to conciliate. (14)

The extent to which unions became less militant and narrowed their horizons during the 1850s is the subject of considerable debate and one which is not the main focus of this chapter. Unions among cotton power-loom weavers were not new in the 1850s and 1860s, but their previous appearance had been ephemeral. Comparisons between past aims and those prevailing at mid-century when permanent organisations emerged are therefore limited in value, although they do emphasise the continuing objective of joint wage control, which for the most part employers had previously denied them. Of course, in the relatively prosperous 1850s, it was far easier for unions, or more especially their leaders, to adopt a more conciliatory tone and even the language of liberal political economy. Wage applications were always more polite than memorials resisting reductions. In fact, during the

Pragmatism vs. Principle

1850s a plethora of evidence exists showing both union moderation and harangues against capitalism and all its evils, but such material needs to be handled with care. Union leaders accepted the arguments of liberal economics only when it suited their purposes. Increased profits justified wage claims, poor profits brought forward the demand for wages being a fixed cost. (15) Similarly, 'sweeping the sham millocracy away', usually came as a threat at the end of a strike fought initially on the grounds of a fairer share of the capitalist profits, when the dispute was already known to be lost. Likewise, co-operation, as an alternative to private enterprise was usually postulated as a balm to ease the wounds of defeat. (16) The militancy or moderation of speeches was dependent partly upon the speaker; trade union leaders being noted for conciliation, whilst paid delegates employed for a strike's duration advocated conflict. Behind all the rhetoric, however, the disputes in the 1850s were essentially over fairly moderate aims. Strikes and lockouts were usually undertaken for modest claims on wage issues, rather than major attacks upon employers' prerogatives.

As with the state of trade, union moderation no doubt influenced the industrial relations atmosphere during the 1850s, but that influence was essentially permissive. Union moderation merely allowed those employers wishing to develop so-called 'better relations' the opportunity to do so. By itself, any new spirit of conciliation coming from the operatives' side cannot explain the different responses of the various employers. The same stimulus of limited aims and objectives, moderate demands, sycophantic memorials and conciliatory overtures, met in some towns with outright rejection, hostility and a refusal by employers even to reply. (17) Neither were the different responses simply a delay in the spread of good practice from progressive employers to the more reactionary ones. Rather, the explanation lies in the employers in the various districts responding to their own particular market position. Simply, employers in high wage paying areas tolerated and encouraged trade unions in order to have them equalise wages between competing districts, while employers in low paying towns were the most actively opposed to the operatives' aims of recognition and a uniform wage list throughout the county. Before attempting to substantiate this hypothesis by elaborating on the actions of employers in the events already described, some understanding of the nature of piece price lists in cotton weaving is necessary.

II. The Evolution of Piecework Wage Lists

Piece rate lists had originated with the old hand-loom weavers as the only reliable method an employer had of paying 'outworkers' beyond their supervision. In the new spinning factories of the late eighteenth century and the powerloom weaving sheds of the 1830s, individual employers usually adopted a list of their own, or one borrowed from a neighbouring mill, as a stimulus

Pragmatism vs. Principle

towards maximising production. Not only did the payments by results system encourage more effort by the weaver, but utilisation of a common list for all the mill operatives in a particular department had ancillary benefits for the employer in other aspects of management. Paying the operatives all the same rate meant no necessity for negotiation with individuals, either when recruited or afterwards. Lists ensured that the various groups of operatives were dealt with collectively in each establishment, a locus of bargaining that the most anti-union employer welcomed and tried to maintain. (18) One's own workpeople were seen as a legitimate group to discuss wage changes with, objection only being raised against the outside interference of a third party. This was dramatically illustrated when one Manchester employer in 1855 discovered, during negotiations with his operatives, that they were acting on the instructions of a union, causing him to throw their petition in the fire and end the talks. (19) Lists also contained graduated scales for a number of variables, with most of the likely changes affecting the operatives' workload and earnings being catered for in the formula. As a result, day-to-day negotiations were obviated, minimising the area of potential conflict within the mill. Thus while the lists operated, the Lancashire cotton industry never successfully developed a system of shop stewards.

The advantages of adopting a common list for the whole town, however, were of a different order. The main benefit of a town list was to take wages out of competition. Labour costs accounted for up to eighty per cent of the selling price of cloth and therefore were a vital element in competition with other employers. Having a common list ensured that in good times employers did not outbid each other for labour and in bad trade a downward spiral of wage undercutting leading to possible disruptions, was avoided. Comparability disputes were minimised and a mechanism created to reduce the influence of labour supply and demand pressures.

Given the advantages it is understandable why it was the employers and their associations who voluntarily introduced town lists, but there were problems. The more widespread the application of a list, the more complicated it had to be, the more difficult for the layman to understand and the more likelihood of imperfections. While plain cloths were basically the same, the different loom makers included modifications, both to the main body of the machine and to its attachments. A list for the Blackburn type of loom, for example, needed to recognise variations for machines entitled Harrison's, Graham's, Hudson's, Dickenson's and Dugdale's, let alone all the other different sizes of attachments. (20) Such a list was beyond the abilities of the most proficient amateur mathematician in the industry and when people began to mix the attachments of different machine manufacturers and create hybrids, a suitable piece price became extremely complex. Individual employers were unable to formulate their own lists or fully understand the ones they used and most operatives could only gauge if their work had been correctly rated when the wage packet arrived. At Great Harwood in 1858, for example, the operatives returned to work believing the settlement over the list prices was fair, only to find take-home pay in some cases reduced by twenty per cent. (21) Similarly at Clitheroe when the weavers demanded and won the Blackburn Standard considerable dissatisfaction arose when it was discovered their old lists paid better on some types of cloth. (22)

Whilst complex, lists did not take cognizance of some important variables, most notably yarn quality, and in consequence it was possible in the late 1870s for Burnley operatives on a low paying list, using better material, to earn more than their contemporaries in Blackburn. (23) Disputes could arise with accusations of discrepancies between lists of twenty-five per cent and, after investigation, over quibbles about the decimal points. Added to these problems was the absence of any method to ensure individual employers abided by their agreement to pay list prices. Without regular policing, piece price list drift could develop in an attempt by an unscrupulous employer to gain competitive advantage and masters' associations simply lacked the personnel to undertake the work. Further, a common wage rate for a town provided a focus for the development of multi-employer bargaining with a representative body of workers, if not a trade union. This is precisely what happened at Blackburn where the first permanent weavers' trade union emerged, acting as a model for all others to follow.

The Blackburn Standard List, known as the Weavers' Charter because of its importance to the weavers' unions, had its origins in the late 1840s. At this time new cloths were being introduced and, in the absence of a generally accepted wage rate, disputes arose as to the correct payment. Initially these disputes were referred to a small group of masters for their ruling, half the arbitrators being nominated by the operatives and half by the employers directly involved. According to Baynes, a local millowner, this system became onerous and after three to four years the two sides of industry in the town appointed representatives and established a United Committee to draw up a standard list for spinning, carding and weaving. (24) Each of these lists was compiled over the next few years, spinning by October 1852 and weaving by August 1853. At that time no formal union amongst Blackburn weavers existed, the negotiations being undertaken by an ad hoc committee of weavers' representatives backed by public meetings. It was only at the end of the Preston Lockout, when Blackburn masters took back the advance of ten per cent given in 1853, that the decision was taken to set up a permanent weavers' union.

Already recognised to some extent before its inauguration in the ad hoc committee, the remit of the new union was to watch for an auspicious moment to regain the lost advance and more especially to monitor and maintain the implementation of the Blackburn Standard List. (25) In this latter purpose the union was fulfilling not only its own aspirations, (for most operatives also wanted common price lists), but also that of the employers,

Pragmatism vs. Principle

helping to solve some of the problems inherent in a general agreement among masters to pay uniform wage rates without the ability to enforce it themselves. What the employers needed was an expert whose time could be spent going from mill to mill calculating the correct prices, an arbitrator of the complicated list clauses. With the jointly agreed Standard List and the creation of a union to ensure individual firms abided by the agreement, employers obtained the benefit of such an expert, who also had the authority to order striking operatives back to work. In Edward Whittle, an ex-member of the <u>ad hoc</u> committee which formulated the list and now Union Secretary, the employers had just the type of person they required to police the agreement. A "quiet unassuming peacemaker attending to the duties for which he was paid", wrote Eccles Shorrocks of Darwen, some years later. (26)

The Blackburn Weavers' Union was formed on the model of a burial club, one penny a week in exchange for £3 on death being the only contractual benefit. Like the Local Philanthropic Burial Society for which Whittle also acted as auditor, contributions were collected door to door, the executive named a Board of Directors and all the lay officials received commission and payments for meetings. The funds enabled Whittle to be paid a full time officer's salary, but were insufficient to sustain a major strike in the town for any length of time. Blackburn's total subscription for one year was not enough for four days benefit for the whole of the membership at the same rate of strike allowance made to operatives at Padiham and Colne. (27) Individual employers might pay Whittle to come and calculate their prices, the amount to be later passed to the union, but the masters as a whole benefited from having their agreement policed at almost no cost to their own association. This junior management role for the Union Secretary implied a level of recognition, but it was an extremely narrow form. The custom was maintained of joint negotiation on list amendments and a sort of understanding prevailed that the Masters' Association would meet the union representative on request, but in the absence of a formal procedural agreement, even these concessions could be withdrawn arbitrarily. (28) It could be argued that recognition was extended not to the union, but merely to the Secretary provided he continued to interpret the list fairly and kept order and discipline. Blackburn employers congratulated themselves on the way they had minimised industrial tension and at the same time solved the problem of list compliance. (29)

Cotton employers in a number of other towns eventually came to follow the example of the Blackburn Masters, the delay being partly explained by the lack of a custom of list wage payments on the level of the town. Newer, growing towns, rarely had a list, but most of the old centres of production had at one time or another some common rate, albeit fallen into disuse. Changes in product and technology necessitated revision and re-establishment, but in practice this was often left undone. The reasons for this are numerous, but most important was the degree of difficulty in constructing a common list. The Oldham Master Spinners, for ex-

Pragmatism vs. Principle

ample, as late as 1870 failed in their attempt to form a town list for minders, because there were simply too many variations to encompass. (30)   Another problem was on whose list should employers agree to equalise.   Understandably, low paying firms were reluctant to lose their advantage and the operatives in high paying establishments were determined not to see a reduction. Such difficulties added to the employers' determination to resist the operatives' claim for ten per cent at Preston in 1853. Suggestions were made by the Spinners' Union that the rise should be made on top of the highest rate in the town, all the rest being equalised at that level.   This was regarded as dictation, justifying total rejection of the major claim.   Within five years, however, the Preston Master Cotton Spinners' Association had passed a rule to exclude from financial compensation or any form of support those firms paying less than the average, and twelve months later brought in its own standard list without industrial conflict. (31)   The problem of who was to get the benefit of equalisation was ameliorated by granting a general increase at the same time, some employers giving more than others. Being jointly negotiated with the unions representing Preston operatives, this was obviously not dictation nor the interference of a third party and apparently, therefore, acceptable.   Further south in the county similar town lists were negotiated, some following strikes over other wage issues, but essentially all without cries of dictation and all involving a level of local trade union recognition. (32)

Not all towns in our period, however, followed Blackburn's example.   In the case of certain towns in the south-east of Lancashire this failure to adopt a list may have been due to the type of competition within the particular area and the predominance of large combined process firms. In the north-east of the county, on the other hand, the opposition engendered related not to competition within the towns, but to competition existing between towns and to the aim of the First Amalgamation to make the Blackburn Standard a universal list in the whole area.   Whereas in Blackburn itself the demand for the standard Universal List was not a contentious issue, outside, in the lower wage paying towns, equalisation was a major threat to their competitive advantage.

III. Competition, Pragmatism and Principle

Part of the explanation of why the idea of a universal list was not something all employers could ascribe to lay not in different levels of wages, but rather in each town's respective products and product markets.   In the 1850s, the geographical separation of the industry, whereby spinning was increasingly concentrated in the south-east of the county and weaving in the north, had already begun.   Further, within the spinning sector fine counts were becoming more and more located around Bolton, coarse and middle counts around Oldham and the low counts and waste cotton in the region of Rossendale.   Similarly, in the

Pragmatism vs. Principle

weaving sector there evolved a greater dependence of particular towns on one type or range of cloth to the exclusion of others. Radcliffe and Pilkington, for example, were concentrating on florentines and nankeens, while up to the late 1840s Blackburn was producing jaconettes and shirtings. Such specialisation affected all the towns in the north-east of the county, with an impact on the operatives' skill level and even the type of loom to be operated. Burnley, for instance, was from the 1850s beginning to concentrate on printers, requiring a narrower loom than that worked at Blackburn.

Over time a town could change its product or become even more specialised in response to market forces, but in the short run it was possible for one town to experience relative dullness of trade, while in another markets were brisk. (33) This was especially true in relation to whether production was for the home market or abroad. Basically, the better quality material went for British consumption and the lower quality cloth for export. Preston, therefore, could be seen as a town dependent upon the home trade, whereas Blackburn and Burnley relied heavily on the production of two types of cloth for India and the rest of the Far East. Specialisation, however, was not yet at a level whereby there was no common production in the various Lancashire cotton towns. Therefore, whilst this goes some way to explaining the difficulties in creating a universal list, the lower wages paid by some towns was the dominant causal factor.

Such differentials engendered animosity between the employers in the various Lancashire production centres, especially when markets were being lost to rivals. (34) Genuine local disadvantage, for transport costs etc., was tolerable, but lower pay was frowned upon as unfair competition when used to poach other towns' trade. It was in the interest, therefore, of higher paid towns to raise those undercutting them, but no means existed to bring this about. An open market and the multitude of manufacturers mitigated against the creation of an effective countrywide cartel, had the low paying towns wanted one. Trade unions could fulfil the function of imposing a common rate on all towns, indeed unless they did so, employers in high paying districts could argue genuinely that they were unable to compete with low payers and must therefore refuse an advance in their own area. (35) Already in the first half of the nineteenth century irregular pressure had been put on the spinners' unions, most notably by Manchester masters, to raise neighbouring towns, but before the 1850s similar action in the manufacturing sector was impossible. However, once the Preston dispute had demonstrated an effective operative weavers' organisation a possible mechanism existed for one group of manufacturers to pressurise another to compete fairly in wage costs.

The first example of the pressure exerted by one town's manufacturers over another to raise wages in our period was during the Preston dispute itself. "The struggle was continued solely on the sufferance of the other employers", claimed the Masters' Defence Association. "It needs but that every employer should cease to pay wages to any who contribute to a strike, in order to render a turn-out impossible", their final report continued. (36) Blackburn Masters, they suggested, were to blame for allowing their operatives to send the bulk of the relief for strikers, while standing aloof from the Defence Association themselves. That it was Blackburn rather than elsewhere which had done this is easily understood, not only had they granted the advance, but on average their wages were already higher. The towns most actively supporting the Preston masters on the other hand were amongst the lowest wage payers, both Rossendale and Burnley being an estimated twelve per cent below Blackburn, and Stockport some seven and a half per cent. (37) What was important too was the sheer size of Blackburn's weaving population, a factor which remained crucial for collections in support of all long strikes until the 1880s. Had Blackburn been a small town, with fewer looms, the size of the collections made in the mills would not have been sufficient to maintain strike pay in the towns where wages needed raising. At the highest rate of semi-voluntary levies then made, contributions from ten working weavers were required to grant five shillings' dispute allowance to one operative on strike. Preston, however, was only the beginning, and once the Blackburn Weavers' Union had grown to encompass surrounding villages, what had been for the most part an inarticulated policy of their masters became overtly expressed.

Outside the Blackburn Masters' Association, towns such as Great Harwood had not been party to the original Standard List agreement, but nevertheless the union was told to 'bring them up' or face reductions in the town itself. (38) Therefore, when the Union struck against an attempt to impose a five per cent reduction for local disadvantage by Great Harwood masters, the Blackburn employers all too willingly allowed mill collections to take place. Even when the local union broke up and the First Amalgamation, created out of the so-called 'out districts', declared its aim to establish the Blackburn Standard as a general list throughout the north-east, the same policy was followed. Prompting the Blackburn Union to give support to the breakaway First Amalgamation at Padiham, Colne and elsewhere, leaders of the Masters' Association promised to stay out of the conflict while those towns paid lower wages. (39) Never quite rejecting the arguments offered by other employers that the question was one of dictation (they continued to advocate that negotiations should be between a representative committee of operatives and employers in each town), they saw no difficulty in allowing their workers to support the strikers financially. (40) Under mounting pressure from the Burnley led Defence Association to join in the resistance by the masters of Padiham, the Blackburn Employers' Association agreed to lay the question before their members, but only after an inspection by their sub-committee of the prices being paid. The results showed only marginal differences between the Standard List and what was earned at Padiham and this effectively ended Blackburn Weavers' Union support and ultimately the strike. (41)

In their action the Blackburn Masters' Association were

clearly pursuing their own self-interest rather than adhering to any principle related to trade unionism or indeed fair competition. By allowing and encouraging hundreds of pounds every week to leave Blackburn in support of strikers elsewhere they effectively diverted attention away from possible wage claims in their own sphere of influence, a factor noted by trade union leaders. (42) In this case limited recognition was not advocated because the employers had discovered the benefits of joint regulation in a straightforward sense: the aim of the policy was to keep trade unions weak in their own town, but strong enough elsewhere to enforce a common wage rate. A similar self-interest lay behind the actions of masters in towns such as Accrington and Chorley when they agreed formally with their operatives to abide by any wage movement which took place at Blackburn. (43) Their production and profits would continue while the main centre was locked in struggle without any costs to themselves, but allowing their operatives to contribute relief. Weavers' organisations in these towns could become effective fund raisers, but experience in normal trade union activity was minimised.

IV. Coercive Anti-Unionism? The Lancashire Masters' Defence Association

Any theory of pragmatism over principle, however, must be able to take account of those opposing trade unions as much as those willing to see their introduction to promote the employers' purposes. To what extent, therefore, can we see in the behaviour of the Masters' Defence Association, merely the working out of their own particular commercial self interest? Certainly there were those who were vehemently anti-union on the grounds of principle, but there is some evidence which indicates at least a cynical rather than genuine opposition to dictation and outside interference. Before the strike at Padiham, employers there had allowed the First Amalgamation General Secretary to visit their mills and had attended open meetings where both sides were present. (44) Offers were made to the operatives to compromise, one employer declaring:

> If there was one principle above another which he recognised in this country, it was the principle of accommodation or conciliation, whatever parties had disputes, the fairest and most legitimate way was to reason together...the very best thing was concession. (45)

It was only when compromise was rejected and attempts were being made to raise subscriptions from masters in other towns that outright opposition to trade unionism and their 'dictatorial' manner took the place of wages as the central issue. The Lancashire Masters' Defence Association was formed during the Padiham dispute following an appeal by the Padiham employers to the nearest town, Burnley, for support. Burnley masters were unable by themselves to levy the amount necessary to pay compensation for those Padiham employers prepared to keep their mills closed and an appeal went out from them to form a new countrywide association. The inaugural meeting in the Free Trade Hall, Manchester, in early June 1859 was essentially a Burnley initiated and organised affair with attendance from masters in Preston, Clitheroe, Great Harwood, Colne, Sabden and Marsden (later called Nelson). (46) Significantly these were all towns where employers had most to lose if the First Amalgamation's aim of making the Blackburn Standard a Universal List succeeded. Absent were the towns of the south-east and mid-Lancashire which paid more than Blackburn, and although Stockport joined later (47), the L.M.D.A. remained predominantly a north-east organisation. Significantly, therefore, Burnley's insistence that the question at stake was one of 'who runs the mills', did not attract support from anybody without a direct financial interest. James Garnett, a Clitheroe employer, expressed their real concern at the first meeting: "they might as well fight the Battle at Padiham than at home". (48)

Up until the Cotton Famine it was the L.M.D.A. who were at the forefront of anti-unionism in cotton weaving. Ignoring their fairly consistent rhetoric, however, even they demonstrated a high degree of pragmatism. Apart from a small number of blackleg unemployed silk weavers from Coventry introduced at Colne, no real efforts were made to bring the disputes they managed to an early close. (49) In their decision to support financially only those whose hands had struck, instead of organising sympathetic lockouts, they not only removed from the market place a considerable amount of cloth, but ensured a firmer price for their own. More importantly, with no concerted attempt being made to stop mill collections and cut off relief, the L.M.D.A. made sure strikers were not forced to return to work for lack of funds. That this was pragmatism not principle is perhaps open to question, but again the views of Garnett provide an insight. After refusing to allow the First Amalgamation Secretary to enter his mill, he later does so, admitting in his diary, "he is much better to do business with than the hands themselves because he can calculate". (50) Once paying the Blackburn Standard he then refused to send aid to the Colne masters declaring there was nothing in it for him. (51)

V.   Conclusions

Obviously, there are limitations to the argument that employers' behaviour towards unions was dependent on competitive advantage. As pointed out earlier, it is necessary to understand the nature of the unions' challenge and what employers were accommodating to. Unions were not totally passive instruments of employers' self interest and manipulation. Whittle might say, "if this union gained its object, and dictation went on in the manner in which it did, it would drive trade and commerce from

Pragmatism vs. Principle

this country". But he was castigated for doing so. (52) As the unions grew they developed the power to challenge employers' customary rights outside the circumstances existing at their emergence and the raison d'etre of their original recognition and accommodation. By 1861, Blackburn employers were complaining, "You weavers are getting too united, you are getting so unanimous we must really make a stand against you". (53) The Masters' Association declined to meet the weavers' leaders (while the operatives refused to take a reduction) and locked out weavers on 44,000 looms in the area until the union dropped its demand for simultaneous short time to accompany the five per cent cut. Cries of dictation were widely raised again, employers entering into a bond with financial penalties for those who opened their mills, claiming, "if they submitted to the terms proposed, (by the union), their mastership would be gone, that their authority as manufacturers would no longer exist". (54) The level of accommodation, therefore, even at Blackburn, was becoming strained by the early 1860s and was dependent on the union continuing to operate in the employers' collective interest. (55)

This formative phase in the evolution of an industrial relations system ended with the American Civil War and the consequential Cotton Famine. Between 1861 and 1864 many of the organisations of both masters and men mentioned above disappeared or became temporarily moribund. The membership of the Blackburn Weavers' Union was halved, and the Lancashire Masters' Defence Association existed in name only. The First Amalgamation, having reached a membership of 24,000 in 1860, fell back to 4,275 in 1863 and the Burnley, Glossop and Ashton Weavers' Unions collapsed. (56) The Blackburn Masters' Association saw some fragmentation with firms paying less than the Standard once the weakened union was unable to secure list compliance. (57)

When the industry re-emerged from the dislocation caused by the Cotton Famine, however, the experience and precedents of the 1850s were built into the industrial relations system that followed. In 1866, the Preston Masters' Association approached Blackburn and together they in turn met with Burnley Masters to establish the North and North-East Cotton Spinners' and Manufacturers' Association (N.C.S.M.A.), which had two main objects. First, to curb union power (strikes for wage increases were then taking place), and second, to develop a common list of wages to be paid throughout the area. (58) Because of objections by the Burnley Masters, who wished to maintain their competitive advantage on printers, the latter proposal was deferred and it was not until 1892 that a Universal List for wages in weaving came into operation, being an average of the rates paid in all three major towns of Blackburn, Preston and Burnley. Although this was calculated by the Secretary of the Weavers' Second Amalgamation (established 1884) the list was forced on the operatives, some of whom suffered wage reductions. The N.C.S.M.A. at the end of the century, however, still only covered thirteen towns and villages and the Weavers' Amalgamation with forty District Associations in membership was expected to ensure all employers in the county paid

Pragmatism vs. Principle

the list. At the same time, within the N.C.S.M.A. area, employers refused to allow a closed shop and resisted all efforts by the union to make itself more effective. (59) Defending what was in the employers' interest - taking wages out of competition in districts outside the N.C.S.M.A. area - the Second Weavers' Amalgamation in the 1890s was kept in a weak, subordinate position in much the same way as the Blackburn Weavers' Union and the First Weavers' Amalgamation had been in the 1850s.

NOTES

This chapter is based on research funded by the Economic and Social Research Council (E.S.R.C.) reference number FOO232204.
1. T. Birtwistle, 38th Colne Strike Bulletin, reprinted in the Blackburn Standard, 27 Feb. 1860.
2. H. Ashworth, The Preston Strike - An Enquiry into its Causes and Consequences, (Manchester, 1854), p. 5. Henry Ashworth Scrapbook, D.D.Pr. 138/87a. Lancashire County Record Office (L.C.R.O.), Preston.
3. Preston Chronicle and Lancashire Advertiser, 20 May, 1854; Manchester Guardian, 27 April; 4, 8 June; 6 Aug., 1853.
4. Blackburn Standard, 17 May 1854. D.D.Pr. 138/87B, Vol. 3, L.C.R.O.
5. Blackburn Standard, 29 Feb. 1860, Oldham Chronicle, 14 Jan. 1860.
6. N. Kirk, The Growth of Working Class Reformism in Mid-Victorian England (London, 1985) p. 257. Blackburn Standard, 27 March, 1, 3, 10 April 1861; Oldham Chronicle, 30 April 1861; Manchester Guardian, 15, 20, 28 Feb., 2, 16, 25, 26, 27, 29 March, 27 April 1861; Manchester Examiner, 29 April, 1861.
7. Accrington Free Press, 24 April, 15 May, 1858; Blackburn Standard, 10 March - 28 July 1858, 29 May 1961. Factory Inspectors Report, R. Baker Esq., 30 April 1861, pp. 38-9. W.A. Jevons, "Account of the Weavers' Strike at Padiham in 1859", in Trade Societies and Strikes. Report of the Committee on Trade Societies appointed by the National Association for the Promotion of Social Science (London, 1860). Manchester Examiner, 21 May 1861. J. Watts, The Workman's Bane and Antidote (Manchester, 1861), pp. 31-48.
8. A. Bullen, The Lancashire Weavers' Union (Manchester, 1984), p. 6.
9. Blackburn Standard, 21 Aug., 16 Oct., 20 Nov. 1858.
10. Blackburn Standard, 21 Aug., 27 Nov. 1858, 23 Feb. 1859. Accrington Free Press, 11 Sept. 1858.
11. Blackburn Times, 26 March 1859. D.D. Sp. Ac. 3990. L.C.R.O. L677 Colne Local History Collection.
12. Oldham Chronicle, 23 Feb. 1861.
13. B.R. Michell & P. Deane, Abstract of British Historical Statistics, (London, 1963), pp. 187-8. J. Watts, The Facts of the Cotton Famine, (Manchester, 1866), p. 53.
14. Blackburn Standard, 25 Oct. 1854, 25 July, 1 Aug., 29

Pragmatism vs. Principle

Aug., 14 Nov. 1855, 3 June 1857, 16 Jan. 1861. Blackburn Times, 21 July 1855, 8 Dec. 1857, 31 Dec. 1859. D.A. Farnie, The English Cotton Industry and the World Market, (Oxford, 1979), p. 84, 48th Colne Strike Bulletin, reprinted in the Blackburn Standard, 8 May 1861.
    15. Blackburn Standard, 29 Feb. 1860, 6 Feb. 1861.
    16.   J. Watts, (1861), p. 45. Blackburn Standard, 20 March 1861. See Blackburn Times, 15 Sept. 1855 for exception.
    17.   Blackburn Standard, 26 Dec. 1860.
    18.   Manchester Guardian, 11 May 1853. Reply of Stockport Masters' Association to the Operatives' Memorial: "I beg to inform you that the course hitherto adopted has been for each employer to receive addresses on the subject of wages from his own workpeople only and that the interference of any general committee is unnecessary."
    19. Manchester Guardian, 15 Nov. 1855.
    20.   Blackburn Times, 9 April 1859. Blackburn Standard, 3 April 1861. Only Harrisons, Dickensons and Dugdales were recognised by the Blackburn Standard List.
    21. Blackburn Standard, 21 July 1858.
    22.   R. Sharpe France (ed.), "The Diary of John Wood of Clitheroe 1860-64" in Transactions of the Historical Society of Lancashire and Cheshire, Vol. 105, (1953), pp. 138-9.
    23.   Textile Manufacturer, 15 March 1884.
    24. Alderman Baynes, The Cotton Trade - Two Lectures, (Blackburn 1857), pp. 70-1. See also E. Shorrocks, Letter to the Working men of Darwen, (Manchester, 1879), p. 11, for a less accurate account.
    25.   Blackburn Standard, 19 July 1854.
    26.   Blackburn Standard, 28th Dec. 1853. Eccles Shorrocks, Letter to the Workpeople of North and North-East Lancashire (2nd edition, Manchester, 1880), p. 4. "If there was any complaint at any mill, he was sent for and the price was soon arranged." See also Textile Manufacturer, 15 April 1884, "It is this impartiality that enables the employers to admit these men into their premises."
    27.   Fifth Half Yearly Report of the Powerloom Weavers' Association (Blackburn, Dec. 1856). Income £376. Cost of supporting 4,000 members for one week at 5/- per head £1,000.
    28.   Blackburn Times, 9 April 1859. Blackburn Standard, 6 Feb. 1861, "they waited upon their masters about some extra headings, their masters told them that they could not meet them on that question because they had not brought up the out-districts".
    29.   Baynes (1857), op. cit., p. 73.   Shorrocks (1880), op. cit., p. 4.
    30. Oldham Master Cotton Spinners' Association, Minute Book, 3 Feb. 1870.
    31.   Blackburn Standard, 29 June, 13 July, 1853. Manchester Guardian, 13 July 1853. Preston Guardian, 22 April, 13 May, 1854. Preston Chronicle, 14 Feb., 3 March 1860. Ashworth, op. cit., (1854), p. 8.   Preston Cotton Masters' Association, Poster, 15 Sept. 1853. D.D.Pr. 138/87B, Vol. 1, L.C.R.O. The

idea of a town list was not anathema to the Preston employers in 1853. The Preston Masters' Association did recommend to its members a general all-round rise of 5 per cent, but suggested that the high paying firms should give less than the lower paying ones, thereby making an approximation "to a uniform rate of wages throughout the town", Preston Employers, Letter Book, 18 Oct. 1853, DDX 1116/3/1 L.C.R.O.

32. Blackburn Standard, 7 Sept., 5 Oct. 1859. Padiham Masters jointly agreed a town list with the local union in March 1860 some six months after the ending of that town's strike. Blackburn Standard, 14 March 1860.

33. Baynes, op. cit., (1857), p. 70. Textile Manufacturer, 15 Jan. 1878, pp. 14-15, 15 Aug. 1879, p. 263, 15 March 1884, p. 85.

34. Manchester Guardian, 16 April 1861. Blackburn Times, 1 Dec. 1855, 19 March 1859. Textile Manufacturer, March 1884, Blackburn Standard 25 Jan. 1860. Preston Masters' Letter Book, 7 June 1886, DDX 1116/3/1, L.C.R.O. Blackburn Times, 1 May 1858: "A Blackburn manufacturer had told him last week, that he was very glad the Harwood men had resisted the reduction on the ground that the Harwood manufacturers had sold goods at a less price in Manchester than the Blackburn manufacturers could afford to do, and this had consequently stopped them from making many a bargain."

35. Colne Strike Bulletin, reprinted in the Blackburn Standard 22 Aug. 1860. Preston Guardian, 24 Sept. 1853. Manchester Guardian, 16 April 1861. Blackburn Standard, 14 Feb. 1860.

36. D.D.Pr., 138/87B, Vol. 3, L.C.R.O.

37. Blackburn Standard, 25 Jan., 29 Feb. 1860. D.D.Pr. 138/87B, Vol. 2, L.C.R.O.

38. Blackburn Standard, 7 April, 1858. Blackburn Times, 1 May 1858. For similar action by employers in other towns see, Manchester Guardian, 21 Nov., 19 Dec. 1855, 16 April 1861.

39. Manchester Guardian, 16 March 1861. Blackburn Standard, 20 March 1861.

40. Blackburn Standard, 14 Aug. 1859. Blackburn Masters' Association admitted, "the principle that all disputes between masters and those employed by them should be regulated between themselves". See the Blackburn Times, 20 Aug. 1859.

41. Blackburn Standard, 14 - 28 Sept. 1859. Blackburn Times, 20 Aug. 1859.

42. Blackburn Standard, 25 Jan 1860: A Bolton Delegate noted: "he fancied the masters rather liked to see a strike in such places as Padiham and Sabden, as it diverted attention of the weavers in such large districts as Bolton and Blackburn from their own interests." See also the Colne Strike Bulletin, reprinted in the Blackburn Standard 27 March 1861: "they know their trade is not flourishing and they would rather live on the contributions of their more reputable manufacturing friends who eager and wishful to keep down the quantity of food you consume seek to fight the battle at a distance." Also Blackburn Standard, 22 Feb. 1861.

43. Blackburn Standard, 6, 20 Feb. 1861. Blackburn Times, 12

June 1858.
44. Blackburn Times, 17 Sept. 1859. Blackburn Standard, 23 Feb. 1859, 14 March 1860.
45. Blackburn Times, 12 March 1859. Blackburn Standard, 23 March 1859.
46. Blackburn Standard, 23, 30 March, 13, 20 July 1859.
47. Preston Employers Letter Book, DDX 1116/3/1, L.C.R.O.
48. Blackburn Standard, 13 July 1859.
49. Colne Masters Levy Book. D.D.Sp.Ac. 3990, L.C.R.O., Preston. Blackburn Standard, 25 July 1860. At a Preston Mill in 1858: "The employer at first would not allow them to collect, but when informed of the position in which the Harwood operatives stood, he had gone into the mill and told them to collect if they liked." Blackburn Times, 15 May 1858.
50. O. Ashmore, "The Diary of James Garnett of Low Moor, Clitheroe, 1858-65. Part 1: Years of Prosperity 1858-60", Transactions of the Historic Society of Lancashire and Cheshire, Vol. 121, 1969, p. 87.
51. M. Brigg (editor), 'A Lancashire Weaver's Journal', The Record Society of Lancashire and Cheshire, Vol. 122, 1982, p. 191, O. Ashmore, (1969), op. cit., p. 90.
52. Blackburn Times, 7 Aug. 1858.
53. Blackburn Standard, 20 Feb. 1861.
54. Blackburn Standard, 13 Feb. 1861.
55. Blackburn Standard, 27 Feb., 6 March 1861.
56. Blackburn Weavers' 10th Annual Report, (Blackburn, Dec. 1864). North-East Lancashire Power-loom Weavers' Association 5th Annual Report and Balance Sheet, (Blackburn, 1863). Webb Trade Union Collection - Section A. Vol. 37.
57. Blackburn Standard, 4 Feb. 1863. Letter from W.H. Hornby.
58. North Lancashire Cotton Spinners and Manufacturers' Association, Minute Book, 11 April, 13, 20 June, 12 Sept. 1866.
59. For more detail on employers' strategies in the later period, see A.J. McIvor, Ch. 1.

Chapter 3

PROTECTING THE INTERESTS OF THE TRADE: WOOL TEXTILE EMPLOYERS' ORGANISATIONS IN THE 1920s

Irene Magrath

Easily distinguished from other kinds of textile production, the wool textile industry remains an umbrella term, encompassing a broad range of products from carpets to fine worsteds. This great diversity of interests has been reflected in the complex development of wool textile employers' organisations in the twentieth century. By 1921 these had come to form part of a set of inter-linked federations designed to protect, maintain and promote the interests of the industry as a whole. The extent to which this organisational unity acted as a constraint upon the ability of individual interest groups to maintain their profitability was one of the vital points at issue in the wool textile crises of 1925 and 1930.

The main concern of this chapter is to examine the complicated structure of wool textile employers' organisations, and to show how it responded to the acute difficulties confronting employers in the 1920s. Given the wide range of market positions occupied by wool textile producers, the study will be approached on two levels. The first will involve a brief outline of the peculiar structure of the wool textile industry, through which changing conditions of trade were refracted, and which together determined very important relationships among and between employers. Secondly, the study will focus on the organisations of product specialisms, the highly differentiated nature and profitability of which provided the complex basis of employer association.

I. Employers' Organisation in Wool Textiles

The associations of employers in Bradford occupied a central role in the textile employers' organisational network. For more than 100 years worsted production, the largest sector of the industry, had been concentrated upon Bradford. So too was the busy merchanting section, according Bradford an importance which was further reinforced by the immediate geographical spread of the industry around it. Around three quarters of British wool textile production was located in the West Riding of Yorkshire. Within this area certain localities were associated with certain products: fine woollens with Huddersfield, low woollen goods with Batley and Dewsbury, worsted spinning with Halifax and Keighley, and worsted production of all kinds with Bradford. In 1935 worsted production made up 57 per cent of total output, of which Bradford alone accounted for 58 per cent. (1)

The major distinction between the woollen and worsted sections of the industry was in the organisation of production. In woollens, where the preparatory processes were fewer, most firms carried out all the stages of production from the handling of the raw wool to the finished product, including dyeing and finishing. (2) In worsteds, on the other hand, there was a tendency to specialise in a single process - combing, spinning, weaving (manufacturing) or dyeing and finishing. There were exceptions as a number of firms combined two or more processes, and a few manufacturing firms, such as Salt's and Foster's, were vertically integrated. (3) Thus, worsted employers might be producers of tops (the combed product), yarn (the spun product) or worsted manufactures/tissues (the woven product), while woollen employers were primarily manufacturers, dependent upon the market for the finished product.

Apart from a few large integrated establishments, the size of the wool textile firm tended to be small - typically employing less than 100 operatives. New entrants could start up with a minimum of outlay by renting room and power and taking in work on a commission basis. In 1926 there were 1,384 firms in the West Riding, 64 per cent of which employed only 18 per cent of total insured operatives employed. (4)

An important feature of the industry was the high incidence of female and juvenile labour, and their particular distribution and mobility within it. It had long been the case that the labour of boys and girls belonged to the spinners. In 1919 it was estimated that juveniles aged between 13 and 18 made up 55 - 60 per cent of all worsted spinning employees. (5) On reaching 18 women might progress to the weaving sheds, and at 16 youths might go on to train for a 'man's' job - perhaps in the combing or dyeing sections or as an overlooker, or they might leave the industry altogether. Accordingly, in spinning, the largest of the worsted sections, much of the workforce was in passage and trade union organisation was weak, as it was in weaving where at least two-thirds of the workforce was female. Only in the craft and male dominated areas did trade unions organise effectively. (6)

The basic differences in the organisation of production between the woollen and worsted sections was particularly important to the way in which employers perceived their trade interests. At each stage of worsted production the product was marketable, so that the market for the intermediate products did not necessarily lie in the subsequent stage of domestic worsted manufacture. Topmakers could either sell their combed tops to spinners at home, or they could export them to an expanding market abroad. Similarly, worsted spinners had the choice of selling their yarn to worsted manufacturers, hosiery manufacturers or customers overseas. Conversely, worsted manufacturers were almost wholly dependent on home produced yarns since these, at least until the late 1920s, were difficult to obtain elsewhere.

This brief outline gives some indication of the factors influencing employers' perception of their 'trade interests'. The degree of trade union activity among employees, the incidence of fellow employer support locally, the trading strategy of employers in supportive processes, and the market for their product, simultaneously affected the ability to maintain profitability. As wool textile producers and fellow employers there was a certain congruence of interest between the sections, but as product specialists and price competitors it was by no means inevitable. Accordingly, the relationship between employers was fluid, to say the least.

Bradford employers first began to organise on a permanent basis from around 1904. (7)   This kind of formal association was not unique to wool textiles, but was adopted by employers in many other industries at about the same time. This is not to suggest that employers had previously been disorganised, or that this was their first or only form of protective action. During the first two thirds of the nineteenth century there were several instances of employers combining on a temporary basis in order to ensure the continuation of favourable trading conditions. (8)   Collective action on the part of employers was rarely necessary as long as workers remained unorganised, and as long as Britain retained its trading advantage over the rest of the world. However, after 1870 the emergence of foreign competition, protectionism, falling prices and increased trade union activity jeopardised the favourable position, and the informal, <u>ad hoc</u> approach to mutual difficulties was no longer adequate.

The threat which changing conditions of trade posed to textile employers provoked a number of collective attempts to preserve profitability. The first evidence of this was in the piece-dyeing employers' cartel in the 1880s. As a section working on a commission basis their 'monopolistic price-fixing' was received with much hostility by their customers, the manufacturers, particularly in view of the downward pressure on prices they were experiencing as a result of foreign competition. (9)   The dyers' joint action was ultimately to find greater acceptability and success in the form of a combine in 1898 - the Bradford Dyers' Association Ltd. Its intentions were:

> to enable the various firms unitedly to meet the more severe trading conditions which were appearing, by affecting economies and improvements in production through the pooling of technical skill and experience and the centralisation of administration, purchasing, distribution and accountancy. (10)

Within the next five years the slubbing dyers, combers, spinners and manufacturers all had made similar attempts, but failed to achieve remotely the 90 per cent involvement of the BDA Ltd. (11)

Wool Textile Employers' Organisations

A second attempt by woolcombers in 1904 did result in a 38-firm combine, but at least half that number remained outside, as well as a number of spinners possessing combing plant.

Although the combine may have been an inappropriate remedy for the problems being experienced by the hundreds of small, often family firms in the wool textile trades, many employers did admit the need for combined action to combat continued trading difficulties. The Home Wool Buyers' Association was established in 1904, federations of spinners and manufacturers in several districts of Bradford in 1907, the Woolcombing Employers' Federation, (which included the combine Woolcombers' Ltd), in 1910, and the Bradford Manufacturers' Federation and further district organisations of spinners in 1913.

The immediate reason for formal associations among employers, for the most part, was the organised demands from workers for increased wages, uniform wages lists, insistence on the employment of union labour only and the limitation of apprentices. The aims of the employers' associations were similar: "to protect, promote and further the interests of members by combined action of the members against combinations of work-people seeking by strikes or other action to impose undesirable conditions of employment." (12) But these organisations were never intended to be purely industrial relations bodies, and their constitutions further provided for action on industrial and commercial matters, Government legislation, disputes with customers, in fact "...any action deemed advisable for the protection and advancement of members' interests". (13)

By 1914 there existed associations of employers in all the main sectors of textile production in Bradford. These were still relatively undeveloped as regards membership - the Woolcombing Employers might boast a membership of around 80 per cent, but spinners and manufacturers had no more than 40 per cent membership. (14) Meetings tended to be called only as circumstances demanded, such circumstances being mainly industrial relations issues, or on a few occasions difficulties with local bye-laws and transport provisions. Similarly, joint conferences were infrequently organised, as many employers disliked the idea of sitting around a table and openly discussing their difficulties with what were, in effect, customers - or, for that matter, competitors.

However, a basic framework of organisation proved of great advantage during the war years, enabling manufacturers, for instance, to solicit large Government contracts (15), and more generally enabling organised employers to act as a medium between Government and the trade. Although Government did actively encourage organisation among employers, this was not the only, or necessarily most important, factor favouring greater organisation. The effects of war aggravated those conditions which had long been precipitating collective action on the part of employers. Increased trade union activity, restricted markets, increased taxation, and intervention in the form of price and supply controls all threatened the basic principles of 'management' and,

47

consequently, profitability. This was nowhere more evident than in the introduction of control to the jute industry in 1915. (16) The need for some voluntary control over prices was the basis of a recruitment drive among Bradford manufacturers in 1915, the focus of discussion at a meeting in favour of a general federation of manufacturers in February 1916, and Government proposals to commandeer the output of spinning concerns an abject reality in April 1916 as worsted spinners considered the more effectual protection of 'the interests of the trade'. (17) The desire of wool textile employers to consolidate and co-ordinate their policies and activities resulted in 1916 in the formation of the Worsted Spinners' Federation Ltd. (W.S.F.) and the Woollen and Worsted Trades' Federation (W.W.T.F.).

By 1920 the W.W.T.F. had 20 affiliated organisations of manufacturers, as shown in Table 3.1. These accounted for 85 per cent of wool textile manufacturing firms, representing a range of product specialists from the fine cloth manufacturers of Huddersfield to the manufacturers of shoddy in the heavy woollen district. (18) The largest single group was the Bradford Manufacturers' Federation (B.M.F.), which represented 25 per cent of their combine manufacturing output. Similarly, of the 9 affiliates to the W.S.F., the Bradford organisation was the largest, representing over 100 firms and more than half the total spindleage. (19)

Wartime conditions also strengthened the tendency of consultation between different groups of employers. These involved Government pleas for co-operation on recruitment, rationing, the postponement of local holidays, and wage claims where it was thought that separate, sectional settlements might, as employers' put it, 'prejudice the interests of the trade'. In 1918 the first of three industry-wide committees was established. The Joint Consultative Board of Textile Employers concerned itself with "matters of general interest to all Textile Employers in the District".(20) In practice its work involved mainly industrial relations matters affecting non-textile workers employed in the textile trades, such as joiners, engineers, firemen and mechanics. Predominantly an association of Bradford textile employers' associations, it did include some 'outside' organisations such as the Yorkshire Dyers' Committee, and a number of large individual concerns such as Lister's, Crossley's and the B.D.A. Ltd.

Its initial aim was to remain as unobtrusive as possible. H.B. Shackleton, the B.M.F. president, did not want his Federation to figure on the Board officially, and it was generally agreed that it should have neither a letter-head nor a secretary. (21) In order to preclude any misunderstanding that the Board was anything more than consultative, all its decisions were to be conveyed to the workpeople by individual federations. The consultative character of the Board made it sufficiently flexible to confer with outside bodies where the interests of Board members were involved. The Board might thus consult with the local Commercial Vehicle Owners' Association on transport difficulties, or the Engineering Employers' Federation on wage rates, when

Table 3.1. Employers' Organisations in the Wool Industry, 1931.

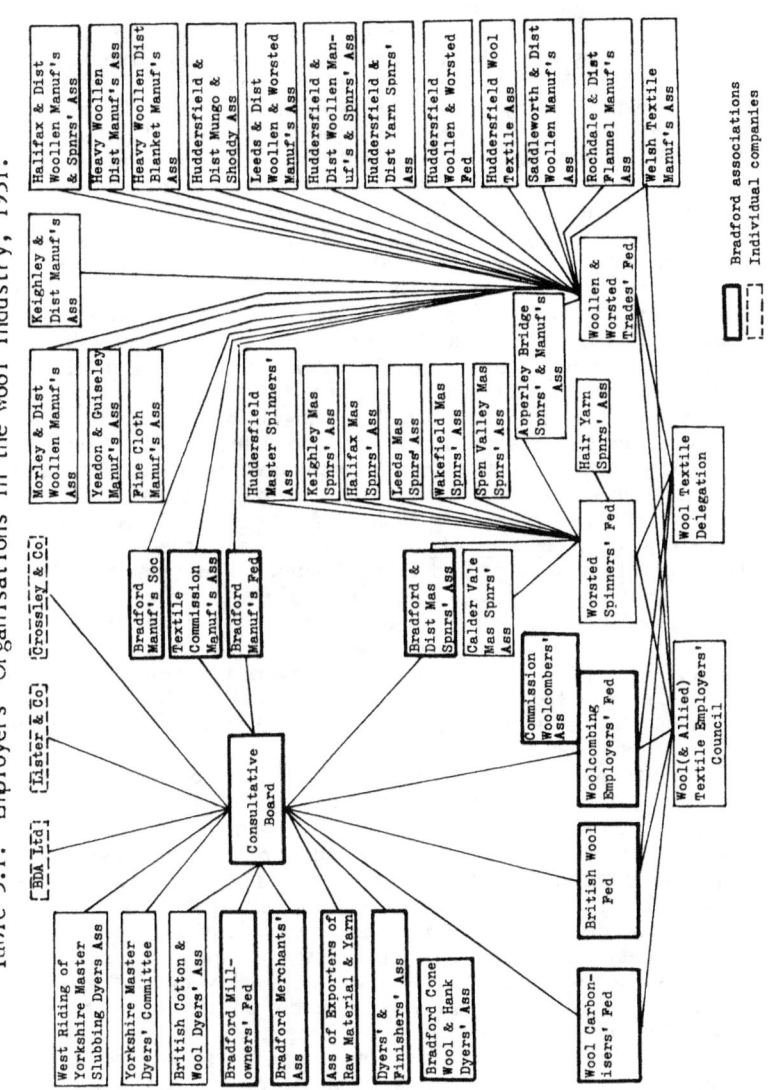

necessary. Its overall strategy, though, was to retain control over wages and conditions of non-textile workers, and not to admit those negotiated by nationally organised trade unions and other employers' organisations.

Fear of outside interference in the affairs of the wool textile industry was one of the major factors behind the formation of the second inter-sectional organisation in 1919. The Wool (& Allied) Textile Employers' Council (W.A.T.E.C.) was made up of the representatives of the employers' organisations affiliated to the Wool (& Allied) Textile Industrial Council formed at the same time. In recommending the establishment of the Government promoted Joint Industrial Council of trade unions and employers to less than enthusiastic members, G.H. Wood, Secretary of the Woollen and Worsted Trades' Federation, had stressed the alternatives: "the question is not will the industry accept the plan of Councils or go on as it pleases? but will the industry control itself, and work out its own future? Or will it be controlled, that is collectivised?" (22) Similar pragmatism was expressed by Worsted Spinners, who felt if a Council was not formed they ran the risk of: "...having foisted upon us a Trade Board under the Trades Board Act, the effect of which would be that Government officials would be introduced on to the Board, and to a certain extent deal with matters over our heads". (23)

Policies on wages and conditions of general effect upon the industry, or a section of it, were to be agreed at the subsequently formed Joint Industrial Council. The employers' side, the Employers' Council, along with the trade unions, was jointly charged with "...ensuring the observance of the decisions of the Council and of the agreements made between Employers and Employees". (24) Although the Employers' Council was designed specifically to speak for the organised wool textile employers as a whole, the power of decision-making had still to be sought from the sectional organisations.

Merger with the Consultative Board was considered, but was rejected by some Employers' Council members because the former included 'outside' organisations and a number of private companies, where the Council was made up of wool textile trade organisations only. The Board members themselves were also against merger, partly because it was felt that local conditions were best discussed by local employers, but also because the Board's real value was in its "elasticity of character, unbound by cumbersome regulations". (25) As the employers' side at the Industrial Council, the Employers' Council on the other hand was bound to abide by its jointly agreed negotiating machinery.

From 1921, issues affecting employers' commercial and financial interests in a more general sense could be referred to a third inter-sectional group, the Wool Textile Delegation. This was formed from the Federation of British Industries Wool Subgroup, the members of which had been meeting as the Wool Textile Association since 1917. Its stated objective was:

Wool Textile Employers' Organisations

The encouragement, promotion and protection of the Industrial and Commercial interests of the Wool Textile Industry, and in particular with a view to obtaining the recognition of the Government as the authoritative body to speak for all matters of commercial and industrial legislation affecting either a Section or the whole of the Industry, except rates of pay and such questions as might be more suitably dealt with by the Industrial Council or other approved or constituted bodies. (26)

However, the Delegation's link with the Federation of British Industries and, thereby, non-textile interests, aroused a certain amount of antipathy towards it. The generally critical conditions of trade during the 1920s meant that issues which might have come within the Delegation's sphere of operation, such as tariff protection, were of such vital importance to the section concerned that they could not be entrusted to a body representing more general interests.

By 1921, wool textile employers were represented at all levels by organisations specifically designed to protect their trade interests. It was still those organisations directly organised around the material conditions of trade which called forth that 'protective' activity. The regional and inter-sectional groups could take no action without reference to the profusion of interest groups which constituted the wool textile industry. The constant shifting of those interests - according to their perceived conditions of trade - produced shifting alliances and relationships, which consequently affected the way in which the elaborate structure of organised activity functioned.

II. Employer Policies and Disunity in the 1920s

Following decontrol of the wool textile industry in 1919 and the return to 'normal' trading, wool textile employers briefly experienced the "largest export trade in woollens and worsteds ever recorded" before the onset of a severe slump in 1921. (27) The unfavourable trading tendencies evident before 1914 were again manifest, but now in more mature form. Trade union activity among textile workers had intensified - co-ordinated in the National Association of Unions in the Textile Trades (N.A.U.T.T.) (28) - and former markets had been absorbed by competitors, or were protected by tariff barriers as those countries sought to meet their own requirements. These factors added up to a decrease in the volume of world trade, the British share of which had previously accounted for 50 per cent of wool textile employment.

By far the worst affected was the trade in worsted cloth manufactures. In 1930 the output of tissues was hardly more than 60 per cent of pre-war production, and during the whole of the inter-war period never achieved again pre-1914 levels. (29) The other sections of the industry did not experience the same pressures upon their profitability, output fell below pre-war levels only in 1929-30. The combing and spinning sections did have difficulties, particularly when the trade ceased to expand after 1928, but never to the extent of those experienced by manufacturers. Emergent competitors first established weaving plants, working on imported intermediate products before further investment in spinning plants and the earlier processes of production. Where export demand for worsted yarns did decline, this was largely compensated for by the increasing amount being absorbed by the home market for hosiery. Less than 50 per cent of worsted yarns were destined for domestic worsted weaving. (30)

In view of the increasing number of textile producing countries and the decreasing volume of world trade, employers resorted to a number of devices in an attempt to maintain profitability. These included a bonus-on-production scheme introduced by Woolcombing Employers - successfully reducing their labour costs of production by 15 per cent, and the adoption of a Terms of Sale and Purchase agreement by spinners, establishing uniform terms on credit, discount and delivery in an attempt to regulate competition and maintain prices. (31) Given the close interrelationship between the worsted sections, however, the very success of such schemes in one section was often a source of irritation in another. Members of the British Wool Federation complained that it was really they who paid the cost of the Woolcombers' bonus through the high rates they were obliged to pay for the wool they had combed on commission. H.B. Shackleton of the Bradford Manufacturers' Federation sympathised, stressing the scheme's essential unfairness: "An aspect of the position which must not be lost sight of is that we were adding to the general costs of the Industry, and paying for labour, such as Woolcombing, an unfair price in comparison with what was being paid for weaving." (32) For worsted manufacturers the bonus-on-production scheme had a double sting. They paid for the bonus once, they contended, as part of the cumulative element of production costs, and again, because the wool was so poorly combed as to require great expense in burling and mending when woven.

Worsted manufacturers were convinced that no other section of the industry was being squeezed as they were. In the vertically organised woollen section manufacturers had greater scope for cost cutting. As the final process in the horizontally organised production of worsteds, the Bradford Manufacturers felt their potential for cost reductions severely restricted. It was they who ultimately paid the cost of the Woolcombers' bonus scheme, suffered the effects of the Spinners' rigidity on terms of sale (particularly credit), and bore the brunt of the Dyers' frequent and 'unwarranted' increases in dyeing charges, and the high price of reads and healds as a result of a price ring operated by their suppliers. (33) Before 1925 the B.M.F. had considered the establishment of its own dyeing plant and distributing outlets, and actually did establish companies to undertake members' burling and mending and the supply of reads and healds. (34)

The element of production costs which received most attention was wages. Since 1919 agreements for the whole industry had been formulated annually at the Industrial Council. In the wake of the slump in 1921, a 5 per cent advance in wages agreed in 1920 had been withdrawn. In 1922 and 1923 the Bradford Manufacturers urged the necessity of a further reduction of the 10 per cent advanced in 1919, to return basic rates to the 1914 level, and the industry to its former competitive position. (35)

Sympathetic to wage reductions, other employers were loath to support the issue to the extent (and expense) of a lock-out, as proposed by the Manufacturers. The Worsted Spinners were quite prepared to settle for a continuation of the old agreement in view of the fact that so many of them were actually working overtime. Privately they were also concerned that reductions in wages would aggravate the shortage of employees consequent upon the abolition of half-time working and the raising of the school leaving age. (36) The British Wool Federation similarly felt that reductions were 'not advisable' as did the Woolcombing Employers, who were obliged to admit that their restraining factor was healthy balance sheets. These two Federations were resolved to resign from the Employers' Council rather than support the Manufacturers and witness mass resignations from their own organisations. (37)

Having warned that "the price they were being asked to pay for the Industrial Council was getting too high", worsted manufacturers acknowledged that unanimity was essential and that a separate agreement was "very dangerous" for them all.(38) The Employers' Council subsequently compromised on the 'stabilisation' of cost of living additions to wages, which had been fluctuating according to the corresponding Board of Trade figure. Similarly in 1924, the Employers' Council used the Cost of Living additions as a means of compromise when the N.A.U.T.T. proposed wage increases on the basis of an upturn in trade. (39) This kind of compromise only temporarily subdued the policy differences between employers, and was a vital point at issue in the textile dispute of 1925.

The three week stoppage in 1925 was the apparent result of the Industrial Council's inability to resolve opposing claims for a 5 per cent advance on wages on the part of the N.A.U.T.T., and a 10 per cent reduction on the part of the Employers' Council. However, having put their claim to the Industrial Council, the Employers' Council had implied a unity of purpose which was by no means the case. The Bradford Manufacturers had wanted to begin negotiations at 20 per cent, and were adamant that their trade could bear nothing less than 10 per cent reductions, at which point they were prepared to lock-out. Not all employers perceived the 10 per cent submission in the same light. During negotiations it became evident that woollen manufacturers in particular were not convinced that the risks attendant upon pursuing reductions, (in view of the counter-claim), were appropriate to their own market position. The Yeadon and Guiseley Manufacturers' Federation 'preferred to go on as at present' rather than face a stoppage. Neither were manufacturers in Morley prepared to face a stoppage. Even if an advance was given, they said, they felt compelled to continue working in order to complete brightly coloured contracts for the East which could not later be sold elsewhere. Rochdale Spinners and Manufacturers, in strong competition with the cotton trade for labour, felt the time 'inopportune' for pressing reductions. (40)

Thus divided on their own wages policy, the Employers' Council found it impossible to continue the course of action upon which it had embarked, that is to press for reductions in wages. Alternatively, having repeatedly stressed the vital necessity of a minimum 10 per cent reduction for the industry's recovery, neither could it withdraw. For employers the point at issue now changed. They had either to support the Employers' Council in bringing the policy which they had initiated to a conclusion, thus maintaining the status of the Industrial Council. Or, on the other hand, they could withdraw that support and take the consequence of its collapse - strengthened trade unions, prejudicial wage settlements and possible interference in the industry's affairs.

Caught in this difficult position, employers chose to post notices of reductions, thereby precipitating a general textile strike. It was, however, primarily a tactical move aimed at maintaining the organisational unity of employers, and not one denoting unity or strength of resolve on the basic issue of wage reductions. On several occasions before and during the three week strike, attempts at mediation by both Bradford's Lord Mayor and the Ministry of Labour met with the reply that the machinery of the Industrial Council was still in existence and third party intervention was, therefore, unnecessary. (41) When both sides of the Industrial Council did agree finally to a Court of Inquiry, the Employers' Council only did so on the proviso that the Court would be confined to consideration of wages only, and that its recommendations would be made binding on both sides.

When the Morris Court reported in November 1925, its recommendations stunned employers. While acknowledging "that the industry is in a depressed state at the present time is not in dispute", it concluded that the evidence was "insufficient to justify a general reduction in wages" or a general increase. (42) The 1924 agreement was to continue to January 1927, terminable thereafter on one month's notice either side. It further recommended greater incentives for piecework, a minimum scale of wages for juveniles, and an overall simplification of the complicated calculation of textile wages.

On reflection, employers admitted tactical errors in their strategy. The Bradford Spinners, Lister & Co., pinpointed two of them:

1. A lack of publicity indicating the employers' point of view, which was a righteous one.
2. That the representatives should have urged the workers' representatives to take a ballot of the workers who it was felt were more than prepared to work at reduced rates. (43)

Wool Textile Employers' Organisations

The Bradford Manufacturers drew several lessons from their experience. They felt that the failure of the lock-out owed much to the strength of the overlookers, and not the operatives themselves. Very importantly in view of their later activities, they also made it clear that they would not again be prepared to consider arbitration. Most other Employers' Council affiliates, and these included the largest group, the Worsted Spinners' Federation, felt equally strongly that a more calculated approach to reductions, designed to take public opinion with them, would have to be pursued, and that a further stoppage must be avoided.

From 1925 onwards, when Britain returned to the Gold Standard, all sections of wool textiles began to experience increasing competition in the home and export markets. The immediate response of the W.S.F. to the 'insane competition' and price cutting it was experiencing in 1926 and 1927, was to encourage members to form trade associations for the purpose of agreeing conversion costs. The Federation was at pains to emphasise that the intention was "to prevent the selling under cost and not the formation of a ring to unduly force prices up". (44)

Price maintenance, though, could only ease the pressure on profit margins to a limited extent and could not increase overall demand. Spinners possessing combing plant attempted to compensate for the loss of spinning business by taking in combing work on a commission basis. The effect of their protective action was to aggravate the position for those combers wholly dependent on commission work. Their response to the effective increase in competition was to form a Commission Woolcombers' Association. Its strategy was to introduce a rebate scheme for customers committing 90 per cent or more of their total combing work to its members, thus keeping machinery active and conversion costs proportionately low. Accused of "compulsion, monopoly and conspiracy" by the British Wool Federation, whose members gave out combing on commission, A.E. Raper of the Commission Woolcombers' Association assured them that the scheme was voluntary "...and there was not any idea of attacking anyone. It was a defensive move to protect the interests of combing in general in the district." (45)

Reductions in production costs were, according to manufacturers, the only solution to the depressed level of demand for their product. The loss of business for them was explained by the cost advantage enjoyed by their competitors, such as France and Belgium, as a result of undervalued currencies and the longer hours and lower wages paid to their operatives. Manufacturers deprecated suggestions in the press and elsewhere that their problem was one of rationalisation, and maintained that rationalisation would "...undermine the technical ability of the trade to meet the nature and variety of demand for its product". (46) Most manufacturers were now agreed that the remedy was in reducing the high level of wages "...which in their opinion were seriously affecting the Industry". (47)

By 1927 Bradford Manufacturers considered their position 'desperate'; of the 400 textile concerns which had gone out of business since 1918, worsted manufacturers constituted the largest proportion. H.B. Shackleton, president of both the B.M.F. and the W.W.T.F. told the Employers' Council it was "... attempting the impossible to try and pay the present rates of wages and do business".(48) In admitting the 'depressed state of the industry' and yet denying them wage reductions, the Morris Court, it was felt, had exacerbated an already bad situation. Manufacturers were obliged to carry the burden of their own excessive wage rates, plus those of the earlier processes which were incorporated in their production costs. The only way to regain lost exports (an indication of the extent of which is shown in Table 3.2), was to reduce wages in all sections, bringing down the price of the finished article and thereby making exports more competitive.

Table 3.2: Woollens and Worsteds - World Exports 1920s (49)

	1924 m. lbs	1928 m. lbs
Tops		
Great Britain	41.1	34.4
France	40.8	54.6
Germany	14.2	23.3
	96.1	112.3
Yarns		
Great Britain	65.9	66.0
France	34.5	61.4
Germany	16.1	23.6
Belgium	20.7	21.0
	137.2	172.0
Tissues		
Great Britain	150.7	107.8
France	61.4	46.9
Germany	22.0	35.2
Belgium	4.0	4.3
Italy	15.1	15.8
	253.2	210.0

By this time, the members of the Employers' Council were more divided on the issue of wage reductions than they had been in 1925. Worsted manufacturers were joined in their resolve to secure nothing less than 10 per cent reductions by the majority of woollen manufacturers, whose export position had deteriorated considerably in the intervening years. Although favouring 'some efforts' to secure reductions, the Federations of Buyers, Carbonisers, Combers and Spinners would not rule out other policy options, and were totally against any course of action which might lead to a stoppage. The opposing tactical considerations of these employers' organisations were particularly evident when, in August 1927, the trade unions brought up the question of tariff protection at the Industrial Council. On the one hand, Spinners welcomed the possibility of safeguarding as an alternative to wage reductions, while on the other, manufacturers perceived it a 'time delaying dodge' on the part of trade unions, the possible benefits of which could only be 'a long way off in time'. (50)

With machinery running at around 65 per cent of full capacity, the manufacturers were no longer prepared to risk their individual profitability in the long drawn-out procedures of the Industrial Council, particularly in view of the lack of resolve of the other sections. The B.M.F. urged the termination of the existing wages agreement claiming that, "...there was a feeling in some districts that the day of general agreements had gone by. Firms had already left their Federations and had altered wage rates to their advantage." (51) Viewed from the less critical market position of the earlier stages of worsted production, the manufacturers' position seemed just the kind of 'drastic action' the Employers' Council representatives had been instructed to avoid. Reluctantly agreeing to the termination of the Morris agreement from November 1927, Worsted Spinners' representatives assured worried members that the only alternative had been disunity and the break-up of the Employers' Council. (52)

The continued organisational unity of employers only thinly veiled the antagonism between them on the vital issue of reductions in production costs. During the following year manufacturers were frequently at odds with the other sectional organisations, who charged them with implementing a policy which was unconstitutional and prejudicial to the interests of the trade. With the ending of the general wages agreement the Employers' Council had agreed that no section should take any action likely seriously to affect the interests of another. (53) Freed of its obligations to specific levels of wages, the W.W.T.F. had immediately recommended individual firms to begin reducing the wages of juveniles, and then general operatives as a means of isolating the overlookers, making it difficult for them to stand out against wage reductions as they had in 1925. The W.W.T.F. maintained that since no agreement was in force, none could be broken, and that only sectional, not individual, action was answerable to the Employers' Council.

The most severe clash between the members of the Employers' Council came in October 1928 when the W.W.T.F. again appealed for united action on the wages issue. The process of individual reductions had proved to be extremely slow, particularly since many manufacturers were not prepared to face the potential risks alone. The Manufacturers backed up their claim to the Employers' Council with figures on the number of bankruptcies since 1924, the extent of unemployment in the industry, the low level of machinery activity, the lower wage rates paid by competitors and "the unenviable position of the British export trade in wool tissues". (54)

Woolcombing Employers confessed themselves still unconvinced that reductions in costs could not be more easily affected through changes in the staffing of machinery, extra hours and tariff protection. The Worsted Spinners held similar views on the possibility of safeguarding, and would only consider a joint application to the Industrial Council if provisions were made for arbitration. The Chairman of their Wages Committee, Colonel Foster explained:

> We thought that we must put ourselves right in the first instance with the public, that any failure again would absolutely wreck our Federation. We don't want a fiasco like the last time. Our people are not for a moment prepared for any stoppage, it is absolutely no use asking them. (55)

The manufacturers were equally determined in their view. Tariff protection, they felt, would not only preclude the possibility of securing wage reductions, but would in itself offer no immediate relief because its effects would take some considerable time to work their way through the sections. Although the manufacturers freely admitted that the co-operation of the other sections was needed to achieve the reductions they deemed necessary, they could not admit the Spinners' conditions for a joint application to the Industrial Council. "Some of us have strong views on Arbitration after 1925", the Employers' Council was informed, "It is very difficult to get an impartial Court. If a similar Court to the last time is contemplated, I cannot imagine a more disastrous procedure." (56) Should anyone have doubted the strength of their resolve, H.B. Shackleton reiterated: "We won't have Arbitration at any price. There is no tribunal worth having in the whole of this Country. We are quite united in regard to that matter - we won't have it at all under any circumstances whatever." (57)

Since the Spinners refused to concede the manufacturers' case, the W.W.T.F. determined to approach the Industrial Council alone. According to its constitution, only the whole of the Industrial Council could negotiate the wages policy of the industry, or any section of it, and the N.A.U.T.T., approached by the manufacturers only, refused to call the Council together. For manufacturers, the possibility of achieving a negotiated reduction was now ruled out. The negotiation of either a general or sectional agreement through the Industrial Council was precluded by the lack of co-operation from the other sectional organisations. To attempt to negotiate a sectional settlement independently of the Industrial Council, would be to reveal that manufacturers did not have the support of other employers, and would weaken their case considerably. Frustrated in what they perceived as strenuous attempts at securing a negotiated settlement, the manufacturers' policy of individual wage reductions accelerated. During the resultant chaos, it was the trade unions' intransigence which their Federation cited as the reason for the lack of negotiations, and their independence of action, and not the strength of difference between employers.

In the early part of 1929 reductions in manufacturing wages proceeded, for the most part, without difficulty. Resistance in the Horbury district of Wakefield had collapsed fairly quickly. Spinners in the Spen Valley area, whose business was concentrated in the declining export market, were particularly impressed by the apparent ease with which manufacturers had affected wage cuts in Leeds, Yeadon, Guiseley and at some firms in their own district. In February 1929 they urged the W.S.F. to adopt a similar policy. Spinners in Bradford considered the time 'inopportune' for such action, in view of current discussions with trade unions on a joint application for tariff protection, as well as the forthcoming elections, and effectively quashed their proposals. (58)

Nevertheless, the antipathy which spinners generally held towards the manufacturers' tactics regarding wages had begun to crumble. From mid-1928 yarn exports had steadily declined and French yarns were entering the home market in ever larger quantities. Doubts as to the validity of continuing to refuse to join with the manufacturers in a general application to the Industrial Council were strengthened by events in the heavy woollen district in April and May 1929. Heavy woollen manufacturers had been particularly badly hit by the loss of exports since 1925, and a group of 9 or 10 of them had made 10 per cent cuts in the basic rates of their general operatives. A trade union ballot had shown only one-third of members prepared to resist, and work had continued without interruption at reduced rates. (59)

The W.S.F. subsequently proposed a general application for wage reductions, withdrawing their conditions regarding arbitration. A general application was now precisely what the W.W.T.F. wished to avoid. Their president explained at length:

> A calling of the Joint Industrial Council would be a disaster and would cut across the movement already started... We do in fact really dread a meeting, general or sectional, of the Industrial Council, as we feel it would almost certainly result in an offer by the Unions of a Cost of Living adjustment. In our view we must get rid of the 10 per cent before we consider the Cost of Living...
> What we feel is that it is desirable that a certain number of resolute men should take the thing in hand and do it. The Wobblers are worse than useless in this case. We should start with 10 per cent, and don't start unless prepared to see the thing through to the end...(but) It should be quite clear that we have made no agreement whatever and that the Unions should get no idea that a 10 per cent reduction was the end. (60)

Although the representatives at the Employers' Council resolved to recommend the manufacturers' policy to their respective Federations, divergences of opinion were now so great that the general situation had become one of confusion. Several members of the British Wool Federation thought the matter could be more easily resolved if the worsted section separated itself from the woollen section. The Woolcombing Employers' Federation contemplated resigning from the Employers' Council and negotiating its own wages policy. In the spinning section a number of employers had followed the example of the manufacturers and attempted individual reductions - some with success, others being forced back at the old rates by strike action. Meanwhile, the irregular pattern of reductions in the manufacturing section had had the effect of intensifying competition between manufacturers and speeding up their strategy of staged reductions.

By late 1929, the general picture was one of chaos. Following a prolonged lock-out at several firms in Calder Vale, scattered stoppages in most other districts and threatened strike action on the part of overlookers generally, the Ministry of Labour appointed a Court of Inquiry under the Industrial Courts Act of 1919. The 'Court' this time consisted of Lord MacMillan only, who, sympathetic to the employers' case, recommended reductions amounting to 9 per cent. Several of the craft unions - particularly overlookers, woolcombers, twisters and power loom tuners - attempted, unsuccessfully, to resist the cuts. With so much of the industry already working on reduced rates, the employers' strategy had isolated, as intended, those elements most likely to resist. Although a few employers did negotiate reductions of less than 10 per cent, within four weeks of the announcement of the MacMillan reductions, the majority of operatives were working at the new rates. (61)

III. Conclusions

Wool textile employers in 1930 had finally succeeded in reducing wages which, they claimed, disadvantaged them in relation to foreign competitors. Yet despite the existence of a complex network of organisations specifically designed to protect 'the interests of the trade', it had taken employers eight years to carry out wage reductions which amounted to no more than two to three per cent of total production costs. The problem in effecting this policy lay not so much in the strength and militancy of patchily organised textile workers but in the employers' consistent inability to agree.

The founding motive of the employers' organisations had been the maintenance and protection of the 'interests of the trade', which referred directly, as the numerous conflicts between employers indicated, to the profitability of specific forms of capital. Given the strong inter-relationship between these in wool textile production, the protection of the interests of one section might be perceived differently in another, as for instance, in the case of the Woolcombing Employers' bonus scheme. Thus, the complicated framework of wool textile employers' organisations, requiring as it did through its link with the

Wool Textile Employers' Organisations

Industrial Council, a certain unity of action, contained severe structural limitations.

During the adverse conditions of the 1920s, employers found it increasingly difficult to respond to disparate trading experiences with uniform policies, which could not be uniform in their effect. In July 1930 Colonel Foster told the Annual General Meeting of the Worsted Spinners:

> I think if anything happens like this again each Section will have to fight and ask for what they want on their own. I do not see how the trade can all come together at the same time, as the conditions between the woollen and worsted trades are totally different. (62)

From these very basic market differences had arisen the crises of 1925 and 1930, resulting in the demise of the Industrial Council, which had insisted upon a unity which, in the market conditions of the 1920s, had little basis in the material conditions of the trade.

NOTES

Particular thanks are due to the Confederation of British Wool Textiles for access to their archives and general helpfulness.

Abbreviations (in text and footnotes):

B.M.F.	Bradford Manufacturers' Federation
W.S.F.	Worsted Spinners' Federation
W.W.T.F.	Woollen and Worsted Trades Federation
W.A.T.E.C.	Wool and Allied Textile Employers' Council

1. Board of Trade Working Party Report, Wool, (London: H.M.S.O., 1947), p. 8.
2. Committee on Industry and Trade, Survey of Textile Industries, (London: H.M.S.O., 1928), p. 162.
3. Tissues or manufactures are frequently used in the trade to refer to the woven product. Employers engaged in weaving cloth are thus usually referred to as manufacturers.
4. Committee on Industry and Trade, op. cit., p. 176.
5. Court of Arbitration (Woollen and Worsted Trades, West Riding of Yorkshire), 18 February 1919, in Worsted Spinners' Federation Minutes, 1919.
6. See J.H. Clapham, The Woollen and Worsted Industries, (London, 1907), pp. 204-9 and B. Drake, Women in Trade Unions, (London, Labour Research Department, 1920), pp. 126-7. For a discussion of the causes of union retardation in the worsted industry see T. Jowitt, Ch. 5.
7. C. Ogden, The History of Bradford, (Bradford, 1934), p. 40.

8. See J.W. Grove, Government and Industry in Britain, (London, 1962), pp. 6-13 and A.J. McIvor, Employers' Associations and Industrial Relations in Lancashire, 1890-1939, (Manchester University Ph.D. Thesis, 1983).
9. E.M. Sigsworth and J.M. Blackman, 'The Woollen and Worsted Industries', in D.H. Aldcroft (ed.), The Development of British Industry and Foreign Competition, 1875-1914, (London, 1968), p. 151.
10. D.T. Jenkins and K.G. Ponting, The British Wool Textile Industry 1770-1914, (London, 1982), p. 180.
11. Worsted Spinners' Combination, Report of a Meeting of Worsted Spinners held at the Victoria Hotel, Bradford, 18 July, 1900, (Pamphlet, 1900).
12. B.M.F. Memorandum of Constitution and Rules, 1913.
13. West Riding of Yorkshire Master Slubbing Dyers' Association, Rules, 1913.
14. These are rough figures based on information in the Minute books of the combers', spinners' and manufacturers' associations 1910-14 and Worrall's Directory for 1910/11.
15. B.M.F., Minutes, December 1914.
16. E.M.H. Lloyd, Experiments in State Control, (Oxford, 1924), p. 36.
17. B.M.F., Minutes, February-June 1915 and February 1916; see also North Bierley and Great Horton Spinners' Federation, Minutes, 12 April 1916.
18. W.W.T.F. Minutes, 12 June 1918.
19. W.S.F. Annual Report, 1919.
20. Ibid.
21. Joint Consultative Board of Textile Employers, Minutes, 8 October 1918.
22. W.W.T.F., Annual Report, 1918.
23. W.S.F., Minutes, 6 December 1918.
24. Wool (& Allied) Textile Industrial Council, Rules, 1919.
25. Joint Consultative Board of Textile Employers, Minutes, 8 October 1918.
26. Wool Textile Delegation, Minutes, 15 July 1921.
27. C. Ogden, The History of Bradford, (Bradford, 1934).
28. J.A. Jowitt & K. Laybourn, 'The Wool Textile Dispute of 1925', Journal of Local Studies, Vol. 2, No. 1, Spring 1982, p. 12.
29. See for example the Index of Production in Board of Trade Working Party Report, Wool, (London, 1947), p. 4.
30. Ibid., p. 22.
31. See Woolcombing Employers' Federation, Minutes, 1920/21, W.S.F., Annual Report, 1921 and Spinner-Combers' Committee Minutes 1920/21.
32. W.S.F., Spinner-Combers' Committee, Minutes, 8 January 1925.
33. Committee on Industry and Trade, op. cit., p. 179.
34. Memorandum on the Wool Textile Industry in Board of Trade (Committee Papers), Sub-Committee on Industry and Trade, 1927 (BTSS/49, Pol. 12).

35. See W.A.T.E.C., Minutes for 1922/23.
36. W.S.F., Minutes, 23 April 1923.
37. British Wool Federation, Minutes, 26 April 1923; and W.A.T.E.C., Ibid., 22 May 1922.
38. W.A.T.E.C., Minutes, 24 May 1922.
39. Ibid., April-July 1929.
40. Ibid., 22 June 1925.
41. W.S.F., Annual Report, 1919.
42. Report of the Court of Investigation concerning the wages position in the Wool Textile Industry (Northern Counties), H.M.S.O., 1925.
43. Bradford and District Master Spinners' Federation, Minutes, 24 August 1925.
44. W.S.F., Annual Report, 1927.
45. British Wool Federation, Minutes, 15 May 1929.
46. The Times, 15 April 1930.
47. W.W.T.F., Minutes, 25 May 1927.
48. W.A.T.E.C., Minutes, 1 June 1927.
49. W.S.F., Minutes, 13 November 1927.
50. W.A.T.E.C., Minutes, 23 November 1927.
51. Ibid., 9 September 1927.
52. W.S.F., Minutes, 15 September 1927.
53. W.A.T.E.C., Minutes, 23 November 1927.
54. Ibid., 9 October 1928.
55. Ibid., 15 October 1928.
56. Ibid.
57. Ibid., 24 October 1928.
58. Bradford and District Master Spinners' Federation, Ibid., 18 April 1929.
59. Yorkshire Observer, 15 April 1929.
60. W.A.T.E.C., Minutes, 14 May 1929.
61. W.S.F., Annual Report, 1931.
62. Ibid., 17 July 1930. For a discussion of the broadly similar process of declining employer solidarity and the collapse of collective bargaining in cotton during the Slump see A. McIvor, Ch. 1, section III.

Chapter 4

COTTON EMPLOYERS AND INDUSTRIAL
WELFARE BETWEEN THE WARS

Steve Jones

Historians of industrial relations have by and large concentrated their efforts on the trade union movement and as a result published material on employers is still a little thin on the ground. (1) However, one of the most fruitful areas of research has been the relationship between employers' labour policy and the development of industrial welfare. It is now acknowledged that industrial welfare, consisting of non-wage services to labour in the form of cash payments such as pensions, profit-sharing and paid holidays or amenities such as canteens, health schemes, housing, and educational and recreational facilities, spread during the late nineteenth and early twentieth centuries. The most recent and the most important work has been undertaken by Joseph Melling. In a number of thoughtful and stimulating pieces, Melling has combined detailed empirical research with a largely Marxist theoretical critique to relate the salient trends in industrial welfare to wider changes in British capitalism. In very broad terms, industrial welfare policy is linked to the production and market conditions in which firms operated, control over local labour markets, and employers' relationship to trade union organisation and industrial conflict, particularly over the labour process. Behind all this, of course, is the employers' need for an efficient and well-disciplined labour force. (2)

In order to assess the content of and motives behind employers' industrial welfare strategy, there is still a pressing need for further studies of particular industries and periods. In fact, Helen Jones has already shown that private occupational welfare expanded quite significantly in the 1920s and 1930s, especially in textile Lancashire, the engineering workshops of London, the lino and paper industry of Fifeshire, and in some of the newer industries of the South East. (3) Again the conclusion is that the main function of welfare schemes was the promotion of discipline and efficiency within the workforce, a view also stressed by Noelle Whiteside and Richard Whipp. (4) It is the aim of this chapter to take the analysis one step further by providing

Cotton Employers and Industrial Welfare

a case study of the cotton trade and industrial welfare. The chapter will trace the development of mill welfare in inter-war cotton, and assess its range and function in managerial operation. Particular emphasis will be given to one form of industrial welfare, namely recreational amenities.

I. Industrial Welfare Schemes in Cotton

The economic history of the Lancashire cotton industry between the wars has been well chronicled. Briefly, Lancashire cotton faced a difficult period of readjustment to new trading conditions. After the post-war boom of 1919-20, the industry was in a state of more or less permanent crisis. In overall terms this is best represented by the reduction in the capacity of the industry. As far as Lancashire is concerned, the number of spindles fell from 60.1 million in 1920 to 40 million in 1939, while for the same period the number of looms fell from 800,000 to 454,000. Obviously, this brought with it a catastrophic decline in the numbers employed: in 1924 there were 572,000 insured employees in the industry as a whole, but only 393,000 by 1938. It is hardly surprising that labour relations also deteriorated, particularly in the period 1928 to 1935 when cotton masters attempted to secure wage reductions and new working arrangements, most notably the more looms system. Interestingly enough, though the industry experienced considerable structural adjustment, partly stimulated by the Government's rationalisation programme, it is doubtful whether it had achieved a viable position even on the eve of the Second World War.

A number of explanations have been advanced for the poor performance of the Lancashire cotton industry. Most commentators agree that the fundamental catalyst was the loss of export markets in India and the Far East, no doubt partly as a result of the dislocation in trade caused by the First World War. For example, by the late 1930s exports of British cotton piece goods were on average only a quarter and yarn only 65 per cent of their 1913 level. Furthermore, undoubtedly the over-capitalisation of mills in the brief boom of 1919-20 created instability, and accentuated the slump in prices once demand fell in the 1920s. William Lazonick has also recently argued that the industry's difficulties were not unconnected to entrepreneurial shortcomings, specifically the failure to replace mule with ring spindles and the Lancashire loom with its automatic equivalent. Lazonick argues that the failure to introduce advanced technologies was related to the structure of the industry; that is, organisation on the lines of vertical specialisation and horizontal competition. (5)

It is difficult to refute Lazonick's findings. However, for the purpose of this chapter it must be added that the cotton industry was not homogeneously structured, but rather differentiated according to trading sector, size of firm and levels of integration. Needless to say, the production of finer grade yarns and fancier cloths held up much better than coarser yarns and plainer cloths. Hence in the 1920s, at least, the fine spinning sector of the industry was more prosperous than the American spinning sector. Equally, there were a number of large integrated concerns which had invested in new spinning and weaving technology, and so therefore were in a stronger competitive position. As we shall see these firms were more likely to invest in occupational welfare.

Given the fact that the cotton industry faced serious difficulties in the inter-war years, it is surprising to find that there were many welfare schemes in operation. Despite the lack of quantitative data, it is clear from the reports of the factory inspectorate, company records and newspaper sources that industrial welfare was practised in the textile districts. This section will trace the most important developments.

As already suggested, industrial welfare in Britain spread from the late nineteenth century. The First World War also witnessed some crucial developments. In particular, the Ministry of Munitions, which sponsored a welfare department, took a great interest in the subject, no doubt realising that good conditions in industry was one way of improving labour productivity, and so contributing to the war effort. By the end of the war, industrial welfare sections were being established throughout Britain, some benefiting from the advice and stimulus of Robert Hyde's newly formed Industrial Welfare Society (I.W.S.). (6) Further consolidation followed in the 1920s and 1930s.

In the pre-war cotton industry, only a small minority of masters had pioneered systematic welfare schemes. Textile employers were clearly opposed to statutory welfare orders, whereby the factory inspectorate would have the legal right to ensure that mills had adequate welfare provision. Broadly conceived, masters were hesitant due to the cost of statutory welfare, the degree of state intervention in managerial prerogatives, and the apparent apathy of the operatives. The two main employers' associations, the Cotton Spinners' and Manufacturers' Association (C.S.M.A.) and the Federation of Master Cotton Spinners' Associations (F.M.C.S.A.), in a conference with officials of the Factory Department of the Home Office, thus protested "that it would be a mistake to make welfare compulsory upon employers, and that if welfare work was to be successful it must be done voluntarily". (7) In fact, as was the case in various other industries, by the mid-1920s, occupational welfare had been introduced on a voluntary basis. The I.W.S. played an important educative and advisory role. Robert Hyde, for example, made a number of speeches and approaches to cotton industrialists in which he appealed for support and urged that welfare matters be an integral aspect of industrial administration.(8) In addition, it is noteworthy that there were local branches of the I.W.S. and the Welfare Workers' Institute. Indeed, in late 1922 and early 1923 the Manchester I.W.S. organised a comprehensive series of lectures on welfare, covering such matters as canteens, medical supervision, factory legislation and national insurance. Certainly, such publicity spawned some positive moves, and mills began to take the initiative.

Initially it was the larger concerns which recorded most progress. The Tootal Broadhurst Lee Company of Bolton, for example, had an extensive welfare machine managed by specialist sections at each end of the company's mills. (9) Most significant was the profit sharing scheme inaugurated in 1919 - dividends on employees' shares were paid throughout the period - and the part-time day continuation school at Sunnyside Mills, which was based on the provisions of the 1918 Education Act and continued on into the 1950s. (10) Facilities were also provided for recreation, as well as dining rooms and dental treatment. A dental clinic was introduced at the Ten Acres Mills in 1926 at a cost of approximately £128 and extended in 1934 for £253. (11) Without doubt the higher management of the company was committed to the principle of industrial welfare. In 1920, Sir Edward Tootal Broadhurst submitted a paper to the International Cotton Congress at Zurich in which he advocated the need for welfare work in the cotton industry. The company was also a regular con-tributor to the I.W.S. (12)

Similarly, the Fine Cotton Spinners' and Doublers' Association (F.C.S.D.A.) - one of the largest British combines in the early twentieth century - made extensive provision for welfare. In 1919 a pension fund for mill operatives was set up, and in the following year the Association appointed a consultant welfare supervisor. (13) By the middle of the 1920s, 30 welfare superintendents had in fact been appointed, and schemes were administered in 42 of the 94 mills owned by the Association. Aside from the pension fund there were programmes covering first aid, canteens, protective clothing, lockers for outdoor clothing, seats, washing accommodation, and recreation. (14) The amount of money spent on welfare work was quite considerable: between 1923 and 1930 £125,000 was transferred from the profit and loss account to the welfare reserve. (15)

Tootal and the F.C.S.D.A. were not the only cotton concerns experimenting with and introducing welfare schemes. For instance, another large combine, the English Sewing Cotton Company, established welfare work on a systematic basis in the immediate post-war period. According to the company's minute books, Welfare Committees had been formed at each of its mill branches, and welfare accommodation purchased. Yet, as will be discussed, recreation was easily the most extensive of the firm's welfare operations. Likewise, the Amalgamated Cotton Mills Trust had a welfare secretary for each of its mills, and provision ranged from rest rooms and canteens to playing fields and social evenings; while Ashton Brothers of Hyde had medical and nourishment schemes, dining rooms, rest rooms, cloakrooms, insurance and savings clubs, and an array of recreational facilities. (16) In overall terms, the evidence suggests a proliferation of welfare projects in varying degrees during the 1920s.

According to the Textile Mercury, whereas in November 1919 welfare work was "beginning to grow in connection with cotton mills", by May of 1920 it was "well established as a definite part of the organisation of a number of cotton mills in Lancashire". (17) The <u>Cotton Factory Times</u> agreed with this view: "There are many signs of a growing interest by mill owners and managers in the welfare of their workers." (18) Clearly, by the mid-1920s occupational welfare was an accepted practice in some cotton districts. In commenting on the general expansion of voluntary welfare, the factory inspector's report for 1925 therefore made particular reference to the cotton industry:

> Perhaps one of the most striking features of this movement is its steady growth in the textile industries, and some of the most striking examples are to be found in the cotton industry in Lancashire...While there is a good deal of prejudice still to be overcome, it is quite evident from these reports that the movement has taken hold, that many employers and managers are taking up welfare questions in one form or another, and sometimes without even looking upon them as welfare, and that a large number of schemes, some modest, some very elaborate, some dealing mainly with inside welfare, others concentrating on outside welfare, are now in operation. (19)

Having said that, it should be appreciated that welfare work experienced a somewhat 'patchy' application. To explain this, schemes need to be related to wider economic and business imperatives.

Above all, it was the state of trade which determined the feasibility of industrial welfare. Generally speaking, welfare was dependent on market conditions and business cycle trends. Occupational welfare in cotton was thus stimulated by the boom of 1919-20, but faltered as trading conditions deteriorated. As one editorial stated: "welfare schemes have been considerably retarded during the long trade depression". (20) Certainly the geographical diversity in the spread of welfare was connected to the trade of the areas concerned. Whilst Bolton concentrated on the relatively more buoyant fine spinning sector and so could afford welfare, Oldham and Blackburn were centres of the badly hit coarse spinning and plainer weaving sectors and so found it more difficult to finance welfare. Therefore, considerable welfare activity was found in Bolton with mill canteens, ambulance rooms and the rest, but less provision in Oldham and Blackburn.

It is true that once welfare sections had been created companies were reluctant to abandon them, though activities were curtailed during the more protracted slump of the 1930s. The F.C.S.D.A. made retrenchments in this decade: losses were made between 1931 and 1933 and, judging from the company minutes, welfare diminished in significance until the Second World War. A number of cotton enterprises reviewed the operation, function, and most important of all, the cost of welfare. Towards the end of 1930 the English Sewing Cotton Company were seeking ways to make canteen arrangements more cost-effective and efficient, "more especially in the reduction of employees' time spent in fetching and carrying food during working hours". (21) Moreover, two years later the company's "Secretary was instructed to make a survey of all expenditure for labour and materials in every section of the Company's welfare organisation"; and it was finally resolved "that, whilst there is no wish to restrict the welfare activities at the Company's mills, the Managers are requested to see that a close watch is kept on all expenditure". (22) Further, in the depressed circumstances of the 1930s, cotton employers opposed the concession of certain welfare or fringe benefits primarily on the grounds of the expenditure involved and "the present unsatisfactory state of the trade" - this was the case with paid holidays. (23) In the last analysis, welfare may be viewed as a dependent variable inasmuch as it relied on the liquidity and productive basis of the enterprise.

Also important in the introduction and continuance of welfare schemes was their function as perceived by employers and managers. The evidence for cotton seems to substantiate the view of Melling and others that industrial welfare functioned to improve labour efficiency. Although advocates of welfarism described its purpose in generally altruistic terms, frequently referring to 'the human side of industry', it was usually conceded that schemes made business sense. Mr. J. Clark, the head of the labour department at Ashton Brothers, was therefore careful to repudiate philanthropic motives: "Let me say at once that my firm strongly resents the imputation of philanthropy in these schemes; we have proved that these efforts to improve conditions and relationships are of immense benefit to the firm as well as the worker." (24) Rest breaks, canteens, medical supervision and even music were cited as methods to improve productivity and increase output. (25) And since efficiency was 'the problem to be solved', it was probably with some satisfaction that one manager recorded that through industrial welfare "the workers went about their work in a far better and more willing manner". (26) More specifically, 'experts' explained that the problem of labour shortage, as it emerged in the immediate post-war years, could be alleviated by using welfare benefits to attract young operatives. (27) In sum, Sir Edward Tootal Broadhurst was correct to stress welfare as a sound business investment inasmuch as it resulted in a healthy workforce, and better time-keeping, reduced labour turnover, and led to a fall in works' disputes. (28) Certainly it is possible that industrial welfare came under pressure not only when profits dwindled and companies became less viable, but also when the rationale behind them disintegrated in a period of high unemployment. In order to assess the function of industrial welfare in a little more detail, this chapter will now examine the important role played by mill recreation.

II. Mill Recreational Facilities

Recreational amenities were perhaps the most popular form of mill welfare. Indeed, in some mills the terms welfare and recreation were almost interchangeable - this was certainly so in the English Sewing Cotton Company. Mills catered for both indoor and outdoor recreation ranging from dances, socials and dramatic performances to sports clubs with playing fields for football, cricket, tennis and so on. Provision was also made for the annual holiday. It has been stated that recreational schemes were of an expensive character and that the growth of commercialised leisure forms such as the cinema made schemes difficult to promote. (29) However, as far as the cotton industry is concerned, mill recreation was far from discouraged. It is true that the cost of recreation was quite high, but even this did not appear to act as a deterrent. How can this be explained?

Recreational provision was widespread among the big combines and those firms with advanced organisation and technology in a secure part of the market. Once again, the F.C.S.D.A. spent considerable sums on recreation. Obviously its market position in the fine spinning sector and its profitable basis, as well as the scale economies achieved by horizontal amalgamation, provided the resources for recreation. By the mid-1920s it had formed football, hockey and swimming clubs, organised football and bowling competitions and provided a considerable number of tennis courts and bowling greens. The first large recreation ground opened by the Association was that of the Musgrave Spinning Company of Bolton, at a cost of between £8,000 and £9,000:

> Mention was made of the opening of the Musgrave Recreation Ground on the previous evening...which was attended by the Executive and various other Directors. There was also a large attendance of the Millworkers. The event had passed very well, and was enjoyed by all those present. The ground included 4 tennis courts, bowling green, football ground, rounders' courts and pavilion. (30)

Support was given to a number of similar projects, and despite the fact that the economic slump of the early thirties curtailed welfare initiatives, company sport still continued to arouse "great enthusiasm". (31)

The English Sewing Cotton Company also sponsored workers' leisure. As an integrated, "well-balanced and comprehensive organisation, embracing nearly all aspects of the cotton industry", the company had an array of recreational schemes at its various mill branches. (32) Clearly, considerable expenditure was diverted to recreation: at the Pendlebury mill in 1923 £460 was sanctioned on two hard tennis courts, pavilion and equipment, and in 1932 £550 on land from the nearby Bridgewater Estates for cricket and hockey fields; at the Stockport mill in 1926 £1,150 was approved for the layout of a bowling green, two tennis courts and a pavilion; at the Skipton mill, also in 1926, £1,750 was sanctioned for a bowling green, four tennis courts and a pavilion; and finally at the Matlock branch in 1929 £3,000 was approved for the provision of a new dining and recreation room. (33) Yet the most extensive facilities were provided at the Belper branch in Derbyshire, which was responsible for the funding and maintenance of the Belper River Gardens. Purchased by the company from the famous Strutt family, the Gardens were an important part of the local recreational milieu. Throughout the period they were used for Bank Holiday fetes - which, though paying concerns, were often spoilt by 'inclement weather' for which insurance cover was taken out - and for functions organised by local charities such as Dr. Barnardo's Homes. Current and capital expenditure on the Gardens was quite high - rowing and motor boats were purchased, labourers employed, and bridges, pavilions and ladies' lavatory accommodation improved. All in all, as the evidence shows, recreation was an important concern of the Company Executive, and accordingly resources were very rarely denied, even during the downturn of the 1930s.

There were other important cotton concerns with recreational programmes, including the Amalgamated Cotton Mills Trust, Ashton Brothers, Bannerman Mills, John Bright & Bros. (Rochdale), John Dugdale & Bros. (Burnley), Greenfield Mills (Darwen), Richard Haworth & Co. (Salford), Burgess, Ledward & Co. (Walkden), the Imperial Mill (Blackburn), Kelsall & Kemp (Rochdale), T. & J. Leigh (Stockport), James Nelson Ltd. (Nelson), and Tootal Broadhurst Lee Company. It would be tedious to outline the nature and range of the respective schemes, but judging from the local papers and the textile press virtually all forms of recreation for both male and female workers were catered for. It is indeed interesting that workshop leagues were established in the 1920s to provide scope for organised competition between mill operatives - in football there was the Blackburn factory and workshops league, the Bolton cotton mills cup and the Stockport workshop competition, while in bowls there was the Tattersall and Palmer cups and a variety of other tournaments. (34)

As already indicated, these companies were able to afford recreation because of their product market and their organisational and technological structure. The Amalgamated Cotton Mills Trust was a large integrated combine which also introduced ring spindle technology, giving it competitive advantages in the market. Both Ashton Brothers and Tootal Broadhurst Lee were integrated and technologically advanced with a stable market niche. During the trade prosperity of 1919-20 when most of the recreational projects were first being promoted, Ashton Brothers had 67,932 mule and 117,560 ring spindles and 4,838 looms, with a relatively good market position due to its technological superiority and hence competitive edge. Similarly, Tootal, another combined firm, had 63,872 mule and 16,364 ring spindles, together with 2,498 looms, and developed on profitable lines throughout the period. (35) By the 1930s the company had excellent facilities for both indoor and outdoor entertainment, including an operatic society and a drama group under the direction of the firm's Newton Heath general manager. (36) And at the end of the decade, it was agreed to spend "a sum not exceeding £3,000 on a new sports pavilion at Newton Heath". (37)

The same pattern can be discerned for those other firms providing recreation. Dugdale and Bros., Richard Howarth, and

Cotton Employers and Industrial Welfare

James Nelson were all integrated enterprises with respectively 66,000, 150,000 and 24,000 spindles, as well as 1,530, 3,200 and 2,400 looms in 1920. It was therefore the leading firms in the industry which embarked on comprehensive recreational programmes, though it must be added that many of the smaller concerns provided facilities for holiday savings clubs, and arranged mill treats, annual excursions and the like.

On the whole it would appear that recreation, like the various other welfare measures, was seen as contributing to labour efficiency. Recreation as a form of industrial welfare was linked to wider aspects of business operation. No matter how altruistic the motives of welfare architects may have been, the company anticipated some kind of 'return' from their investment. In the final analysis recreation clubs were viewed as ways of safeguarding and regenerating a productive workforce. As Sir Edward Tootal Broadhurst expressed it: "factory operatives who...use their leisure in healthy, physical and intellectual pursuits, are an undoubted advantage to the cotton industry, as they are to any other". (38) With recreation, however, the analysis needs to be taken one step further. Since a number of historians have examined leisure as a form of 'social control', it may be illuminating to focus on the control functions of mill recreation.

III. Recreation Provision as a Form of Social Control

In capitalist society, social control is one of the means by which the ruling class is able to secure and reproduce its economic, political and ideological dominance: though it must be added that the reproduction of class rule is the site of struggle and contestation and is never static or inevitable. From a Marxist perspective this definition of control has much in common with Gramsci's concept of bourgeois hegemony and Althusser's 'Ideological State Apparatuses', both of which attempt to explain the ideological legitimacy of capitalism. (39) And it is in a similar way that social control has been applied as an explanatory concept in a number of fields of historical inquiry. (40). However, if all social phenomena involve some element of control, then the concept has little value as a mode of explanation. Not surprisingly, the concept has come under fire from both Marxist and non-Marxist historians alike. (41) Nonetheless, in the context of this discussion it is possible to view mill recreation as a form of social control for companies sought to channel operatives into safe, responsible and edifying leisure activities. Presumably, social control could have acted on two separate, though mutually reinforcing, levels.

In the first place, cotton operatives were one of the many categories of workers which achieved the shorter working week in the immediate post-war period. After a short trade dispute in the summer of 1919, which was prolonged by the spinners' union, the basic weekly hours in the industry were reduced from $55\frac{1}{2}$ to 48 (the operatives also received a 30 per cent increase on list by way of wage compensation). Under such conditions the employers were clearly apprehensive about the use to which the newly-won leisure time would be put. According to the Textile Mercury: "The shorter working week has brought new problems and responsibilities to employers and work people." (42) In brief, masters were responsible for weaning their workforce away from those activities, especially gambling and drinking, which resulted in ill-health, absenteeism, poor time-keeping, and which interfered with production. As H.H. Payne countered, "every firm has the opportunity of encouraging its employees...to spend their leisure time reasonably". (43) Because "the hours spent away from work are too often misused" it was to be the role of the welfare supervisor to "be the focus of all social and athletic activities of the worker". (44) Recreation was promoted with this 'control' function in mind, and, to be sure, successes were recorded: "By the provision of facilities for recreation, many textile firms in Lancashire have enabled their workpeople to spend their leisure time under healthgiving conditions, so that they return to the mills physically and mentally refreshed". (45) In the case of Ashton Brothers, the Medical Officer of Health for Hyde commented that the firm had "taken earnest steps in recent years to improve the physique of its employees" through the provision of a gymnasium, recreation club and a wide range of sports facilities. (46) Equally, Mr. G.A. Barnes, a director of the F.C.S.D.A., acknowledged that the recreation ground of the Musgrave Spinning Company "would be of the utmost benefit both to the workpeople and to the firm itself". (47) Employers regarded holidays in a similar light, and to this end Sir John Grey, the chairman of the C.S.M.A., agreed that the annual break from work conferred a "change of scene, freshness, physical and mental, and restoration of health". (48) However, a qualification needs to be registered here as, clearly, recreational responsibilities and activities of the mill were not allowed to interfere with production. The English Sewing Cotton Company, for example, protested that mid-day addresses to operatives, general welfare duties and the annual camp of the Territorial Army, should not impede work. (49)

The second level at which mill recreation operated as a form of control can be discussed in terms of class relations. Patrick Joyce, in his enterprising study of factory culture in later Victorian England, has shown that big employers organised all variety of leisure activities and cultural events. In a stimulating discussion, Joyce asserts that this form of industrial paternalism, supported by economic expansion and peaceful industrial relations, was an important factor in the deference and subordination of the factory proletariat. (50) He goes on to suggest, however, that by the close of the century factory paternalism had been shattered by the growth above all of a commercialised leisure industry. (51) From the observations already made, it is clear that paternalism survived for much longer than Joyce implies. At least in the fine spinning sector, paternalism had evolved from the level of the individual firm to the more bureaucratised level of the multi-mill, combine structure. It is true that by the inter-war period mill recreation had been recast, but it was still being used as a way to forge links between masters and men, and more importantly to reduce conflictual industrial politics.

The captains of industry were often sympathetic to welfare work precisely because it was thought to encourage class consensus. As one mill manager asserted: "The more they did in the movement the better co-operation they would have between the workers and the management." (52) Certainly, leaders of the industry were quick to point out that welfare "tended to greater cohesion between employer and employed", and resulted in "a much better feeling and greater unity...among the workers and the staff". (53) Recreation was an integral aspect of all this, providing the opportunity for masters and men to come together at mill functions, sports days, excursions and the like. Although some welfare benefits functioned as part of a firm's internal labour market and drove wedges between operatives and staff - paid holidays, for instance, were provided for white-collar but not blue-collar workers - social activities sought to transcend divisions at work.

It is also possible that a programme of welfare capitalism was adopted as a way of gaining identity and support in the wider community. Jonathan Boswell after all has discussed the 'informal social control' exercised over business conduct in the years between 1880 and 1939. In a broadly non-Marxist discourse Boswell argues that business had social and ethical responsibilities in the community. (54) To be sure, business philanthropy had not died by the inter-war years and Quaker employers in particular still exerted an influence on business affairs. (55) Evidence indeed suggests that cotton employers subsidised many local bodies and charities, and played a role in the social, political and religious affairs of the community. Most crucially, however, business promoted recreation in order to gain the backing of their workers and public opinion in the locality. (56) In spite of the fact that the English Sewing Cotton Company was a little reluctant to allow 'outsiders' to use mill recreational facilities, their Bank Holiday fetes can be seen in this light. Not only were they a form of company publicity, but also an extension of the corporate spirit into the community. (57) Furthermore, masters assisted local (and national) celebrations and events. Paid holidays were therefore granted on the occasion of George V's Jubilee in 1935 and George VI's coronation two years later. (58)

More significant still, company recreation was used to counter the growth of anti-capitalist sentiment. Holidays with pay may have nourished the occasional community spectacle, but they were also granted to undermine trade union strength. (59) Moreover, it is possible that recreational schemes spread during the industrial unrest of 1919-20 because they were assumed to be a means of political incorporation into the bourgeois social order. At a time when the Home Office was carrying out surveillance of revolutionary activity in the North West, sport was pronounced as a factor in political stabilisation. (60) Presumably, to use the words of John McConnel of the Fine Spinners, sport and welfare would encourage "harmony and peace between the classes". (61) Note also the sentiments expressed in one local newspaper editorial, at the height of the more looms dispute in 1932:

> It is generally acknowledged that football provides one of the finest antidotes to unrest in this country, and creates in the mass a sense of sportsmanship that no other games can possibly do. In such an atmosphere the possibilities of a settlement of Lancashire's cotton problems are considerably strengthened. Employers and operative meet on common ground as lovers of the winter pastime, and win, lose, or draw, ill-will and prejudice disappear when both sides "play the game". (62)

It is debatable whether sport has ever been a source of class collaboration (63), though it is important nonetheless that the ruling elite viewed it this way. However, in the final analysis it must be emphasised that control over labour was achieved principally by the re-imposition of managerial authority at the place of work, by wage reductions, and by unemployment: industrial welfare played only a secondary role.

Mill recreation, so it appears on the surface, acted as a medium of control by guiding workers into healthy and re-generative pastimes, and by binding workers and the community at large to the corporate entity. At this stage, however, a number of caveats are necessary. The purpose of mill recreation may well have been that of social control, yet it is doubtful whether it ever functioned on this level. True, workers' printed addresses and testimonials were genuinely grateful for the efforts of the masters. The employees of Sunnyside Mills, Bolton, thanked Harold Lee "for the many advantages we have enjoyed through your thoughtfulness for our welfare", while the recreational provisions of the Greenfield Mill, Darwen, were said to stand "for the better life and for better conditions for the workers". (64) Also relevant here, recreational facilities, far from being imposed by the employers, were sometimes provided in response to the demands of the operatives themselves, as happened at mills in Pendlebury, Skipton and Stockport. (65) More than this, once schemes had been established operatives, not employers, often controlled them. This was an established principle in many companies. In opening Tootal's new sports ground and pavilion, Captain A.W. Smith, a director of the company, reminded the workers that the ground "belongs to them and is for their benefit". (66) William Howarth, managing director of the F.C.S.D.A., made a similar point:

> As regards recreation for the workers it was not desirable that this should be controlled by the Welfare Superintendents, as the policy of the Association was that all means for recreation and canteens should be provided, and started from the Welfare Fund, but that afterwards they should be controlled and maintained by the workers themselves. (67)

Cotton Employers and Industrial Welfare

Even when managerial prerogatives remained, workers could reappropriate company facilities and use them for their own ends, divorced from the initial designs of the employer. In brief, the extent to which operatives could be overtly or covertly manipulated by management can be exaggerated.

Many workers, of course, resented the incursion of employers into their leisure time. There was a long-established tradition of self-help and independence among the operatives of Lancashire, which extended into relative autonomy in the recreational and cultural sphere. As employers like J. Thorpe, W. Howarth, F. Holroyd and W. Hamer suggested, "the Lancashire operatives were too independent to have the pleasures of life mapped out for them in any spoon-fed way". (68) Indeed, union officials opposed welfare where it threatened independent labour organisation. (69)

Lastly, mill recreation never dominated the social life of the locality. There was a plethora of alternative leisure amenities. At Belle View Mills, Skipton, for example, at least initially the workers "did not desire that any welfare organisation should be established (as) there were plenty of counter attractions...on the amusement side". (70) Equally, the extensive sports facilities of James Nelson Ltd. - one of the largest textile firms in North East Lancashire with 2,200 employees in the mid-1920s - failed to undermine working class organisations. (71) The Nelson branch of the Independent Labour Party, for instance, associated as it was with the Clarion, the Socialist Sunday Schools and the local Weavers' Association, was a self-contained unit providing all those social and cultural needs that the labour community required. (72) Elsewhere a number of what may be loosely termed counter-cultural organisations existed: for instance, the Stockport Labour Brotherhood and the Hyde Socialist Church. (73) Moreover, though as we have seen commercial forms did not exactly replace mill forms of recreation, they were a source of competition for operatives' spare time. In textile areas such as Rochdale, Bolton and Hyde, with fairly extensive company facilities, commercialised enterprise was certainly penetrating the leisure domain. (74) Needless to say, employers were unable to achieve total control over the life and leisure of their workforce.

IV. Conclusions

This chapter has shown that the cotton industry, or at least important sectors of it, shared in the expansion of industrial welfare in the inter-war years. As a staple industry, dependent on exports for its living, cotton was severely hit after the First World War by the loss of overseas markets and increased foreign competition. For those loss-making firms resources were not provided for elaborate welfare schemes, though some of the nineteenth century rituals of factory life such as picnics and outings survived. It was those larger firms with a more buoyant market position and efficient industrial structure which afforded private occupational welfare. For these firms, the primary function of industrial welfare was one of economic efficiency. Objectively, welfare moulded a more reliable and productive labour force.

In the more detailed treatment of mill recreation, welfare was also examined as a form of social control. Roy Hay has explained that control and considerations of economic efficiency are interrelated, making it "difficult to distinguish where efficiency ends and control begins. The creation of a docile labour force, which responds swiftly to economic incentives, involves both control and efficiency." (75) With mill recreation, therefore, control helped to promote labour health and productivity. Yet control had extra dimensions. By encouraging rational recreation under the control of the firm, some employers thought they could gain ideological consent, forge links with the community and assuage feelings of class hostility. No doubt, benevolent employers were also genuinely concerned about the well-being of the working class. Even so, control through industrial welfare and recreation was difficult to secure, precisely because operatives were not industrially or politically impotent. Welfare failed to prevent disputes at the point of production - companies such as Ashton Brothers and the English Sewing Cotton Company still experienced strikes despite their welfare efforts. Indeed, it is testimony to the resistance and independence of cotton workers that many of their institutions remained intact, particularly during a time of wage-cuts, short-time working, unemployment and a quite inventive, and incorporative, industrial welfare policy.

NOTES

I would like to thank the Northern Spinning Division of Courtaulds Ltd., the Tootal Group P.L.C., and the British Textile Employers' Association for access to their records. I would also like to acknowledge the helpful comments of Arthur McIvor.

1. See A.C. Howe, The Cotton Masters, 1830-1860, (Oxford, 1984); A.J. McIvor, 'Employers' Organisation and Strikebreaking in Britain, 1880-1914', International Review of Social History, XXIX (1984), pp. 1-33. See also W.R. Garside and H.F. Gospel, 'Employers and Managers: Their Organizational Structure and Changing Industrial Strategies', in C. Wrigley (ed.), A History of British Industrial Relations 1875-1914, (Brighton, 1982), pp. 99-115; H.F. Gospel and C.R. Littler (eds.), Managerial Strategies and Industrial Relations: An Historical and Comparative Study, (London, 1983).

2. See, for example, J.L. Melling, 'British Employers and the Development of Industrial Welfare, c. 1880-1920: An Industrial and Regional Comparison', (unpublished Ph.D. thesis, University of Glasgow, 1980); idem, 'Employers, Industrial Welfare and the Struggle for Work-Place Control in British Industry, 1880-1920', in Gospel and Littler, Managerial Strategies, (1983), pp. 55-68.

3. H. Jones, 'Employers' Welfare Schemes and Industrial Relations in Inter-War Britain', Business History, XXV (1983), pp. 61-75.

4. Ibid; N. Whiteside, 'Industrial Welfare and Labour Regulation in Britain at the time of the First World War', International Review of Social History, XXV (1980), p. 327; R. Whipp, '"The Art of Good Management": Management Control of Work in the British Pottery Industry, 1900-25', International Review of Social History, XXIX (1984), p. 379.

5. W. Lazonick, 'Competition, Specialization, and Industrial Decline', Journal of Economic History, XLI (1981), pp. 31-8; idem, 'Industrial Organization and Technological Change: The Decline of the British Cotton Industry', Business History Review, LVII (1983), pp. 195-236.

6. E.D. Proud, Welfare Work: Employers' Experiments for Improving Working Conditions in Factories, (London, 1916); J. Lee, The Principles of Industrial Welfare, (London, 1923); E.T. Kelly (ed.), Welfare Work in Industry, (London, 1925). For the I.W.S., see R. Hyde, Industry was my Parish, (London, 1968), pp. 68-105; E. Sidney, The Industrial Society 1918-1968, (London, 1968), pp. 3-35.

7. Greater Manchester County Record Office, Cotton Spinners' and Manufacturers' Association, Chairmen of Local Associations, Minutes, (hereafter cited as C.S.M.A. Minutes), 17 September 1920, 14 December 1920; C.S.M.A., Minutes, 19 January 1921; Federation of Master Cotton Spinners' Associations, Annual Report, 1921, pp. 16-21. It should be noted that affiliates of the F.M.C.S.A. thought this question was 'for the Federation to deal with'. See John Rylands Library, Manchester; General Committee of the Ashton and District Cotton Employers' Association, Minutes, 23 February 1920; Harold Cliff (Secretary of the Oldham Master Spinners' Association) to Chief Inspector of Factories, 5 March 1920; Committee of the Glossop, Hyde and District Cotton Employers' Association, Minutes, 13 September 1920; Manchester Central Library Archives Department, M 127/1/12-32; Executive Committee of the English Sewing Cotton Company, Minutes, (hereafter cited as English Sewing Cotton Company Minutes), 8 September 1920, 8 November 1920. Statutory welfare orders could be made under the 1916 Police, Factories etc. (Miscellaneous) Provisions Act for any class of factory and by 1932 24 orders had been made. Annual Report of the Chief Inspector of Factories and Workshops for the year 1932, (hereafter cited as Factory Report, Cmd 4377, pp. 63-64.

8. See Textile Mercury, 13 September 1919, p. 241; 9 July 1921, p. 38; 3 December 1921, p. 636; 29 April 1922, p. 403; 7 February 1925, p. 128; Cotton Factory Times, 3 April 1925, p. 3; 18 February 1927, p. 3.

9. Tootal Group P.L.C., Spring Gardens, Manchester, file on Tootal Broadhurst Lee Company, n.d.

10. Textile Mercury, 23 August 1919, p. 182; 30 August 1919, pp. 191-2; Skinner's Cotton Trade Directory of the World, (Manchester, 1941), p. 365; Bolton Public Library, ZTBL/9, Records of

Tootal Broadhurst Lee of Sunnyside Mills.
11. Manchester Central Library Archives Department, M 461, Mills Management Committee of Tootal Broadhurst Lee Company, Minutes, (hereafter cited as Tootal Minutes), 23 February 1926, 25 September 1934.
12. E.T. Broadhurst, 'Welfare Work in the Cotton Industry', in Proceedings of the Tenth International Cotton Congress, Zurich, (June 1920). Tootal Main Board, Minutes, 14 March 1922, 6 July 1937; Tootal Finance Company Minutes, 4 April 1932.
13. Stockport County Borough Express, 29 May 1919, p. 6; Factory Report for 1920, Cmd 1403, p. 81.
14. Factory Report for 1925, Cmd 2714, pp. 48-50; Factory Report for 1928, Cmd 3360, p. 59.
15. Courtaulds Ltd., Northern Spinning Division, Manchester, Fine Cotton Spinners' and Doublers' Association, Main Board Minutes, (hereafter cited as F.C.S.D.A. Minutes), 22 July 1924; and calculated from the Company's Annual Reports. See also A.C. Howe, 'Dixon, Sir Alfred Herbert (1857-1920): Cotton Manufacturer', in D.J. Jeremy (ed.), Dictionary of Business Biography, II (London, 1984), pp. 107-12.
16. Textile Mercury, 12 June 1920, p. 655; 11 October 1924, p. 331; 'Open Conference: Welfare Work', Journal of the British Association of Managers of Textile Works (Lancashire Section), X (1919-20), pp. 31-41.
17. Textile Mercury, 22 November 1919, p. 494; 1 May 1920, p. 488. A further sign of growing interest is the fact that representatives of the C.S.M.A. attended a Home Office conference on industrial welfare. C.S.M.A., Minutes, 18 June 1920.
18. Cotton Factory Times, 12 November 1920, p. 1. Cf. E.D. Newcomb, 'Welfare Work in Textile Factories', Textile Mercury, 13 August 1921, p. 169, where it is claimed that Lancashire was "near the bottom of the welfare ladder".
19. Factory Report for 1925, Cmd. 2714, p. 48. See also Factory Report for 1924, Cmd. 2437, p. 59; Factory Report for 1926 Cmd. 2903, p. 54; Factory Report for 1927, Cmd. 3144, p. 67; F. Nasmith, 'Twenty-one Years Survey', The Textile Recorder, 15 December 1925, pp. 49-51. It is also suggestive that a new textile journal appeared in 1925 under the title, Health, Welfare and Safety.
20. Textile Mercury, 2 June 1923, p. 469. See also 'Welfare Workers' Institute', Textile Institute Journal, XIII (1922), p. 8; Factory Report for 1928, Cmd. 3360, p. 58.
21. English Sewing Cotton Company Minutes, 21 October 1930.
22. Ibid., 10 June 1932, 17 June 1932, 28 June 1932, 22 July 1932, 12 October 1934. See also F.C.S.D.A., Executive Directors' Minutes, 17 January 1935, 31 January 1935.
23. See Minutes of Evidence Taken Before the Committee on Holidays with Pay, 1937-38, pp. 123-35; Textile Weekly, 29 April 1938, p. 572; 3 June 1938, p. 744; 1 July 1938, p. 4; 19 August 1938, p. 224; 11 November 1938, p. 648; F.M.C.S.A., Annual Report, 1938, pp. 15-16; C.S.M.A., Minutes, 22 March 1938, 22 April 1938. For further details, see S. Jones, 'The Lancashire Cotton Industry

and the Development of Paid Holidays in the Nineteen Thirties', Transactions of the Historic Society of Lancashire and Cheshire, CXXXV (1986).

24. 'Open Conference: Welfare Work', p. 35. A similar view was expressed in the Textile Mercury, 11 September 1920, p. 256: "We are speaking from a business rather than from a sentimental point of view, for it can be conclusively proved that welfare adds not only to production and efficiency, but to goodwill between employers and workpeople." See also Textile Mercury, 2 September 1922, p. 181; 11 October 1924, p. 323.

25. Textile Mercury, 27 March 1920, p. 335; 29 April 1922, p. 403; 1 July 1922, p. 17; 13 December 1924, p. 551. For a general discussion of industrial health in this period see A.J. McIvor, 'Manual Work, Technology and Industrial Health, 1918-39', Medical History, 31, 1987, pp. 160-89.

26. Miss Voysey, 'Welfare Work from the Welfare Workers Point of View', Textile Institute Journal, X (1919), p. 165; English Sewing Cotton Company, Minutes, 16 May 1919.

27. See Stockport Advertiser, 30 May 1919, p. 4; English Sewing Cotton Company Minutes, 5 September 1919, 8 September 1919, 10 September 1919, 12 September 1919; Textile Mercury, 24 December 1921, p. 655.

28. Textile Mercury, 12 June 1920, p. 654.

29. Minutes of Evidence Taken Before the Committee on Industry and Trade 1924-1929, I, Evidence of the I.W.S., 21 January 1925, p. 195; Jones, 'Employers' Welfare Schemes', p. 72.

30. F.C.S.D.A., Executive Directors' Minutes, 9 July 1925; Cotton Factory Times, 17 July 1925, p. 4. The Musgrave Spinning Company held annual sports days and swimming galas. Cotton Factory Times, 29 July 1927, p. 4; 23 September 1927, p. 4.

31. F.C.S.D.A., Executive Directors' Minutes, 24 September 1925, 26 August 1926, 18 July 1929, 30 January 1936, 8 April 1937; Finance Committee Minutes, 29 March 1951; Behind the Distaff: An Account of the Activities of the Fine Cotton Spinners' and Doublers' Association Ltd. Manchester (Manchester, n.d. 1945?), p. 93; M. Rooff, Youth and Leisure: A Survey of Girls' Organisations in England and Wales (Edinburgh, 1935), p. 66.

32. H.E. Blyth, Through the Eye of a Needle: The Story of the English Sewing Cotton Company, (Manchester, n.d. 1947?), pp. 21, 79.

33. English Sewing Cotton Company, Minutes, 19 July 1922, 15 January 1923, 29 April 1926, 6 August 1926; 26 August 1926, 8 October 1926; 7 January 1929, 7 June 1929, 23 December 1932, 2 July 1934.

34. Textile Mercury, 4 August 1923, p. 116; 30 August 1924, p. 195; Cotton Factory Times, 1 May 1925, p. 4; 13 May 1927, pp. 3-4; Stockport Advertiser, 8 May 1925, p. 6; Cheshire Daily Echo, 2 February 1929, p. 3; English Sewing Cotton Company, Minutes, 9 May 1930, 26 June 1933, 12 April 1937.

35. Figures are taken from Worrall's Cotton Spinners' and Manufacturers' Directory for Lancashire, 1920. See also, M.W. Dupree, 'Broadhurst, Sir Edward Tootal (1858-1922): Cotton Man-

ufacturer' in Jeremy, Dictionary, I, pp. 452-7.
36. Cotton Factory Times, 15 April 1927, p. 2; Unity, August 1930, p. 12.
37. Tootal, Mill Management Committee Minutes, 23 May 1939.
38. Textile Mercury, 12 June 1920, p. 655.
39. Q. Hoare and G. Nowell (eds.), Antonio Gramsci: Selections from the Prison Notebooks, (London, 1971); L. Althusser, 'Ideology and Ideological State Apparatuses. (Notes towards an Investigation)', in Lenin and Philosophy and Other Essays, (London, 1971), pp. 121-73.
40. See J.R. Hay, 'Employers' Attitudes to Social Policy, and the concept of "Social Control", 1900-1920', in P. Thane (ed.), The Origins of British Social Policy, (London, 1978), pp. 107-25; E. and S. Yeo, 'Ways of Seeing: Control and Leisure versus Class and Struggle', in E. and S. Yeo (eds.), Popular Culture and Class Conflict 1590-1914: Explorations in the History of Labour and Leisure, (Brighton, 1981), pp. 128-54; C. Critcher, 'The Politics of Leisure - Social Control and Social Development', in Work and Leisure: The Implications of Technological Change, (Edinburgh, 1982), pp. 43-53.
41. G. Stedman Jones, 'Class expression versus social control?: A critique of recent trends in the social history of "leisure"', History Workshop, IV (1977), pp. 162-70; F.M.L. Thompson, 'Social Control in Victorian Britain', Economic History Review, XXXIV (1981), pp. 189-208.
42. Textile Mercury, 30 October 1920, p. 422.
43. H.H. Payne, 'The Industrial Welfare Movement: Its Principles and Its Influence on Industrial Relations', Textile Institute Journal, XIV (1923), p. 280.
44. R.R. Hyde, 'Factors in Industrial Welfare Work', Textile Mercury, 9 July 1921, p. 88.
45. Textile Mercury, 29 Sept. 1928, p. 203.
46. Stalybridge Local History Library, CA/HYD/880/15, Borough of Hyde, Annual Report of the Medical Officer of Health, 1920, pp. 5-6.
47. F.C.S.D.A., Main Board Minutes, 24 July 1925.
48. Minutes of Evidence Taken Before the Committee on Holidays with Pay, Evidence of the C.S.M.A., 5 October 1937, q. 1444 at p. 133.
49. English Sewing Cotton Company, Minutes, 11 December 1918, 24 November 1919, 22 July 1921, 13 June 1927.
50. P. Joyce, Work, Society and Politics: The Culture of the Factory in later Victorian England, (Brighton, 1980), especially ch. 4.
51. Ibid., pp. 186, 338-9.
52. Textile Mercury, 15 November 1919, p. 485.
53. Textile Mercury, 24 December 1921, p. 655; English Sewing Cotton Company, Minutes, 22 January 1922. As Sir Alan Sykes, chairman of the the Bleachers' Association, stressed in formally opening one firm's sports facilities: "It did not matter whether it was the employer or the employed, capital or labour, they could not succeed unless they pulled together, because they

were interdependent.", Cotton Factory Times, 29 April 1927, p. 1.
54. J. Boswell, 'The Informal Social Control of Business in Britain: 1880-1939', Business History Review, LVII (1983), pp. 237-57.
55. J. Child, 'Quaker Employers and Industrial Relations', The Sociological Review, XXII (1964), pp. 293-315.
56. See, for example, F.C.S.D.A., Main Board Minutes, 14 May 1919; Executive Directors' Minutes, 10 April 1924, 24 September 1925.
57. See Melling, D. Phil. thesis, I, p. 241; S.D. Brandes, American Welfare Capitalism, 1880-1940, (Chicago, 1976), pp. 75-82; C. Sabel and J. Zeitlin, 'Historical Alternatives to Mass Production: Politics, Markets, and Technology in Nineteenth Century Industrialization', Past and Present, no. 108 (1985), p. 151.
58. Tootal, Mill Management Committee Minutes, 5 March 1935, 16 February 1937; Stalybridge Local History Library, TU/6/1/46, Minutes of the Manchester District of the S.E. Lancashire and Cheshire Weavers' and Winders' Association, 18 March 1935, 8 April 1935; English Sewing Cotton Company, Minutes, 15 March 1937, 12 April 1937; F.C.S.D.A., Directors' Minutes, 8 April 1937; C.S.M.A., Central Committee Minutes, 12 January 1937, 2 March 1937, 13 April 1937, 4 May 1937; Textile Weekly, 9 April 1937, p. 460.
59. A. Fowler, 'Trade Unions and Technical Change: The Automatic Loom Strike, 1908', North West Labour History Society, Bulletin 6 (1979-80), pp. 48-9; D.C. Coleman, Courtaulds, An Economic History, II (Oxford, 1969), p. 447.
60. PRO CAB 24/96 (C.P. 462); CAB 24/117 (C.P. 2316). The C.S.M.A. was in fact contacted by organisations set up to counter revolutionary propaganda. C.S.M.A., Central Committee Minutes, 19 August 1919, 28 December 1920.
61. Textile Mercury, 19 June 1920, p. 684.
62. Ashton-Under-Lyne Reporter, 27 August 1932, p. 6. Cf. Ashton-Under-Lyne Reporter, 12 July 1930, p. 8.
63. See R. Miliband, Marxism and Politics, (Oxford, 1977), pp. 51-2; Stedman Jones, 'Class Expression', p. 169.
64. Tootal Group P.L.C., Spring Gardens, Manchester, Printed Address from the Employees of Messrs. Tootal Broadhurst Lee Co. Ltd. Sunnyside Mills, Bolton, 10 October 1917; C.D., 'Factory Life: Improving the Workers' Lot at Darwen', Cotton Factory Times, 23 January 1925, p. 1.
65. English Sewing Cotton Company, Minutes, 8 December 1921, 31 May 1922, 2 August 1922, 11 February 1926.
66. Cotton Factory Times, 7 August 1925, p. 4.
67. F.C.S.D.A., Main Board Minutes, 25 September 1925. See also English Sewing Cotton Company, Minutes, 18 June 1919, 4 March 1920; Blyth, Through the Eye of a Needle, p. 81.
68. Textile Mercury, 18 December 1920, p. 625. At about the same time the employers also complained that welfare "accommodation or facilities would not be utilised by the workers", C.S.M.A., Minutes of a Conference, 19 January 1921.

69. See, Yorkshire Factory Times and Workers' Weekly Record, 3 August 1922, p. 3. On union responses to the economic slump see A. Fowler, Ch. 6.
70. English Sewing Cotton Company, Minutes, 22 March 1920.
71. For details of the facilities, see Cotton Factory Times, 9 January 1925, p. 2; 4 November 1927, p. 2; Textile Mercury, 24 October 1925, p. 428; 27 August 1927, p. 256.
72. Stanley Iveson, interview with the author, 11 September 1981; Nelson Leader, 1938, passim; A. and L. Fowler, The History of the Nelson Weavers Association, (Nelson, 1984), p. 8.
73. Stockport Public Library Archives Department, B/MM/3/20-23, B/X/7/12; Working Class Movement Library, Manchester, F4 Box 3, F27 Box 6.
74. P. Wild, 'Recreation in Rochdale, 1900-40', in J. Clarke, C. Critcher and R. Johnson (eds.), Working Class Culture: Studies in History and Theory, (London, 1979), pp. 40-60; J. Power, 'Aspects of Working Class Leisure During the Depression Years: Bolton in the 1930s', (unpublished M.A. thesis, University of Warwick, 1980); S.G. Jones, 'Recreational and Cultural Provision in Hyde between the Wars', in A. Lock (ed.), Looking Back at Hyde, (Tameside, 1986). See generally, S.G. Jones, Workers at Play: A Social and Economic History of Leisure, 1918-1939, (London, 1986).
75. Hay, 'Employers' Attitudes', p. 110.

Section II.

TRADE UNIONS AND LABOUR

Chapter 5

THE RETARDATION OF TRADE UNIONISM IN THE
YORKSHIRE WORSTED TEXTILE INDUSTRY

Tony Jowitt

In April 1914 G.D.H. Cole and W. Mellor described trade unionism in the British wool textile industry as being

> ...still in its infancy...none of the pressing problems that affect it have been satisfactorily handled. Craft prejudice, narrowness of outlook, suspicion and 'benefit-hunting' are rampant. Indeed compared with any other industry or occupation this branch of the textile trade of England is lamentably backward. (1)

This assessment followed a number of similar statements in the last quarter of the nineteenth century and the first decade of the twentieth century, both from participants in the struggle for unionisation and outside observers. In the latter category was the German social investigator, von Schulze-Gaevernitz, who in the 1890s stated:

> Although the oldest English industry, it is still badly organised, partly because it is subject to numerous changes of fashion and to foreign competition, partly because almost seventy per cent of the workers are women - as a general rule the conditions resemble those of Lancashire fifty years ago...Their position is insecure and miserable. (2)

This comparison between the highly unionised and well organised Lancashire cotton industry and the low levels of union membership in the Yorkshire woollen and worsted industries has continued to fascinate historians: "In the Yorkshire woollen and worsted industry the weakness of trade unionism presented a remarkable contrast to the strength of the amalgamations on the other side of the Pennines." (3)

The numerical disparity between the two industries was striking. In 1900 there were 167,666 cotton trade unionists compared with 8,797 union members in wool textiles. Although the early twentieth century saw a significant increase in wool textile unionisation with a three-fold increase between 1901 and 1911, the respective totals of 274,538 members in the cotton industry and 23,102 in wool textiles still reflected a wide disparity. In 1911 slightly more than 45 per cent of the cotton labour force were trade unionists compared with 10 per cent in wool textiles. (4) Even more striking was the high level of female membership in the cotton unions, whereas in Yorkshire the number of women trade unionists was minimal until after 1910. In 1914 there were some 210,272 female trade unionists in the Lancashire cotton industry compared with 7,695 in the woollen and worsted industries. (5)

Trade unionists in the West Riding were acutely aware of the weak state of local textile trade unionism and advanced a number of reasons for it. Amongst these were: the high proportion of women in the labour force; the large number of small firms in direct competition with each other which retarded employer collaboration and the development of formalised collective bargaining; the high proportion of young people and adolescents in the mills; the fact that no two mills paid similar wages or determined wage levels in the same way, making worker comparison and co-operation between mills very difficult; the depressed state of the worsted industry in the late nineteenth and early twentieth century; the hostility of West Riding employers to trade unions and the blacklisting of labour militants; the development of social exclusiveness amongst individual trades and crafts; the power structure within the mills where overlookers and charge hands were the primary determinants of promotion and employment prospects; and the continuing power of paternalism and employer hegemony, which had dominated the middle decades of the nineteenth century, and remained a potent force in the West Riding textile towns and villages up to the First World War.

Before examining these specific factors it is necessary to provide a brief historical analysis of the development of the worsted industry and its impact on labour and labour organisations. (6)

From the later middle ages the West Riding of Yorkshire has been an important centre of domestic woollen cloth production. In particular the Pennine valleys had provided a fertile breeding ground for the mass growth of the industry. In the eighteenth century this had been supplemented by the introduction of the worsted industry in the western part of the Riding, in the area to the north and west of its three centres in Halifax, Bradford and Keighley. In addition to geographical concentration, the West Riding worsted industry, from the outset, manifested a different organisational framework to that of its sister woollen industry. Whereas the woollen industry was organised essentially on a small scale with a large number of individual producers, the worsted industry was dominated by a small number of large merchants and manufacturers who controlled the production of worsted cloth. As one commentator said: "The small independent clothier never existed in the worsted industry". (7) Rather, there was a sharp division between the influential and wealthy merchants and those to whom they put out their wool, "an army of wage dependent domestic workers who virtually formed a rural-industrial proletariat". (8)   The reasons for this different organisational form lay in the later introduction of worsted production, superimposed on an older industry; the use of long stapled wool, which was both more expensive and less readily available than that commonly used in woollen cloth production; and finally the fact that worsteds did not require the expensive and highly complicated finishing processes that were associated with woollens and dominated by the wealthy and powerful urban merchants.

By the late eighteenth century the Yorkshire worsted industry was dominated by a small number of large merchants, men like John Hustler of Undercliffe, Bradford.   These worsted merchants wielded immense influence locally, not only through the wealth that the trade generated, but also through the power that they could exert on the labour force through the Worsted Acts.   These acts, introduced in the 1770s, dealt with the particular problem of outwork, and specifically the problem of embezzlement by an army of domestic combers, spinners and weavers, who could not be directly supervised.   There is little doubt that these acts, which laid the onus of proof on the accused rather than the accuser, provided a powerful weapon against labour militants. In the late eighteenth century the once powerful Woolcombers' Association was increasingly threatened by them and by the end of the century labour organisations were in a very much weakened state. (9)

The final blow to the pre-industrial heritage of trade unionism and trade societies came with the mechanisation of the worsted trade.   Between the 1790s and the 1850s the Yorkshire worsted industry was transformed from a domestic hand trade to a fully mechanised factory industry.   In the process of mechanisation the industry became concentrated on a smaller number of urban centres, in particular Bradford which in 1800 was the location of one small solitary spinning mill.   By 1850 there were some 129 mills in the Bradford area and within the parish were to be found 40.9 per cent of English worsted factories, 44.2 per cent of the spindles, 54.1 per cent of the power looms and 45.2 per cent of the factory labour force. (10)   In addition to this process of concentration, mechanisation brought about both de-skilling and the development of a labour force which was predominantly female and youthful.   The worsted industry, much more than both the woollen and the cotton industry, relied very heavily on female and juvenile labour. In worsted spinning juvenile and female labour worked the throstle and the cap, whereas the spinning mule was manipulated by male labour.   Similarly, worsted weaving employed higher proportions of female workers than woollen and cotton weaving.   In 1833 John Wood's spinning mill, the largest in Bradford, employed 527 workers, of whom only 38 were male, and employed only 16 workers older than twenty, and not one of these was male. (11)   The development of a predominantly youthful and female labour force was to be an enduring feature of the worsted industry.   The Factory Acts of the mid-nineteenth century did not alter significantly the composition of mill labour. In 1873 Daniel Illingworth's Whetley Mills employed 943 workers of whom only 287 were aged over eighteen and 383, one-third of the labour force, were half-timers under the age of twelve. (12) In 1911 the Bradford factory labour force was still predominantly female and young, particularly in the spinning and weaving sections, which accounted for the majority of the worsted textile labour force.

Table 5.1: Percentage Composition of the Textile Labour Force in Bradford in 1911 (13)

	MALES		FEMALES	
	under 18	over 18	under 18	over 18
Combing/Carding	3.1	60.9	2.4	33.6
Spinning	20.2	9.4	31.7	38.7
Weaving	5.6	14.3	10.9	69.2
Dyeing	10.1	82.9	1.2	5.8

The development of a mechanised industry, particularly when the bastions of male hand labour, hand combing and weaving, were threatened, was opposed by local labour leaders. This was seen most clearly in the Bradford strike of 1825, a twenty-three week long epic struggle in British labour history, which saw the defeat of the weavers and combers, the destruction of the last vestiges of trade union strength and the onset of a period of employer diktat. (14) From 1825 through to the late 1840s, the period which witnessed the most traumatic changes, the West Riding was a centre of working class radicalism and agitation, with workers enrolling in large numbers in the Factory Reform Movement, the Anti-Poor Law agitation, trade unionism, Owenism and finally in Chartism, all in an attempt to curtail the power of the new factory owning elite. (15) Throughout the period the general recourse was towards political activity, either through the demand for the vote and political representation, or for interventionary legislation. There was a heritage of political, rather than economic activity which developed in the West Riding, which although subdued in the mid-Victorian period, was to be resurrected towards the end of the century.

The process of mechanisation largely saw the eradication of trade unionism in the worsted industry. Only in some skilled trades could workers wield enough power to develop their own protective organisations, as with the woolsorters and supervisory workers. Unlike the Lancashire cotton industry, which saw the development of the mule spinners as a powerful and effective force in the industry, the worsted industry underwent a more thorough de-skilling process and a weakening of the position of workers in the factory. From the 1820s worsted trade unionism was in a very weak position, from which it only recovered slowly throughout the course of the nineteenth century as Table 5.2 shows.

Retardation of Trade Unionism in Worsted

Table 5.2: The Formation of Worsted Trade Unions in the Nineteenth Century

1820s	1830s	1840s	1850s	1860s	1870s	1880s	1890s
1	2	2	2	4	2	6	6

The slow growth of trade unions in the nineteenth century was a clear reflection of the weak and divided nature of the labour force. Up to the 1870s, trade unionism, if indeed it can be referred to as such, was confined to the skilled and supervisory workers. The vast majority of these organisations were mutual benefit societies, providing for the insurance requirements of their members and a defence of their craft skill. Although many employers abhorred the concept of worker combination per se, amongst the more progressive manufacturers there were those who supported trade unions of skilled workers. Not only were these groups the N.C.O.s of the textile mill, crucial for the organisation of production and the supervision of other factory workers, but in addition their organisations were seen as fitting into the general pattern of self-help and self-improvement agencies of the period. No such benevolence was extended to the great mass of unskilled and semi-skilled textile workers. The coming of a wider based trade unionism, primarily concerned with wages and conditions of work, had to wait until the last quarter of the nineteenth century.

Table 5.3: Trade Unions Formed in the Yorkshire Wool Textile Industry with the Dates of Formation, and Membership in 1910 (16)

Trade Union	Date of formation	Membership in 1910
1. Overlookers Friendly Society	1827	merged with No. 9 in 1905
2. Managers and Overlookers Institution	1833	823
3. Bradford Woolsorters Society	1838	312
4. Bradford Stuff Makers Up	1843	120
5. Bradford and District Power Loom Overlookers Society	1844	931
6. Warehousemans Philanthropic Society	1850	merged with No. 25 in 1909
7. National Dyers and Finishers (originally called Huddersfield, Bradford and Barnsley Dyers)	1851	3874
8. Huddersfield and Dewsbury Power Loom Society	1861	384
9. Managers and Overlookers Society	1862	843
10. Yorkshire Twisters and Drawers In	1862	877
11. Leeds Cloth Pressers	1864	170

Table 5.3 (continued)

Trade Union	Date of formation	Membership in 1910
12. Leeds and District Power Loom Overlookers Society	1866	134
13. Halifax and District Power Loom Overlookers Society	1866	89
14. Huddersfield and District Cloth Pressers	1872	250
15. Huddersfield Warehousemen	1875	103
16. Bradford Pressers	1876	285
17. Amalgamated Society of Dyers	1878	10538
18. Leeds, Halifax and Bradford Stuff Pressers	1880	633
19. General Union of Textile Workers (originally called Huddersfield and District Power Loom Weavers and Woollen Operatives Association)	1881	4535
20. Halifax and District Warp Dressers Association	1887	42
21. Bradford and District Warp Dressers	1887	926
22. Yeadon, Guiseley and District Factory Workers Union	1889	569
23. National Union of Woolsorters	1889	1826
24. Bradford and District Machine Woolcombers	1890	6500
25. Amalgamated Society of Stuff and Woollen Warehousemen	1894	343
26. Huddersfield Healders and Twisters	1896	389
27. Leeds and District Warp Dressers and Twisters	1898	348
28. Bradford Wool Top and Noil Warehousemen	1899	900
29. Bradford and District Card Grinders and Setters	1902	121
30. Huddersfield and District Warpers Association	1907	220
31. Keighley and District Power Loom Overlookers Association	1908	123

Why then was trade union growth so retarded in the West Riding worsted textile industry? Of all the reasons cited the most popular has been that which stressed the high proportion of women workers in the industry. Women workers provided the majority of the labour force, and both activists at the time and later writers have stressed that they presented a major obstacle to unionisation. The 1914 Annual Report of the General Union of Textile Workers said that its low levels of membership were "because a large number of women are employed in the textile industry". (17) Union activists like Ben Turner accused male textile workers of keeping "their wives and daughters outside the trade unions". (18)

Retardation of Trade Unionism in Worsted

There was clearly a continuing hostility to working women, and a constant struggle to ensure that they did not find work in the more skilled and better paid jobs. The Yorkshire Warp Twisters made this the central tenet of their strategy, fighting two successful strikes in 1899 and 1902 to prevent the introduction of female workers into their area of work. During the First World War it stated that its members would work any length of overtime or work at other firms rather than accept the introduction of female workers. (19)

At the same time it is clear that employers were introducing women into an increasing number of areas in the mills, due primarily to the fact that they could be paid lower wages. As W.H. Drew observed: "There are scores of able-bodied men, competent men, who are unable to obtain employment in consequence of the competition of women." (20) Wages in worsted factories were sharply differentiated in terms of men and women. Where workers undertook the same or very similar tasks women were paid less than male workers and, as D. Busfield shows in Chapter 8, even in areas where women were clearly undertaking skilled work, as in burling and mending, their wages were lower than those of men in less skilled jobs. (21) And yet this in no way adequately explains the low levels of unionisation. The Lancashire cotton industry employed a similar proportion of female workers and similarly discriminated between male and female wages, and yet at the same time women made up a significant proportion of trade union members, and in weaving provided a majority of the membership. Further it was women workers who had played a crucial role in late nineteenth century textile disputes and in the formation of the General Union. The Dewsbury strikes in the 1870s and early 1880s had been led and staffed by women workers, and yet, as Maria Bottomley shows in Chapter 9, they were surprisingly absent within a short period. (22)

Women workers were rarely encouraged to join trade unions or to participate in them. Yorkshire textile leaders consistently made this opposition felt, particularly during the 1890s, by pursuing a policy of excluding married women workers from the industry: "Let one woman do one share of work, one spinner mind two sides, keep them out of the mill who can afford to stay at home, and then there would be less out-of-work factory operatives."(23) Not until around 1910 did the union consciously set about trying to enrol large numbers of women.

Less often mentioned as a cause of trade union retardation, but of great importance, was the high proportion of young workers. Of all the textile industries the worsted trade depended the most heavily on children and adolescents. The figures from Whetley Mills in 1873 (see Table 5.4), a typical example of a large worsted factory in Bradford, clearly show the youthful nature of the labour force, with 40.6 per cent of the total labour force being aged under twelve and 69.6 per cent under eighteen.

Although clearly there was a rise in the age of the worsted labour force in the late nineteenth century, because of the introduction of compulsory elementary education and the raising of the school leaving age, the number of youngsters in West Riding mills remained high. In 1907 there were more than 5,000 half-timers, children aged under 13, working in the Bradford mills. (24) The trade unions were generally not interested in these groups recognising that large numbers of young males would leave the industry when they reached the age when adult wages were payable. However, unlike their counterparts in the Lancashire cotton trade unions, Yorkshire trade unionists actively campaigned against half-time work, recognising its impact on general wage levels.

Another factor often cited to explain trade union weakness was, paradoxically, the weakness of the West Riding textile employers. The worsted industry as it had emerged from the period of mechanisation had been characterised by a business structure which included a small number of large firms, usually integrated mills, and a large number of small, specialised firms, often concentrating on one sector of production. In the later nineteenth century it was these larger mills which were most severely affected by the changed trading situation. In the late nineteenth and early twentieth century there emerged an increasing process of disintegration in the worsted sector. (25) Faced by a hostile trading situation, and in particular by the rise of foreign competitors, usually protected by high tariffs, there was a movement towards the supplying of foreign competitors with semi-manufactures. This saw the splitting up of integrated units and an increased role for commission firms, producing in its wake extreme competition, particularly in the commission sector leading to undercutting and the impossibility of establishing district wage standards. In Lancashire, employers' amalgamations acted as a powerful incentive to trade union growth and the development of collective bargaining, whereas in the West Riding intense competition between manufacturers made this very difficult.

Significantly the one area of the trade which saw the development of employer co-operation also saw the greatest amount of unionisation. The development of controls on prices in the dyeing sector through the formation of the Bradford Dyers' Association (B.D.A.) in 1896, saw the mass growth of trade unionism and the development of collective bargaining arrangements and standard district wage levels. This arrangement in the dyeing sector was the only instance of formalised collective bargaining in West Riding textiles, whereas in Lancashire, by 1900, the cotton spinning and weaving employers had accepted the full panoply of formalised collective bargaining. (26)

The historical development of the industry in a large number of small interlocking units had produced a situation of extreme diversity. Different mills paid different wage rates and had different systems of wage payments. This made it very difficult to develop extra-factory groups, as it was hard to make comparisons. W.E. Forster, in explaining the reasons for the absence of strikes in the worsted industry before the Select Committee on Masters and Operatives in 1856, observed: "...very much to the exceeding variety of good that are made in our

Table 5.4
COMPOSITION OF THE LABOUR FORCE AT WHETLEY MILLS, BRADFORD, JANUARY 1873 (27)

	Short Timers										Full Timers										Women 18 & above		Men 18 & above	
	Boys					Girls					Boys					Girls								
	8	9	10	11	12	8	9	10	11	12	13	14	15	16	17	13	14	15	16	17	S	M	S	M
Shed Carding & Combing												1	2	1	1	1				9	23	19		
Shed Roving																				3	10	7		
Shed Drawing												1					5	5	5	8	3	3		
No.2 Drawing												1	2				2	3	4	7	19	5		
Spinning No.1	2	3	3	5	2		1	1	2	2	2	1		2		1	1	1	2	1	3	1		
Spinning No.3	7	11	10	15	9	5	9	8	6	16	6	5		2		7	8	8	2		7			
Spinning No.4	3	11	14	10	9	4	8	12	13	7	6	3	3	1		11	7	5	1					
Spinning No.5	2	13	12	15	7	5	11	4	9	8	5	3	1		1	7	10	3	6	3	3			
Spinning No.6		12	12	8	9	1	3	3	7	11	6	5	3	2	2	2	10	6	3	3	7	2		
Twisting		2	3	6	3		1	3	3	1	3	2	2			3	2	3	3	3	8	6		
Reeling									1	2		1	1			2	2	3	2	3	8	6		
Sorter etc.													1	2									14	20
Men in Mill												1	2	1									34	75
Office					1						1												3	1
totals	14	52	54	59	40	16	33	31	37	47	28	21	16	14	6	34	47	41	35	31	91	49	51	96
Overall Total	219					164					85					188					140		147	
	383										273													
	656																							
																								943

Retardation of Trade Unionism in Worsted

district; the same sort of goods is not made by many masters and consequently there is not the same list of wages to pay and differ about". (28) In addition, employers had little incentive to establish district wage levels, operating as they did their own personalised wage payments system. As late as 1925 the Court of Inquiry into the 1925 wool textile dispute found the wages system an almost impenetrable morass.

Throughout the period the industry was bedevilled by a continuing sectionalism. Workers had very clear ideas of the status of different jobs in the mills. This was carried out into the community, for as Ben Turner said:

> The weaver was looked down upon by the overlooker...a woollen spinner and a woolsorter despised the average man in ordinary grades of labour...the woolsorter had his special chair in his special snug at his customary public house and a wool-comber or a labouring factory worker had to be above the ordinary if he was allowed in that place. (29)

Workers were overwhelmingly concerned with differentials and with maintaining these rather than with working for the general improvement of the wages and conditions of all textile workers. Indeed, the formation of trade unions sometimes stemmed directly from sectional concerns. As one correspondent to the <u>Yorkshire Factory Times</u> said, the formation of the Huddersfield Warpers Association stemmed from the belief that "their craft was of high importance and that they were of superior character to some of the other mill operatives". (30)

Even within particular occupations there were sharp divisions between different kinds of workers as evidenced by the continuing split between the Bradford Woolsorters' Society and the National Union of Woolsorters, which did not finally merge until 1920. (31) Even within the General Union of Textile Workers, ostensibly committed to overall trade unionism throughout the industry, there was clear evidence that its preoccupations were often of a sectional character. As G.H. Wood wrote: "The present policy of the General Union and its tiny fellow unions is absolutely sectional. One day it is willeyers and fettlers, another it is warpers, a third it is weavers, but always at different places." (32)

The sectionalism and the hierarchical nature of the industry made the overlooker into a powerful figure. He it was who determined who should get promotion and who should be kept on at times of unemployment or short-time working. As such they could provide a powerful bulwark against the trade unionism of the ordinary workers, through their power to hire, fire, discipline and promote the mill workers under them. Overseers and skilled workmen invariably favoured relatives, turning certain occupations into family affairs. As the Bradford and District Warp Dressers stated in 1911: "Of course when a learner has to be taken, we shall always give preference to members' sons, relatives, other things being equal". (33) Unlike the Lancashire cotton industry where the overlooker's power was circumscribed, to some extent, by the use of sub-contracting systems, the worsted industry rarely adopted this pattern of employment. In the worsted industry, the greater proportions of female and young workers gave a greater power to the male overlooker. Also, the movement towards greater managerial control, and the tendency to by-pass the overlooker, which was occurring in other industries in the late nineteenth and early twentieth centuries, was rarely witnessed in the worsted trade, probably as much as anything due to the different company form. The movement towards limited liability companies in Lancashire was only tardily followed in the West Riding worsted industry and a dwindling family presence in mill management may even have led to an increased role for the overlooker. Oral evidence for the early part of the twentieth century certainly reflects the power of the overlooker and his all-pervading influence. (34)

A further factor which severely constrained trade unionism in this period was the increasingly poor situation of the Yorkshire worsted trade, and in particular of the Bradford trade after the mid-1870s. Between the 1840s and the early 1870s the worsted trade had flourished with Bradford as the great beneficiary of the growth and expansion of the British worsted industry. This trade was built on the production of mixed fibre worsteds, using the cotton warp with a whole range of other fibres including alpaca, mohair, silk, wool and angora, in the production of women's cheap dress goods for export. From the 1870s this trade was adversely affected by a number of factors. First, there was a change in fashion, away from the stiff lustrous mixed fibre worsteds towards the softer all-wool worsteds, a sector of the market which had been largely ceded to the French producers. The second problem was the rise of worsted industries elsewhere in Europe and the U.S.A. The great bulk of these industries were developed behind protectionist tariffs, culminating in the 1890s with the passage of the McKinley and Dingley tariffs which cut Bradford exports to the U.S.A. by 40 per cent and 72 per cent respectively. (35)

The general impact of these changes on the Bradford trade have been analysed in some detail by Dr. Sigsworth. Essentially, the Bradford trade made the decision not to compete directly with the French product. To do this would have required the re-equipping and reorganisation of the industry with the introduction of French combing and drawing machinery; and more importantly the introduction of the mule into the spinning sector. Not only was re-equipping during the period of the 'Great Depression', with its sluggish business activity and low profits, a difficult proposition, but in addition it would have required major changes in the structure of the labour force. Unlike the Lancashire cotton industry, the worsted industry had not utilised the mule and its accompanying skilled male labour, but instead used the throstle and the cap frame employing female and juvenile labour. To a great extent the essential and continuing logic of the worsted industry throughout its history was a constant attempt to cheapen the cost of the labour component.

The response of the worsted manufacturers was to retain their

Retardation of Trade Unionism in Worsted

existing equipment and system of production and to use these to develop new products such as men's suitings, overcoatings and furnishing fabrics; to turn to new markets, in particular Imperial markets, which were unable to erect tariff walls, and most importantly to supplying foreign worsted manufacturers with semi-manufactured goods. In an oft quoted statement, J.H. Mitchell, one of the foremost spokesmen of the Bradford trade in the late nineteenth century, pinpointed this changed situation. In his evidence to the Tariff Commission in 1905 he said:

> This shows a steady determination on the part of the nations of the Continent to take from us more and more of these commodities which are almost raw materials and into which hardly any skilled labour has been entered and less of those finished products which employs the most highly skilled and best paid...No country can begin to lay down plant immediately it requires capital and skilled workmen, and it takes a generation really, to develop an industry like that. They are doing it, but they put all their money practically and all their experience into manufacturing first and their development has been enormous. (36)

The export figures for woven fabrics, yarns and tops (combed wool) clearly show a movement back down the production cycle.

Table 5.5: Exports of Worsted Stuffs, Yarns, Tops and Alpaca and Mohair Yarns, 1866-1905 (37)

Years	Stuffs (lbs.)	Worsted Yarn (lbs.)	Tops (lbs.)	Alpaca and Mohair Yarn
1866-70	227,621,000	33,425,000		965,000
1881-85	195,200,000	33,255,000		9,300,000
1891-95	138,352,000	48,947,000	10,591,000	15,203,000
1901-05	102,695,000	51,695,000	36,633,000	13,005,000

There was, therefore, an increasing proportion of workers in the spinning and combing sectors, the former the province of juvenile workers and the latter recognised as having the worst working conditions in the industry. In woolcombing, workers on the night shift worked from 5.15 p.m. till 6 a.m., often without any recognised meal breaks and in temperatures of over $100°F$. In addition they were casual workers, with no permanency of employment, having to report each evening to see whether there was any work available. One reliable observer in the 1890s estimated that the night combers averaged no more than $3\frac{1}{2}$ nights per week, and earned an average of 14s. per week. (38)

During this period of transition it is clear that even without major technological innovations profitability was increased. The two great costs in worsted production were raw materials and wages. Some manufacturers clearly profited through speculation in raw wool but the great bulk of savings was extracted from the labour force. The pressure on the labour force was coupled with a factor which is more difficult to analyse, the demise of paternalism.

W.H. Clapham, talking about the low level of unionisation, had no doubt that an important reason for it lay in

> ...what are commonly called patriarchal relations between masters and men. In some of the old family businesses, strikes are unknown. Two of the larger employers in the worsted business stated in evidence before the Labour Commission in the nineties, that there had never been a strike in their mills and that so far as they were concerned unions might have been non-existent. (39)

During the 1850s there had emerged in the West Riding a movement amongst the leading manufacturers, Nonconformist ministers and Liberal leaders to deal with the social and political tensions that had been so apparent in the 1840s. This took a number of forms ranging from the model village schemes of men like Titus Salt at Saltaire and Edward Akroyd in Halifax, through to a whole range of smaller initiatives like works' trips, and support for mill cricket teams, brass bands and welfare facilities. It was a conscious attempt to re-integrate the working classes in the textile towns and villages and was coupled with a range of events outside the mill such as the sponsoring of adult education, mutual improvement societies and temperance societies, and with the development of class conciliation in the revamped Liberal Party which emerged in the third quarter of the nineteenth century. (40) The leading figures both in the mill and in the community were the large manufacturers. It was premised on the concept of the mill as the family and it was so much a part of the life of these leading manufacturers that in 1880, when H.W. Ripley was confronted by a strike at Bowling dyeworks, he clearly expressed his shock at their behaviour:

> Many of you, grandfathers, fathers and sons, have worked at Bowling all your lives, and this is the first occasion on which you have during long series of years, ever assumed a hostile attitude. I appeal to you not to listen to the advances of men who really know nothing about you and have not your real interests at heart. (41)

For its success paternalism required a continuing and active involvement in the daily life of the factory and its surrounding community. But it was this commitment which declined towards the end of the century. Many of the first generation manufacturers died, to be replaced by sons who had little aptitude for textiles and wished to move away from the West Riding. The desire for a different type of life-style was strikingly clear. The majority were educated at public schools and at Oxford and Cambridge, and aspired not to a career in the mill but to the armed services, the professions, a political career or simply the life of a gentleman of leisure. This pattern of development is too widespread to detail in full but two examples might serve as illustrations. Hugh Ripley, son of the great Bowling dyeing magnate, H.W. Ripley, was educated at Cheltenham and followed a career in the army; and Percy Holden Illingworth, son of prodigious entrepreneurial forebears in Henry Illingworth and Mary Holden, was educated at Jesus College, Cambridge, was well known as a rugby player and big game hunter, and later became an important Liberal politician. This movement into different careers was paralleled by a movement away from the West Riding. Throughout this period West Riding manufacturers were investing heavily in landed estates. The Fosters of Black Dyke Mills bought Hornby Castle amongst other estates; Angus Holden purchased the Nun Appleton Estate; Francis Willey, Blyth Hall; Francis Crossley, the Somerleyton Estate in Suffolk; and largest of all, Samuel Cunliffe Lister spent close to three-quarters of a million pounds on two North Yorkshire estates. These developments inevitably saw a lessening of interest in the firm and the local community. Increasingly, the priority became the extraction of as much money as possible from the family firm for expenditure upon 'conspicuous consumption' elsewhere. (42)

The decline of paternalism and the harsher economic conditions of the period combined to produce an increased pressure on the worsted labour force. There were constant attempts to replace male workers by female workers, to increase the juvenile component of the labour force and to increase the speed of machinery and hence improve productivity: "One weaver will now mind in two looms as much as 11,000 to 12,000 ends for practically less wages than were once paid for minding two looms with a matter of 800 ends each." (43) In addition, the number of workers per machine was increased. In mohair spinning one operative per frame was replaced by one operative for every six machines and workers constantly complained about a deterioration in their conditions. One correspondent to the <u>Yorkshire Factory Times</u> drew a parallel with the sweated trades: "From the woolsorter to the half-timer there is a system of unfairness and jobbery practised that would not be tolerated in any other industry that is outside the sphere of the sweating commission." (44) The decline of paternalism and the associated changes in the West Riding worsted industry clearly heralded a movement towards collective organisation by the workers. The movement out of the trade and the district was at its height during the 1880s and 1890s, and this period witnessed a great upsurge in trade union formation and membership in the West Riding. However, there was clearly no massive expansion in local trade unionism, largely because of the structural weaknesses of local textile workers.

A further problem with which trade unionists had to contend was low wages. Wages in the West Riding worsted trade were lower than those in Lancashire and generally lower than those in the West Riding woollen industry. W.H. Drew, the Bradford textile trade unionist, firmly believed that low wages were the prime cause of low trade union membership levels:

> I have my own opinion about it, and it is this, that when people get down to the pitch to which the textile operatives are in the West Riding, they have very little heart, for anything. They think that it is no use organising, and in many instances, I am compelled to say that they cannot afford even the small sums of the subscription. We have ample proof of this in the fact that if our members get three months in arrears, as a rule we lose them. They cannot pull up again, and they see the difficulty and lapse out. (45)

Union dues could present a sizeable financial outlay from low and committed wage packets. In the early twentieth century the General Union of Textile Workers slashed union dues, in an attempt to recruit more members. A long letter to the Yorkshire Factory Times in 1909 catalogued in detail the appallingly low wage levels:

> Out of 31,000 men...5,200 earn less than a pound a week - mainly wool washers, combers, piecers, stuff weavers and general labourers. This is bad enough but there are 8,000 women earning less than 10s a week and over 21,000 earning less than 12s a week...Put bluntly there is sweating going on. (46)

Coupled with low wages there was the recurring problem of unemployment and under-employment, particularly the latter, with short-time working being an almost endemic feature of the trade. (47) In January 1894, in the midst of depression, the Bradford Unemployed Emergency Committee found that 58,558 persons, or 27.1 per cent of Bradford's population, were suffering the effects of total or partial unemployment. (48) Possibly of greater continuing consequence was the problem of short-time working. The problems of under-employment in wool combing have already been mentioned, but the greatest problems were to be found in the weaving sector. Weavers were hired by the piece, and often in periods of bad trade would be kept waiting for the next piece. The Wages Census of 1886 asserted that weavers annually lost 10 per cent of their income through broken time. The Bradford manufacturers conducted their own survey in 1891 which found broken time, representing 9.3 per cent of total working hours, or a loss of about five weeks' wages. (49)

Finally, a good number of employers, for a variety of reasons, were strongly opposed to trade unions and manifested this by a system of blacklisting militants. As W.H. Drew explained to the Royal Commission on Labour in 1892, his trade union and political activity in the early 1890s had meant that: "For about five months it was utterly impossible for me to get employment no matter where I went, although I knew that there were looms standing, the cry was "No" and it was only when I found an employer who was really fast for weavers that I got employment." (50) Employer hostility was also reflected in the fact that it was almost impossible to collect union dues at the workplace: and they had to be collected outside working hours at workers' homes. Shop floor organisation and controls therefore stood little chance of developing. (51)

Textile trade unions were therefore faced with a number of interrelated problems which severely retarded membership. The response of the existing organisations was varied. The older sectional unions, such as the Twisters and the Warp Dressers, continued to remain essentially small friendly societies overwhelmingly concerned to safeguard the position of their own individual trade. The major concern was with the apprentice system, but also with the safeguarding of their position. The Bradford Warp Dressers' Association provided men for employers and held itself responsible for the work of its members. Many of these bodies had high levels of unionisation: the Bradford Stuff Pressers had 90 per cent unionisation in 1895, the Warp Dressers just under 50 per cent and the Bradford Twisters' Society about 55 per cent. As one writer said: "...unions were separated one from the other. There was little feeling of community of interest and often the secretaries did not know each other." (52)

The second type of trade union, emerging in the late nineteenth century, was the industrial union, which enlisted everybody in a particular type of textile work irrespective of their status or position. The two unions most closely associated with this development were the Amalgamated Society of Dyers (founded in 1878) and the Bradford and District Machine Woolcombers (founded in 1890) - woolcombing was almost entirely confined to the Bradford district. Both operated generally in horizontal segregated areas, which both allowed for more control at the workplace and also for a much greater identity of interest amongst the workforce than was possible in the general union. The A.S.D. and the Woolcombers were greatly assisted by developments amongst the employers. Both industries were dominated by commission working and in an attempt to combat price wars and low profit levels they developed price cartels in the Bradford Dyers Association and Woolcombers Ltd. Once this system was in operation employers found it useful to make general industry wide agreements with the workers so that labour costs were equalised between firms. In addition, there would seem to have been an increase in profit margins which may have led to a more benevolent attitude towards trade unionism. By the beginning of the twentieth century the A.S.D. had close to 100 per cent unionisation in the piece dyeing sector and had the first collective bargaining agreement and standard wage scales in operation. The situation was more confused in woolcombing, but after the formation of Woolcombers Ltd. in 1904 the workers, through a series of militant strikes, enforced wage increases on the employers and had about 50 per cent unionisation by 1914.

The third type of trade unionism that was followed in the West Riding was general unionism in the General Union of Textile Workers and the Yeadon and Guiseley Factory Workers' Union. The latter is of less importance in this discussion as it was essentially an amalgamation of dyers and woollen workers in a relatively small area. The General Union aimed to enlist all woollen and worsted workers but up to the First World War only managed to recruit a small proportion of textile workers. It was much weaker in the worsted section than in woollens. To the exasperation of union leaders like Ben Turner, the worsted towns of Bradford, Halifax and Keighley proved a stony ground for trade unionism in contrast to the much stronger woollen towns of the heavy woollen district and Huddersfield. As Turner said, the union had "full time women organisers and full time men organisers. It has initiated policies for adult weavers and menders for which neither the weavers nor the menders care a tinker's curse or showed practically a jot of interest in anything done for them." And he concluded, "...the work is enough to make any Christian feel inclined to swear at the backwardness of the Bradford textile operatives". He expressed similar sentiments about Halifax which he called "a hopeless area", and Keighley, which he stigmatised as "a blackleg area". (53)

The slow growth of trade unionism up to the First World War was the cause of another major difference between the Yorkshire and the Lancashire textile unions. Although the Lancashire cotton unions generally had a large membership, they took a moderate political stance. In Yorkshire, the much smaller trade unions brought in their wake a commitment to independent labour politics. As James Hinton has written:

> It is significant that the I.L.P. emerged out of a defeated strike in Bradford, and that the West Riding of Yorkshire, where trade unionism was particularly weak, remained for many years its strongest area of support. The growth of socialist politics in the 1890s represents...a search for political solutions where industrial ones had failed. Behind this lay the incompleteness and weakness of trade union organisation. (54)

The strength of the I.L.P. in the West Riding and in particular in the two worsted towns of Bradford and Halifax stemmed directly from the failure to develop coherent and viable trade unionism and from the experience of the Manningham Mills strike of 1890-1.

Throughout the period from the 1840s there had been few industrial disputes in the West Riding textile industry. Disputes generally involved few workers, were confined to individual mills or departments, and were short in duration, ending usually in fairly rapid capitulation. Where larger disputes did emerge they tended to take on the aspect of a much wider community struggle by evoking an emotional response that transcended the immediate reason for the dispute. They therefore often had important consequences, as in the Dyers strike in Bradford in 1880, and the strikes in the 1870s and 1880s in Huddersfield and Dewsbury which had led to the formation of the General Union.

The Manningham Mills strike, 1890-1, was to fit into this

pattern for it took on the aspect of an emotional crusade and was to have a crucial impact on the development of working class politics. The actual events of the strike have been recounted on a number of occasions and here the author simply wishes to look at the consequences of the strike for local trade unionism and labour politics. (55)

The strike symbolised extremely starkly the division between capital and labour. On the one side there was the largest employer in Bradford, Samuel Cunliffe Lister, and behind him the great mass of local textile employers and local politicians of both the Tory and Liberal parties. On the other side were some 4,000 workers, the vast majority of whom were young, female and non-unionised. For support they could count only on a tiny band of local socialists and some of the West Yorkshire textile trade union leaders. As the <u>Yorkshire Factory Times</u> wrote: "The operatives have from the first been fought not only by their own employers at Manningham but by the whole of the monied class of Bradford." (56) The strikers, advised by other West Yorkshire trade unionists not to strike because of their lack of organisation and finance, were eventually defeated. However, they held out for close to four months and their militant and emotional campaign served to polarise the local community and to politicise local workers, as the dispute changed from a struggle about wages to a major confrontation about civil liberties and the rights of workers.

The strike clearly outlined the weakness of local trade unionism and showed to many of the participants the necessity of an independent working class political party which could provide a local political structure in which trade unionism could operate. The hostile actions of local councillors and magistrates showed, as Fred Jowett, the first Labour M.P. for Bradford, clearly stated, that "the people of Bradford saw plainly, as they had never seen before, that whether their rulers are Liberal or Tory they are capitalists first and politicians afterwards". (57) As a direct result of the strike sprang, first, the Bradford Labour Union and subsequently the Bradford Independent Labour Party.

Up to the First World War the Independent Labour Party became the main vehicle for local working class advances. Within months of its formation the I.L.P. was represented on the local council and the School Board. In 1906 Bradford had its first Labour M.P. and by 1914 the I.L.P. was polling around 40 per cent of the vote in local elections. However, the success of the I.L.P. did not mean that there was a divorce from trade unions or trade union issues. At the heart of West Yorkshire independent labour politics was a close and enduring alliance with the trade unions. Trade unionists recognised the need for a political programme, and from the early 1890s local trades councils were generally committed to an independent working class party. They saw that trade union growth depended to some extent on the creation of a local and national political context that was not inimical to trade unions. At the same time, local I.L.P.ers perceived that only with trade union assistance could they hope to grow: in particular, they needed trade unions' financial and organisational support. Most local textile trade union leaders, such as Alan Gee, Ben Turner and W.H. Drew, were committed I.L.P.ers, recognising the need to develop strategies on both the industrial and the political fronts.

Up to 1914 textile trade unionism in the Yorkshire woollen and worsted industries remained limited in size and functions. There were some thirty different trade unions, many with minuscule memberships. The major reason for the plethora of unions and their overall weakness lay in the structural constraints surrounding the industry, the composition of the labour force, the authority structure in the mills and the highly competitive and unstable nature of the trade. At the heart of the problem lay the fact of sexual demarcation. Around 60 per cent of the worsted labour force was female. Women workers were generally low paid and confined to unskilled and semi-skilled jobs and were perceived by many male workers and active trade unionists as **the** major problem. In particular, married women workers, who made up between 10 and 15 per cent of the labour force, were openly denounced as a blockage to better conditions and higher wages. Trade unions, even when ostensibly committed to the representation of all workers, did little to attack or break down this sexual demarcation.

The great transformation of the position of the trade unions occurred during the First World War and was the result of outside intervention. In 1914 the General Union of Textile Workers had 12,950 members. By 1919 it had 63,828 members. In addition, by the end of the war, the trade unions had developed a combined negotiating body in the National Association of Unions in the Textile Trades (N.A.U.T.T.) which operated in a collective bargaining structure established on the Whitley joint industrial council format. Although clearly the major thrust of these developments emanated from war-time conditions and the intervention of the state, even before the onset of war significant changes were occurring within the trade.

In particular, the sectionalism of the Yorkshire textile unions was breaking down. In 1909 the first working agreement between the Bradford Woolsorters' Society and the National Union of Woolsorters was arranged. By 1910 the three overlookers' and managers' societies had amalgamated. In 1911 the Yorkshire Federation of Power Loom Overlookers was set up. In 1914 a number of different textile unions centralised their activities by moving jointly into Textile Hall. But the clearest expression of inter-union co-operation and a recognition of the inter-dependence of trade union activity was shown in the assistance that the Amalgamated Society of Dyers gave to the Woolcombers in 1911, both in the provision of financial help and in the loan of Joseph Hayhurst, one of the most prominent trade unionists in Bradford, to work for the Woolcombers.

The progress that trade unionism made in the Yorkshire worsted and woollen industries in the second decade of the twentieth century ironically produced for the first time a strong trade

Retardation of Trade Unionism in Worsted

unionism at the point when the West Riding textile industry began the process of decline. The high water mark of wool trade unionism occurred in 1920: from that point, although unionisation increased, the overall size of the industry began to decline in the face of foreign competition, the decline in world trade and the inter-war depression. (58)

NOTES

1. G.D.H. Cole and W. Mellor, 'Sectionalism and Craft Prejudice, Yorkshire's Need for the Greater Unionism', Daily Herald, 14 April, 1914, reprinted in Leeds Weekly Citizen, 24 April 1914, cited in J. Bornat, 'An Examination of the General Union of Textile Workers 1883-1922', unpublished Essex University Ph.D., 1981.
2. G. von Schulze-Gaevernitz, Social Peace: A Study of the Trade Union Movement in England, (London, 1893), p. 192.
3. H.A. Clegg, A. Fox, A. Thompson, A History of British Trade Unions since 1889, (Oxford, 1964), p. 33.
4. Trade union membership levels have been taken from Board of Trade (Labour Department), Report on Trade Unions in 1900, Vol. LXXIV, 1901 and Report on Trade Unions, 1908-10 with comparative statistics for 1901-10, XLVII, 1912-13.
5. B. Drake, Women in Trade Unions, (London, 1920; reprint 1984), p. 238.
6. For the historical development of the West Yorkshire woollen and worsted industries see, H. Heaton, The Yorkshire Woollen and Worsted Industries, (Oxford, 1965); J. James, A History of the Worsted Manufacture in England, (London, 1857); E.M. Sigsworth, Black Dyke Mills - A History, (Liverpool, 1958); D.T. Jenkins and K.G. Ponting, The British Wool Textile Industry 1770-1914, (London, 1982).
7. H. Heaton, op. cit., p. 297.
8. P. Hudson, 'Proto-Industrialisation: the case of the West Riding Wool Textile Industry in the 18th and early 19th Centuries', History Workshop, 12, 1981, pp. 38-9.
9. For John Hustler and his role in gaining and administering the Worsted Acts, see W. Hustwick, 'An Eighteenth Century Woolstapler', Journal of the Bradford Textile Society, 1956-7. For other leading individuals in the trade and their business activities see E.M. Sigsworth, William Greenwood and Robert Heaton, 'Two Eighteenth Century Worsted Manufacturers', Journal of the Bradford Textile Society, 1951-2.
10. Parliamentary Papers, 1850, XLII, p. 460 cited in J. James, op. cit., p. 609.
11. Answers of John Wood, jun., Bradford in Answers of Mill Owners to Queries, C.1, p. 121 - Factory Inquiry Commission, Supplementary Report, Employment of Children in Factories, Part II, reprinted in Irish University Press (Dublin), Industrial Revolution, Children's Employment, vol. 5, C.1, p. 121.
12. E.H. Illingworth (ed.), The Holden-Illingworth Letters,

(Bradford, 1927), p. 489.

13. Census of England and Wales, 1911, Vol. X, Occupations and Industries, Part II, p. 664.

14. For the 1825 strike see J.T. Ward, 'A Great Bradford Dispute', Journal of the Bradford Textile Society, 1961-2; E.E. Dodd, 'The Bradford Strike of 1825', Journal of the Bradford Textile Society, 1966-7 and J. Smith, 'The Strike of 1825', in D.G. Wright and J.A. Jowitt, Victorian Bradford, (Bradford, 1982). A similar situation occurred in the Scottish cotton industry with the Glasgow spinners' strike in 1837 which Hamish Fraser argues ushered in a period of trade union weakness for decades. W.H. Fraser, 'The Glasgow Cotton Spinners, 1837', in J. Butt and J.T. Ward (eds.), Scottish Themes, (Edinburgh, 1976).

15. For the political and social ferment in the West Riding in the 1830s and 1840s see D.G. Wright, 'Politics and Opinion in Bradford 1832-80', unpublished Leeds University Ph.D. thesis, 1966.

16. Full details about trade union formation and membership levels in the woollen and worsted industry are to be found in The Board of Trade (Labour Department), Reports on Trade Unions.

17. Annual Report of the General Union of Textile Workers, 31 December, 1914. The position of women within the industry and the woollen trade unions has recently been analysed in J. Bornat, 'Lost Leaders: Women, Trade Unionism and the Case of the General Union of Textile Workers, 1875-1914', in A.V. John, ed., Unequal Opportunities: Women's Employment in England 1800-1918, (London, 1986). This essay provides a powerful analysis of the role of women textile workers, particularly in the Huddersfield and Heavy Woollen areas, and a fine analysis of the relationship of the male trade union leaders and the women workers.

18. B. Turner, The History of the General Union of Textile Workers, (Heckmondwike, 1920), p. 127.

19. Labour Organisation in the Woollen and Worsted Industries - anonymous typescript lodged in Bradford Central Library, p. 35.

20. Parliamentary Papers, 1892, XXXV, Royal Commission on Labour, Evidence of W.H. Drew.

21. For a fuller exposition of male/female wage and skill differentials see D. Busfield, ch. 8.

22. For the role of female workers in the development of textile trade unionism in the Heavy Woollen district in the 1870s see M. Bottomley, ch. 9.

23. Yorkshire Factory Times, 1 March, 1895.

24. Interdepartmental Committee on Partial Exemption from School Attendance, Minutes of Evidence, Cd. 4887, (1909), q. 1398.

25. For the problems affecting the large integrated worsted mills after 1873 see E.M. Sigsworth, Black Dyke Mills, pp. 118-24. For the particular difficulties at Salts, see R. Sudddards (ed.), Titus of Salts, (Bradford, 1976), pp. 35, 40-1.

26. For the ongoing problems of employer disorganisation, see I. Magrath, Ch. 3.

27. E. H. Illingworth, op. cit., p. 489. S stands for Single

and M for married workers.

28. Select Committee on Masters and Operatives (Equitable Councils of Conciliation), 1856, XIII, reprinted in Irish University Press (Dublin), Industrial Relations, Vol. 7, p. 108.

29. B. Turner, About Myself, (London, 1930), p. 130.

30. Yorkshire Factory Times, 9 March, 1916.

31. Labour Organisation in the Woollen and Worsted Industries, op. cit., p. 9.

32. H. Wilmott, 'The Labour Unrest and the Woollen Trades', Socialist Review, November 1910, pp. 214-15.

33. Labour Organisation, op. cit., p. 40.

34. Oral testimony of Bradford mill workers is lodged, both on tape and transcript, in the Bradford Heritage Recording Unit, 140-148 Manningham Lane, Bradford.

35. For the problems affecting the mixed fibre worsted trade, and the consequences of American tariffs see G. Firth, 'The Bradford Trade in the Nineteenth Century', in D.G. Wright and J.A. Jowitt, Victorian Bradford, pp. 22-33, and E.M. Sigsworth, Black Dyke Mills, pp. 72-102.

36. Tariff Commission Report, para. 1601.

37. Cited in E. Sigsworth and J.M. Blackman, 'The Woollen and Worsted Industries', in D.H. Aldcroft (ed.), The Development of British Industry and Foreign Competition 1875-1914, (London, 1968), p. 135.

38. Bradford Trades Council Minutes, 56D 80/11/3 (lodged in Bradford Archives). Inquiry into the Conditions of Employment of the Bradford Operative Woolcombers (1899) - evidence of S. Shaftoe.

39. J.H. Clapham, The Woollen and Worsted Industries, (London, 1907), p. 207. For a thought provoking analysis of paternalism in the northern textile districts see P. Joyce, Work, Society and Politics: The Culture of the Factory in Later Victorian England, (London, 1980). He argues that paternalism was crucial to the acceptance of the capitalist system of production and the legitimation of social inequality. His work on the West Riding is neither as detailed nor as satisfactory as that for Lancashire.

40. For an analysis of the paternalism of some West Riding manufacturers during the mid-nineteenth century see J.A. Jowitt (ed.), Model Industrial Communities in Mid-Nineteenth Century Yorkshire, (Bradford, 1986).

41. Bradford Observer, 6 February, 1880.

42. For further examples of this retreat both from the trade and the locality see J.A. Jowitt and R.K.S. Taylor, Bradford 1890-1914: The Cradle of the Independent Labour Party (Bradford, 1980), p. 8.

43. Bradford Observer, 31 December, 1888.

44. Yorkshire Factory Times, 2 August, 1889.

45. Parliamentary Papers, 1892, XXXV, Royal Commission on Labour, Evidence of W.H. Drew.

46. Yorkshire Factory Times, 22 April, 1909.

47. For an examination of politics and the labour movement see J. Hinton, 'The Rise of the Mass Labour Movement' in C.J.

Wrigley (ed.), A History of British Industrial Relations 1875-1914, (1982), pp. 25-8.
48. Bradford Unemployed Emergency Committee, Manifesto, (Bradford, 1894).
49. Parliamentary Papers, 'Wages of the Principal Textile Trades', LXX, pp. xiii-xxi; Bradford Observer, 3 February 1892.
50. Parliamentary Papers, 1892, XXXV, Royal Commission on Labour, Evidence of W.H. Drew. For a general discussion of employers' coercive victimisation tactics against labour in this period see A.J. McIvor, 'Employers' Organisation and Strikebreaking in Britain 1880-1914', International Review of Social History, XXIX, 1984, Pt. 1, pp. 19-23.
51. For an analysis of the difficulties of collecting union dues at the workplace, see J. Bornat, op. cit., p. 58.
52. Labour Organisations, op. cit., p. 66.
53. B. Turner, The History of the General Union of Textile Workers, (Heckmondwike, 1920), pp. 124, 127, 156.
54. J. Hinton, (1982), op. cit., p. 31.
55. For the Manningham Mills Strike and the development of the I.L.P., see J. Reynolds and K. Laybourn, 'The Emergence of the Independent Labour Party in Bradford', International Review of Social History, XX, Pt. 3, 1975; K. Laybourn, 'The Manningham Mills Strike: Its Importance in Bradford History', Bradford Antiquary, 1976; C. Pearce, 'The Manningham Mills Strike, December 1890-April 1891', University of Hull Occasional Papers in Economic and Social History, 1975; K. Laybourn, 'Trade Unions and the Independent Labour Party: The Manningham Experience', in J.A. Jowitt and R.K.S. Taylor, Bradford 1890-1914; D. Howell, British Workers and the Independent Party 1888-1906, (Manchester, 1983); K. Laybourn and J. Reynolds, Liberalism and the Rise of Labour, (London, 1984).
56. Yorkshire Factory Times, 1 May, 1891.
57. The Labour Journal, 7 October 1892.
58. For trade unionism in the wool textile industry in the 1920s see J.A. Jowitt and K. Laybourn, 'The Wool Textile Dispute of 1925', The Journal of Local Studies, Vol. 2, No. 1, Spring 1982.

Chapter 6

LANCASHIRE COTTON TRADE UNIONISM
IN THE INTER-WAR YEARS

Alan Fowler

The history of cotton trade unionism in the twentieth century has attracted very little attention from labour historians. H.A. Turner's history of cotton trade unionism, written in 1962, (1) remains the standard account and yet it has very little to say about a key period in the history of cotton trade unionism - 1918 to 1932 - when the unions were involved in eight major industrial disputes. Given this level of industrial unrest amongst cotton operatives, why did contemporaries dismiss them as a spent force and why have labour historians implicitly followed this evaluation? The aim of this chapter is to show that in fact the unions remained a crucial element in the struggle between labour and capital in the inter-war years and that the General Strike did not end industrial conflict in Britain in the period between the wars. A major wave of industrial unrest took place in textiles between 1929 and 1932 and it was this, rather than the General Strike, that was the last industry-wide conflict in that period. Why were the cotton trade unions able to maintain this level of response in a period when the rest of the trade union movement was relatively quiescent? An explanation has to be sought in both the development and structure of the cotton unions themselves and also in the underlying economic and social consequences for the British textile industry of the restructuring of the world economy in the inter-war years.

I. Cotton Workers and their Unions

The cotton industry, horizontally rather than vertically organised, was divided into two major sectors, spinning and weaving. The structure of the cotton trade unions reflected the sectionalism of the industry, though all the cotton unions belonged to the United Textile Factory Workers' Association (U.T.F.W.A.), a political pressure group modelled on the Factory Reform Movement of the 1840s.

107

Cotton Trade Unionism

The Amalgamated Association of Operative Cotton Spinners was the largest elite group of workers in the industry, as well as the wealthiest trade union in the country, with a membership of approximately 25,000 in 1914 (see Table 6.1). They earned around £2 per week in 1906 and were considered by contemporaries to be part of the aristocracy of labour. They were all male and opposed to any women working in the spinning room. Their trade union was organised on essentially exclusive lines, concentrating on controlling the supply of labour, though they were not formally craftsmen in the sense of having to serve an apprenticeship. The system of job training in the industry was to work as a 'little piecer' and then a 'big piecer' before becoming a spinner, a process which could take more than a decade. Moreover, there was considerably less chance of a job at the end of the period than in the case of an apprentice. The spinner operated two mule spinning machines working as a team with the aid of a little and big piecer. The piecers were not employed by the firm but were sub-contract labour actually employed by the spinner himself. The spinner as head of the team was paid piece rate and divided the wage up between himself and his two helpers. However, the piecers were paid day rate and the wage did not vary according to production. As a result the piecers received no monetary compensation for the intensification of the work process - the speeding up of machinery and the use of longer, more spindle mules - which was taking place in the late nineteenth century.

The little piecer was normally a juvenile starting work as a half-timer and moving up to become a big piecer in his mid-teens. The big piecer became eligible to become a spinner in his early twenties, but the period he served as a piecer depended upon the opportunities available to become a spinner. James Mawdsley, Secretary of the Spinners, told the Royal Commission on Labour in 1891 that only one out of three trained piecers became spinners. For many operatives piecing was a dead end job. It was difficult to bring up a family on a big piecer's wages as the spinner ensured that the largest share of the wage earned by the team went to himself. The problem of the big piecer became more and more acute with the inter-war depression, because as the industry contracted, opportunities to obtain promotion to minder of a pair of mules became much scarcer. (2)

The Amalgamated Association of Weavers was unusual in that a majority of its members were female and with a total membership of 200,000 in 1914 they were the second largest union in Britain (see Table 6.1). They were an open union organising the largest single group of workers in the cotton industry. Unlike spinning, weaving was essentially labour intensive and was not thought by contemporaries to require the same level of skill. Indeed, the weaver was viewed as a semi-skilled machine minder. Crucial to the prosperity of the weaving communities was the family wage. Average individual earnings in the industry were around 28/- per week in 1914 but the fact that husband, wife and children worked guaranteed a far higher family wage than industrial earnings would suggest. Whether the consequence of women working in the mill was a far higher infant mortality rate in Lancashire than the country generally, was a constant source of debate amongst contemporaries. (3) Certainly there are many accounts of women working very late into pregnancy and resuming work very quickly after childbirth. There is no doubt, however, that part of the price paid for high family wages was child labour. Half-time work for children over the age of ten in the late Victorian period, and over the age of twelve post-1900, continued until 1921. Whenever the cotton operatives were consulted about the half-time system they voted for its retention because for them it was a crucial part of the family wage.

There was no comparable system of piecers in weaving. Entrants to the industry, usually half-timers, initially earned nothing for the early months when they were learning the skill. In fact, normally their parents would pay the weaver a small sum to cover the cost of tuition, despite the fact that the weaver would benefit from increased production and therefore increased wages because of the trainee's contribution. Having learned the skill a young weaver, still an early teenager, would begin working one loom, advancing to two or three looms as the skill improved and finally, on adulthood, take charge of four looms. Normally, as the trainee weaver completed learning the trade, his or her mother would cease to work and the children made up her contribution to the family wage. By the late nineteenth century the practice was for a weaver to work four looms, which represented a marked increase in productivity on the early nineteenth century standard. The more looms worked, the higher the wage paid, as the weaver, like the spinner, was paid piece rate. (4)

The Amalgamated Association of Cardroom, Blowing and Ring Room Operatives has received little attention from historians. It organised workers in the preparatory stages of spinning, cleaning, preparing, combing and twisting the raw cotton before it was spun into yarn. The Cardroom Amalgamation (established in 1886 and the seventh largest union in Edwardian Britain), has been characterised by H.A. Turner as an open union and while it had a large membership, 60,000 in 1914 (see Table 6.1), and organised all the operatives in the Card, Blowing and Ring Rooms irrespective of job or level of skill, its main rationale was to raise the status and pay of the strippers and grinders. These were the elite, key groups of male workers amongst an overwhelmingly female membership of the Amalgamation. The eventual aim appears to have been a status comparable with the spinners and all other goals of the union were subordinated to it. By 1906 the strippers and grinders had raised wages to around 30/- per week, just above the average industrial wage and generally better than wages in weaving. Despite the growing status of the strippers and grinders, workers in the cardroom were generally looked down upon by their fellow cotton operatives, especially the women workers in the cardroom, who lacked the status of women in weaving. (5)

Cotton Trade Unionism

Table 6.1: Trade Union Membership in the
Cotton Industry, 1900-1938

Year	Spinners[1]	Cardroom[2]	Weavers[3]
1900	18,348	22,197	81,500
1913	23,713	52,113	179,391
1921	23,628*	80,638	224,219
1929	21,613*	60,633	155,074
1938	13,161*	47,228	95,455

Sources: (1) Amalgamated Association of Operative Cotton Spinners. A. Fowler & T. Wyke, The Barefoot Aristocrats (Littleborough, 1987), pp. 242-4.
(2) Amalgamated Association of Card, Blowing and Ring Room Operatives. A. Bullen & A. Fowler, The Cardroom Workers' Union (Rochdale, 1986), p. 177.
(3) Amalgamated Weavers' Association. A. Bullen, The Lancashire Weavers' Union (Rochdale, 1984), pp. 72-3.
* Figures for spinner membership only. From 1920 piecers were "full" members of the union.

The pattern of industrial relations was different in spinning and weaving and this hindered the development of co-operation on industrial matters. Before the 1890s wages were paid according to town lists and these could vary considerably. (6) By the 1890s, however, there was growing uniformity. The weavers had a single list (the Uniform List) and the spinners automatically followed the movement upwards or downwards of the Oldham or Bolton list. The spinners and weavers negotiated with different employers' organisations. The spinners negotiated with the Federation of Master Cotton Spinners' Association and the weavers negotiated with the Cotton Spinners and Manufacturers' Association. Until the First World War there was no uniform wage movement between the two sectors of the industry and therefore spinners and weavers did not become directly involved in each other's industrial disputes. (7) The war was responsible for two major changes in cotton trade unionism. Firstly, the system of collective bargaining was radically altered with the introduction of industry-wide collective bargaining. This was the indirect result of the setting up by the government of the Cotton Control Board in 1917. Secondly, the war prompted important changes in working conditions, most notably the introduction of the 48-hour week and the abolition of the half-time system. (8)

However, the optimism of 1919 was crushed by the onset of economic crisis in the summer of 1920, a crisis that was to last for twenty years. The dimensions of these changes in economic fortunes are summarised in Table 6.2. The economic downturn essentially reflected the decline of the Lancashire cotton industry and was deepened in 1929 by the onset of the world depression and the consequent collapse of world trade. However, the fundamental problems of Lancashire remained the same in the 1920s and 1930s - the spread of industrialisation in the under-developed world combined with the growth of economic nationalism which cut off Lancashire markets. These trends were stimulated and accelerated by World War One and, though the developments were visible before 1914, they were obscured by the prosperity of the Edwardian age, especially with the expansion of the Indian market between 1900 and 1914. Lancashire's competitive advantage over the world would have ensured the slower development of this trend had not the war restricted the capacity to export. The war stimulated economic nationalism as new textile producers sought to develop their own markets through protection. Crucial to this was India which effectively had fiscal independence from 1917 onwards and used this freedom to erect tariff barriers and protect her own industry. (9)

These long term changes in the world economy were inevitable and consequently it was beyond the ability of Lancashire to arrest the decline of its staple industry. However, there were factors internal to the cotton industry which heightened the crisis of the inter-war years and had a disastrous effect on the cotton industry's competitiveness in the world. The most important of these factors was the re-capitalisation of the industry during the period of the immediate post-war boom. (10)

Table 6.2: The Cotton Industry in the Inter-War Years

Year	Production Cloth m. sq. yds.	Exports Piece Goods m. sq. yds.	Machinery Spindles million	Machinery Looms 000s	Labour 000s
1912	8,050	6,913	61.4	786	621.5
1938	3,126	1,449	42.1	495	393.0

Source: Working Party Report: Cotton Board of Trade, 1946, p. 6. Table 1.

II. Trade Union Responses to the Depression

The trade union response to the depression was shaped by employer policies. As Arthur McIvor has outlined in Chapter 1, employers responded to the crisis of the inter-war years in a number of ways. The most significant was to seek wage cuts, which were implemented in 1921, 1922, 1929, 1932 and 1935 (weaving). By 1922 the post-war advances of the operatives had been wiped out leaving them with the 48 hour week as the only permanent gain of this period. By 1922 real wage levels were no higher than in 1914 and this remained true until the mid-1930s. The cotton operatives had not received large advances during the war and the post-war boom. Wages caught up with prices only in 1920 and this period lasted for just a matter of weeks when the wage advance of 1920 was wiped out by the general introduction of short-time working in the industry. The operatives did not share in the post-war boom except in terms of increased employment levels.

Employers were also concerned with the question of hours. They had bitterly resented the introduction of the 48 hour week in 1919 and made two major attempts to increase hours worked in 1928 and 1932. Neither of these attempts was successful but employer hostility to the 48 hour week was an underlying feature of the period and accounts for the concern of the operatives to have the 48 hour week legalised. Since the first Factory Acts the hours of work of the cotton operatives had been laid down by Act of Parliament and they looked to parliamentary rather than industrial action on this issue. The employers had conceded the 48 hour week against the background of the foundation of the International Labour Organisation and the Washington Convention of 1919 when it was generally assumed that Britain would ratify the Convention and therefore legalise the 8 hour day. When this failed to happen the employers realised they had made an unnecessary concession and repeatedly tried to revoke it, while the operatives continued to look collectively to Parliament for legislation. The employers probably assumed when they granted the 48 hour week that the loss of hours would be offset by productivity gains, but the traditional technology of the industry had reached its maximum capacity around the turn of the century and there was thus no increase in productivity after 1919. (11)

The massive debt incurred during the re-capitalisation of the industry during the short post-war boom ensured that there was no capital available for the introduction of new technology during the 1920s and 1930s. Unable to introduce new technology, the employers looked to changes in work practices to increase productivity. The most important was the introduction of the more looms system in weaving. Between 1928 and 1932 the weaving employers sought to persuade the Weavers' Amalgamation of the benefits for weavers in working eight or six looms instead of the traditional four. This process of persuasion was only successful after a period of major labour unrest in the industry.

The original aim of the more looms system had been to achieve a saving on wages of about 30 per cent by using a different wage system to that of the Uniform List, but within eighteen months of the new system operating, this differential had been reduced on the employers' initiative to only 10 per cent, thus effectively ending any advantage. The more looms system had been designed by the Burnley employers to reduce the industry's costs, but in fact it opened a bitter price war between individual employers which was only ended by state intervention in the form of the Cotton Manufacturing Act of 1934. The more looms system could only be operated by certain employers because of technical difficulties. Those producing fine cloths found that the cloths were not suitable for the more looms system, while other employers whose cloths were more suitable, discovered that the spacing of machinery in their factories did not lend itself to the system. There were also additional costs that were involved in the introduction of the more looms system, which though small compared with the cost of introducing automatic looms, still led many small employers to hold back from initiating change. The response of these employers was to introduce the system of wage payment without actually introducing the more looms system, thus imposing a wage cut on those operatives working the traditional complement of four looms, and generating a vicious price war between manufacturers. Initially, the employers' organisation was prepared to turn a blind eye to this undercutting of wage agreements in the hope of forcing the weavers to the negotiating table. However, as the practice grew, it threatened to undermine the employers' organisation itself, and although individual employers continued with the more looms system, the major employers' organisations abandoned it as the panacea for the industry's problems. (12)

There was no comparable attempt to alter work practices in spinning. There are a number of possible explanations for this difference. Mule spinning was less labour intensive than weaving on the Lancashire loom and potential savings to employers in spinning from cuts in labour costs were considerably less than savings held out to employers in weaving. In spinning there was an easily available form of new technology, ring spinning, which had already been introduced by 1914 and represented approximately a fifth of the industry's capacity. Ring spindles were worked by cheap female labour organised by the cardroom and not the spinners' union. Ring spinning had advantages for production of coarse yarn for the cheaper end of the market and it therefore made sense to introduce ring spindles rather than alter work practices for the mule spinners. However, an examination of the pattern of investment in the inter-war period shows that while there was a rise in ring spindles as a percentage of total spindles, from 20 per cent to 35 per cent by 1939, there was no major substitution of ring spindles for mule spindles. In fact, ring spindles were scrapped in the inter-war years, probably because those firms that had introduced new machinery were the very same firms where speculation had taken place in the 1920 boom. They were, therefore, heavily burdened by debt and needed to rationalise urgently. A further explanation of the failure by employers to change work practices is that in the very sector where Lancashire still remained strong, fine spinning, the mule still had considerable advantages over ring spinning and it was quality rather than price that gave Lancashire its predominant position in these markets. A change in work practice might well undermine the skill of the operative, the basis of success in the luxury trade. It may also be that the strength of the spinners' union discouraged employers from altering work practices. The spinners' union was always a stronger union than the weavers and it is possible that, confronted with the 'craft' practices of such a well organised and crucial sector of the labour force, spinning employers were reluctant to take on an issue with no guarantee of success. Savings from the introduction of new technology in the industry would have been greatest if both ring spinning and automatic looms had been introduced, together with a high draft system in the cardroom. Such rationalisation would have required the whole industry working together which was impossible given its horizontal divisions. (13)

A further factor in the employers' failure to attempt to change work practices in spinning was their decision instead to use inferior raw cotton. Employers in both spinning and weaving used 'bad' material as a means of saving money. This was not a new device and consisted of buying cheap raw cotton which was difficult to work. There had been regular complaints from the operatives about bad materials before 1914 and these complaints continued during the depression of the 1920s. Lazonick has argued that for the period before 1914 this was a substitute for technical change. If employers were able to use poor quality raw materials, yet keep up previous levels of productivity, they were effectively raising the productivity of the operative without any increase in the rate of pay. (14)

Trade union complaints about fining also continued during the 1920s. Weavers were normally fined for producing faulty cloth though they were the only group of cotton workers to be affected by this system. They bitterly resented fining, arguing that they were being held responsible for the faults of other workers and the faults of the materials they worked with. Though fining, like bad materials, was a problem that aroused considerable resentment from operatives before 1914, there appears to have been a sharper response in the 1920s, culminating in the Nelson Lockout of 1928 and a number of legal cases which the operatives lost. (15)

There were two major waves of labour unrest in the Lancashire cotton industry: in 1918-21 and again in 1929-32. The first wave of strike action had its origins in the wartime experience of the cotton operatives. Falling real wages and rising profits during the war, combined with a growing expectation of a 'land fit for heroes' after 1918 led to a wave of militancy.

The most significant feature of the war for trade unionism in general was the shortage of labour, but in the cotton industry it was the shortage of raw cotton supplies - due to the low priority given to raw cotton in the allocation of shipping space - rather than labour, that was crucial to the political economy of the industry. The crisis in the supply of raw cotton reached its height in the summer of 1917 when the government was forced to intervene to set up the Cotton Control Board to ration the supply of raw cotton. The Board devised not only a system for rationing raw cotton, but also a means of levying the industry to provide unemployment pay for operatives. This saved the industry from crisis in 1917, but the employers wanted to use the Board as a mechanism for restricting wage advances (16), and all this at a time when they were making uniquely high profits. The result of the employers' tactics was an explosion of labour unrest between the summers of 1918 and 1919 including the first general strike by all cotton operatives. As a result of these industrial actions, cotton operatives were able to raise their wages above the 1914 level and at the same time achieve the major breakthrough of the 48 hour week, a goal they had been seeking since the early 1890s. The introduction of the 48-hour week brought an end to the system of starting work before breakfast at 6.00 a.m. This was particularly significant in an industry which had a large proportion of women workers.

There was a national wave of labour unrest in the years 1918-21 and the militancy of the cotton operatives was part of this general movement of labour, though the period covers a variety of experiences: war, post-war boom and onset of depression. The unrest in the cotton industry began as a trade union offensive attempting to make good the losses of the war and to achieve the historic aim of the 48-hour week. It ended as an employers' offensive to wipe out the post-war gains of the operatives and restore the industry's prosperity through wage cuts. Industrial defeat for the cotton operatives in 1921, combined with the cost of meeting both strike and unemployment pay during these years, convinced the cotton unions that further resistance was counter-productive and would actually undermine their organisations. Exhausted, they accepted a wage cut in 1922 without dispute and between 1922 and 1928 industrial relations in cotton textiles were quiescent. (17)

The second wave, 1929-32, is more interesting. Industrial conflict in Britain was rapidly declining after the General Strike, yet against the unpromising background of the world depression textile workers of Lancashire and Yorkshire raised a bitter resistance to their employers' traditional policy in times of crisis of cutting the textile workers' wage. In 1928 the employers returned to the offensive against labour hoping both to reduce wages and increase hours. Between 1929 and 1932 textiles accounted for three-quarters of the total days lost due to strike action. Why did the cotton unions resist when it appeared to be so unlikely that they would be successful and in a period when the rest of the trade union movement was in retreat? Clegg has suggested that the explanation is to be found in the extent of wage cutting in textiles, which was greater than that of other industries. (18) This rather economistic explanation does not do justice to the cotton operatives. It is true that cotton operatives suffered greater wage cuts than employees in other industries, but along with this went an intensification of the work process, illustrated by the operatives' complaints about bad materials and fining, that forced the cotton unions to take a stand. These developments reached their height in employer attempts to impose the more looms system on weaving operatives. (19)

The long term consequence of the more looms system was seen by the operatives as leading to unemployment or under-employment as the demand for labour declined with higher productivity. More importantly perhaps, the more looms system threatened the continuation of the 'family wage' in cotton which had been the basis of the pre-1914 prosperity of the cotton operatives' community. Traditionally, married women had continued to work in textile production, especially in weaving where they formed the overriding majority of the labour force. It is clear from the 1931 ballot of the weavers that the membership was strongly opposed to the introduction of the more looms system. The union leadership, however, appears to have been prepared to make a deal with the employers on the basis that the more looms weaver would receive adequate remuneration to replace the family wage. Adult males with family responsibilities would supply the majority of the labour force for the more looms system. It was even suggested that unmarried women in the textile districts should seek work as domestic servants to solve unemployment and under-employment in Lancashire. Ironically, this suggestion came from Margaret Bondfield, the first woman Cabinet Minister. The intensification of the labour process with the introduction of the more looms system in weaving was consciously, or unconsciously, accompanied by an ideology that saw the solution to depression and unemployment in a sharpening of the sexual division of labour, relegating Lancashire women to the home, and thereby destroying the degree of independence they had managed to achieve as autonomous wage workers. (20)

The conflict between labour and capital was greatest in weaving because the militancy of the weavers remained intact until 1932. The centre of industrial militancy in weaving was northeast Lancashire, especially Nelson. Nelson, with its concentration on fine cloth, was protected against the depression of the 1920s which mainly hit Blackburn, heavily committed as it was to the Indian market and cheap cloth production. The fine trade concentrated largely on the home market and the luxury markets in Western Europe and the Dominions, which held up relatively well in the 1920s, and even in the 1930s the crisis was nowhere as deep as that suffered by the coarse trade with its reliance on the Far East. The relative insulation of Nelson from the depression preserved the pre-1914 traditions of industrial militancy and political radicalism in the area, and during the inter-war years the town became known in Lancashire as 'little Moscow'. (21) As Table 6.3 indicates, union membership in Nelson fell at a considerably slower rate than the major centre, Blackburn.

In spinning, unlike weaving, the pre-1914 centre of industrial militancy, Oldham, was not protected from the economic crisis. In fact Oldham, as the centre of American cotton spinning, bore the brunt of the economic crisis of the 1920s. The effect of this was to decimate trade union membership (see Table 6.3) and destroy Oldham's militancy. This helps to explain why the labour unrest of 1929-32 was led by the weavers, in contrast with the earlier wave of industrial militancy - 1918-21 - which was led by the spinners. Oldham's militancy, which had been the basis of the renewed war and post-war militancy of the spinners, collapsed with the slump of 1920. Oldham concentrated on the production of

Cotton Trade Unionism

coarse yarns for the Indian and Far East markets and the economic crisis of the industry was concentrated on that sector. By 1932 it was the traditionally moderate Bolton, where trade union membership held up rather well, that was leading the opposition to wage cuts. Bolton produced fine yarns and had a similar market position in spinning to that of Nelson in weaving. (22)

Table 6.3: Cotton Trade Union Membership in Blackburn, Bolton, Nelson and Oldham, 1900-1937

Year	Blackburn[1] Weavers	Bolton[2] Spinners	Nelson[3] Weavers	Oldham[4] Spinners
1900	10,700	4,779	6,000	6,319
1913	19,500	5,708	17,000	8,963
1920	20,000	5,892*	18,000	9,538*
1929	15,990	6,122*	16,000	8,090*
1937	8,172	5,270*	11,000	5,131*

Sources: (1) Blackburn Weavers' Association. Amalgamated Weavers' Association, Annual Report, 1900, 1913, 1920, 1929, 1937.
(2) Bolton Spinners. A. Fowler and T. Wyke, The Barefoot Aristocrats, pp. 242-4.
(3) Nelson Weavers' Association. A. and L. Fowler, The History of the Nelson Weavers' Association, (Nelson, 1984), p. 120.
(4) Oldham Spinners. Fowler and Wyke, The Barefoot Aristocrats, pp. 242-4.
 * Figures for spinner membership only. From 1920 piecers were "full" members of the union.

The characteristic form of industrial dispute changed during these two waves of labour unrest. Traditionally in the nineteenth century, the main type of dispute had been the town strike or lockout. Certain towns were seen by both employers and unions as the key to determining general wage levels in the industry - Manchester in the first half of the nineteenth century and increasingly Oldham in the second half. In weaving, wage agreements tended to follow the movement of the Blackburn list. By the late Victorian period the sectional dispute was becoming significant: the 1878 lockout encompassed both Blackburn and Burnley, while the Brooklands dispute of 1892-3 included Oldham and surrounding towns. The new feature of the inter-war years was the emergence of the general strike affecting both sections of the industry. This was due to the growing co-operation of the two employer organisations coupled with the impact of state intervention in the form of the Cotton Control Board during the war. A growing belief in the efficiency of industrial unions may also have helped to encourage cotton trade unions to co-operate more on industrial questions. The cotton unions even went so far as to debate changing the United Textile Factory Workers' Association from a legislative pressure group into an industrial union, though opposition from the leadership of the cardroom and from the rank and file of the spinners, ensured that this did not happen. (23)

The experience of the three general disputes in the industry, however, did not augur well for future industrial co-operation. All three disputes ended with considerable internal disunity. Turner suggested that this was due to sectionalism (24), but the reality was that in all three cases the activity of the union leading to the break-up was informed by a need to avoid rank and file rebellion against the executive. In 1919 and 1921 it was the attitude of the Spinners' Amalgamation which led to the break-up of the cotton operatives' unity and, in 1929, the weavers were responsible for the break away from the other unions. (25)

After 1932 the cotton unions increasingly looked to political rather than industrial solutions to the industry's continued decline. The United Textile Factory Workers' Association took on the role of evolving an economic policy for the industry. (26) The unions do not appear to have given a great deal of thought to the industry's future development before 1914, but the impact of the depression was such that it became crucial for them to develop their own strategy for the industry in opposition to that of the employers. This became especially important with the rise of the Labour Party and the possibility of a Labour Government coming into office.

The miners' success in forcing the Government to hold an inquiry into the problems of their industry and the consequent report of the Sankey Commission which exposed the mineowners' culpability became the model on which the cotton unions developed their policy. (27) The cotton trade unionists believed that it was the recapitalisation of the industry during the post-war boom which was responsible for the crisis in the trade and not the high level of wages as the employers continually claimed. (28) Throughout the 1920s the cotton unions called for a government inquiry into the industry and this became part of the Labour Party's programme in 1928. Textile Lancashire returned a majority of Labour seats in the 1929 election for the first time. All the major towns returned Labour M.P.s and the election was the culmination of a steady swing to the left that had been occurring in Lancashire throughout the 1920s. (29)

The Labour Government of 1929 failed to appoint a Commission of Inquiry into the cotton trade and instead appointed a sub-committee of the newly-formed Economic Advisory Committee. The failure to set up a full scale Commission of Inquiry was really a result of the Labour Government bending to objections from the cotton employers who did not want an open and public debate about the industry. The employers claimed this was because they did not want trade secrets to be revealed, but in fact they were reluctant to have an open discussion on any aspect of the cotton trade as evidenced by their similar refusal to have a public hearing at the

1929 Board of Arbitration on Wages. The public discussion they wanted to avoid was about recapitalisation. In the event the report, which was unsympathetic to the cotton trade unionists, was irrelevant, since absolutely no action was taken on any of its recommendations. (30)

The world depression and the industrial defeats of 1929-32 forced the cotton unions to re-think their strategy for the industry. However, their new policy had to be worked out in the hostile climate of Labour's defeat in 1931 and a general swing to the right in textile Lancashire. Initially, they argued for a return to the World War One experience with the setting up of a Cotton Control Board for the industry, but when this received little support from the employers they moved to a demand for full socialisation. This was in line with T.U.C. thinking after 1931 when Congress was also demanding nationalisation of coal, iron and steel. (31) Although socialisation of the cotton industry became part of the Labour Party's programme at the 1935 General Election, it was not a popular demand among cotton operatives, and the unions quickly moved to concentrating on achieving an agreement with the employers on a joint approach with them to the government for legislative action to alleviate the problems of the industry.

III. State Intervention and Politics in the Inter-War Years

The economic crisis of the inter-war years placed a great strain on collective bargaining in the cotton industry, leading to a growth in state intervention in industrial relations. This major change took place after 1929. The Master Spinners' Federation decisively rejected state intervention in both 1919 and 1921, but by 1929 was forced to accept it. (32) Initially, the change was brought about by the election of a Labour Government and its insistence on intervening in the labour disputes of 1929 and 1931. The National Government continued this form of intervention and, after two disputes in 1932, proposed that there should be new conciliation schemes in both weaving and spinning. These were both introduced as a further tier in the system of collective bargaining and involved an outside and independent chairman, who effectively arbitrated between the two sides, and one nominee from each of the employers and the unions. The new conciliation scheme worked well in weaving and became a permanent feature of the bargaining process, but was dropped in spinning after three years because of the opposition of the spinners. The introduction of the conciliation schemes in the industry occurred at the same time as an improvement in the performance of the British economy and the cotton industry. 1932 also saw the stabilisation of collective bargaining in the cotton industry. It is difficult to judge whether this stabilisation was a result of improved mechanisms for collective bargaining or of improvements in economic conditions. (33)

The most important form of state intervention in industrial relations, however, was legislative. The Cotton Manufacturing Act of 1934 legalised weavers' wages, though largely on the employers' terms. This was a novel form of legislation for the National Government and was seen at the time as essentially experimental. It legalised the wage agreements reached via the bargaining machinery already established for the industry. Firms outside the employers' organisations were legally bound to pay the wage rates agreed and this affected about one-third of employers. The employers' organisations favoured the legislation because they were concerned about competitors undercutting them. The unions supported the legislation because, after the 1931 crisis, cotton operatives were being forced to accept lower wages than those collectively agreed, or face unemployment. These wage reductions could take many forms, one of which included forcing employees to buy shares in the firms they worked for, though this was later declared illegal under the Truck Acts. The weavers' participation in the scheme was opposed by the T.U.C. because they were concerned that once the Bill reached the Commons, it would be amended in ways detrimental to trade unionism because of the large Conservative majority. At the cost of further wage reductions the legislation did stabilise wages and brought to and end the crisis of collective bargaining. (34)

The growth in state intervention was associated with the National Government of the 1930s. The social consequences of the world depression were devastating but did not produce a swing to the left in the political attitudes of cotton operatives. In the 1920s, political opinion in Lancashire had slowly moved to the left and by 1929 all the major textile constituencies were returning Labour M.P.s. However, this position was reversed in the 1930s when the National Government won most of the seats in textile Lancashire. The National Government's victory in 1931 was not surprising but Labour had expected to recover in 1935, and even many Conservatives expected them to pull back some support. (35) Recent historians, notably Stevenson and Cook, have suggested that the success of the National Government in the 1930s was partly due to the prosperity caused by the rise of new industries. (36) The National Government's success in Lancashire cannot be explained in these terms, for in Lancashire such prosperity never existed in the 1930s. Its success can be explained only in terms of the dismal failure of the Labour Government of 1929-31.

Lancashire was central to the experience of the 1929-31 Labour Government in a number of ways. Unemployment was a major problem in Lancashire; India, a major pre-occupation of the Government, was also central to Lancashire's future; and at the same time great hopes were placed on the Clynes Committee bringing forward a solution to decline in the cotton industry. Unemployment continued to rise throughout the period; the Gandhi boycott added to the industry's problems; and the Clynes Committee produced no significant results. Added to this was the fact that the Government's intervention in industrial relations in 1929 and 1931 had proved detrimental on both occasions to the interests of the cotton operatives. In 1929 it was the Government arbitrator who recommended the wage cut, and in 1931 it was the Cabinet which tried to persuade the weavers to accept the more looms system. Also, as previously noted, in 1931 the Minister of Labour was recommending weavers to leave the industry and to move into domestic service. This produced cries of outrage from the women weavers of Lancashire, who saw domestic work as sweated labour and an affront to their dignity. Work as domestic servants for wealthy people was no substitute for the independence and status women had achieved as weavers. Disillusion with the Labour Party was evident by the early 1930s and would probably have seriously undermined Labour's position in Lancashire without the help of Ramsay McDonald. (37)

The National Government introduced three major pieces of legislation in attempts to solve the problems of the cotton industry. It was actually building on Labour's traditions of intervention, in fact going much further than Labour was prepared to, in an attempt to consolidate its electoral support in Lancashire. The legislation was corporate in the sense that it attempted to bring together employers, trade unions and government and was therefore unique in terms of peacetime legislation. The Government was not prepared to introduce legislation without agreement from both employers and trade unions. This formula was extremely successful in the 1934 Cotton Manufacturing Act which legalised weavers' wages. The Government then attempted to fashion a similar agreement between employers and trade unions for the spinning industry to promote the reduction of surplus capacity. The Spindles Act of 1936 created a system of compensation for owners who were prepared physically to destroy excess spindles. The compensation fund was created by raising a levy on all working spindles. The cotton unions opposed the Act because it failed to provide compensation for operatives who were made redundant through spindle-smashing. A number of employers also opposed the Act, particularly those who had moved to vertical organisation, owning both looms and spindles. The combined opposition of the trade unions and this section of the employers turned what the government had envisaged as an uncontentious piece of legislation into a major political issue in Lancashire.

The lesson the government learned from this was that any future legislation would have to cover the whole industry and not one section of it, and that the total support of the trade unions and employers would have to be negotiated before any proposed legislation reached the statute book. This explains the long negotiations between employers, trade unions and government prior to the passing of the 1939 Cotton Industry Act. This Act was more classically corporate legislation in that it provided not only for the physical destruction of excess capacity but also for the setting up of a Board to supervise the industry on which representatives of the cotton unions, employers and government were to serve. It also envisaged some form of compensation for those operatives who lost their livelihood through the decisions of the Board. In fact, the provisions of the Act were never implemented because of the outbreak of War in 1939. (38)

Cotton Trade Unionism

IV. Conclusions

The political and industrial defeats of the cotton operatives were caused by the massive decline of their industry. Membership of the cotton trade unions was approximately halved between 1920 and 1939. The United Textile Factory Workers' Association claimed a membership of 400,000 in 1921 but by the late 1930s this had been reduced to below 200,000. The Amalgamated Association of Operative Cotton Spinners, whose membership with the addition of piecers had peaked at 55,000 in 1921, had fallen by 1939 to 30,000. Membership of the Amalgamated Association of Card Blowing and Ring Room Operatives had similarly peaked in 1921 at 80,000 but had fallen to 40,000 by the end of the 1930s. The Amalgamated Weavers' Association, whose membership had reached the figure of 225,000 in 1921, had fallen even more dramatically to 86,000 in 1939. Symbolic of this irreversible decline, the cotton operatives' newspaper, the Cotton Factory Times, closed in 1937.

One of the major effects of the economic crisis of the inter-war years was to reduce the cotton operatives' wages. The spinners, who had earned approximately £5 in 1920, were reduced to £3.10s.0d. by 1932. The problem of the piecer system increased as the industry contracted, leaving many adult males as big piecers permanently earning less than 30/- per week. Weavers who earned around £3 in 1920 earned less than £2 in 1937. These figures must be compared with the average labourer's wage of £2, and £3.10s.0d. for the skilled worker in the 1930s. (39) They suggest that the spinner who had been earning well above the average craftsman's wage in 1914, now earned approximately the same, and the weaver had been reduced to less than the wage of the general labourer compared with a pre-1914 position of being equal to the average industrial wage and well above the poverty level. In fact, many weavers and piecers in spinning earned little more than they could have received on unemployment pay. The impact of short-time working, under-employment and unemployment, combined with the fall of wage rates as the result of employers' lockouts, account for this change. The effect of this was to reduce significantly the prosperity of the Lancashire cotton communities. Their reputation as one of the better-off sections of the British working class came to an end in the inter-war period and, increasingly, their living standards were reduced to the level of traditional sweated workers. (40)

What is surprising, however, is the continued level of resistance by organised workers in the 1920s and 1930s to employers' cost cutting policies. This high level of trade union militancy can be explained by a number of factors. Firstly, there was the long tradition of trade unionism amongst cotton operatives. Though the emergence of modern mass cotton trade unionism was in the 1880s, this was merely the culmination of organising efforts that began in the early nineteenth century. The cotton unions were central to local communities in the North-West in a way that has been rarely discussed by historians. Secondly, employers' proposals for the industry encountered bitter opposition from the operatives because of the general belief that it was the massive speculation between 1918 and 1920 which had created the crisis of the 1920s. Thirdly, the level of wage cuts was high, as Clegg has argued, but the most critical factor was that the employers' proposals threatened the family wage. In an industry where, apart from the spinners and possibly the strippers and grinders, the male wage was not sufficient to feed a family, it was crucial that women, married and unmarried, should work. The more looms system threatened this, as did proposals that women cotton operatives should seek work in domestic service. It was the threat to women workers and the family wage that was behind weavers' militancy, and this in turn kept up the demands of workers in spinning. Finally, certain markets, especially for fine goods, held up during the slump and workers in areas producing for those markets were able to maintain militant attitudes towards employers. Nelson was an area where levels of production and therefore employment held up reasonably well, and the town's militancy of the 1919-21 period was rekindled between 1929 and 1932. In contrast, Oldham, a coarse spinning town which suffered badly through loss of markets and high unemployment during the slump of the 1920s and 1930s, failed to generate a radical, militant response.

NOTES

My thanks to Arthur McIvor, Tony Jowitt, Terry Wyke, Neville Kirk and Lesley Fowler for comments on an earlier draft.

1. H.A. Turner, Trade Union Growth, Structure and Policy, (London, 1962).
2. For spinners and piecers see A. Fowler & T. Wyke (eds.), The Barefoot Aristocrats (Littleborough, 1987); J. Jewkes & E.M. Gray, Wages and Labour in the Lancashire Cotton Spinning Industry (Manchester, 1935) and J.L. White, Limits of Trade Union Militancy (Westport, U.S.A., 1978).
3. See, for example, A. Clarke, The Effects of the Factory System (1899; reprint Littleborough, 1986), pp. 119-28.
4. For weavers, see A. Bullen, The Lancashire Weavers' Union (Rochdale, 1984); A. & L. Fowler, The History of the Nelson Weavers' Association (Nelson, 1984); E. Thornton, Some Memories (unpublished typescript, 1986) and J.L. White, op. cit.
5. For cardroom, see A. Bullen & A. Fowler, The Cardroom Workers' Union (Rochdale, 1986) and J.L. White, op. cit. On women in cotton see M. Savage, ch. 11.
6. The origins of town wage lists and formal industrial relations systems have been analysed by A. Bullen in ch. 2.
7. For employer organisations in cotton, see ch. 1 and A.J. McIvor, 'Employers' Organisations and Industrial Relations in Lancashire, 1890-1939', (Ph.D. thesis, University of Manchester, 1983), ch. 8. See also A.J. Bullen, 'The Cotton Spinners' and Manufacturers' Association and the Breakdown of the Collective

Bargaining System in the Cotton Manufacturing Industry, 1928-35', (M.A. thesis, University of Warwick, 1980).

8. United Textile Factory Workers' Association Legislative Committee, Minutes, 1918-1919. For a more detailed discussion of industrial relations in cotton during World War One, see A. Fowler & T. Wyke (eds.), op. cit., ch. 8.

9. See J. H. Porter, 'Cotton & Wool Textiles' in N.K. Buxton & D.H. Aldcroft (eds.), British Industry Between the Wars (London, 1979), pp. 25-47.

10. The classic account of the immediate post-war period is G.W. Daniels & J. Jewkes, 'The Post-war Depression in the Lancashire Cotton Industry', Journal of Royal Statistical Society, 91, 1928. For the trade union view, see United Textile Factory Workers' Association, Inquiry into the Cotton Industry (Blackburn, 1923).

11. Jewkes & Grey, op. cit., ch. III.

12. For a more detailed analysis of the more looms system, see A. & L. Fowler, op. cit., chs. V and VI; A. Bullen, op. cit. and also J.H. Riley, 'The More Looms System and Industrial Relations in the Cotton Manufacturing Industry, 1928-35', (M.A. thesis, University of Manchester, 1981).

13. See W. Lazonick, 'The Cotton Industry' in B. Elbaum & W. Lazonick (eds.), The Decline of the British Economy (Oxford, 1986) and W. Lazonick, 'Industrial Organisation and Technical Change: the Decline of the British Cotton Industry', Business History Review, Vol. 57, 1983.

14. W. Lazonick, 'Industrial Relations and Technical Change: the Case of the Self-Acting Mule', Cambridge Journal of Economics, Vol. 3, 1979; W. Lazonick & W. Mass, 'The Performance of the British Cotton Industry, 1870-1913', Research in Economic History, Vol. 9, 1984.

15. A. & L. Fowler, op. cit., ch. IV.

16. See H.D. Henderson, The Cotton Control Board, (Oxford, 1922).

17. A. Fowler & T. Wyke, op. cit., chs. 8 & 9.

18. H.A. Clegg, A History of British Trade Unions since 1889, Vol. II, (Oxford, 1985), p. 523.

19. The main union documentation of the more looms disputes is at Lancashire Record Office, Amalgamated Weavers' Association Collection, DDX 1123/6/2/363.

20. See United Textile Factory Workers' Association, Report of the Annual Conference (1931), pp. 68-72 for government pressure on weavers. For more looms and women, see A. & L. Fowler, op. cit., pp. 63-6 and the Amalgamated Weavers' Collection, Lancashire Record Office, DDX 1123/6/2/352. Also J. Liddington, The Life and Times of a Respectable Rebel (London, 1984). See also M. Savage, ch. 11, for a discussion of women and militancy in the inter-war period in cotton.

21. See A. & L. Fowler, op. cit., chs. I & IV and J. Liddington, op. cit., Ch. III.

22. A. Fowler & T. Wyke, op. cit., ch. 9.

23. United Textile Factory Workers' Association, Annual Reports, 1920, pp. 11-13; 1921, p. 19; 1922, pp. 16-18; 1923, pp. 11-15. United Textile Factory Workers' Association, Annual Conference Reports, 1919, pp. 10-22; 1920, pp. 58-64; 1921, pp. 74-7; 1922, pp. 15-28; 1923, pp. 10-32.
24. H.A. Turner, op. cit., pp. 325-31 for his account of the inter-war years.
25. See A. Fowler & T. Wyke, op. cit., pp. 156-60 for 1919 dispute and the role of shop stewards in spinners' militancy. For the 1921 dispute see Amalgamated Weavers' Association Collection, Lancashire Record Office, DDX 1123/6/2/124. For 1929 see the same Collection DDX 1123/6/303.
26. United Textile Factory Workers' Association, Annual Conference Reports, 1933, pp. 60-7; 1934, pp. 39-52, 70-4; 1935, pp. 18-26.
27. United Textile Factory Workers' Association, Annual Report, 1928, (1 June - 31 Dec.), pp. 9-10; Annual Conference Report, 1929, pp. 61-9.
28. See Z. Hutchison, 'The Trusts Grip Cotton', Independent Labour Party Pamphlets, New Series, No. 28, 1920.
29. A. Fowler & T. Wyke, op. cit., p. 168. For 1929 elections results see Labour Year Book, (1930; Reprint, Brighton, 1973), pp. 254-7.
30. A. Fowler & T. Wyke, op. cit., pp. 172-73; see also the Economic Advisory Council, Report of the Committee on the Present Condition and Prosperity of the Cotton Industry, Cmd. 3615, (London, 1930).
31. Trades Union Congress, Cotton, The T.U.C. Plan for Socialisation (London, 1935); E. Barry, Nationalisation in British Politics: the Historical Background (London, 1965), pp. 310-54.
32. For a general discussion of the role of the Ministry of Labour in the inter-war years, see R. Lowe, Adjusting to Democracy (Oxford, 1986), pp. 76-131.
33. For the Midland Hotel Agreement see Amalgamated Weavers' Association Collection, Lancashire Record Office DDX 1123/6/2/362.
34. For the 1936 wage negotiations see Amalgamated Weavers' Association Collection, Lancashire Record Office, DDX 1123/6/2/436; E.M. Gray, The Weavers' Wage, (Manchester, 1936), ch. II.
35. J. Stevenson & C. Cook, The Slump (London, 1979), p. 251.
36. Ibid., pp. 1-7, 8-30, 265-82.
37. United Textile Factory Workers' Association, Annual Conference Report, 1931, p. 65 (which refers to the electoral slump in Lancashire at Municipal elections). See also the Labour Year Book (1931. Reprint, Brighton, 1973), pp. 365-71.
38. See United Textile Factory Workers' Association, Special Conference Report, 12 January 1939 for the cotton unions' discussion of the Act.
39. See J. Jewkes & E.M. Gray, op. cit., pp. 201-02 and E.M. Grey, op. cit., p. 31.
40. G.D.H. and M.I. Cole have shown that of 28 major industries cotton experienced the fourth largest percentage fall in wage rates between 1920 and 1934. Average weekly wage rates

(not earnings) in cotton in 1934 were just 53 per cent of 1920 rates. Larger falls occurred in Wool and Worsted (51 per cent), Coal (42 per cent) and Iron and Steel (42 per cent). See G.D.H. and M.I. Cole, The Condition of Britain, (London, 1937), p. 246.

Chapter 7

WORK, WAGES AND INDUSTRIAL RELATIONS IN
COTTON FINISHING, 1880-1914

Arthur McIvor

The cotton industry has been the subject of intensive investigation and the focus of contentious debate amongst social and economic historians of all orientations. For reasons which are obscure, however, the finishing sector, incorporating the bleaching, dyeing and calico printing processes, has been overlooked consistently and, as a result, knowledge of the industry beyond weaving remains sketchy. (1) G. Turnbull's classic, A History of the Calico Printing Industry in Great Britain (1951) remains the only really useful monograph. Part of the reason for this neglect lies in the fact that the chemical processes involved in finishing differentiate it distinctly from spinning and weaving. Some official nineteenth century government reports even classified finishing in the 'non-textile' industrial category. Undoubtedly, the size of the sector has also contributed to its neglect. Cotton spinning and weaving were much more significant to the economy of Lancashire, providing more than ten times the jobs generated by finishing. Nevertheless, an industrial sector which employed no less than 55,000 in 1914 merits due attention. This chapter attempts to rescue some aspects of the social history of cotton finishing from anonymity and presents a rough-hewn overview, focusing on the experience of work and wages in the industry, and the evolution of trade unionism and industrial relations during the phase of industrial maturity, 1880-1914. The first section briefly outlines industrial structure, employment patterns and work processes. Section II looks at the experience of the craft artisans in the industry and briefly assesses some of the dimensions of unilateral craft control over work. This is followed in Section III with an analysis of work, wages and unionisation amongst the semi- or lesser skilled bleachers and dyers. Finally, the experience of the small minority of female workers in the industry is assessed in Section IV.

Work, Wages and Industrial Relations

I. The Cotton Finishing Industry

After the loom, cotton cloth was either exported in the 'grey' state or cleaned and finished within Britain for the market. Prior to the late eighteenth century the finishing of cloth was a long, laborious process. Bleaching was achieved by subjecting the material to a succession of natural cleansing agents and then exposing the 'pieces' in open fields - or 'bleachcrofts' - to the natural bleaching power of the sun for anything up to several months. Cloth was dyed using natural dyestuffs and patterns printed on to the calico by highly skilled workmen using engraved hand held wooden blocks. These time-honoured techniques were revolutionised, however, in the late eighteenth and early nineteenth centuries with the development of steam power, chemical bleaching, machine roller printing, mechanical singeing, mangling, washing and drying, and, from the mid-1850s, the discovery of artificial dyestuffs. These chemical and engineering innovations enabled the industry vastly to expand its productivity and absorb the increased output of yarn and cloth emanating from the crucial technical developments of the self-acting spinning mule and the power loom. (2)

The cotton finishing industry developed in close proximity to cotton spinning and weaving, the two major centres being west Scotland and Lancashire. Finishing in Scotland declined with the stagnation of the cotton sector north of the border from the 1850s. Whilst the 1911 Census records 20,865 workers in the bleaching, dyeing, printing and allied industries in Scotland, it is evident that the majority was involved in the finishing of other textiles than cotton. (3) Nevertheless, there remained a number of major cotton finishing firms in Scotland, including the United Turkey Red Company, a combine of four firms, based in the Vale of Leven, employing 2,600 in 1914, and with a pre-war reputation for fierce, irrevocable opposition to trade unionism.

The main centres of the expanding cotton finishing industry in the North-West of England were Bolton, Manchester, Salford, Bury, Radcliffe and Stockport. 167 of the 230 firms within Lancashire and Cheshire in 1884 were situated in these towns. (4) Most of these companies were small jobbing concerns. However, in the late 1890s there were around 45 bleaching and dyeing firms each employing between 100 and 500 workers and 5 firms - R. Ainsworth; T. Cross; Deakins; W. Buckley; P. Reid - each employing over 500. (5) By the 1900s, the finishing industry was characterised by a high degree of combination and direct price control. In response to the ruinous depression of the 1880s and 1890s measures were taken in an attempt to eliminate excess capacity and regulate product price. The Bleachers' Association was established in 1900 amalgamating 60 firms, employing in total 10,000 workpeople. The dyeing sector was very small in Lancashire and its concerns either remained independent, merged (as combined process firms) into the Bleachers' Association or were absorbed into the Yorkshire based combine, the Bradford Dyers' Association Ltd. (1898), which had three large works in Salford, Ardwick and Wigan employing around

1,000. The Calico Printers' Association (C.P.A.) was created in November 1899, encompassing 46 printing firms, 13 merchants and over 80 per cent of the printing capacity of the industry. After closing down a number of small, inefficient units, output of the C.P.A. amounted to 52 per cent of all printed cloth produced in Britain between 1901 and 1914. (6)

Multi-process firms continued in existence in cotton finishing, but the trend up to 1914 and beyond was towards horizontal specialisation and a division between the bleaching-dyeing trade and calico printing. The industry was also divided by the nature of the product, its markets and the finish traditionally associated with particular companies. A number of firms dyed yarn, whilst the majority bleached and finished 'grey' cloth from the loom, those specialising in the home market usually requiring the most elaborate and more costly finishes. A significant feature of the industry was its dependence on the merchant, who purchased and warehoused the 'grey' cloth from cotton weavers and commissioned out the material to bleachers, dyers and calico printers, depending on the type of finish clients requested. Cotton finishing was thus a 'service' industry which neither controlled the purchase of its basic raw material nor had any but marginal influence on the timing and flow of orders. One important result, with implications for industrial relations, was that labour costs as a proportion of total production costs in cotton finishing were extremely high.

Because of the tendency to aggregate statistics for the textile finishing sector as a whole in both the Census (after 1891) and the Factory Inspectors' Reports, it is difficult to obtain accurate series of statistics on numbers employed in the cotton sector alone.

Table 7.1: Numbers Employed (Cotton Calico Printers, Dyers and Bleachers), 1881 and 1891

	Male	Female	Total
1881	22,750	3,932	26,682
1891	26,103	5,005	31,108

Source: Census, 1881, 1891
Notes: These figures under-represent actual numbers employed because they exclude Scotland and undefined textile finishing workers and miscellaneous labourers. In 1881, for example, there were 11,799 undefined textile dyers, scourers, bleachers and calenderers not included in the above figures. It is unlikely, therefore, that the British cotton textile finishing industry employed less than 35,000 in 1880.

Work, Wages and Industrial Relations

After the 1891 Census the nearest one can get to identifying employment in the cotton finishing sector is to analyse the returns for Lancashire.

Table 7.2: Numbers Employed in Textile Finishing in Lancashire, 1901 and 1911

	1901		1911	
	male	female	male	female
Bleaching	8,198	2,095	8,202	1,647
Dyeing	7,092	473	7,234	788
Calendering	4,059	1,203	12,076	4,626
Printing	7,626	647	7,481	504
Total	26,975	4,445	34,993	7,565

Source: Census, 1901, 1911
Notes: Problems of under-representation of the entire cotton finishing sector, and changes in classification criteria, continue. For example, the 1911 figures for calendering are suspect. It is unlikely that less than 55,000 were thus employed in the cotton finishing industry in Britain in 1914.

Turnbull provides a detailed description of the bewildering series of processes and transformations which the 'grey' cloth underwent before re-emerging in its finished state. (7) Something of the complexity of the occupational structure can be gauged by the fact that the Amalgamated Society of Dyers, Bleachers, Finishers and Kindred Trades regularly monitored the earnings of 66 distinct occupational groups in the 1890s. (8) However, the major work processes might be summarised thus:

1. Preparation: continuous piece stitching; singeing; dressing.
2. Bleaching; washing; 'chemicking'.
3. Dyeing; washing.
4. Mangling; drying; stoving.
5. Calendering; stretching; damping.
6. Beetling and stiffening.
7. Printing - engraving (hand and machine); pattern printing (more than 90 per cent of which was by machine rather than the older block technique).
8. Making up and 'finishing'; mending; silking; folding; packing.

Work experience varied widely not only because of the wide range of processes, but also because of product diversity and local specialisms (e.g. Bolton - home market; Manchester - export), lack of technological standardisation and the customary sexual division of labour. However, a marked divergence in experience existed between the larger group of predominantly semi- and lesser skilled labourers employed in the earlier and intermediate processes of preparation, bleaching and dyeing, and, on the other hand, the relatively privileged, well paid craft artisans in the engraving and pattern printing departments. The 1906 Wages Inquiry provides one indication of the extent of these divisions. The average adult male weekly earnings in cotton finishing were 28s.10d. This hid wide variations, however, between around 20 per cent of the workforce who earned over 30 shillings, and averaged around £2 (predominantly foremen, printers, engravers, and the best beetlers and stiffeners) and the other 80 per cent, whose earnings ranged between 15 and 30 shillings and averaged less than 25 shillings. (9)

II. The Craft Artisan Elite: Calico Printing

The experience and status of the craft artisans in the cotton finishing industry before World War One contrasted markedly with that of the mass of bleach and dye workers. Craftsmen exercised more discretion and authority at work; and they enjoyed relative job security, lighter work, and higher wages, and usually toiled in a less unhealthy work environment. Two groups in particular were in a privileged position: the engravers and the calico printers. Traditionally these were apprenticed crafts, where strong trade societies securely controlled entry, hence maintaining skilled labour scarcity and high earnings.

Engravers held a pivotal position within the finishing occupational hierarchy as they were responsible for sketching, etching and cutting the print designs and patterns on to blocks and copper rollers. They had achieved a 35 shilling minimum guaranteed wage by 1906, a 56 hour working week, regulation of overtime working (with extra payment) and strict control of apprentice numbers to a ratio of one to every four journeymen. (10) Foremen engravers could obtain quite astounding earnings: a Calico Printers' Association survey of six firms in 1910 reported weekly wage rates of up to £7.7s.0d. (11) Tight control over entry to the trade enabled the engravers to escalate earnings in periods of trade buoyancy and tight labour markets, for example, over 1910-14. The Society of Master Calico Printers complained in 1911: "Members find that the men are willing to sell themselves to the highest bidder and that wages are running up in an alarming manner". (12) When the Master Engravers' Association attempted to control this situation and impose a degree of regulation in 1913, almost 2,000 engravers struck work for two months. The employers' opposition dissolved and the engravers returned to significant wage advances and an affirmation that the employers accepted the conditions laid down in the union rule book. (13)

The calico printers also occupied an elite position within the trade and are a good example of a group of workers who exercised an extremely high degree of control over their labour process and virtually regulated working conditions unilaterally in the industry. Average earnings in 1906 reached 46s.6d for machine printers in England, which made them the highest paid group of workers in the industry below the supervisory grades. (14)

The power of the calico printers in the late nineteenth century derived essentially from their complete control of recruitment in the trade and their extremely well organised trade union, the Amicable and Brotherly Society of Machine Printers (hereafter cited as Printers' Union). This union was formed in 1840 and organised the elite machine printers in a 'closed', exclusive organisation which failed to recruit the mass of lesser skilled employees in cotton printworks. (15) It covered virtually all machine printers and had a small membership of 950 in 1899. (16) There were just less than 1,000 calico printing machines in Britain at this time - all but a very small number being utilised for one shift only. The Printers' Union was powerful enough to dictate unilaterally working conditions. As one employer noted in 1906: "Hitherto the trade has been compelled to adopt Rules framed by the men without having taken any part in their discussion." (17)

Juveniles entered a seven year apprenticeship in calico printing usually between the ages of 20 and 25, after having worked in the trade as tenters or shifters for several years. The Printers' Union enforced a strict apprenticeship ratio in the 1880s and 1890s of no more than one trainee to every three journeymen. Moreover, in response to the formation of the Calico Printers' Association in November 1899 and the scrapping of excess capacity (which threw over 10 per cent of members out of work) the Printers' Union introduced an embargo on any new apprentices for two years and subsequently imposed severe limitations, refusing to sanction additional apprentices at any firm unless members were fully employed. This policy continued up to World War One, with only a two year moratorium (when there was a return to a 1:3 ratio) over 1911-12. (18) This effectively undermined any attempt by employers to replace labour during industrial disputes.

The cotton finishing employers adopted, in general, a passive and conciliatory attitude towards their pivotal skilled labour and their lack of control over recruitment. Few employers risked precipitating a strike and, as the Annual Reports on Strikes and Lock-Outs indicate, stoppages were rare in this sector of the industry. The creation of the Calico Printers' Association in 1899, and the Society of Master Calico Printers (S.M.C.P.) in 1905, constituted a challenge to workers' unilateral control. Some of the smaller constituent firms saw the consolidation of business structure and employers' organisation as an opportunity to seek confrontation, make a stand to reduce labour costs and wrest control over work from the union, even to the point of initiating a lock-out. (19) However, the C.P.A. remained conciliatory in its labour relations policy, invariably counselled caution and concession within the S.M.C.P., and explicitly accepted the status quo prior to World War One. The main thrust of C.P.A. labour rationalisation was the extension of piecework systems of wage payment, especially over 1910-14. This was done with full union co-operation and a guaranteed day rate during experimental piece-rate trials. (20) On the apprentice/recruitment question the C.P.A. advised member firms to apply directly to John Holt, general secretary of the Printers' Union, if they required additional labour. The Labour Exchanges Act, 1909, appeared to be a boon to management, enabling them to secure labour without going to the union. However, in practice, unemployed calico printers boycotted the Exchange and the union retained firm control of its traditional labour clearing house functions. There is no evidence, for example, of constant utilisation of the Exchanges by the C.P.A. and the two recorded requests made for calico printers before 1914 could not be filled by the Labour Exchange in Manchester. (21)

There are other clear indications of the power and privilege of the craftsmen in calico printing prior to World War One. Firstly, a survey of S.M.C.P. firms in 1905 found that, with only two exceptions calico printers received time-and-a-half pay for overtime - a rate enjoyed by no other group of workers in the industry. A campaign to reduce this rate was completely ineffective and was quietly dropped by mid 1906. (22) Secondly, the union extended strict controls over nightwork, reported to be growing in incidence over 1900-14, especially amongst smaller firms. (23) Thirdly, the machine calico printers retained an extraordinary degree of control over their labour process and the pace and rhythm of work. Employer attempts to monitor more closely and oversee production were fiercely resisted as in the work 'booking' dispute of 1908. (24) Fourthly, the bargaining power of labour *vis a vis* capital in calico printing was clearly indicated during the 1908-9 recession, when the S.M.C.P. initiated a campaign to create a Brooklands style jointly negotiated working agreement between management and men. Some members of the S.M.C.P. wanted to use the recession to initiate a trade lock-out to wrest control from the union. In the event, however, the S.M.C.P. backed away from precipitate action and accepted an agreement on the union's terms, incorporating as its basis "the general working conditions existing in the various printing shops of the Calico Print Trade". (25)

Evidence suggests, therefore, that despite the rationalisation of business structure inherent in the formation of the C.P.A. in 1899, the scrapping of excess capacity and the consolidation of employers' organisation with the formation of the S.M.C.P. in 1905, the calico printing and engraving craftsmen and their unions retained firm control, and thus their position of power and privilege within the cotton finishing workforce, right up to 1914. High union membership density linked with firm, almost absolute, control over entry to the craft, lay at the core of the calico printers' bargaining strength. Moreover, the machine printing craft was under no serious threat from technological change. Employers' resistance was also weakened by poor collective organisation amongst firms and by labour shortages, which almost entirely neutralised any possibility of successfully replacing labour during strikes. Employers were also often under severe pressure from merchants regarding delivery of goods (especially for export); and because clients often specified the special 'finish' of a particular firm it was difficult on any work except the roughest to get orders executed at another plant in the eventuality of a strike. (26) Finally, it might be hypothesised that the dominant, semi-monopoly position of the C.P.A., and its ability to influence (if not always directly to fix) product prices, encouraged it to adopt a labour relations strategy characterised by flexibility, aversion to conflict and a willingness to accept, or at least not radically to challenge, the status quo.

III. Bleach and Dye Workers

The majority of employees in cotton finishing were male labourers or semi-skilled workers involved in bleaching, dyeing, washing and cleaning the cloth. Job training periods were relatively short, discretion and autonomy minimal, and the task range prescribed. Work tasks essentially pivoted around the carrying, manipulating, guiding and monitoring of the cloth, stitched together to form continuous 'ribbons', as it passed through the bleaching kiers, dye vats and cisterns, washing and scouring machines, steam powered mangles, stretching machines and tin cylinder drying machines. Labour processes varied enormously and defy generalisation. However, what is clear is that work in this section of finishing was characterised by its physically arduous and fatiguing nature.

This is a difficult assertion to quantify or substantiate. However, it may be significant that in a Factory Inspectorate survey in 1912, dyeing came next to top of a league table of industries involving the lifting of heavy weights, likely to cause injury. (27) The sick pay, superannuation and accident claims files of the Operative Bleachers and Dyers (Bolton Amalgamation) also indicate that hernias and ruptures were a common occupational hazard. (28) Great variation in temperature in workrooms was also normal (up to 110 degrees) and the work environment was usually hot and damp, the result partly of steam emission from the machinery. Exhaust fans were reported by the Rochdale Factory Inspector to be invariably wrongly positioned and ineffective. (29) Physical and mental overstrain was exacerbated by long and irregular working hours, the 'speed-up' of machinery and insecurity of employment. Phases of inactivity and underemployment alternated with frenetic periods of 'hard graft' in an attempt to honour rush orders from merchants. Illegal overtime working and time 'cribbing' were also frequently recurring offences in bleaching and dyeing, noted by the Factory Inspectorate. (30)

Clearly, the industry also had a poor safety record if judged by the evidence of accidents in the Factory Inspectors' Reports, the union files and, indeed, the minute books of the employers' accident insurance company, the Bleachers and Dyers Mutual Indemnity Company. 1,636 accidents, 30 of which were fatal, were reported to the Factory Inspectorate for the entire textile finishing industry in one year, 1910. (31) Dr. Niven, the Medical Officer of Health for Manchester, scheduled the bleaching and dyeing trade in third place behind chemicals and glass manufacture in his statistical analysis of the relative mortality record of Lancashire industries. (32) Accidents often occurred as a result of limbs, clothing and hair being caught up in unfenced machinery, vats and kiers, especially where it was difficult (before electricity) to cut off power quickly. Uneven, wet and slippery floors also added to the danger, particularly where kiers and vats were flush with the floor, rather than raised several feet from it. Scalding and burns were commonplace, not least because of explosions, faulty valves and lack of steam pressure gauges on kiers and drying cans, which, it was alleged, were neither regularly tested nor properly maintained. At least up to 1901, these machines were not covered by Factory legislation and not required to be inspected. (33) The following terse statement from the bleaching employers' accident insurance records for one year, 1906, is indicative of the heavy toll on life and limb:

> The accidents may be summarised as follows: 4 injuries to the eyesight; 5 cases of burns; 25 cases of scalds; 14 cases of injury to the head; 19 cases of injury to the arms; 30 cases of injury to the body; 29 cases of injury to the feet; 37 cases of injury to the legs; 3 cases of rupture; 6 cases of sprains; 73 cases of finger trapping; 5 cases of blood poison. (34)

All of the five fatalities for which the company paid financial compensation in the same year were juvenile plaiters. These were all killed in the bleachcroft, where accident rates were particularly high, not least because employers failed to initiate preventive action to raise safety standards. (35)

To the death and injury toll of accidents must be added the harvest of disability and mortality caused by industrial disease. The superannuation and sickness files of the Bolton Amalgamation provide a chronicle of occupationally related diseases and illnesses, including rheumatism (especially of the feet and legs), rheumatic gout, sciatica, bronchitis, chronic asthma and ulceration of the skin. There was an ever-present danger of poisoning by inhalation or skin contact with the chemicals and materials being used to clean, bleach and dye the cloth, a danger exacerbated by poor ventilation and inadequate floor drainage in many firms. (36) As late as 1911, the Factory Inspectorate was still encouraging finishing employers to provide exhaust ventilation linked with every machine, rather than the usual single fan per room. Some firms were forced to provide milk in an attempt to ease throat and gastric problems associated with the inhalation of dangerous fumes and dust. Skin contact could have tragic effects. One commentator reported in 1911:

> In many cases the women and girls are working under the most shocking conditions I have ever come across. In one department girls work all day with their bare feet in cold water. In another case I have seen a girl with flesh burned off her hands by working with caustic soda. This girl suffered great agony...But this is only one case; there are others. I have seen girls arms with holes burned in them by chrome. (37)

A Home Office inquiry in 1906 estimated that around 47 per cent of those dyeworkers in the mixing and preparation departments were poisoned to a greater or lesser degree by the materials used. (38) In this same year the dyeing industry was scheduled as a 'dangerous trade' under the Factories legislation, thus tightening regulations and making it easier to obtain financial compensation in the eventuality of chlorine, chrome and aniline poisoning. The emphasis remained, however, on compensation rather than prevention.

Apart from the health risks, bleaching was amongst the poorest paid of finishing tasks. Wage standardisation was rare, workers being invariably paid what the market would bear, with allowances for experience, strength and output. Three features of the wage system are noteworthy. Firstly, payment by time rather than piece was most common, though payment by results was spreading rapidly in the decade preceding World War One. (39) Secondly, in the 1880s, weekly pay days were rare, most workers being paid on a fortnightly or monthly basis. (40) Thirdly, up to the turn of the nineteenth century, a system existed whereby workers were not paid for cloth which went into stock, rather than to the market, until such stocks were sold. (41) Not surprisingly, by the First World War, bleaching, and especially croft work, had become an unpopular and despised occupation. William Barlow, who started work in 1914 recalled how recruitment occurred at the Starr Bleachworks in Bolton: "If your father didn't work there the only job you got in the bleachworks was in the croft, which nobody wanted." (42) Indeed, work in bleaching and dyeing was generally considered to be an inferior choice to employment in the cotton spinning mills and weaving sheds, where work in 1900 by comparison was less physically demanding and better paid, where health and safety provisions were more extensive, and where working hours were shorter and annual holidays greater. Why was this the case? Part of the answer lies in the relative strength of trade unionism in the various cotton processing sectors.

In the late nineteenth century, trade unionism remained much weaker in the cotton bleaching and dyeing trades than in cotton spinning and weaving. In 1899, there were 26,000 cotton cardroom workers, 40,000 cotton spinners and 112,000 cotton weavers unionised; whilst union membership in the whole of the textile finishing sector amounted to only 17,110. (43) Perhaps half of this number were cotton finishers, representing an average union density of less than 20 per cent of potential members at the turn of the century. Of course, averages often obscure as much as they illuminate. The major exception, already noted, was the calico printers, who had a very high union density similar to the cotton spinners. Bleachers and dyers found it much more difficult to sustain trade unionism, which was crucially undermined by employer opposition, victimisation, the overstocked nature of the labour market, and trade union fragmentation. The emergence of a mass labour movement occurred only in the decade immediately prior to World War One. By 1914, there were over 70,000 trade unionists across the whole textile finishing sector.

The 8-9,000 or so cotton finishing workers who were union members in the 1890s were distributed amongst a disparate cluster of organisations:

Table 7.3: Trade Unions Recruiting Cotton Finishers, 1890s

1. Operative Bleachers and Dyers (Bolton Amalgamation). Formed 1866. 4,400 members, 1899, in 10 Lancashire branches. Membership largely confined to cotton bleaching/dyeing.

2. National Society of Dyers and Finishers (Bradford). Formed 1851. 3,033 members in 1909, 1,416 (47%) of which were in 9 Lancashire branches.

3. Amalgamated Society of Dyers (Bradford). Formed 1878. 7,724 members in 1909, around 1,000 in 3 Lancashire branches. Predominantly recruited wool dyers.

4. Radcliffe Cotton Skein Dyers, Bleachers and Sizers. Formed 1866. 276 members, 1899.

5. Dressers, Dyers and Finishers Association (Salford). Formed 1833. 753 members, 1895. Collapsed 1899-1900.

6. Operative Calendermen, Embossers and Schreiners Society (Manchester). Formed 1872. 116 members, 1906.

7. National Union of Calico Printers' Labourers (Bury). Calico Print Workers Union (Manchester). Both had a brief existence in the 1890s. Joint membership at peak, 1896, was 360.

8. Amalgamated Union of Engravers to Calico Printers. Formed 1872. 106 members, 1886; 1,798 members, 1913.

9. Amicable and Brotherly Machine Printers Society. Formed 1840. 903 members, 1895.

Sources: Board of Trade Reports on Trade Unions; Bolton Amalgamation Reports and Balance Sheets; Annual Reports of the National Federation of Bleachers Dyers and Kindred Trades.

Work, Wages and Industrial Relations

In 1896 a number of these unions (including the first four on the above list) formed a loose federal organisation, the National Federation of Bleachers, Dyers and Kindred Trades. By 1907, this federation covered 17,500 workers. However, it was an uneasy alliance in which the constituent members closely guarded their autonomy. A move to merge and create a single industrial union for textile finishers had to be abandoned in 1903 to prevent a breakaway split of two of the major constituent organisations. (44) Union fragmentation continued seriously to weaken the bargaining power of labour in bleaching and dyeing right up to World War One.

The union which recruited most of the organised cotton finishers, outside the craft artisan group, was the Operative Bleachers and Dyers (Bolton Amalgamation). This union was formed directly after the Lancashire Cotton Famine in 1866, and by 1871 its membership had grown to 1,034 in eight branches. H.A. Turner has suggested that this was a 'closed' union (on the model of the cotton spinners' union), based initially on a group of relatively skilled workers in the finishing trade processing the fine yarn cloths around the Bolton district. (45) The union included in its objects that: "We are pledged to secure uniform working hours, a fair and legitimate remuneration and the elevation of our trade to an average standing with other branches of industry."(46) The union campaigned and applied pressure on employers in the last quarter of the nineteenth century to abolish the truck system, non-payment for stock and monthly pay days, with, by 1900, some success. For example, weekly pays, rare before 1890, were common (though not universal) by 1900.

Evidence suggests that throughout the last quarter of the nineteenth century the Bolton Amalgamation concentrated on its extensive friendly society functions and its campaigning and pressure group role. Strikes were rare in the trade and undertaken only in the last resort. The reports of the union from the 1870s to the 1890s indicate a clear commitment to a conciliatory, anti-strike strategy. Witness, for example, the union statement in 1887: "We are ever anxious to avoid all undue contention with employers and strongly deprecate strikes, and hope we shall continue to steer clear of them, as they are invariably harrassing, embittering and unprofitable and entail untold suffering on all involved in them." (47)

This strategy was undoubtedly dictated by union weakness. After an initial phase of growth, membership stagnated through the 1870s and 1880s, when only a very small minority of cotton bleachers was organised. Many employers refused to employ trade unionists and victimisation was reported to be rife. (48) In marked contrast to cotton spinning and weaving, industrial relations in the last quarter of the nineteenth century was characterised by quiescence and stability. J.C. Scholes referred to this in his history of Bolton in 1892:

> If it can be said with force that happy is the industry that knows not trade disputes and ruptures of a surety the bleaching, dyeing and print trades of Bolton and district

should be called 'happy'. In no branch of labour have fewer disturbances occurred in the relations between employers and employed. (49)

None of the long list of major strikes and lock-outs before 1899 cited in the First Annual Report on Strikes and Lock-Outs (based on G. Howell's research), occurred in textile finishing. (50)

However, whilst clearly strikes were uncommon in this sector, the image of quiescence and stable industrial relations projected above is not entirely accurate. Conflict did erupt sporadically at individual plants and when stoppages did occur they were often characterised by heavy picketing, violence, legal action and a legacy of bitterness. Bolton Amalgamation membership doubled over 1889-93 and broadened out to encompass lesser skilled workers, at the peak of the trade cycle, and these years witnessed a cluster of strikes and some labour successes. At Hepburn and Co. Bleachworks in Ramsbottom 127 female and over 70 male workers struck work for 24 weeks in 1892 with full Bolton Amalgamation support in an attempt to resist wage reductions of varying intensity across work 'sets' from 10-40 per cent. After a lockout threat by the Master Bleachers' Association the union executive agreed to conciliation, negotiating new price lists for the works (which incorporated wage reductions averaging 9 per cent) and a guarantee of re-employment for all regular workers. Wage cuts across the industry followed. (51)

Almost 100 workers were involved in a strike at Blair and Sumner's Mill Hill Bleachworks in Bolton in 1893. The issue was non-payment for work which went into stock, rather than to the market. Payment for work done had been delayed longer than a year, workers had left and never received moneys owed, and some employees had never been paid for damaged goods, despite the fact that these were later sold as substandard by the firm. The company retorted by importing blackleg labour at a generous remuneration of 8d. per hour. Two factors, however, undermined the employers' position. Firstly, public opinion favoured the union. The Bolton Journal, for example, declared that non-payment for stock work was "totally indefensible." (52) Secondly, the 40 or so non-unionist women in the finishing department refused to blackleg and left work in sympathy. After four weeks the management settled by agreeing to the total abolition of the stock system.

The Carrbrook Printworks Strike at Buckton Vale, near Stalybridge, provides a good example of the power of large employers in the industry and the effectiveness of strikebreaking tactics. The Bolton Amalgamation called out 540 bleachers and dyers at Carrbrook (out of a total workforce of 1,100) on 29 August 1895 in support of a wage rise claim. The union proceeded by organising picketing and fund raising, imposing an additional levy of 6d. per week on all employed union members. The firm responded by hiring a professional strikebreaker, Graeme Hunter, who proceeded with military precision, calculated cunning and ruthless efficiency to break the union's resistance. By the middle of October Hunter had drafted in over 600 blacklegs from Manchester and Scotland, and billeted these on the premises in specially constructed sheds. Powerful searchlights were used at night, the outer fence around the plant was electrified and a photographer engaged to provide prints of activists and those committing offences. Police protection was arranged and additional police drafted into the town. Physical attacks on blacklegs, strikers and police took place and the local police court was kept busy with intimidation and assault cases, which were met with fines and several terms of imprisonment of up to three months. The scale of the successful strikebreaking operation and the onset of winter demoralised the strikers and in mid-December the union agreed to call off unconditionally their action. The company simply informed the strikers that they had a new workforce and that old hands would be re-employed only when and if vacancies occurred. The Carrbrook Printworks was a major employer in Buckton Vale and the 1895 conflict devastated the local community. (53)

It is perhaps significant that on these three important labour-management confrontations in 1892, 1893 and 1895 the Bolton Amalgamation failed to call an industry-wide strike. Clearly, one of the most significant features of industrial relations in the later nineteenth century in bleaching (in marked contrast to cotton spinning) was that the union lacked the resources to initiate general stoppages and confined itself to sustaining and supporting pivotal individual plant strikes. This was clearly a period of employer hegemony and labour weakness, indicated most starkly by the relative ease with which lesser skilled union labour and strikers could be replaced. Of the 21 strikes in cotton bleaching and dyeing recorded in the Annual Reports on Strikes and Lock-Outs compiled by the Labour Department of the Board of Trade over 1888-99 only six had any degree of success, the other fifteen being settled by total labour 'submission', usually after strikers had been wholly or partially replaced by blacklegs. Moreover, re-employment after a strike was selective. The best replacees were usually retained, whilst labour militants were singled out and victimised in the region.

The balance of power in cotton bleaching and dyeing altered quite markedly in labour's favour during the decade immediately prior to World War One. As an examination of the workers' journal, the Cotton Factory Times indicates, labour began to successfully encroach into customary managerial prerogatives and rights. Several pieces of evidence substantiate this assertion. Firstly, the data in the Annual Reports on Strikes and Lock-Outs indicates clearly both an increased strike proneness and greater labour success rate over 1905-14. A crucial union success was achieved in 1907 when the Bolton Amalgamation presented its first general wage claim to the Employers' Federation of Bleachers (E.F.B.) and, after selective strikes (five firms) and the threat of wider action, obtained an 8 per cent rise across the industry for beetlers. (54) Seven strikes were recorded by the Board of Trade in 1910 in cotton bleaching and dyeing, twelve in 1911, and, after a lull in 1912, thirteen strikes in 1913 (up to October).

Work, Wages and Industrial Relations

Much of this action was spontaneous and unofficial and created tensions within unions between the leadership and rank and file activists. The Bolton Amalgamation leadership remained committed to utilisation of the rudimentary disputes procedure (a Conciliation Board had been established in 1907) and protested strongly against the increasing incidence of independent rank and file initiatives:

> We feel it incumbent upon us to enter a strong protest against the growing tendency of members striking without official authority and desire it to be understood that such actions, if persisted in, can only lead to chaos and loss of prestige by undermining the standing of the Executive Council as the appointed and recognised authority to negotiate matters in dispute. (55)

To discipline members, strike pay was refused, as in the Littleborough dyers strike in 1914.

Secondly, union recognition was being extended substantially over 1905-14 to firms which had previously been anti-union. The Wage Agreements File of the Bolton Amalgamation clearly indicates that an increasing number of firms in the trade were committing themselves to a union-employer negotiated standard company wage structure. (56) Moreover, the union succeeded in its 1907-8 campaign to improve the wages of labourers in printworks and gained formal recognition from the C.P.A. and the S.M.C.P. as the negotiating body regarding the wages of such workers. By the end of 1908 the S.M.C.P. had conceded that altered circumstances necessitated acceptance of a standard minimum wage list for all labourers in member firms' printworks. Indeed, the principle of a 21 shillings minimum wage for such labour was being accepted rapidly by finishing employers over 1912-14. (57)

Thirdly, other substantive successes in wages and working conditions were achieved. In 1907, after a threat of industrial action, working hours were reduced to 55½ per week and annual holidays increased by two days, bringing the finishing industry totally in line with cotton spinning and weaving. After the short depression of 1908-9, upward wage drift characterised the years 1910-14 with the finishing employers' organisations, the E.F.B. and the S.M.C.P., unable to prevent wage escalation. For example, "damaging precedents" were conceded by individual firms regarding beetlers wages in 1912 and regarding the concession of time and a quarter pay for overtime over 1913-14. In 1910 the finishing unions also obtained a long sought after reform: inclusion of the industry in the Particulars Clause of the Factory Act. Furthermore, on the eve of the First World War bleachworkers were pressing further into managerial terrain - claiming a bonus for nightwork, abolition of overtime and control over internal promotion procedures in an attempt to neutralise favouritism and prevent management bringing in outsiders. On the latter issue the E.F.B. commented: "This has of recent date been carried so far as to suggest that many working men absolutely deny the right of an employer to use his own discretion as to who is the proper man to fill a vacancy." (58)

The evidence therefore suggests that labour bargaining power in cotton finishing increased markedly in the decade before 1914 and that what Carter Goodrich has called 'the frontier of control' was being pushed inexorably into traditional managerial terrain. Why was this so? How had the situation changed compared to the 1880s and 1890s? To a degree the increasing militancy of bleach and dye workers in the immediate pre-war period was a reflection of a deeper rooted malaise: 1910-14 witnessed a strike wave in British industry of unprecedented proportions, influenced by a release from legal constraints, a broader penetration of syndicalist ideology and 'direct actionism', increased price inflation which eroded real wage levels, very tight labour markets, accelerating union membership and disillusion with the record of the Labour Party in Parliament. Most of these factors affected the cotton finishing industry in varying degrees, though it perhaps ought to be noted that there is no evidence to suggest that syndicalism had any but a marginal influence amongst the Lancashire cotton workers.

However, the changes which occurred within the cotton finishing labour movement over 1905-6 were crucially important preconditions for the subsequent phase of militancy. The Bolton Amalgamation was reorganised over this period with a new, energetic General Secretary, Alfred Smalley, and a new permanent appointment, Robert Kay, as Organising Secretary. A Journal was also established and a recruitment drive initiated. (59) Membership increased rapidly thereafter, thus improving tactical resources and encouraging a more militant strategy in 1906-7 on the beetlers' wages, working hours and holidays issues. Massive successes in 1907 on these questions, coupled with the establishment of a Conciliation Board which formalised trade union recognition, brought in more new members, and the organisation made the crucial shift from representing less than 20 per cent of the workforce in 1905 (5,250) to representing around 50 per cent in 1913 (17,525). 1907 was a crucial year which alone saw an influx of more than 5,000 new members to the union. (60)

The decade before World War One witnessed, therefore, a challenge from labour which resulted in some improvement in wages and working conditions in cotton bleaching and dyeing, the emergence of a mass labour movement and a much broader and deeper rooted recognition of trade unions and their rights. However, whilst employers were clearly on the defensive, this period was still undeniably one of capitalist hegemony. Indeed, over 1905-14 employers in this sector strengthened and consolidated their own organisations, which broadly adopted a conciliatory, flexible and de-escalating labour relations strategy, whilst attempting to improve labour productivity and the wage for effort exchange by extending payments by results systems. Industrial relations, moreover, remained essentially decentralised. Where company wage lists were established and negotiated between trade unions, the company and the employers' organisation rates were quite often 'personalised' to the extent of naming individuals in agreements and their specific time or piece wage rate. Whilst union action was beginning to erode this system (witness the 21 shilling labourers' minimum), nevertheless right up to World War One the E.F.B. continued to claim that "wage demands of a general nature are unacceptable". (61) The old industrial relations system thus died hard.

IV. Female Cotton Finishing Workers

An important feature of the cotton finishing industry, which distinguishes it from other branches of the textiles sector, is the small proportion of females to males employed (see Table 7.4). Female labour was hired by most finishing firms to undertake a range of specific sex-stereotyped tasks - most notably involving hand and machine needlework. Female designated tasks included stitching pieces of cloth to form continuous lengths, sewing silk borders, ribboning and embroidery (termed tambouring), burling and mending, light washing, folding and parcelling. Most female workers were concentrated in the making-up or 'finishing' department - perhaps two-thirds of the total. In the Lever Bank Mill in Bolton in 1891, for example, 35 out of 54 female employees were 'finishers'. Similarly, at Slater and Co., Bolton in 1899, 51 out of 59 women workers were in the making-up department. (62) This kind of distinct sexual division of labour was common to many sections of textiles, though it assumed different forms.

Table 7.4: The Textile Workforce by Gender, 1891

	male	female
Cotton finishing	84%	16%
Cotton spinning and weaving	40%	60%
Wool	50%	50%
Worsted	37%	63%
Silk	35%	65%

Source: Census, 1891

Jill Norris and Deirdre Busfield have recently suggested that female occupations, irrespective of genuine skill content, were devalued, both in terms of status and pecuniary reward. (63) This appears to be true of female employment in cotton finishing. The 1906 Wages Inquiry indicates that adult female workers' average weekly earnings in cotton finishing were 14s.10d, just over 50 per cent of adult male average earnings of 28s.10d. Moreover, skilled and highly complex female tasks such as burling, mending and tambouring commanded under 19 shillings a week in the 1900s, a lower wage than the average male labourers' earnings of 20s.5d. Women were also much more likely than men in cotton finishing to have their remuneration tied directly to their output, hence intensifying their workload. Of 2,333 women and girls surveyed in 1906 in cotton finishing, 1,269, or 54 per cent, were paid by the piece. The corresponding figure for men and boys was 19 per cent on piecework out of 10,314 surveyed. (64)

Why were female wages so poor? The wide wage differentials in cotton finishing (wider than wool and other sections of cotton) were undoubtedly symptomatic of a deep-rooted belief in late Victorian and Edwardian society that female labour power was worth less than male labour power. This conviction was rationalised by employers and management in all kinds of ways: by the argument that male wages should enable support of a dependent family whilst female earnings were 'supplementary'; by reference to female 'inferiority' in physique, strength, and general standards of health, which reduced productivity; and by arguing that female workers lacked commitment and experience because factory work was usually a short interlude before marriage, child bearing and domestic responsibilities. Women had undergone a long socialisation process which had effectively impressed an acceptance of inferiority and subordination upon them. Female cotton finishers, for example, rarely, if ever, openly challenged the fundamental reasoning behind the huge wage differentials between the sexes. This is not to imply, however, that female labour was intrinsically any less militant than male. Despite low levels of unionisation, female workers were involved actively in a number of the major conflicts of this period and could play a decisive role, as in the case of Blair and Sumner's strike in 1893, and the United Turkey Red Company strike (Vale of Leven, Scotland) where over a thousand women struck work in 1911 to gain general wage rises, improvements in work conditions and union recognition. (65)

Table 7.5: Female Membership of Trade Unions in Textiles, 1899 and 1913

	1899	1913
Textile Finishing	325	9,453
Cotton Preparation	20,516	53,317
Cotton Spinning	1,669	1,857
Cotton Weaving	77,391	155,910
Wool and Worsted	1,604	7,738
Silk	177	4,247
Hosiery	2,086	4,070
Linen and Jute	8,102	20,689
Total	111,870	257,281

Source: Abstract of Labour Statistics, 1915, Cd. 7733, pp. 202-3.

As Table 7.5 indicates, in common with women in silk, wool and worsted, female cotton finishers were poorly organised up to 1900. The attitude of established trade unions in cotton finishing to female membership differed markedly, though most discriminated against women to a greater or lesser extent. The Machine Printers' Union, in typical elitist skilled craft society manner simply barred women from membership before World War One. This embargo effectively kept women out of the occupation in England, though in Scotland, where trade unionism had a weaker hold, women were employed on the rougher types of machine printing. (66) The Amalgamated Society of Dyers, Bleachers and Finishers (Bradford) barred women from membership until 1909, when it established special female sections with lower contributions (2d. per week) and lower rates of benefit. (67) The Bolton Amalgamation changed its rules to allow female members in 1891, explicitly because unorganised women were recognised as potential blacklegs during strikes. (68) Membership was free, though 2d. a week gained access to some of the unions' benefits (though not superannuation or accident pay). The female section of the Bolton Amalgamation remained extremely weak through the 1890s and membership was only 477 in 1905, representing around 5-7 per cent of all Lancashire female cotton finishing workers. From this point on, female membership grew steadily, aided by a more positive recruiting policy within the union and by the campaigning support of the Women's Trade Union League. In 1905, for example, two W.T.U.L. organisers, Mary MacArthur and Ada Nield Chew spent a week each speaking and recruiting female finishers in Bolton and Middleton respectively. (69) Female membership of the Bolton Amalgamation thus almost tripled between 1905 and 1908 to 1,381 members and more than doubled again by 1914 to 2,867 members. As a result, women constituted around 16 per cent of total Bolton Amalgamation membership on the eve of World War One.

Despite this surge in female membership evidence suggests that the finishing unions failed to address issues which were of especial interest to women, and particularly that they failed to press for any serious erosion of the wide differentials between male and female earnings. Tacitly, therefore, the male-dominated unions in cotton finishing effectively colluded in the underpayment and undervaluation of female labour power. This was true, for example, of the Bolton Amalgamation. Women appear only rarely in the collective bargaining agreements between the union and individual firms and usually only in the context of setting a maximum adult rate of 15 shillings per week. This was actually 3 shillings below the 'standard' rate laid down in many of these same agreements for 18 year old male workers and yard labourers. Moreover, there are a number of examples amongst these agreements of male workers gaining rises whilst women's rates remained stable, and of the union agreeing separate male and female rates for the same work. (70)

The massive influx of female members into the Bolton Amalgamation over 1912-14 provided the impetus for an initiative by the union, which took up the issue of female wage rates in the spring of 1914, protesting to the Employers' Federation of Bleachers that 15 shillings was not being paid at a number of firms and making a formal claim for a 17 shillings minimum weekly wage for adult women workers. The employers rejected the claim, arguing that to raise female labour costs would force them to decasualise female work and shed labour: "There are a large number of girls whose time is barely occupied but whose services cannot be retained if a higher standard is fixed, many of them doing work which would be too highly paid at this standard." (71) Significantly, after this rebuff in March 1914 the union chose not to press forward with a campaign or with direct action to force employers to concede a minimum wage of 17 shillings for women workers. Nevertheless, wage agreements were being negotiated over this period with individual firms establishing minimum wage rates of 21 shillings for male labourers over 20 years old. Women clearly remained in a subordinate position within the Bolton Amalgamation: the voting power of females was one-third that of males (based on financial contributions); local branch committees included very few women and the National Executive had no female representation at all. (72) There appears to have been neglect, apathy and even discrimination at work here in respect of the position and interests of the minority of female workers in the cotton finishing industry.

V. Conclusions

This chapter provides little more than a brief, cursory reconnaisance of work, wages and industrial relations in cotton finishing before World War One. This industry provides further evidence that fundamental divergences in work experience existed between highly skilled craft artisans and lesser skilled bleachers and dyers, and between male and female employees. The workforce, in other words, was divided both by skill and gender. Craftsmen like the engravers and calico printers retained a position of privilege, high status, high earnings and firm control over the labour process right up to 1914, primarily because of three factors: firstly, strong trade unions; secondly, almost total control over entry to pivotal occupations within the finishing process. This control continued with only marginal erosion even after business 'rationalisation' and labour shedding over 1899-1901, and the establishment of Labour Exchanges in 1909. Thirdly, the drive of cotton printing employers' to rationalise and control work was muted and largely ineffective before World War One because of the weakness of employers' organisations and the conservatism and caution of the dominant combine in the trade, the Calico Printers' Association Ltd., which shirked a radical challenge to unilateral craft control over the labour process. This, it has been argued, was primarily the result of the semi-monopoly market position of the C.P.A., which enabled it to pass relatively high labour costs on to product prices.

By contrast, the work experience of the lesser skilled

bleachers and dyers was characterised by physically arduous and dangerous toil, which was poorly paid, with invariably a narrowly prescribed task range and little autonomy or control over production flows and work rhythms. The correlation between work and ill-health was particularly stark in bleaching and dyeing, with a high accident rate, evidence of debilitating industrial diseases and fatigue and overstrain. Clearly, safety standards were low and there appears to have been little appreciation of the welfarist maxim that improving workers' health and well-being reaped rewards in terms of increased productivity. Up to at least the middle of the 1900s, trade unionism remained extremely weak in this sector and control over entry was virtually non-existent outside the most complex tasks of beetling and calendering. Hence employers were able to keep labour costs low and, in the event of industrial action, invariably succeeded in replacing strikers with imported, blackleg labour. Only in the decade immediately prior to World War One was employer hegemony significantly eroded as membership of trade unions accelerated, strike action increased, wages rose and the employers extended recognition of the union and accepted the principle of a 21 shilling minimum wage for male workers over 20 years.

The minority of female workers in cotton finishing found themselves, not surprisingly, at the bottom of the occupational hierarchy, confined largely to extremely low paid, repetitive, monotonous, casualised tasks. Females were barred from entering craft occupations like calico printing in England, despite the fact that the employment of women on such work in Scotland clearly indicated that females did not intrinsically lack the strength or aptitude to perform such work. Where women did perform genuinely skilled work, they were usually paid less than a male labourer's wage. Moreover, evidence indicates that the unions of cotton bleachers and dyers discriminated against women. These unions failed to recruit women before the 1890s and then established subordinate sections and failed to address the interests of female employees. In particular, little was done to redress the enormous wage differentials which existed between male and female earnings. This survey of cotton finishing therefore tends to confirm what Jill Norris and Deirdre Busfield have suggested for silk and wool: namely that employers and trade unions alike have colluded in the undervaluation of female labour and the customary sexual division of labour.

In one other significant way work experience varied markedly in cotton finishing. Unlike cotton spinning and weaving, the finishing sector lacked any significant degree of wage uniformity resulting from formal collective bargaining, substantive wage agreements and a disputes procedure in the nineteenth century. This was partly because trade unionism was so weak in cotton bleaching and dyeing and partly because employers' organisation was so poorly developed in calico printing. Despite the creation of centralised Conciliation Boards in the 1900s, the industrial relations system in practice remained rudimentary and largely decentralised right up to World War One. Andrew Bullen has suggested that relative wage uniformity and a sophisticated industrial relations system emerged early in cotton weaving because employers recognised that in a highly competitive industry strong trade unions could perform a useful role in disciplining members and enforcing standard wage lists, thus taking wages out of competition between employers.(73) In cotton finishing, giant combines were able to exert a considerable degree of control over final product prices and thus were able to pass on higher wage costs more easily. Hence such combines lacked the incentive to encourage trade unionism, develop a formal substantive industrial relations system or even, until later, a sophisticated disputes resolution procedure. Wage standardisation between firms in cotton finishing was thus extremely limited and wide differences in remuneration and working conditions between product sections, towns and separate companies continued to characterise the industry through to World War One.

NOTES

I would like to express my thanks to Alan Fowler and Tony Jowitt for comments and particularly to Andrew Bullen for research aid, comments and a number of references. This chapter is based on research funded by the Economic and Social Research Council (E.S.R.C.) reference number FOO232204.

Abbreviations

C.P.A.	Calico Printers' Association Ltd.
S.M.C.P.	Society of Master Calico Printers
E.F.B.	Employers Federation of Bleachers
B.D.M.I.C.	Bleachers and Dyers Mutual Indemnity Company Ltd.
F.I.R.	Annual Report of the Chief Inspector of Factories
A.S.D.	Amalgamated Society of Dyers, Bleachers, Finishers & Kindred Trades
Printers' Union -	Amicable and Brotherly Society of Machine Printers
Bolton Amalgamation -	Bleachers, Dyers and Finishers (Bolton Amalgamation)

    1. Two examples of this neglect of cotton finishing are H.A. Turner, Trade Union Growth, Structure and Policy: A Comparative Study of the Cotton Unions, (London, 1962) and J.L. White, The Limits of Trade Union Militancy: The Lancashire Textile Workers, 1910-14 (Westport, U.S.A., 1978).
    2. G. Turnbull, A History of Calico Printing in Great Britain (Altrincham, 1951), pp. 12-30.
    3. 17th Abstract of Labour Statistics (U.K.), 1915, Cmd. 7733, p. 295. On the industry in Scotland see J. Butt and K. Ponting, eds., Scottish Textile History (Aberdeen, 1987).
    4. Worralls Cotton Spinners' and Manufacturers' Directory, 1884.

5. B.D.M.I.C., Minutes, 28 June 1898 (Greater Manchester Record Office).
6. The Monopolies and Restrictive Practices Committee, Report on the Process of Calico Printing, (London, 1948), Appendix 7, p. 114. See also the Cotton Factory Times, 30 Nov. 1906, p. 4.
7. See G. Turnbull, op. cit., pp. 42-3 and ch. 4. The subsequent and final processes of making-up and packing could be either performed by the finisher or, as Alan Fowler has shown, directly by the merchant who also warehoused the finished product. See A. Fowler, 'Twentieth Century Trade Clubs: A Study of Cotton Trade Unionism', Textile History, No. 4, 1973, which analyses unionisation amongst these employees.
8. A.S.D., Occupations and Wages Lists, 1894-1903, Bradford Local Archives, 126.D77/8. See also the Bolton Journal, 2 Sept. 1893, p. 8.
9. Earnings and Hours Inquiry, Vol. I, Textiles Trades, 1909, Cmd. 4545, pp. lxxii-iii; 226-7.
10. Agreement, 19 Jan. 1905, between the Engravers' Union and the Master Engravers Association. C.P.A., Correspondence File No. 167, C.P.A. Archives, Manchester Central Library.
11. C.P.A. Survey, 9 May 1910. C.P.A. Correspondence File No. 76.1., C.P.A. Archives.
12. S.M.C.P., Minutes, 5 Jan. 1911 (Greater Manchester Record Office).
13. Board of Trade, Annual Report on Strikes and Lock-Outs, 1913, p. 135; C.P.A. Correspondence File, 167.
14. Earnings and Hours Inquiry, op. cit., p. 226. Makers-Up occupied a similar position amongst the 'labour aristocrats' of the cotton textile industry. See Fowler, (1973), op. cit., pp. 86-7, 90.
15. H.A. Turner, op. cit., p. 176.
16. Board of Trade, Report on Trade Unions, Cmd. 422, 1900, pp. 62-3.
17. S.M.C.P., Minutes, 5 Feb. 1906.
18. Ibid., 4 Sept. 1906; 8 Nov. 1906; 4 Nov. 1910; 5 Jan. 1911; 16 Jan. 1912; 13 Jan. 1913. C.P.A., Managing Directors' Minutes, 1 Oct. 1901 (C.P.A. Archives M75). Bolton Journal, 17 May 1907.
19. S.M.C.P., Minutes, 1 March 1907.
20. A.S.D., Piecework Particulars at the Branches of the C.P.A. Ltd. File, Bradford Archives, 126.D77/12.
21. C.P.A. Correspondence File 10.1 (C.P.A. Archives M75).
22. S.M.C.P., Minutes, 17 Oct. 1905; 23 Oct. 1905; 18 May 1906; 27 Feb. 1908.
23. Ibid., 12 Oct. 1911; 2 Feb. 1912; 2 Dec. 1913.
24. Ibid., 26 March, 1908; 17 July 1908; 3 Dec. 1908.
25. Ibid., 29 Jan. 1909; 1 March 1909; 30 March 1909. The Working Agreement is reprinted in full in G. Turnbull, op. cit., pp. 333-5.
26. See the correspondence between merchants and the C.P.A., 11 Nov. and 12 Nov. 1913, in C.P.A. Correspondence File 167, C.P.A. Archives M75.

27. F.I.R., for 1912, Cmd. 6852, 1913, p. 92.
28. Bolton Amalgamation, Superannuation Files, FT/1/Box 2. Bolton Local Library Archives Dept.
29. F.I.R., for 1905, Cmd. 3036, 1906, p. 150; F.I.R., for 1912, Cmd. 6852, 1913, p. 81; F.I.R., for 1913, Cmd. 7491, 1914, p. 13.
30. See, for example, F.I.R. for 1890-91, Cmd. 6720, 1892, pp. 73-5. On the 'speed-up' of machinery since 1890 see Cotton Factory Times, 30 Nov. 1906, p. 4.
31. F.I.R. for 1910, Cmd. 5693, 1911, p. 233. See also the Bolton Amalgamation, Report and Balance Sheet, 31 October 1913 (Bradford Archives Dept.). For further insights into accidents at work see J. Burns, Tragedy of Toil, Clarion Pamphlet, No. 29, London, 1899; T.A. Brocklebank, Mammon's Victims, (n.d., c.1910-14) and P. Bartrip and S. Burman, Wounded Soldiers of Industry (Oxford, 1983).
32. F.I.R., for 1900, Cmd. 668, 1901, p. 305.
33. Ibid., p. 288; F.I.R. for 1911, Cmd. 6239, pp. 113-14; F.I.R. for 1912, Cmd. 6852, p. 89. The Home Office Accidents Committee added two other causal factors: the 'carelessness of workpeople' and the 'increased speed and pressure of work' (including piecework). See the Report of the Departmental Committee on Accidents, Cmd. 5535, 1911, pp. 13-14, 18-21.
34. B.D.M.I.C., Minutes, 19 Oct. 1906. (Greater Manchester Record Office).
35. F.I.R., for 1912, Cmd. 6852, 1913, p. 88. On employer and state policy regarding industrial health see A.J. McIvor, 'Employers, the Government and Industrial Fatigue in Britain, 1890-1918', British Journal of Industrial Medicine, Vol. 44, 1987. And, on a later period, A.J. McIvor, 'Manual Work, Technology and Industrial Health, 1918-39', Medical History, April 1987, Vol. 31, pp. 160-89.
36. B.D.M.I.C., Minutes, 17 Feb. 1909; C.P.A. Correspondence File 46.6 (Doctors Fees), C.P.A. Archives M75; F.I.R. for 1910, Cmd. 5693, 1911, pp. 63, 87, 94, 102, 128.
37. Forward, 9 Dec. 1911 (letter from G. Dallas, referring to conditions at the United Turkey Red Company).
38. Bolton Journal, 18 May 1906. For an interesting comparison see T.Wyke, 'Mule Spinners' Cancer', ch. 10 in A. Fowler and T. Wyke (eds.), The Barefoot Aristocrats (Littleborough, 1987).
39. Earnings and Hours Enquiry, op. cit., pp. lxxii-iii. 82 per cent of surveyed textile finishing workers in 1906 were paid by time.
40. Bolton Journal, 27 Dec. 1890, p. 8.
41. Ibid., 31 Dec. 1881, p. 8; 14 Nov. 1885, p. 5.
42. William Barlow, born 1901. Oral recording No. 42, 15 Oct. 1981, Bolton Oral History Project (Bolton Local Library).
43. Board of Trade, 17th Abstract of Labour Statistics, Cmd. 7733, 1915, pp. 200-1. See also H.A. Turner, op. cit., p. 173.
44. National Federation of Bleachers, Dyers and Kindred Trades, Balance Sheet and Report, 4 April 1903. Ref. 126.D77/84,

Bradford Archives.
45. H.A. Turner, op. cit., p. 177.
46. Bolton Amalgamation, Report, 12 Nov. 1872 (Bolton Library Archives, FT/1/Box 2).
47. Ibid., Report, 12 Nov. 1887. See also the Bolton Journal 21 June 1907.
48. Ibid., Report, 12 May 1883.
49. J.C. Scholes, History of Bolton (Bolton, 1892).
50. Board of Trade, First Annual Report on Strikes and Lock-Outs for 1888, Cmd. 5809, 1889, pp. 21-9.
51. Bolton Amalgamation, Reports, 20 April 1892; 30 Oct. 1892; Press Cuttings File.
52. Bolton Journal, 2 Sept. 1893, p. 8.
53. The strike is reported in detail in the employers' journal, Textile Mercury, 14 Sept. 1895, p. 216; 12 Oct. 1895, p. 297; 19 Oct. 1895, p. 317; 2 Nov. 1895, p. 357; 9 Nov. 1895, p. 376; 14 Dec. 1895, p. 476. See also the Cotton Factory Times, 30 Aug. 1895, p. 5, and 4 Oct. 1895, p. 8, and the Board of Trade, Annual Report on Strikes and Lock-Outs for 1895, pp. 148-9 (case 747). On strikebreaking in general over this period see A.J. McIvor, 'Employers' Organisations and Strikebreaking in Britain, 1880-1914', International Review of Social History, XXV, Pt. 1, 1984 and A.J. McIvor, 'Employers' Organisations and Industrial Relations in Lancashire, 1890-1939' (Ph.D. thesis, Manchester University, 1983), especially Ch. 6.
54. Bolton Amalgamation, Report, 31 April 1907; 31 Oct. 1907; Bolton Journal, 26 April 1907; 27 Dec. 1907. The growing militancy of the finishing workers is well documented in the Cotton Factory Times; see, for example, 22 June 1906, p. 8; 31 Aug. 1906, p. 3; 5 Oct. 1906, p. 5; 26 Oct. 1906, p. 4; 30 Nov. 1906, p. 4; 5 Apr. 1907, p. 4; 15 Nov. 1907, p. 5; 6 Dec. 1907, p. 3.
55. Bolton Amalgamation, Report, 31 Oct. 1913, and repeated 31 April 1914.
56. Bolton Amalgamation, Wage Agreements, (Bradford Archives, File 126.D77/107).
57. E.F.B., Minutes, 4 April 1913; 29 April 1913; 22 July 1913. S.M.C.P., Minutes, 10 Jan. 1908; 17 Jan. 1908; 27 Feb. 1908; 3 Dec. 1908. C.P.A., Correspondence Files, Letter C. Roberts to J. Christie, 6 Nov. 1911.
58. E.F.B., Minutes, 20 Nov. 1913. On the other challenges to employers' rights see E.F.B., Minutes, 6 March 1912; 29 Oct. 1912; 31 Jan. 1913; 8 May 1914.
59. Bolton Amalgamation, Report, 31 Oct. 1906. Smalley later defected to the employers, becoming Secretary to the Employers' Federation of Bleachers in 1915 and a representative on their Executive Committee.
60. Bolton Amalgamation, Reports and Balance Sheets, 1905-14, Bradford Archives, 126.D77/114; Cotton Factory Times, 21 June 1907, p. 8.
61. E.F.B., Minutes, 4 March 1913; 9 Sept. 1913.
62. Lever Bank Mill, Piecework Wages Account Book, 1886-92.

(Bolton Library Archives, ZLB/13/8) Slater and Co. Watermead Works, Wages Book, 1899 (Bolton Library Archives ZSL/27).
63. See D. Busfield, ch. 8 and J. Norris, ch. 10.
64. Earnings and Hours Inquiry, op. cit., pp. 226-7.
65. C.P.A. Correspondence File 209, C.P.A. Archives M75 (Manchester Central Library). On women in Scottish textiles see E. Gordon, Women and the Labour Movement in Scotland, 1850-1914, (Ph.D. thesis, Glasgow University, 1985) and E. Gordon, 'Women, Work and Collective Action: Dundee Jute Workers, 1870-1906', Journal of Social History, Sept. 1987.
66. G. Turnbull, op. cit., p. 224. A similar position existed in making-up where collective organisation of female assistants to male craft artisans was insignificant before the creation of a separate female society in 1908. See A. Fowler, (1973), op. cit., p. 88.
67. A.S.D., Report, 9-10 Oct. 1909 (Bradford Archives, 126.D77/5).
68. Bolton Journal, 7 Feb. 1891, p. 7; Bolton Amalgamation, Report, 30 April 1891.
69. Bolton Journal, 20 Oct. 1905, p. 3; Bolton Amalgamation, Report, 31 Oct. 1905.
70. Bolton Amalgamation, Wage Agreements, (Bradford Archives File 126.D77/107). See, for example, Agreement numbers 40, 47, 54, 55, 57, 61, 79 and 84.
71. E.F.B., Minutes, 24 March 1914.
72. B. Drake, Women in Trade Unions (London, 1920; Virago edition, 1984), p. 137.
73. See A. Bullen, ch. 2.

Section III.

WOMEN IN TEXTILES

Chapter 8

SKILL AND THE SEXUAL DIVISION OF LABOUR
IN THE WEST RIDING TEXTILE INDUSTRY, 1850-1914

Deirdre Busfield

In the last ten years historians have shown an increasing interest in the subject of "skill" and in particular in its role in explaining working class stratification. (1) However, throughout the debate the relationship which women workers have had with skill has been largely, or even completely, ignored.(2) Most writers seem satisfied that if they invoke "custom" or "tradition" they have said all there is to be said on the issue of women and skill. In fact, of course, this simply begs more questions than it answers. As Ester Boserup has pointed out in her study of women in both developed and developing countries, the pattern of sex roles, with men in the skilled and supervisory work and women doing the unskilled and subservient jobs, is not a universal norm but is found only in modern, urban economies. (3)
   The majority of women in manufacturing industry in the nineteenth century were "unskilled" or at best "semi-skilled" workers.(4) They commonly earned between one-third and one half of men's wages. (5) This ratio improved only very slowly in the twentieth century and in the late 1960s women still earned less than two-thirds of men's wages. After the Equal Pay Act of 1970 women's earnings rose sharply in relation to men's and stood at over three-quarters in 1977, but since this peak they have begun to decline again. (6)
   Women's low pay was (and is) frequently blamed on the unskilled nature of most of their work and this, Victorians argued, was due to the fact that girls were unwilling to undergo the long periods of training necessary to make them skilled. Women were said to have an "insuperable reluctance" to becoming skilled workers, to sacrifice a little immediate gain for something permanently better in the future. (7) This argument essentially blames women themselves for being low paid. Yet it is clear that even when women did qualify as skilled workers - primarily in the sewing trades - they were not rewarded in the same way as their male counterparts. Skilled male workers usually earned between 50 per cent and 100 per cent more than unskilled workers; they had considerably more job security than other workers and they were

153

Skill and the Sexual Division of Labour

usually people of some authority in the factory or workshop. They saw themselves, and were seen by others, as being superior to the mass of ordinary workers. (8) In contrast, highly skilled women, who had undergone long apprenticeships to become dressmakers or milliners, were compensated with long hours, low pay and irregular employment. Skilled women commonly earned less than unskilled male workers. (9)

It would seem doubtful, therefore, that categorising jobs as "skilled" or "unskilled" gives an objective description of the work content or training involved. Recently, it has been argued that conventional descriptions of jobs in terms of skill are, in fact, "saturated with sexual bias" and it is frequently the sex of the worker, rather than the job the worker does, which determines the way in which it is described. (10)

I. What is Skill?

The word skill is frequently used, but generally with a very imprecise meaning. It is not at all uncommon for workers to be described as "skilled" simply because they earn high wages. There are essentially two ways of looking at the concept of skill. Skill can be defined objectively as "any combination, useful to industry, of mental and manual qualities which requires considerable training to achieve". (11) These qualities include manual facility and knowledge of tools and materials. The traditional way of acquiring such skill was by a long apprenticeship, although by the nineteenth century informal arrangements and various forms of on-the-job training had become more important, especially in the textile trade. Skill, using this definition, is genuine, and the higher status and earnings accorded to skilled workers are a justified reward for their investment in training, and a reflection of their importance in the production process.

However, skill can also be "socially constructed". That is, the description "skilled worker" is essentially a label, denoting social status, which distinguishes one worker from another in order to claim for him special privileges. This is commonly seen as the result of the efforts of a group of workers to improve their own position in the labour force. For example, it has been argued that shipbuilding became, and remained, "skilled" work, whereas docking did not, because shipbuilding workers, unlike dockers, were able, through strong trade union organisation, to exercise control over the manning of machinery and to exclude both management and other workers. (12)

II. How Justified are Skill Definitions?

In the West Riding wool textile industry, as in most other industries, there was a clear demarcation between "men's work" and "women's work" and the two did not, in general, overlap. The majority of women were employed in the intermediate processes -

Skill and the Sexual Division of Labour

feeding the carding engines, worsted spinning, doubling and hanking, warping - and also in the two finishing processes of burling and mending. Men were employed primarily in the initial and finishing processes - woolsorting, willeying and fettling, scouring and milling, raising the nap and shearing, pressing and packing. They were also the spinners in the woollen industry, and overlookers were invariably male. Only in some types of weaving and in machine woolcombing did men and women do the same job, and even here distinctions were often made in the work done by the sexes; for instance, men were said to do "heavier" types of weaving.

Virtually all the jobs done by men in the industry have been described as "skilled" at some time or other, especially by the men themselves, while relatively few women's jobs have been so described, and even those that were did not receive the recognition of high wages. (13) However, a detailed examination of the various occupations in the industry suggests that only woolsorting, an all-male occupation, and mending, an all-female occupation, could really be classed as requiring a high degree of genuine skill.

Woolsorting, the first stage of the manufacture of wool textiles, involved separating the raw wool into different qualities according to such factors as fibre length, strength and softness. Sorting was one of the few occupations in the wool textile industry in the nineteenth century which still required an apprenticeship. It appears that, in the fourteenth and fifteenth centuries, women had been woolsorters; indeed, a statute of 1554 declared that the experience of sorting "consisteth only in women as clothiers' wives and their women servants". (14) However, at some time between the sixteenth and late eighteenth centuries, woolsorting was taken over by men. This seems to have coincided with the growing organisation of the wool trade, and the move away from the sorting of wool by clothiers and their families in their own homes, to the sorting of the raw material by workshop-based employees of the woolmen and wool staplers (the dealers who acted as middlemen between the growers and the manufacturers and exporters). (15) Once they had taken over the occupation the men succeeded in maintaining their monopoly by refusing to impart their skill to women.

Mending, the only all-female occupation in the textile industry to be regularly described as "skilled", was one of the last operations to be carried out on a finished piece of cloth. It involved removing all the imperfections - broken ends were repaired, knots which had been put in by spinners and weavers were removed and the ends sewn in, uneven patches were completely unpicked and replaced. It was dependent on the skill of the mender whether a piece of cloth could be sold at full price as "perfect" or whether it had to be marked down as "imperfect".

Skilled though it was, mending did not require an apprenticeship or any kind of formal training. It was assumed that all girls had been taught some sewing from their mothers, or at school. The special type of sewing required in mending was

Skill and the Sexual Division of Labour

learned by simply watching an experienced mender for some time and then "picking-up" the skill by trial and error, starting on simple pieces and gradually progressing to more difficult ones. It would appear that men were never employed in mending though, of course, many men in the tailoring and boot and shoe industries were highly proficient with the needle and would presumably have been capable of the work.

Both woolsorting and mending were handicrafts using little in the way of mechanical aids; both required a high degree of judgement to be exercised by the worker who had to have a close knowledge and understanding of the materials. Both types of worker operated without close supervision or discipline and in both jobs there was a minimum of subdivision of labour. Both jobs required considerable training; the fact that, in the case of the mender, most of the training was carried out at home rather than in the workplace does not alter this fact. It is interesting to note that while the importance (and probably the difficulty) of mending seems to have been increasing during the late nineteenth and early twentieth centuries, the skill content of woolsorting appears to have been declining, since around this period firms of spinners and staplers began to reduce the amount of fine sorting they did and "sorting in bulk" became more common. (16)

The status of the woolsorter remained high, however. They were respected members of the textile factory workforce who, with the woolspinners, were said to have "despised the company of men in ordinary grades of labour". (17) Menders had once been "the female aristocrats of the textile industry", but by the end of the century the growth of commission mending (carried out by specialised firms rather than on a manufacturer's own premises) and the increasing use of younger workers, had led to a decline in the position of the mender. The competition between commission mending firms resulted in a lowering of wages, increasing use of overtime, and a growing amount of home working by menders which the women, few of whom were members of a trade union, were powerless to resist. (18).

The difference in the position of the mender and the sorter is clear from the average wages of the two groups. In 1886 woolsorters in Bradford earned just over 28 shillings a week while in Leeds and Huddersfield the figure was around 26 shillings. Menders in Huddersfield and Bradford, on the other hand, earned an average of 14s 9d., while in Leeds it was only 13s 10d. In 1906 menders in Huddersfield apparently averaged 17s 4d, although in Halifax it was only 15s 1d. and in Bradford 15s 3d. Sorters in Huddersfield earned 27s 10d., in Halifax 29s 5d. and in Bradford 32s 1d. (19)

The sexual division of labour in spinning is one of the most interesting in the textile industry because it had been, for generations, a female speciality which, after mechanisation, came to be divided into two distinct types - one performed by young girls and boys and described as "unskilled", and one carried on by adult men and described as "skilled".

Hand spinning involved the continual drawing out and twisting of the yarn and required considerable skill to produce a thread of consistent quality. It has been said that at one time virtually every cottage in the land had its spinning wheel, but not every spinner was equally skilled, as is clear from the constant complaints from clothiers about the variable quality of the yarn they received. (20) The first successful spinning machine, the "jenny", did not reduce significantly the skill required by the spinner although it did enable her to increase greatly her output by the operation of a number of spindles - initially eight - simultaneously. Small jennies were used widely in the cotton and woollen industries by women in their own homes, but when larger machines, with 60, 80 or even 130 spindles were produced they were generally grouped together into workrooms and small factories and were operated by adult men with the aid of children to piece together the broken ends.

It has been argued that before the invention of the jenny "the force of custom prevented men from engaging in any appreciable numbers in what was regarded as women's work". Men began to spin "only when a new machine appeared, the effective management of which demanded both strength and skill. The new machine was the jenny." (21) Leaving aside the unlikely suggestion that women were incapable of the skill involved in operating the jenny, we have the contention that this machine required the strength of adult men. In fact, the strength requirement of the jenny seems to have been limited, since, unlike the slubbing billy and the mule which came later, the spindles on the jenny were fixed and did not have to be pushed and pulled by the spinners. This issue of strength will be returned to shortly, but it seems clear that (as in the case of woolsorting) the crucial change for women was not the development of a new technology as such, but the shift of production out of the family home and into workshops where many women, especially married women with children, were unable to follow.

The jenny was not suitable for producing very fine yarn, nor for the highly-twisted worsted yarn, which continued to be spun on the one-thread wheel until Arkwright's water frame was adapted to accommodate it in the late eighteenth century. The frame, and the throstle which developed out of it, considerably reduced the skill content of spinning; the operator's job was simply to replenish the slivers, piece together the broken ends and remove the bobbins when filled with yarn. In the worsted trade in the nineteenth century throstle spinners were primarily young girls and boys under 18 years old, with a few adult women also involved. (22)

The introduction of Crompton's mule, greatly improved the mechanised spinning of fine cotton yarn and softly-twisted woollen yarn. On the mule the spindles, several hundred of them, were mounted on a moving carriage which the spinner pulled towards him as he drew out the yarn and inserted the twist, and then pushed back again as he wound the yarn onto the cop. While the mule reduced the amount of skill required to spin it did not, at this stage, become a simple mechanical process and the spinner was required to exercise a degree of skill and judgement at various

Skill and the Sexual Division of Labour

points in the operation. From their introduction, first in the cotton industry and later in wool, the mules were operated by adult men who are generally described as "highly skilled". (23) In the cotton industry the mule spinners became an elite among the factory workers, and while the status of wool spinners was probably not as high, they were still considered (along with wool-sorters) to be a "cut above" the rest of the workforce. (24)

Why did women not become mule spinners? Certainly mule spinning was more skilled than throstle spinning, but it seems unlikely that it was more skilled than either jenny, or for that matter, hand spinning. In any case, in the 1830s a self-acting mule was invented which greatly simplified the process of spinning and its designers undoubtedly believed that it would henceforth be operated by women and children. (25) In fact, the male spinners, in general, successfully resisted the introduction of female labour and continued to monopolise the occupation, although they did accept the "speeding up" of the machinery and an increased number of spindles. (26) Before the introduction of the "self-actor" women were employed on small mules in some areas, and after the 1830s a system existed whereby teams of women, supervised by male overlookers, operated mules in the Glasgow cotton industry and in the woollen industry in the west of England. However, this was very much the exception to the rule. These women were never referred to as "spinners" but described as "piecers" although they did essentially the same work as the male mule spinners. (27)

There are a number of other factors which might explain why mule spinning became virtually an all-male occupation. Returning to the question of strength, it does seem that operating the early, manual mules was a strenuous operation which might have been beyond the physical capabilities of most women. (28) The problem with this argument is two-fold. Firstly, as Cynthia Cockburn has pointed out, although in general women are less strong than men, they have also been excluded from a variety of activities which would have increased physical ability. From early childhood boys are taught to develop their muscles and to become more "physically effective" than girls. (29) In any case, at the same period when women were excluded from mule spinning and other jobs in the textile industry because they were "too heavy", women and quite young girls were employed to haul loads of coal weighing up to 10 cwt. underground in mines in eastern Scotland and parts of England (30) And, of course, it is the case that not all men are strong. (31)

The second point to be made about strength is that in a mechanised industry sheer physical strength should be irrelevent for most jobs. The essence of the period which we call the Industrial Revolution was, as Peter Mathias has said, to give "increasing freedom from the old traditional limitations of nature, which had been imposed upon the economy in all previous ages". (32) The Industrial Revolution meant freedom from reliance on water and windpower and from "the limitation of strength in animal power or human muscle". Or, as William Lazonick put it, if it were merely the superior strength of men which was preventing the use of cheaper and more docile women workers in spinning, then "the enterprising capitalists of the day would surely have found ways to eliminate the strength factor in the operation of the mule". (33)

Another factor which, it has been argued, made mule spinning a male occupation relates to the exercise of authority. Skilled craftsmen were usually in a position to exercise authority over others in a factory or workshop; women workers seldom were. Lazonick maintained that because mule spinners had to direct a team of other workers they had to be male. Men, he argued, were more "productive" in this supervisory role because they were able to command the "respect" of their assistants and could provide the necessary discipline, and physical punishment, to keep them working at maximum output. (34) This question of authority could apply to a number of other occupations in the textile factory, most obviously to overlooking; women were never considered as overlookers.

To sum up so far, most jobs in the wool textile industry, apart from sorting and mending and some engineering occupations, could be said to have required only a "knack" or a "technique" which could be learned with only a little training, followed by a period of repeated practice to attain maximum speed and efficiency. Manual ability was limited and a relatively small amount of thought was generally required. (35) While not, of course, arguing that there was no genuine skill in any men's work, it is true nevertheless that, time and again, work of this routine nature has been described as "skilled" when performed by men, and as "unskilled" or "semi-skilled" when performed by women - and remunerated accordingly.

In some cases men have been described as "skilled" simply because they earned higher wages than women. In other cases what was referred to as skill in relation to men's work was no more than physical strength, or the exercise of authority. It is also the case that skilled work, when done by women, has been undervalued. As Maxine Berg has pointed out, women are often said to be preferred for some jobs because of their "nimble fingers", their delicacy of touch, their powers of concentration on tedious processes, but these abilities are never classed as skills and are certainly never rewarded with high wages. (36) Jill Norris has proposed the concept of "social destruction" of skill, in contrast to the "social construction" of skill. By this she means the systematic devaluation of a skill possessed by a worker simply because that worker is a woman. (37) Mending in the wool textile industry would appear to encapsulate this concept.

III. Why Did Women Not Acquire Skill?

When considering this question it is necessary to keep in mind the two concepts of skill and to realise that women failed to acquire both genuine and socially constructed skill. In those cases where skill was genuine, the most obvious way to exclude women was to deny them the necessary training. The traditional

Skill and the Sexual Division of Labour

method of acquiring skill was by the completion of an apprenticeship and this has remained a requirement for many skilled trades right up to the present day. Apprenticeship served two main purposes - it was a method of transmitting and maintaining standards of craftsmanship, and it was a way of restricting entry to a trade in order to ensure an artificial shortage of a skill and so keep wages high. Much of the recent debate over skill has centred on the extent to which the trade union regulated apprenticeship of the nineteenth and twentieth centuries has served the second rather than the first of these functions. (38)

There is little evidence about girls and craft apprenticeship in its early period, but it does seem that some were enrolled as apprentices and admitted to the craft gilds on completion of their terms, especially in the textile trades, (although most of the skilled trades open to women, such as millinery, upholstery and muff-making, were not organised into gilds). However, from the mid-fifteenth century onwards it appears that women were gradually excluded from the male-dominated gilds. (39) Many women continued to receive informal training in skilled crafts from their fathers but, in general, they were taught only enough to make them useful as assistants and not enough to allow them to pursue a craft independently. (40) In any case, if they attempted to work on their own, outside the family, without having completed an apprenticeship, they could fall foul of the law. (41) Thus, long before the period under consideration here, women had been denied craft training. The sexualisation of skill is by no means a new phenomenon.

In the nineteenth century informal, on-the-job training was the most important way of acquiring skill in the textile industry. Many textile workers entered the industry as half-timers at the age of 11 when they usually worked as "doffers", exchanging the full bobbins of yarn for empty ones on the spinning frames. Once they were 13 they became full-timers. In the worsted industry such youngsters would be spinners until about the age of 18 when the girls would move into drawing, winding, reeling or warping or, alternatively, would become weavers, with a few going into burling and mending. Some boys would train as woolsorters, willeyers and fettlers, warp dressers and weavers and a few would become overlookers. In general there was much greater concern about the future of factory boys than of girls, especially in the early decades of the twentieth century when there was considerable public debate about "blind alley" occupations for boys. (42) Employers often made some form of arrangement with a boy's parents, agreeing to see that he was taught a specific trade in a certain period of years. (43) Boys were not encouraged to stay in the industry after their mid-teens unless they were to be trained in this way. On the other hand, the training of girls appears to have been haphazard and generally had little to do with the employer. A girl either picked up knowledge over the years by watching older workers, or else her parents paid a small sum for her to be taught by an experienced worker. (44)

Another factor which, it may be argued, held girls back from

Skill and the Sexual Division of Labour

obtaining skilled jobs was their generally poor educational attainments. Certainly the Factory Inspectors pointed out that many girls never attended school at all in the days before compulsory education. They were often employed as nursemaids, or kept at home helping with housework or younger children until they were old enough to work full-time. Boys, on the other hand, were more likely to begin work as half-timers and so receive some education, however rudimentary, since half-day attendance at school was compulsory for all factory children. (45)

Even after compulsory education was introduced, girls were often kept away from school to help at home - either on a regular basis, such as every wash-day, or for long periods at a time. (46) Once at school, most girls would learn something of the 3 Rs but there was also great emphasis placed on teaching them domestic skills, since it was believed that compulsory attendance at school made it less likely that these would be learned at home. (47) Nor could any deficiency of the day-school system be easily remedied by attending at adult evening classes, as those which were available to women were, until the early twentieth century, highly restricted. Reading and writing plus domestic subjects such as cookery and sewing were virtually all that was offered to women since the organisers, whether middle class philanthropists or working class men, shared a common view that although adult education for men should be aimed at improving them both as individuals and as workers, adult education for women was often intended to fit them to be the wives and mothers of the future. (48)

IV. The Role of the Trade Union

It is undoubtedly true that in the nineteenth century the male-dominated trade unions played a major role in the exclusion of women from a variety of skilled (and not so skilled) occupations by, for example, refusing to accept female apprentices or by denying women membership of the union which controlled entry to a particular trade. The battle over access by women to skilled jobs was perhaps most bitter in the printing trade but unions representing workers as diverse as miners and carpet weavers, tailors and engineers, metal workers and bookbinders, fought to exclude women from their employment. (49)

In 1829 the male mule spinners' conference declared that "no person or persons be learned or allowed to spin except the son, brother or orphan nephew of spinners and the poor relations of the proprietors of the mills".(50) From this period onwards male mule spinners succeeded in strictly controlling entry to their trade, excluding women, enforcing apprenticeship and seniority rules and resisting the efforts of employers to "deskill" their occupation. H.A. Turner has been most influential in propounding the view that groups of workers who have built strong trade unions have been able to maintain, or in some cases even create, skill, in the face of hostile employers whose interests lay in the unrestricted access to, and so cheapening of, industrial skills.

Skill and the Sexual Division of Labour

He argued that workers were skilled or unskilled "according to whether or not entry to their occupation is deliberately restricted and not, in the first place, according to the nature of the occupation itself" and he believed that the mule spinners were a classic example of this. (51)

It is sometimes suggested that the hostility of male trade unions (and the craft gilds before them) towards women workers was not because they were women per se, but because they were unskilled workers who were being used by the employer to "dilute" the craft skills of the men. (52) And yet, the trade unions (and gilds) were quite prepared to share their skill with properly regulated male apprentices - it was only females they excluded. In addition, it is the case that women were only available to be used as agents of deskilling because male workers insisted that they had a right to earn higher wages than women. In particular, it was argued from about the middle of the nineteenth century onwards that the man should be considered as the "breadwinner" of the family and so be paid a "family wage", i.e. one that was sufficient to support a dependent wife and children. The converse of this was that women were paid very low wages, justified on the grounds that they were supported, at least partially, by a husband or father. They were thus available as a pool of "cheap labour". (53)

V. The Role of the Employers

The ability of unions to deny women access to skill was limited by the extent to which they controlled employment conditions in their trade. A number of writers have argued that, contrary to Turner's thesis, most unions were not able to impose skill definitions - and the consequent wage differentials - on employers who were determined to resist them. (54) Therefore, as Charles More has said, where social construction of skill by trade unions took place "there had to be acceptance, if not active compliance, from employers". (55)

It is certainly the case that the male mule spinners' union in the woollen industry was by no means as strong as its counterpart in the Lancashire cotton trade and it is hard to see how it could have enforced the skill differentials if employers had been determined to resist them. Yet, as in the cotton industry, mule spinners in the West Riding woollen industry were all relatively highly paid men. Woolsorters had a weak union in the late nineteenth century and yet employers made no systematic effort to introduce cheaper, female labour into sorting. Male weavers in the Huddersfield area were better organised than elsewhere in the West Riding but their union was still not strong. Yet, as one Huddersfield manufacturer told the Royal Commission on Labour in 1892, it was "the custom of the district" to give women only simpler, cheaper types of weaving and reserve more complicated, higher paid work for men. (56) A number of textile employers refused to employ married women, a frequent demand by male trade

Skill and the Sexual Division of Labour

unionists who claimed that they were taking jobs from men "who were the legitimate breadwinners". (57) It is perhaps significant that "prejudice against married women is strongest in Huddersfield", which was also the area where the men's union was strongest. (58)

Employers may have feared the costs involved in a dispute with their male workers; but, on the other hand, the costs involved in paying male workers so much more than women must have been high in an industry where anything up to 50 per cent of the workforce might be male. Alternatively, employers may have believed that women were simply less productive workers than men. Sidney Webb certainly argued in 1891 that "where inferiority of earnings exist (between men and women doing the same work) it is almost always co-existent with an inferiority of work". (59) Webb, and others, argued that women's "net advantageousness" (his phrase) to an employer was less than men's because of the restrictions (particularly on night work and overtime) placed on women's work by the Factory Acts; the inability of women workers to perform simple repairs on their machine or to "tune" their looms; and the fact that women could not be promoted to senior positions since "male operatives would not accept a woman supervisor". Women were also said to be more subject to absence through ill-health, their bosses could not "swear comfortably" at them, and they tended to "go off and get married just as they were beginning to be of some use". (60)

There are two main problems with this argument. In the first place many of the disadvantages attributed to women workers were red herrings. The ability to tune looms was unimportant in many textile factories as loom engineers were employed to do this work. There is no evidence that the Factory Acts prevented textile firms from working more hours than they wished since the Bradford woolcombers' solution of operating men-only night shifts was presumably open to them. Men were more prone than women to absence through drunkenness, and were equally likely to leave their jobs, albeit not on account of marriage. In the second place, many of the problems apparently associated with women workers should have discouraged employers from hiring any at all. In fact, of course, employers, especially in the textile industry, were quite willing to hire large numbers of women in those occupations which were seen as suitable "women's work". The cheapness of women's labour, their apparent willingness to perform routine, monotonous work, and their renowned "docility", would appear to have overcome any disadvantages where these jobs were concerned.

On the whole, it would seem that employers were willing to accept their male workers' assumption of superiority over their female workers except where, as in the case of the printing industry, the men demanded what were considered to be totally unrealistic wage differentials.

VI. The Sexual Division of Labour

The sexual division of labour, both in the home and at the workplace, was so deep-seated that, leaving aside the real obstacles in their paths, it was virtually impossible for women to aspire to skilled jobs where those jobs were clearly recognised as "men's work". Even today, those who lament the scarcity of women in skilled occupations - especially in the engineering and scientific fields - are liable to be told, "But women don't want those jobs". Undoubtedly, in the nineteenth century many women would not have wanted to do the skilled work done by men, even if it had occurred to them that they were capable of it. For example, an investigator in a 1904 survey of women in the printing industry said that when women were asked why they did not attempt certain jobs which were clearly within their capabilities, they usually replied, "Why that's men's work and we shouldn't think of doing it", this reply being given with "a toss of the head and a tone insinuating that there was a certain indelicacy in the question". (61)

In general, "men's work" and "women's work" did not overlap and the implication was that this division of labour was somehow "natural". In fact, of course, ideas about what is "women's work" vary greatly, not only over time and across cultures, but also from region to region and industry to industry within the same period and society. In one society tree-felling will be an exclusively male occupation but in another exclusively female. Cooking in one culture is an all-female occupation and an all-male occupation in another. (62) In nineteenth century Northumberland and Durham it was not considered suitable for women to work in the coalfields but this was normal practice in Wigan, St. Helens and Lancashire, while in the Black Country brickmaking was a women's trade, but in Lancashire it was an all-male preserve. (63)

VII. Skill and Masculinity

The nineteenth century feminist Cicely Hamilton said that "women's work is the kind of work which men prefer not to do". (64) Equally, "men's work" is "men's work" because men say that it is, and "men's work" is "skilled" and "women's work" is "unskilled" for the same reason. It is quite clear that working class men (and in particular the male-dominated trade union movement) have been in the forefront of the struggle to deny women access to skilled jobs. Male workers appear to have identified skill status with masculinity and consequently to have felt a deep personal need to label their work as skilled in order to differentiate it from women's work, so maintaining existing power relations both within the home and at work. (65)

In the clothing industry in the inter-war years, for example, male machinists - who were largely Russians and Poles who had been excluded from the genuinely skilled jobs by their immigrant status - fought successfully to have the work they did defined as

Skill and the Sexual Division of Labour

"skilled" and so distinguished from women's machining which was classified as "semi-skilled". This struggle over the skill label was apparently closely associated with the men's need to maintain their traditional authority within their families, an authority which would have been undermined were they to have been denied superior status to women. (66) Similarly, in the modern printing industry, the introduction of new technology has meant that male printers no longer operate linotype machines but tap out text on computer terminals with keyboards like typewriters. As a result many men feel degraded at having to do work which is essentially no different from that performed by women typists. They feel that their identity as men is threatened by the change. (67) If skilled status is so important to a man's self-respect, one might ask how men compensate who are clearly in jobs which are unskilled? The evidence would suggest that they gain satisfaction from doing heavy manual labour which is clearly beyond the physical capabilities of most women. (68) The man wielding the pickaxe has no doubts that he is in a masculine job.

Women's failure to acquire skill, and the earnings and status which go with it, is essentially a reflection of their position in the wider world and in particular their subordinate role within the family; the sexual division of labour in the workforce simply mirrors that within the home and family, and from the late nineteenth century onwards women were fixed even more firmly than before in the domestic sphere. It has been argued here that working class men on their own could not have constructed skill against women and that they were supported, tacitly or openly, by their employers. This is the result of the patriarchal nature of our society. All men, both as employers and as workers, have a vested interest in maintaining the patriarchy since they control all avenues of power - economic, military, religious, etc. But, as Heidi Hartmann has pointed out, our society is also hierarchical, with men of different classes, races and ethnic groups occupying different places in the hierarchy. And, she commented, "hierarchies 'work' at least in part because they create vested interests in the status quo." Those at the higher levels "buy off" those at the lower levels by offering them power over those still lower. "In the hierarchy of patriarchy all men, whatever their rank in the patriarchy, are bought off by being able to control at least some women." (69)

VIII. Conclusion

The term skill has been used, at least in the textile industry, largely as a way of distinguishing between men's and women's work and not as an objective description of the requirements of a job. In reality there was very little difference in the skill content of much of the work done by men and women but, as it was important to men to maintain superior status in the workforce, the label "skilled" was employed. Male occupations were thus upgraded and female occupations were downgraded. Where genuine skill did

Skill and the Sexual Division of Labour

exist in some all-male occupations men succeeded in reserving it for themselves by the exclusion of women from apprenticeships and other forms of training. Elsewhere, women were denied membership of the trade union which controlled entry to a particular occupation. In the final analysis though, it was often the employers' willingness to support conventional skill definitions which relegated many women to the ranks of the unskilled. In some cases women's work was skilled but their skill was undervalued. Other occupations open to women - particularly in the sewing trades - were greatly overcrowded and as a result the skill involved lost the scarcity value necessary to produce higher wages. All these factors were compounded by the lack of worker organisation in women's trades both before and after industrialisation. (70)

In the textile industry in the nineteenth century traditional measurements of skill such as apprenticeship had largely disappeared. However, the male workers' need to see themselves as superior to the women with whom they worked had not; indeed, in an increasingly hostile work environment, it was probably growing, and the patriarchical nature of society was both a cause of, and a means of facilitating, this need. Where possible the most skilled jobs were reserved for men - but in the absence of skill the process was reversed and men's jobs were simply labelled as skilled.

NOTES

1. Interest in skill has gathered pace since the publication of H. Braverman, Labor and Monopoly Capital (London, 1974), although the issue of skill and the division of the working class was raised much earlier by E.J. Hobsbawm in "The Labour Aristocracy in Nineteenth Century Britain" in Labouring Men (London, 1964).

2. Those who have written on the issue of women and skill have tended to publish in feminist or sociological books and journals and it has, apparently, been easy for "mainstream" historians to overlook their work. See, for example, A. Coyle, "Sex and Skill in the Organisation of the Clothing Industry" in J. West (ed.), Work, Women and the Labour Market (London, 1982); A. Phillips and B. Taylor, "Sex and Skill; Notes Towards a Feminist Economics" in Feminist Review, 6, 1980; V. Beechey, "The Sexual Division of Labour and the Labour Process; a Critical Assessment of Braverman" in S. Wood (ed.), The Degradation of Work? (London, 1982).

3. E. Boserup, Women's Role in Economic Development, (London, 1970), p. 140.

4. J.D. Milne, Industrial Employment of Women of the Middle and Lower Ranks, (London, 1870), pp. 207, 236. See also, S. Alexander, "Women's Work in Nineteenth Century London: a Study of the Years 1820-50" in J. Mitchell and A. Oakley (eds.), The Rights and Wrongs of Women, (Harmondsworth, 1976), pp. 72-4.

Skill and the Sexual Division of Labour

5. In the 1886 wage census women's average wage was 10s.10d. compared with the men's average of 25s.5d; in the 1906 census women earned an average of 12s.5d. while men earned 30s.4d. See; Rates of Wages in the Principal Textile Trades, Parliamentary Papers, 1889 LXX; Rates of Wages in the Minor Textile Trades, P.P. 1890 LXVIII; Wages of the Manual Labour Classes, P.P. 1893-4 LXXXIII; Inquiry into the Earnings and Hours of Labour of Work-People, P.P. 1909 LXXX; War Cabinet Committee on Women in Industry; P.P. 1919 XXXI.

6. Equal Opportunities Commission, Eighth Annual Report, (Manchester, 1983), pp. 89, 91.

7. H. Bosanquet, "A Study in Women's Wages" in Economic Journal, 12, 1902, p. 49; G.M. Oakeshott, "Artificial Flower Making" in Economic Journal, 13, 1903, p. 130.

8. J. Burnett (ed.), Useful Toil, (London, 1974), pp. 266, 449; E.J. Hobsbawm, op. cit., pp. 275, 291-2, 346.

9. Royal Commission on Labour, P.P., 1893-4, XXXVII, p. 89; E. Cadbury, M.C. Matheson and G. Shann, Women's Work and Wages, (London, 1906), p. 132.

10. Phillips and Taylor, op. cit., p. 79.

11. This is the definition used by C. More, Skill and the English Working Class, 1870-1914, (London, 1980), p. 15.

12. H.A. Turner, Trade Union Growth, Structure and Policy (London, 1962), pp. 114, 164-5, 194. R. Penn, "Skilled Manual Workers in the Labour Process, 1856-1964", in Wood (ed.), op. cit., p. 100.

13. For example, Fettling - R.C. on Labour, P.P., 1892, XXXVI, pt. 1, p. 19; Mule spinning - W. English, The Textile Industry (London, 1969), p. 165; Milling - C.W. Whewell, "Milling and Milling Machinery" in J. G. Jenkins (ed.), The Wool Textile Industry in Great Britain, (London, 1972), pp. 168-9; Warp-dressing - R.C. on Labour, P.P., 1892, XXXV, p. 216.

14. E. Lipson, The History of the Woollen and Worsted Industry, (London, 1921), p. 34.

15. P.J. Bowden, The Wool Trade in Tudor and Stuart England, (London, 1962), pp. 80, 92. See also, K.G. Ponting, The Wool Trade, Past and Present, (Manchester, 1961), p. 11.

16. R.C. on Labour, P.P., 1892, XXV, pp. 252-3.

17. B. Turner, About Myself, (London, 1930), pp. 130-1.

18. Yorkshire Factory Times, 19 April 1895, 3 May 1907.

19. Wages in the Principal Textile Trades, P.P., 1889, LXX; Inquiry into the Earnings and Hours of Workpeople, P.P., 1909, LXXX.

20. J. James, History of the Worsted Manufacture in England, (London, 1857), p. 312; Lipson, op. cit., pp. 64-5.

21. S.D. Chapman, The Cotton Industry in the Industrial Revolution, (London, 1972), p. 59.

22. R.C. on Labour, P.P., 1892, XXXV, pp. 272, 429, 438-9.

23. e.g. H. Catling, "The Evolution of Spinning" in Jenkins (ed.), op. cit., p. 111; English, op. cit., p. 165; I. Pinchbeck, Women Workers and the Industrial Revolution, 1750-1850, (London, 1930), p. 148.

24. See note 17 above.
25. A. Ure, The Cotton Manufacture of Great Britain, (London, 1836), p. 199.
26. H. Catling, op. cit., p. 49.
27. W.H. Fraser, "The Glasgow Cotton Spinners, 1837", in J. Butt and J.T. Ward (eds.), Scottish Themes, (Edinburgh, 1976), p. 97; K.G. Ponting (ed.), Baines' Account of the Woollen Manufacture of England, (Newton Abbott, 1970), p. 164; W. Lazonick, "Industrial Relations and Technical Change; the Case of the Self-Acting Mule" in Cambridge Journal of Economics, 3, 1979, p. 244.
28. Lazonick, op. cit., pp. 234-5.
29. C. Cockburn, "The Material of Male Power" in Feminist Review, 9, 1981, p. 44.
30. First report of the Children's Employment Commission (Mines), P.P., 1842, XVII, pp. 165-6.
31. The Bradford Socialist, Fred Jowett, weighed only 7s. 11bs. at the age of 20 but, believing that confidence was the most important factor in carrying heavy weights, he trained himself to be an overlooker and carry beams of up to 150lbs. each. F. Brockway, Socialism over Sixty Years (London, 1946), p. 21.
32. P. Mathias, The First Industrial Nation, (London, 1969), p. 143.
33. W. Lazonick, "Historical Origins of the Sex-based Division of Labour Under Capitalism; a Study of the British Textile Industry During the Industrial Revolution", Harvard Institute of Economic Research, Discussion Paper no. 479, 1976, p. 10. In fact, of course, non-human power (first water and later steam) was quickly harnessed to the mule which virtually removed the strength requirement; men, however, continued to monopolise mule spinning although they came to operate pairs of mules instead of one.
34. Lazonick, "Industrial Relations", op. cit., pp. 229, 243.
35. Turner, Trade Union Growth, op. cit., p. 111.
36. M. Berg, The Age of Manufactures, 1700-1820, (London, 1985), p. 152.
37. J. Norris, chapter 10. October 1984.
38. eg. More, Skill and the English Working Class, op. cit., and "Skill and the Survival of Apprenticeship" in Wood (ed.), op. cit., argues that, in general, apprenticeship was an efficient method of imparting skills which were valued by employers. Turner, op. cit., holds that skill is socially constructed by trade unions.
39. Pinchbeck, op. cit., p. 121; O.J. Dunlop, English Apprenticeship and Child Labour, (London, 1912), p. 151; A. Clark, The Working Life of Women of the Seventeenth Century, (London, 1919), p. 103; H. Heaton, The Yorkshire Woollen and Worsted Industries, (Oxford, 1920), pp. 38-9.
40. Pinchbeck, op. cit., pp. 282, 160-1; Dunlop, op. cit., pp. 148-9.
41. Heaton, op. cit., p. 103.
42. H. Hendrick, "A Race of Intelligent Unskilled Labourers", History of Education, 9, 2, 1980.
43. See volumes of employment records of T. & M. Bairstow,

worsted manufacturers of Keighley, Leeds Archives Dept.
44. R.C. on Labour, P.P., 1892, XXXV, p. 315; M. Hartley and J. Ingilby, Life and Tradition in West Yorkshire, (London, 1976), pp. 41-2.
45. Half Yearly Reports of the Factory Inspectors, P.P., 1863, XVIII pp. 22-3; 1868-9, XIV, p. 37.
46. The suffragist, Hannah Mitchell, for example, received only "a fortnight's schooling" in the 1870s. H. Mitchell, The Hard Way Up, (London, 1968), p. 46. See also, A. Davin, '"Mind That you do as you are Told" : Reading Books for Board School Girls, 1870-1902' in Feminist Review , 3, 1979, p. 98; E. Roberts, A Woman's Place , (Oxford, 1984), p. 34.
47. C. Dyhouse, "Social Darwinistic Ideas and the Development of Women's Education in England, 1880-1920" in History of Education, 5, 1, 1976, p. 46; also her, "Good Wives and Little Mothers; Social Anxieties and the Schoolgirls' Curriculum, 1890-1920" in Oxford Review of Education, 3, 1, 1977, p. 21.
48. J. Purvis, "Working Class Women and Adult Education in Nineteenth Century Britain", History of Education, 9, 3, 1980, p. 198.
49. B. Drake, Women in Trade Unions, (London, 1920), pp. 20-1, 32-5, 115-17.
50. Quoted in J. Liddington and J. Norris, One Hand Tied Behind Us, (London, 1978), p. 51.
51. Turner, op. cit., p. 114.
52. Dunlop, op. cit., p. 144; Drake, op. cit., p. 9.
53. H. Land, "The Family Wage" in Feminist Review, 6, 1980; M. Barrett and M. McIntosh, "The Family Wage; Some Problems for Socialists and Feminists", Capital and Class, 2, 11, 1980.
54. More, Skill and the English Working Class, op. cit., ch. 7; D.J. Lee, "Skill, Craft and Class; a Theoretical Critique and Critical Case" in Sociology, 15, 1981.
55. More, Skill and the English Working Class, op. cit., p. 163.
56. R.C. on Labour, P.P., 1892, XXV, p. 288.
57. eg. George Thomson, a partner of Thomson & Sons Ltd., Woodhouse Mills, Huddersfield, said he employed no married women on principle, and women already employed by him who got married had to leave their job within six months. R.C. on Labour, P.P., 1892, XXXV, p. 288; Yorkshire Factory Times, 6 December 1889.
58. R.C. on Labour, P.P., 1893-4, XXXVI, p. 102.
59. S. Webb, "The Alleged Differences in the Wages Paid to Men and to Women for Similar Work", Economic Journal, 1, 1891, p. 657.
60. Ibid., p. 645; E. Rathbone, "The Remuneration of Women's Services", Economic Journal, 27 1917, pp. 58-9. See also, M. Fawcett, "Review; Women in the Printing Trades: a Sociological Study, edited by J.R. McDonald", Economic Journal, 14, 1904, and her "Equal Pay for Equal Work", Economic Journal, 28, 1918; F.Y. Edgeworth, "Equal Pay to Men and Women for Equal Work", Economic Journal, 32, 1922.
61. J. R. McDonald (ed.), Women in the Printing Trades, (London, 1904), pp. 65-6.

62. A. Oakley, Sex Gender and Society, (London, 1972), p. 128.

63. J. Lewis, Women in England, 1870-1950: Sexual Divisions and Social Change, (Brighton, 1984), pp. 149-50.

64. C. Hamilton, Marriage as a Trade, (1909), quoted in W. Beveridge, John and Irene: an Anthology of Thoughts on Women, (London, 1912).

65. One might ask what compensation women factory workers were expected to have, especially as they monopolised the most boring, routine types of work? The answer would be that women were expected to gain their primary fulfilment from their families and so were much less dependent than men on their employment to provide them with a personal identity.

66. B. Burnbaum, "Women, Skill and Automation; a Study of Women's Employment in the Clothing Industry, 1946-72" (unpublished paper) quoted in Phillips and Taylor, op. cit., p. 82.

67. C. Cockburn, Brothers. Male Dominance and Technological Change, (London, 1983). This attitude might also explain why men apparently found it so appalling if they were in the position of having to do housework. The Yorkshire Factory Times constantly stressed how "degrading" it was for men to have to cook, clean or look after children.

68. Cockburn, op. cit., pp. 139-40.

69. H. Hartmann, "The Unhappy Marriage of Marxism and Feminism; Towards a More Progressive Union" in Capital and Class, 8, 1979, p. 11.

70. Roger Penn has argued that: "Where workgroups were unable to establish control through social exclusion before the introduction of factory automation no secure basis existed from which to resist changes in the labour process and to establish skilled trades." See, "Skilled Manual Workers" in Wood (ed.), op. cit., p. 90.

Chapter 9

WOMEN AND INDUSTRIAL MILITANCY: THE 1875 HEAVY WOOLLEN DISPUTE

Maria Bottomley

> It's time we stuck up for ahr trade an
> Just made it a livin' for men
> We could do it bi' true combination -
> In fact it just rests wi' oursen   (1)

Women textile workers in Yorkshire have been represented almost without exception as a liability and an obstacle to unionisation. Running throughout trade union history there is often an assumption that women simply did not regard 'work' in the same way as men; that they were not expected to remain in work, leaving to get married and have children; their earnings were looked upon as supplements to the family income, the real 'breadwinners' being the family's male members whilst women's paid work was secondary to their real role as wives and mothers. For men, on the other hand, work was a primary consideration; being a man and being a worker were two sides of the same coin. (2) Men were therefore prepared to make sacrifices to protect their position as workers, by paying union dues or striking, for example, which women, who did not value their role as paid workers, would not do. Any industry which employed large numbers of women was generally viewed with dismay by unions and their historians. Women workers prevented men from organising, put them out of work and dragged down their rates of pay. As the Yorkshire Factory Times commented, they were used by employers "as tools to effect the ruin of their husbands and brothers". (3)

Since women workers were unlikely to organise if left to their own devices, it followed that men needed to take this important task upon themselves, leading the women by example. In 1907 J.H. Clapham surveyed the woollen and worsted industries and noted the weakness of trade unions. He saw the decline in the number of men working together as being partly responsible for this since, he claimed, "it may be taken as an axiom that the organisation of women is never likely to be complete where that of men is defective". (4)

This chapter investigates, in some detail, the 1875 strike in the heavy woollen district, a strike which was overwhelmingly a women's strike showing that women were capable of organising themselves and male workers, that women workers felt attacks on their role as workers as keenly as any man, and that they were just as aware of the need for a permanent union and were prepared to work and fight for it. More importantly, the strike also indicated the kinds of sacrifices that women were prepared to make in defence of their rights and the social pressures they had to face when they did so. Such pressures rarely appear in the lists of reasons as to why women were 'poor' union members, but to be aware of them makes it clear that the apparent reluctance of women to unionise and agitate was not necessarily due to their lack of interest or unwillingness to make sacrifices, but rather to the fact that union activity was considered to be 'a man's question' and therefore unsuitable for women.

The heavy woollen district of the West Riding of Yorkshire consisted of several small towns, around the two commercial centres of the district, Batley and Dewsbury. The area derived its name from the nature of the cloth produced in its mills which differentiated it from its neighbours such as Huddersfield and Bradford. It had been a mainly agricultural district until the early nineteenth century when Benjamin Law developed a process to produce shoddy, and subsequently mungo, from rags to make rag wool which could then be woven into cloth. (5) The new invention was regarded initially with horror by local manufacturers but it was taken up very rapidly because of the large profits that could be reaped through its use. Indeed, by the end of the century rag wool was widely used throughout the woollen industry.

Batley, where Law developed his invention, changed from a 'mere hamlet' to a town with a considerable industry. (6) Its population increased four-fold and the general impression of the town in the mid-nineteenth century was one of growth and prosperity. Samuel Jubb, already in 1860 writing the history of the shoddy trade, stressed the liberal provision of institutions for the "intellectual, moral and religious interests of the people" - churches, schools, the Mechanics Institute, a Town Hall and a savings bank. This prosperity was also reflected in the wages of those employed in the shoddy trade which were said to be higher in this area than in those making finer cloth or than in other areas producing shoddy. (7)

The period up to the early 1870s was generally one of expansion and high profits for local millowners. Herman Burrows, a local manufacturer, wrote of this period as being particularly prosperous for young men setting up in business. He referred to the beneficial economic effects on the area of the Franco-Prussian War, which had resulted in large government contracts for blankets and clothes. However, by 1875 this prosperity "had pretty well worked itself out. Demand had fallen off. Times were difficult in the trade." (8) Market reports in the local press claimed that the 1874 season had been "the worst that has ever been known" and that manufacturers were "apprehensive" that 1875 would not prove any better. Anxious to protect their profits, millowners in the

Women and Industrial Militancy

heavy woollen district appear to have decided that the burden of the recession should be met by their workers.

Early in the new year the local manufacturers' association drew up a new statement of prices to be paid to weavers in the district. (9) The first indication that this was going to cause trouble came on 1 February when weavers at two mills in Batley, Taylor's and Stubley's, struck work when they were informed of the new wage rates. Throughout the week weavers in several other mills in the town walked out as the statement was posted in the sheds. On Friday, the action spread to the neighbouring town of Dewsbury when 300 weavers walked out of Mark Oldroyd's mill claiming that the new statement would mean a reduction of two to three shillings a week. (10)

The manufacturers' association met to discuss the situation and decided that unless the dispute was settled there would be a general stoppage from Saturday, February 13th. It was agreed to meet with representatives of the weavers although the feeling of the manufacturers was very strongly against giving any higher rates, "the present prices allowing no margin for profits". (11) Up to this juncture there was nothing remarkable in the dispute, it being very similar to countless others both in textiles and in other industries. However, at this point the weavers' strike began to develop the feature that made it extremely unusual - its leadership by women.

The introduction of the power loom had opened up weaving as an occupation for women. In the heavy woollen district, a late-comer to the textile trades, power loom technology diffused rather slowly and male weavers were reluctant to leave their handlooms where they were still able to make a good living. (12) Manufacturers therefore used women weavers. The effect of this, according to Sam Jubb, was that "women are quite at a premium in the labour market". (13) It became established practice for heavy wool weaving to be a predominantly female occupation (14), and as Jubb stated, "the wages of females have advanced in a marked degree since the introduction of the power looms". (15) A weavers' strike in the heavy woollen sector would, therefore, inevitably be a women's strike, and in the first week of February 1875 that was the case in Dewsbury and Batley, although a small number of men was also involved. However, the action did not remain confined to the weavers for it soon included virtually all the textile workers in the area as the dispute was transformed into a lock-out. The women weavers, however, maintained a central role as leaders throughout the dispute and, indeed, beyond it.

They assumed this role on the first day of the dispute. The weavers from Stubley's and Taylor's, male and female, held a meeting which broke up without taking any decisions. Dissatisfied, a number of women got together and decided to form themselves into a committee. When the all-male committee representing the Oldroyd strikers was formed at the end of the week, the two groups met to decide on representatives to meet the employers' association. Out of that meeting emerged an all-woman committee of seventeen weavers which eventually met with the employers. As the strike progressed an Executive Committee was formed composed of twelve women to match the twelve men on the Executive Committee of the manufacturers' association.

After the first flurry of activity, many weavers returned to work to finish pieces they had on their looms. This done, they held a meeting on Wednesday of the second week. More than a thousand weavers met to discuss the masters' threat of a lock-out. They met that threat with one of their own: that they would 'stand out' as from 13 February, the day of the lock-out. The manufacturers' association had by now taken to meeting daily and, on hearing of the weavers' decision, declared it "suicidal, seeing that trade is bad and stocks are heavy". (16) Several manufacturers had recently received cancellations of large orders for the United States, where a tariff bill on woollen goods had recently been enacted.

The first offer from the employers was that the weavers could return to work for a month at the old rates whilst a joint committee negotiated a new price list. This was rejected by the weavers. When the suggestion was put to a meeting, one woman stood up and called upon her colleagues not to be fooled: "Were weavers to go back a month to their work they would liberate the masters who had contracts to fulfil, but that would fasten themselves and that they must not do." (17) On the Saturday the masters locked their mills, escalating the dispute from a weavers' strike to a lock-out which affected the majority of textile operatives in the district.

Leadership of the workers remained in the hands of the all-female Executive Committee. Amongst the group, two women were beginning to gain prominence: the president of the committee, Mrs. Hannah Wood and the treasurer Mrs. Anne Ellis. Although as the strike progressed more women came forward to chair and address meetings, it was Hannah Wood and Anne Ellis who were the most prominent figures mentioned in the local press. Both were at pains to point out that this was the first time that they had ever been involved in a labour dispute, although Hannah Wood would later say that the question of a union was one that had interested her "for quite some time". It was Hannah Wood who suggested the formation of an Executive Committee to match that of the manufacturers and showed herself to be familiar with the proceedings of the meetings: putting resolutions, seconding them, taking notes, introducing speakers, giving a vote of thanks and so on. Anne Ellis was described as the main spokeswoman at the early meetings with the manufacturers' association.

Once the strike was coupled with a lock-out the women were having to deal with extremely large numbers of people. It was estimated that 25,000 workers were now involved in the dispute and most of these were people who had been locked out because the weavers had refused to return to work. The majority thus had no immediate grievances with the masters. Somehow, the weavers' committee had to convince them of the validity of the weavers' cause, to retain solidarity and to negotiate with the manufacturers' association. At the first mass meeting of the weavers on the Wednesday before the lock-out, the women faced the difficulty of their position head-on. "This dispute as to wages is more of a man's question than a woman's", said a female weaver, "but we have taken it into hand." "Women are not public speakers", said another, giving the lie to her own words, "but this time they had begun a thing and when women began a thing, they went through with it." (18)

There was an ambivalence about the role the women were playing. One correspondent to the local paper voiced his abhorrence but not all the locals disapproved of what was going on in their district. When male speakers did address meetings they usually included a word of congratulation for the stand taken by the women. On those occasions when the committee openly sought the approval of the workers, votes of confidence would often be proposed by one of the men present. "There was something going on in Dewsbury that never did in another place or country", said one old man, with obvious approval, "ladies coming to the front and talking on labour and they could not find another place in England where they had done that." (19)

This novelty about the strike obviously attracted attention, and the weavers' committee began receiving support from those outside the district and the industry. One of the first 'outsiders' to make an appearance on the platform with the women was J.C. Cox, who had been the unsuccessful Radical candidate for the Dewsbury parliamentary constituency in the previous year. (20) His involvement with the strike caused some controversy for he was known to have friends amongst the Liberal manufacturers who had supported his parliamentary campaign. Cox, however, was keen to support the striking workers and spoke often and at length in their favour. He was also responsible for involving another 'outsider' in the dispute when he informed the National Union of Working Women (N.U.W.W.) about events in Dewsbury and Batley. They sent their secretary, Mr. H.M. Hunt, who arrived in Dewsbury during the fourth week of the strike. His principal concern was to enrol the weavers' into the N.U.W.W. and he remained in the area until the end of the strike. His presence had some influence on the weavers committee for the subject of unionisation becomes a more frequent topic of discussion at the weavers' meetings after his arrival. (21)

Since the meeting between the masters' association and the weavers' committee in the second week of the strike, there had been no contact between the two sides. The manufacturers had taken their stand by offering the weavers the option of returning to work at the old rates of pay, whilst representatives of the two sides negotiated a settlement. This offer came too late, for the weavers had already drawn up their own statement - 'the blue tariff' - which was presented to the manufacturers. (22) This was rejected and 'the blue tariff' became the battle cry of the strike, with the weavers refusing to go back with anything less. Following a meeting at which the two sides failed to come to terms, there was a total break in communication. On the surface this appeared to be due to the non-acceptance of 'the blue tariff', but in fact, during the two meetings of the manufacturers' association and the weavers' committee in the first fortnight of the strike, another issue had surfaced. It was an issue which proved far more effective in keeping the two sides apart than any disagreement over prices paid for weaving.

The first meeting had gone well for the women and they were optimistic about its outcome. This positive impression seems to have been created simply by the fact that "they were received as if they were the highest ladies in the land". The manufacturers' association assumed, perhaps, that as they were dealing with "a few poor deluded women" (as one manufacturer was reputed to have described them), they would only need to apply charm and good manners and that would settle the matter. Unfortunately, they misjudged the all-female weavers' commitee, for when they met a second time to discuss the association's proposal, they found their offer was being refused. The benevolence came to an abrupt end. The women walked out of the meeting claiming they had been "grossly insulted". (23) A later reference by Anne Ellis to this meeting, saying she had been told "she had cheek" to be involved in such matters, suggests that the insults, which neither side made public, were of a personal nature and directed at the committee as women meddling in affairs which did not concern them.

At a meeting in Heckmondwike later in the strike Mrs. White, an Executive Committee member, told her audience that "the only objection" the masters had to increasing wages "was that they did not like to say they had been beaten by women. The masters, however, would be beaten in the long run." (24) This was the attitude that gave the strike its impetus, that pushed the women on, gave them the determination to continue the fight and was the crucial issue along which the battle lines were drawn. For both the employers and the weavers the fact that the conflict was being fought on one side by women and on the other side by men, assumed as great a significance as the question of wages. As the strike wore on, Hannah Wood reported the masters as saying "if they had had men to deal with the dispute would have been settled long since". (25)

The rift between the two sides, caused by the 'insult' of that second meeting, lasted two and a half weeks. In material terms the prolonging of the strike caused great hardship for those either on strike or locked out. Yet, in other ways, it was an important breathing space for the weavers' committee. Free from the immediate concern of negotiating with the manufacturers' association, and now fired with an even greater determination to win, the interval proved to be invaluable. The longer the strike went on the more they grew in confidence and in their abilities to lead and to organise. As the strike developed, so did the women of the Executive Committee.

There appeared, then, to be no prospect of an immediate settlement of the strike and this presented the committee with two main problems. One was the alleviation of the hardship which most of those on strike or locked out were by now facing, and the other was to keep up the morale of those on strike, and to try to maintain the support of those locked out. They dealt with their first problem by organising collections and relief payments: these began immediately the decision to stand out was taken. Not all the mills in the district had been locked for there was some division amongst the manufacturers, particularly in Batley, where a number of mills remained open. Those still at work, therefore, were able to help support those out on strike. The women also sent out collectors to various surrounding districts, receiving financial support from the weavers of Huddersfield amongst others. Money also came in from anonymous sympathisers, radicals like J.C. Cox and the local Co-operative Society. (26) Difficulties arose over the distribution of these funds for it was decided that the weavers should have priority and that money would be paid to them before anyone else. This was obviously an unpopular decision amongst those locked out and caused some ill-feeling. Having made this decision, the committee then had to set about administering the strike pay. There was not enough money to pay everyone, so payments had to be discretionary, 3 shillings being given for the relief of small families, 4 shillings and 5 shillings for those that were larger. (27)

In an attempt to retain solidarity, the Executive Committee called, attended and addressed meetings which also provided opportunities for interested parties and local 'figures' to take the platform and have their say. The meetings were often rowdy; police were present at some of them, although the only violence reported throughout the strike was of a verbal, rather than a physical, nature. At first, when handling these meetings, the women of the committee were undeniably timid. The only one amongst them who seemed to have any confidence at all in her ability to speak to large crowds (the usual attendance appears to have been several thousand), was Anne Ellis. Most of those who took the platform at the earliest meetings were men. With the exception of Mrs. Ellis, the other committee members, including Mrs. Wood, confined themselves to making very brief introductions to these male speakers and equally brief votes of thanks. Their own words usually consisted of an apology for being there and taking up their time, an insistence that they were not really used to doing this sort of thing, and a simple plea for them all to stick together and support the strike. However, as the strike went on, this changed. Addressing large gatherings daily, sometimes twice daily, gradually drew the women out. Their contributions to these meetings became longer and less apologetic. The number of men who addressed these meetings dwindled, until it was they who were confined to passing votes of thanks, or resolutions confirming support for the Executive Committee. More of the committee came forward. The names of Mrs. Ellis and Mrs. Wood continued to feature heavily in the local press, but the names of other women - Mrs. White, Mrs. Abernethy, Mrs. Marsden, Kate Conran - began to appear more frequently.

The strike committee worked hard at encouraging their supporters to stick together but by the third week of the strike many were beginning to suffer and numerous examples of hardship were cited at meetings, compounded by a worsening in the weather. (28) Inevitably, there were calls from all sides for the two committees to resume contact and, eventually, the weavers' committee agreed to a meeting on condition that they did not have to deal with those members of the masters' committee whom they had met with earlier. When this condition was not agreed to, the women stipulated that the press be present throughout the meeting. As a result, the conference which took place between the two committees on 1 March, is recorded in detail in the local paper.

By this stage, the women had drawn up a list of demands which they presented to the manufacturers' association. Heading the list was the statement that they would not accept anything below that stated on the blue tariff. Further, they wanted any statement of wage rates that was agreed to be posted in every shed and any 'irregular practices' that might undermine such a statement to be stamped out; and the number of strings to be woven, to be stated and paid for, thus making it difficult for the length of a piece to be misrepresented.(29) The manufacturers denied all knowledge of any such practices but agreed that should such practices be found to exist they would, of course, be stopped. Agreement on wage rates, however, was not so readily reached. The manufacturers did agree to an advance of $\frac{1}{2}$d. on their previous offer but this was turned down by the weavers on the grounds that this offer also included a $\frac{1}{2}$d. reduction for the dressing of warps. Once again the two sides reached stalemate. The action of the Executive Committee in turning down this offer received overwhelming support when put before workers' meetings, and praise from 'outsiders' like Cox and Hunt. "What a will of power and brain they possessed", declared Cox, referring to the women of Batley and Dewsbury. "He thought they had rather astonished the masters." (30)

Groups of local men, however, began to question the leadership and undermine the strike. On the same day that Cox was extolling the praises of the strike committee, a public meeting was called 'anonymously' in the Market Place at Batley. It was addressed by a number of local dignitaries: Alderman Marriot, Mr. Neal, a member of the local School Board, and Mr. Exley the sanitary inspector, who all expressed their desire to see the dispute brought to a speedy conclusion. They decided that one way of achieving this would be to set up a third committee to act as intermediary between the existing committees. This new committee was to be made up of "six or seven sensible men...who were capable of dealing with this matter". (31) A few days later another 'public' meeting was held, this time addressed and attended by the working class men of the town. The main speaker was Mr. Hunt, who was supposedly in town to enrol the female weavers into the N.U.W.W., but who urged the audience to join the Woollen Operatives' Union. This was said to have existed in the district three years previously but membership had dwindled until there were only six members left. The strike and lock out had aroused interest once again in the idea of a union. Even though this was largely due to the efforts of the women weavers, the opportunity of joining this union was only offered to the male workers. (32)

It appeared that men of all classes were beginning to tire of the women's public profile. The manufacturers thought them 'deluded', the middle classes thought them not 'sensible', and the working men of the town seem to have perceived no continuing trade union role for the women workers after the strike. On all sides it was being made clear that whilst female involvement in the strike itself might be acceptable, any attempt by the women to enter into the arena of decision-making on a more permanent footing was out of the question. This would be an invasion of the territory that was reserved for issues that were 'a man's question', whether that man be a master, an alderman or a textile operative. It was an attitude summed up by one letter writer to the press when he heard the weavers' committee were refusing to meet with the manufacturers' association. "I have no wish to be hard on the poor women of the committee," he wrote, "although I think them very much out of their place." (33)

The women of the Executive Committee increasingly mooted the idea of establishing a permanent trade union. The arrival of Mr. Hunt gave impetus to their discussions and the subject was now raised at every meeting in an effort to ascertain the views of the weavers. Initially, the idea was to join the N.U.W.W. but some of the Executive, particularly Mrs. Wood, were not happy with this suggestion as it would have excluded the male weavers. Before the women could give their full attention to the setting up of their weavers' union, however, they found themselves overtaken by events when, on March 10th, the manufacturers decided to open up their mills. The day before the lock out was due to end, the weavers' executive called mass meetings in Batley and Dewsbury. They explained what the manufacturers' offer of a ½d. advance meant and urged the weavers to continue their strike. There appears to have been no question of asking other workers who had been locked out to stay out in support of the weavers. Resolutions to continue standing out were carried unanimously and when the mills were opened the following day the papers reported that none of the weavers returned to work.

The confidence and determination of the leadership had clearly developed during the dispute, and this was reflected in their conduct during the last phase of the strike. On the day before the lock-out was due to end the weavers had called mass meetings, first in Batley, to be followed by one in Dewsbury. The first meeting went on much longer than intended and by the time the Dewsbury meeting began, it was nightfall. A large crowd of about 9,000, the majority of whom were men, had gathered to hear what the executive had to say. Hannah Wood stepped onto the wagon which was being used as a platform and delivered a passionate speech to this rowdy crowd urging any weavers amongst them not to go back in when the mills were opened. Having done that, she then turned on the manufacturers, whom she described as cowards for issuing their statement without facing the weavers' committee - "they dare not" she said. "No doubt some are at the meeting", she went on, "and they will know my opinion of those who attended the

Executive meeting this afternoon. They could not for shame attend a weavers' meeting in the daylight so hung down their heads and slunk into the crowd in the dark." (34) The following day some of the manufacturers accepted the challenge and did attend a daytime meeting. Mrs. Wood acknowledged their presence and went on to remark that she felt in no way threatened by it. (35) Her outspoken statements at the meeting had greater significance, for around this time Hannah Wood received a couple of threatening letters.

Further pressure was exerted on the female weavers by an influential body of male workers, the tuners, who were both supervisory workers and loom mechanics and as such could persuade and intimidate the weavers under them. The tuners had been holding meetings since the middle of the strike, although they had declared themselves neutral as regards the dispute. (36) This neutral stand came into question when, in the closing days of the strike, they began to pressurise the weavers into returning to work. The local paper, reporting on a meeting held in Dewsbury, noted the presence of several tuners who, it was said, had come to listen so that when work was resumed "they could pick on those they deemed obnoxious". The reporter went on, "Their presence evidently had an influence, for no woman except Mrs. Wood ... could be got to deliver a speech. She, however, did not exhibit the "white feather" but peformed her duty with courage...indicating her great influence with both men and women." (37) Taking the platform, Mrs. Wood explained that she was alone because the other members of the committee were attending other meetings; and then she went straight into her attack. First, she turned her attention to men in general. The <u>Batley Reporter</u> paraphrased her speech: "There had been a great deal of chaff about weavers turning soft, and much of it had been in public houses by men who it seemed to her, wanted them to do so, but she hoped the weavers would take no notice of such talk." She then turned on the tuners. Throughout the week, this group of men, according to Mrs. Wood, had been "running about to the weavers' houses" telling the weavers their masters wanted to see them and to "never mind Mrs. Wood". Unfortunately for them, the weavers had stuck together and told their masters and tuners "we shall stick by our Executive and the blue tariff". (38)

Apart from the efforts of the tuners, the weavers' committee were having to deal with other pressures on the weavers to return to work. The manufacturers' association had revised their list yet again, increasing the rates they were offering by 1d. This was still rejected by the weavers' committee, as it fell below the rates of the blue tariff. This revision had been forced on the employers' association, said the weavers, by 'defectors', as some of the Batley owners had offered prices above the average. In an effort to hold the manufacturers together the Dewsbury and Ravensthorpe prices had been brought up to the Batley rates and a revised scale drawn up which all the manufacturers agreed to stand by. The weavers' committee saw this as evidence that the manufacturers' association was "breaking up piecemeal" although this was hotly denied. Instead, it was claimed that it was "certain of the weavers who were giving way". This difference of opinion centred on the return to work of weavers at two Batley mills: Stubley's and Ellis'.

The firm of Joshua Ellis had been a thorn in the side of the manufacturers' association throughout the strike. It was known to pay above average wages and Mr. Ellis was reported as saying that far from wanting to reduce his scale, he wanted to see the manufacturers' association bring theirs up to it! He was considered "a gentleman" by the strikers and they quoted Mr. Ellis as pouring scorn on the manufacturers' association's claims of the difficulties caused by "foreign competition". The weavers' committee said that both Ellis' and Stubley's mills had accepted the blue tariff. The employers' organisation denied there had been any defections, but that Ellis' had simply offered their old rates and weavers had returned on their own accord without any backing from the Executive Committee. There was an element of truth in both arguments and both sides were being careful not to give the whole picture of what was happening.

The manufacturers' association, facing problems with individual members, called meetings with their own workers in attempts to persuade them to return, using the tuners as go-betweens. One master had promised his workers "a knife and fork tea party" if they returned at the old rates. (39) Although they had little success, this put great pressure on the workers' Executive Committee, which saw these individual mill meetings as a direct attack on their position, and instructed the weavers that such meetings should be avoided. They even went to some lengths to break up such meetings. (40)

Even so, not all the weavers were able to withstand the pressure to return, particularly when the manufacturers' association presented their revised and improved wage tariff. Although the weavers' committee claimed a victory at Stubley's and Ellis', weavers were returning to work at mills where the blue tariff had not been agreed. Two days before the strike ended, the committee was forced to admit that weavers were starting to go in and "more than they liked under the circumstances". There were claims that some had been forced to go back by threats to the employment of fathers, husbands and brothers. (41) Whatever the reason, the weavers' executive had to face the fact that holding out for the blue tariff was not going to be successful. Although some of those who returned to work had done so for the blue tariff, others had returned for no statement at all. In this deteriorating situation, the weavers' committee came up with a solution which opened the way for negotiations with the manufacturers' association.

The dispute had centred on the prices paid and reductions proposed for one particular type of work - reversibles. This type of work was more complicated than others and required a greater degree of skill from the weavers, who expected to be paid on a higher rate when weaving this type of cloth. Prices paid for the other two major types of cloth produced, devons and plains, had never been at issue. However, at this juncture, the weavers'

Executive Committee introduced them into the dispute claiming that rates paid for weaving such cloth were too low. They put forward the compromise that if prices paid for devons and plains were improved, they would be willing to accept slightly lower rates than those they were claiming for weaving reversibles. This proposal by the weavers formed the basis for a settlement of the dispute on 18 March 1875. The agreement was regarded as a victory for the weavers. Mark Oldroyd grudgingly admitted "they might have achieved a slight conquest and the masters have had to give in a little", although he qualified this by adding "The loss was great on both sides and it would take years to redeem that loss." (42) Officially the strike ended that day. Minor disputes arose spasmodically over the following few weeks, as individual mill owners tried to ignore the agreed statement, but these appear to have had little impact. The negotiated settlement was an 'equalisation', which meant that some of those previously earning above average wages returned to reduced wages. Although only applying to a minority of workers it caused some bad feeling.

For the women of the Executive Committee, the ending of the strike meant they could return to their discussions on the formation of a union for the district. At the final strike meeting Anne Ellis, who was the keenest advocate of unionism amongst the weavers, announced that they had organised books for enrolment, had laid down some basic rules and formed a connection with a sick and burial fund. At that point, however, the issue of joining the N.U.W.W. or forming a new union for weavers, had still not been resolved, despite various proposals on the matter being voted upon at strike meetings. At some point between the end of the strike and April 3rd, the Executive Committee finally decided to form a new local union for weavers, (a decision which prompted a bitter letter to the local paper from Mr. Hunt). On 3 April, a mass meeting was held to inaugurate the new union, The Dewsbury, Batley and Surrounding Districts Heavy Woollen Weavers' Association.

Until its amalgamation with the Huddersfield weavers' union in 1883, the history of the union in the heavy woollen district is vague. In 1920, Ben Turner had in his possession the minute books and other papers from the first years of the union. These he reprinted in his history of the General Union of Textile Workers (G.U.T.W.). (43) From this information it is possible to glean that in those early years, the women who founded the union were gradually replaced by men. In the minutes for April 1875, only women are recorded as being present. Gradually, more men appear in the minutes quoted by Turner, and by October 1881, the officers and committee appointed consisted of six men and seven women. Only two names from the days of the strike remain, those of Anne Ellis and Mrs. Abernethy. The amalgamation in 1883 with the male-dominated Huddersfield weavers' union effectively put an end to the involvement of the women of the heavy woollen district and it is the names of Allan Gee, Ben Turner and W.H. Drew which are most closely associated with the union from this point on.

The marginalised role women played in this union, and its successor, the G.U.T.W., through to 1914 has been analysed elsewhere by Joanna Bornat. Only four of the new 1883 Executive Committee of ten members were women. One of these was Anne Ellis, who became a representative of the new union to the Trades Union Congress in 1883 and 1884 and campaigned vociferously for women's rights. However, her involvement with textile unionism ended soon after being sacked and victimised from her job in Dewsbury in 1885, though she remained an active suffragette throughout her life. Female membership of the Huddersfield union and the G.U.T.W. remained relatively high through to World War One, though as Bornat has noted, their role remained confined "typically at the lower levels", with male colleagues in control and positions of authority. (44)

The women in the heavy woollen district had demonstrated in 1875 that they believed in the value of collective organisation, spent time discussing the issue and worked hard to establish a union. Some, like Anne Ellis, believed passionately that workers needed to band together if they were to have strength and never gave up the fight for this principle. Most of the women, however, were not able to turn their ideals of the strike into commitment once it was over. All along it had never been forgotten that the women, by participating in the strike, were taking it upon themselves to interfere in what was, essentially, "a man's question". The women justified their position by claiming the situation had been forced upon them and that, in a sense, they had no choice. Once the strike was over their involvement no longer had this justification and their 'freedom' to choose was restored. To continue pursuing their new role in the world of 'work' would have meant issuing a fundamental challenge to the accepted order of things. Throughout the strike, men of all classes had made it clear that such a challenge would not be issued by ensuring the women's involvement remained restricted to the strike. Few men had taken any direct part in the strike action. When they did involve themselves, this usually took the form of men-only meetings. Others explained that few men participated "out of respect for the ladies...they did not want to usurp the power of the ladies because there never was such a thing in England before as ladies taking the stand they had taken." (45) Others probably had real fears for their own jobs. The one man who did actively participate in the strike action, Mr. Henry Chambers, was sacked, and threats to the jobs of their male relatives was one of the reasons given for the return to work of weavers before the strike officially ended.

Above all, the one thing that did keep men out of the strike, and which also restricted female involvement to the strike only, was the implicit 'conspiracy' which existed between masters and working men. This manifested itself most overtly in the relationship between the employers and the tuners, but it also existed in a more subtle, but powerful form in the social pressures which conditioned women into believing that in taking responsibility for their work, an economically important part of their lives, they were somehow 'out of their place'. Two days before the strike ended, Mrs. Wood told a meeting that "it had not been altogether pleasant for them (the women) to take the part they had done". They had been accused of being "brazen" and of "having cheek", for standing on platforms and addressing meetings. For her own part she had, she said, "felt it very much". (46) The social pressures that implied 'decent' women did not do such things must have been great.

How much greater such pressures would become if the women went on actively to choose to adopt such 'brazen' attitudes, to choose not to be satisfied with the roles assigned to them as wives and mothers, without the justification of the strike. How could a woman justify a continued interest in such issues just for the sake of it? No doubt also the women missed the mutual support they would have received as participants in the strike, and as members of the committee. Without this it would have required tremendous strength of purpose to ignore taunts of being 'brazen' and 'cheeky'. Far from being unwilling to make sacrifices to defend their rights as workers, such a defence required women to make far greater sacrifices than would be asked of any man. A woman's involvement in such issues meant her whole character, her morality, her 'decency', would be questioned. In today's society such values, and the importance attributed to them, still suffice to keep many women 'in their place'. Such attitudes also ensure that women, such as those who participated in and led the strike of 1875, remain 'hidden from history'. This is far less than they deserve.

NOTES

1. B. Turner, 'The Fast Loom Weyver's Rhyme', in Dialect and Other Pieces From a Yorkshire Loom (Heckmondwike, 1909), p. 44.

2. For examples see Parliamentary Papers, 1892, XXXV, Royal Commission on Labour, evidence of A. Gee, B. Turner and W.H. Drew re female employment in textiles. Also H.A. Clegg, A. Fox and A.F. Thompson, History of British Trade Unions since 1889 (London, 1964).

3. Yorkshire Factory Times, 19 July 1889.

4. J.H. Clapham, The Woollen and Worsted Industries (London, 1907), p. 204. For more detail on the causes of trade union weakness in worsted see J.A. Jowitt, ch. 5.

5. This is a very simple explanation of a rather more complicated process. For more detail see N.C. Gee, Shoddy and Mungo Manufacture (Manchester, 1950).

6. The inscription on Law's gravestone in the graveyard of Batley Parish Church credits him with this transformation.

7. S. Jubb, The History of the Shoddy Trade: its Rise, Progress and Present Position (Batley, 1860).

8. H. Burrows, A History of the Rag Trade (London, 1956), p. 47.

9. Although the manufacturers' association is often referred to in newspaper reports, I have as yet been unable to find any other source of information about it. A small piece in the Batley

Reporter in February 1875 written in answer "to numerous enquiries" stated that approximately fifty local manufacturers were members.

10. Batley Reporter (hereafter cited B.R.), 6 February 1875.
11. Ibid.
12. S. Jubb, op. cit., pp. 84-5. Jubb's figures show that there were still 1,200 handloom weavers in Batley in 1860 compared with 500 power loom weavers. The former could earn 18s. per week, the latter 9s. per week.
13. Ibid., p. 88.
14. Ben Turner told the Royal Commission on Labour that women outnumbered men 4:1 and during the strike the general opinion was that 75 per cent of the weavers were women.
15. S. Jubb, op. cit., p. 88. Also, D.N. Thompson, Shoddyopolis - the Rise of a West Riding Woollen Town (unpublished dissertation, 1978, lodged in Batley Library), cites statistics from A.L. Bowley in 1902 that show that rates for female weavers in Batley in 1870 were considerably higher than those in surrounding districts where weavers were more likely to be men.
16. B.R., 13 February 1875.
17. Ibid.
18. B.R., 20 February 1875.
19. Ibid.
20. C.J. James, M.P. for Dewsbury (Brighouse, 1970), p. 84.
21. There is a misleading reference to the role played by the N.U.W.W. during the weavers' strike in S. Rowbotham, Hidden from History, p. 60. This is not the impression given by the women leading the strike.
22. So called because it was written on blue paper. It was an attempt to bring about a standard rate of pay throughout the district.
23. B.R., 20 February 1875.
24. B.R., 20 March 1875.
25. Ibid.
26. A statement of the strike accounts is reprinted in B. Turner, A Short History of the General Union of Textile Workers, (Heckmondwike, 1920), pp. 91-4.
27. B.R., 20 March 1875. This gives a vivid account of the actual process of the distribution of relief at Batley Carr.
28. Ibid.
29. The number of strings in a piece determined its length and therefore the weaver's wages. Employers could claim that a smaller number of strings had been woven and so pay less for a piece than the weaver deserved.
30. B.R., 27 February 1875.
31. Ibid.
32. B.R., 13 March 1875.
33. B.R., 27 February 1875.
34. B.R., 13 March 1875.
35. Ibid.
36. B.R., 27 February 1875.
37. B.R., 20 March 1875.

38. Ibid.
39. Ibid.
40. B.R., 13 March 1875. This account relates how one meeting was disrupted by a bell man who was paid to cry "Don't take heed of them" throughout the meeting.
41. B.R., 20 March 1875.
42. Ibid.
43. B. Turner, op. cit., pp. 101-8.
44. J. Bornat, 'Lost Leaders: Women, Trade Unionism and the Case of the General Union of Textile Workers, 1875-1914', ch. 7 in A. John (ed.), Unequal Opportunities: Women's Employment in England, 1800-1918, (Oxford, 1986), pp. 211-15. See also J. Bornat, 'An Examination of the General Union of Textile Workers, 1883-1922 (Ph.D. thesis, Essex University, 1981).
45. B.R., 27 February 1875.
46. B.R., 20 March 1875. For further discussion on the attitude of male dominated trade unions to female membership see D. Busfield, ch. 8 and A. McIvor, ch. 7, Section IV. See also J. Bornat, op. cit.; B. Drake, Women in Trade Unions (London, 1920); K. Boston, Women Workers and the Trade Unions (London, 1980); S. Lewenhak, Women and Trade Unions (London, 1977); D. Rubinstein, Before the Sufragettes (Brighton, 1986), E. Roberts, A Woman's Place (Oxford, 1984).

Chapter 10

"WELL FITTED FOR FEMALES." WOMEN IN THE MACCLESFIELD SILK INDUSTRY. (1)

Jill Norris

A visiting clergyman, the Reverend Edwin Sturdee, who was taken round a Macclesfield silk mill in 1899, was greatly impressed by

> The general appearance of the workers, so neat, so well dressed, that as I said to my guide, 'These girls could stand just as they are behind the counter of any draper's shop in London.' 'Their character is influenced by their employment,' observed the Vicar (i.e. of Macclesfield)...'They are refined and ladylike in every way.' (2)

These sentiments were echoed a quarter of a century later by James Arnold, a local silk manufacturer:

> No industry can compete with it (silk) for beauty, for healthy conditions under which the operatives work, and for its refining tendencies. The fact of the eye and hand seeing and handling such a beautiful textile leaves its mark on all those who are engaged in it...We should be a great asset to the nation, absorbing a large number of females in a healthy, remunerative and beautiful occupation. (3)

Two main points emerge from these descriptions. Firstly, women were evidently important to the silk industry. They were highly noticeable, a group who attracted comment rather than being lost in the shadow of male workers. Instead, both observers equate the workforce with women; "the workers" leads directly on to "these girls", and "the operatives" is followed by "a large number of females". Men silk workers, in contrast, are not mentioned.

Secondly, silk was considered a very suitable industry for women. It is described as having both positive physical qualities - "healthy conditions" - and intangible advantages. Both observers considered that the work had a "refining" effect upon those engaged in it, Arnold specifically equating the influence

Women in the Macclesfield Silk Industry

with the fine quality of the textile. This attitude is summed up by another Macclesfield employer, G.N. Heath, who in giving evidence in 1923 to the Board of Trade Inquiry into the Silk Industry spoke of "an industry so beneficial particularly to females".

The British silk industry, although of importance in the eighteenth century, declined during the nineteenth, and consequently historians have paid it little attention. However, the quotations given above suggested that conditions within it were sufficiently unusual to provide a contrast with other industries, and hence to shed some light on the questions of women's employment. By exploring the images of women silk workers and the reality that lay behind them, it will be possible to consider issues relevant to women's industrial position in general. At the same time it will provide a contribution to a neglected area of textile history.

By the end of the nineteenth century Macclesfield was the chief centre of the silk industry in Britain. Its origins are however obscure; the earliest references are to the making of silk buttons in the late seventeenth century. Women's work appears to have been of great importance at this stage; the buttons probably consisted of wooden foundations covered with twisted patterns of silk and other exotic threads by women and children working in their homes. A button merchant, who took the work out to button makers in the villages around Macclesfield is recorded in the early eighteenth century as saying that, "An active and diligent woman could earn four shillings a week". (4)

There was also a certain amount of 'smallware' (narrow fabric) weaving, and again this seems to have been largely women's work. When new looms were introduced which could weave six or eight strips at a time, "In October 1673; the women of Macclesfield 'rose in a mob' and burnt some looms, and when their leaders were arrested, released them from prison".(5) Women were thus not only the first silk workers but also the first recorded as taking part in industrial action in the area.

The silk industry was one of the earliest to move to factory production. The first silk mill in Macclesfield was built in 1743 for a button merchant, Charles Roe, and was soon followed by others. These mills were for 'throwing' or processing silk yarn from imported skeins of raw silk for the use of the Spitalfields weavers in London. Women were an important part of the factory workforce. A local historian wrote in 1817 that, "About forty years ago, or in the year 1776, the wages paid to the Millmen and Stewards was seven shillings a week, that of women employed as doublers, three shillings and sixpence." (6)

Women remained important to the silk industry in the early nineteenth century, although the handloom weaving of broad silk, which developed in Macclesfield in the 1790s, was largely a male occupation. The 1841 census records 3,676 males and 3,681 females working in silk. By 1851, changes in the town boundaries led to the recording of 4,887 males and 4,674 females, again approximately equal numbers for each sex. Macclesfield was very much a

Women in the Macclesfield Silk Industry

one-industry town. Cotton had appeared as a possible rival to silk at the end of the eighteenth century, but it never expanded beyond a minor industry, alongside textile engineering and flour milling. In 1851, according to Molly Spink's analysis of women in Macclesfield at this date, 71 per cent of all jobs done by women were in silk. (7)

The decline of the British silk industry after the Cobden treaty of 1860 exposed it to foreign competition, saw a change in the proportions of men and women workers. Figures for Macclesfield alone are unfortunately not available, but of 17,643 silk workers in Cheshire in 1871, only 37 per cent were male. Contraction continued during the late nineteenth century, and by 1901 the total number of Cheshire silk workers was only 8,720, of whom 33 per cent were male.

As the silk industry shrank, it became concentrated in fewer centres, of which Macclesfield was the most important. In the early twentieth century the town was still dominated by silk, although there had been some diversification, notably into commerce and transport. Jobs in these were, however, mainly taken up by men, and women remained concentrated in the silk industry, which by now included rayon, or artificial silk. It also included a substantial clothing section; many silk manufacturers had from the 1870s onwards developed making-up departments producing scarves, ties and other items. There were also some clothing firms which had no connection with the silk industry, but unfortunately it is not possible to separate the numbers employed in these. A woman working in a silk firm might be engaged in throwing, weaving, or garment making or in a number of ancillary occupations, and would refer to all these as being 'in the silk'.

The census data for 1921 indicate clearly the importance of women workers to the Macclesfield silk industry by this date. They formed 66 per cent of its workforce, with the proportion being much higher in the making-up departments. This would explain the high visibility of women workers to commentators on the silk industry.

The other conclusion which can be drawn from these figures is that the silk industry was of great importance to women in Macclesfield. Some 71 per cent of those women in paid employment worked in silk in 1921, and it is reasonable to suppose that there were substantial numbers of former silk workers who were at that date out of the labour market or in other occupations such as charring. If professional and white-collar jobs are excluded, so that working-class occupations alone are considered, the dominance of silk becomes even more striking. For working-class girls leaving school in Macclesfield in the inter-war years there was very little choice. This is borne out by the oral evidence: a woman who began work in 1934 explained, "Well at that particular time there was nothing, only the silk for women, you see". (8) In Macclesfield, women and the silk industry were of great mutual importance. The industry depended on female labour, and women looked to the mills for employment. Work in silk was the common experience.

Women in the Macclesfield Silk Industry

Table 10.1: Occupations in Macclesfield, 1921

	Male	Female
Silk and related occupations:	2,863	5,450
inc: textiles	2,372	3,682
makers of textile goods and articles of dress	491	1,768
Other occupations:		
inc: transport	1,045	31
commerce, finance etc.	1,139	445
professional	295	364
domestic servants	13	501
Total employed:	8,156	7,680

Source: Census, 1921

With such a limited range of available occupations over several generations, the question of the suitability of the silk industry cannot have been uppermost in the minds of Macclesfield women. Yet, as we have seen, it was the quality which particularly impressed several observers, who contrasted the silk workers favourably with the usual image of factory girls, the image given in Elizabeth Gaskell's novels or in this description by a middle-class evangelical, Lettice Bell:

> There is no mistaking her in the streets. The long day's silence is made up for the moment she is free, by loud and boisterous laughter, and a flow of language peculiar to her and her alone. No pavement ever seems quite wide enough for her requirements, as she strolls along from side to side, arm in arm with two kindred spirits. She is apparently born minus a sense of shyness. Why live in a free country if she cannot accost every man that looks likely to afford a hopeful butt for her sarcasm, or to stand her a drink? (9)

Explicit comparisons were made between women workers in silk and cotton. The correspondent of the Morning Chronicle, Angus Reach, who visited Macclesfield in 1849, wrote that, "The silk girls seem to belong to altogether a superior and more refined class of society than the female cotton workers". He attributed this directly to the work they did:

> The work is cleaner, and in many respects is well fitted for females, who are able to dress with far more neatness and propriety than the girls in the cotton factories. In several of the silk mills which I have gone over the girls were dressed rather in the style of milliners' apprentices than of

ordinary female operatives. (10)

It is worth considering in some detail the work that the women in the silk mills actually did. Reach described a division between women's and men's jobs, and also the places in which they worked:

> About one half of the labouring population of Macclesfield work at home, and the other half in the mills. The home labourers are exclusively weavers; the mill labourers are principally engaged in throwing, doubling and other processes ...in preparing the threads which are intertwined by the loom. By far the largest proportion of the mill population is female, the weavers who work looms in the mills being inconsiderable in number, compared with those who work at home.

He described a few jobs for men among the throwing processes, but these were obviously a small minority. In the mid-nineteenth century nearly all the weaving was done by hand, by both men and women, and handloom weaving at home continued until the 1930s, and in mills until 1981. (11) Apart from this, the division of labour in the mills remained much the same for the next century. (12)

When the raw silk arrived in a mill, it was first washed, to remove dirt and excess gum. Once dried it was subjected to a variety of processes collectively known as 'throwing' (including winding and doubling), which thickened and twisted the thread until it reached the required strength and resilience. (This is qualitatively different from spinning in that silk is wound from the cocoon in a continuous filament, while the short fibres of wool or cotton have to be spun together to make a thread.) Most of the workers engaged in the throwing processes were women. The yarn might then be dyed, a male occupation. Before weaving, the lengthways warp threads had to be arranged in order, and this was almost entirely a woman's job. Weaving, as stated above, might be done by either sex, although women predominated. It might be plain, or the richly-patterned jacquard designs. Some yarn was used for knitting, though this was relatively unimportant in the Macclesfield industry. The cloth would then be dyed, if this had not already been done in the yarn, or printed, an exclusively male job. Making up the finished cloth was almost entirely women's work. The numbers of men and women doing each job are given in Table 10.2.

It is possible to distinguish certain categories of men's and women's jobs. Men's work was either dirty or heavy work (washing, dyeing), supervisory, or skilled, in the technical sense of having served an apprenticeship, a point to which I shall return later. Women's work, in contrast, was mainly semi-skilled machine-minding.

Women in the Macclesfield Silk Industry

Table 10.2: Silk & Clothing Workers in Macclesfield, 1921

	Male	Female
Silk		
Employers & Managers	142	10
Foremen & Overlookers	183	65
Weavers	575	730
Winders, Cleaners & Doublers	35	981
Hosiery & other machine knitters	62	326
Lookers & Examiners	6	68
Dye mixers and Dyers	357	5
Printers	47	-
Jacquard Punchers & Card Setters	27	-
Reelers, Beamers & Warpers	13	240
Makers of Textile Goods & Clothing		
Employers & Managers	53	23
Foremen & Overlookers	12	23
Dress & Blouse makers	1	213
Embroidery Machinists/workers	93	240
Sewers, Stitchers, etc	12	973

Source: Census, 1921

The main exception was weaving. Strictly, a weaver learned 'on the job', taught by watching and assisting another weaver, a process taking only a few weeks. However, it was claimed that the ability to do the job properly only came after years of practice. Joel Downes, the secretary of the National Silk Workers' Association, gave evidence to the Board of Trade Enquiry:

> I am speaking for the moment of power-loom silk weavers, and by saying that it is a mixed occupation I mean that women can be as skilled as men and earn the same money...I want you to realise that in order to become skilful power-loom weavers it takes five or six or seven years.

A sense of skill and pride in their work comes through the recorded memories of former weavers, as for instance: "I had never been fetched in over my work, and they often gave me special things to do - jobs that nobody else would tackle. We did some lovely work there. I did one that was all open - and little knots - lovely when it was done." This woman had her standards: "Some places wanted you to work four looms, but I said it couldn't be done. You couldn't keep the quality up with four loom weaving, and I only ever did two." (13) Another woman who had worked as a smallware weaver, making gold braid, said:

> Difficult, yes, very exacting work, but very satisfactory when you took it off and it came out right when you'd stood over it

Women in the Macclesfield Silk Industry

...If you were conscientious and you knew your work was wrong it was very upsetting...I've wanted perfection you see, and weaving is one of the things where if you really do give your mind to it you can get as near perfection as you know. (14)

Warping was another job done by women which required considerable ability and which was not easily learned. A warping manager described the training girls received:

The trainee would stand with a skilled operator for a while, perhaps three weeks or a month, and then we would try her on her own with her teacher supervising, and the machine slow...I could soon tell whether they've got the talent for the job it's no use otherwise. You can do so much damage with a bad warper ...Some of them you had to reject eventually, and find a simpler occupation somewhere else in the department. (15)

In contrast, women who worked at machine-minding jobs in the throwing mills had little training and did not mention job satisfaction. Instead, they talked about the company they found at work. One winder said: "We all got on well together. And we used to sing, and all that, you know, it was jolly. Yes, we had some good times... It is noisy, but you get used to the noise...I remember we all used to be singing in harmony." (16)

For a minority of women, then, working with silk was a positive experience. They liked their work because they liked what they made and the sense of skill and achievement in making it. But this sense of satisfaction was by no means confined to women. Weaving was also done by men, and some of the most creative and complex processes were exclusively male occupations, notably designing and printing. A far higher proportion of female than male workers were in jobs that required little skill or training and provided little satisfaction. The silk industry was no especial benefactor to women in this aspect, at least.

A consideration of the material rewards of working in silk brings the same conclusion. Wage rates were determined according to two criteria, skill and sex. The list included in the evidence to the 1923 Inquiry is divided into two scales, men's and women's. Within these scales are gradations which reflect the degree of skill involved. The highest male rate given is 76 shillings per week, paid to power-loom overlookers, followed by 60s 5d to dyers and going down to 54 shillings for "other workers". The female list shows much less variation. The highest rate was for warpers, at 37s 6d; other jobs paid between 31 shillings and 33 shillings except for winding at 29s 6d. In other words, the differential based on sex was much greater than that based on skill.

Once again weavers form an exception. Their rates do not appear in the 1923 list, since that only includes time rates while weavers were paid, literally, by the piece. The Power Loom Weavers' Price List agreed between manufacturers and union in 1912 is a lengthy and complicated document, tabulating different rates according to the type of cloth, number of warp threads, number of colours and so forth. A weaver's earnings could, therefore, vary considerably from week to week. As Downes stated to the 1923 Inquiry, men and women weavers were paid at the same rate. The Price List explicitly states in its rules that there was equal treatment for men and women:

> Should any work be standing for which there is no Weaver, and should any Weaver be playing (i.e. not working) altogether, it is advisable for the Committee to see that the Weaver who has played the longest be allowed to weave the same until he or she (my emphasis) shall have earned 10s., and then allow the next on turn to earn the same.

It seems that most kinds of cloth were woven by either men or women. However, there were some exceptions; the 1919 Arbitration Award for the silk industry included a clause which stated, "The list prices for certain classes of cloth which is (sic) more suitable for men to work are to be reviewed and increased by approximately 10 per cent". (17) There is no other evidence on fabrics woven exclusively by men, and it is probable that they were only a small minority of total production.

Although the weavers' wages were so variable, there are some indications of what might be expected as a week's pay. Downes told the inquiry that (in a time of slump) rates could vary from £2 0s 3d down to £1 0s 3d, and ten years later Florence Holden, a Macclesfield weaver featured in a BBC broadcast Workers in Europe, stated that, "A good weaver with good conditions can earn £2 10s or more. But on the other hand you can drop much lower." (18) An average wage would probably be about 40 to 45 shillings a week. This rate is substantially higher than that of any other category of women workers, while at the same time being appreciably lower than that of any men. The weavers' rate lies between the usual scales for men and women, and this may be taken as reflecting the fact that weaving was the one job done by large numbers of both women and men. For most women the beneficial effects of working in the silk industry were not to be found in their wages.

Although the weavers' skill was recognised among workers in the silk industry, it was not acknowledged officially. Weavers did not receive articles of apprenticeship and 'serve their time', and, as shown above, they were not paid at the rates of other skilled workers. Charles More (19) has developed a complex analysis of skill, distinguishing between 'genuine skill', defined as a "combination of manual skill and knowledge", and "socially constructed skill", whereby the label of 'skilled' (with its financial rewards) is applied to workers on external grounds such as tradition or the ability to bargain with employers. More cites the cotton spinners as an example. Given that the silk weavers evidently possessed 'genuine skill' that was not recognised financially, it is perhaps appropriate to introduce a concept of the 'social destruction of skill', whereby a worker's abilities are systematically devalued at the same time as they are utilised

Women in the Macclesfield Silk Industry

by the employer.

Along with low wages, the silk industry offered low status to its women workers. Table 10.2 indicates that very few women held positions of authority. Only 88 women, compared with 195 men, were classified as 'foremen and overlookers' in a workforce composed mainly of women. Photographic evidence suggests that while men might supervise other men, mixed groups or groups otherwise composed entirely of women, women were only to be found in charge of all-women groups. The correlation of authority with masculinity lies outside the scope of this study; here it is important to notice the relative paucity of opportunities for promotion for women, compared with men.

While supervisory posts were difficult for women to achieve, the status of employer or manager was almost impossible. Only 33 women came into this category in the 1921 census, compared with 195 men. Male employers and managers, in the twentieth century at least, were recruited largely from the sons of silk manufacturers, but there were certain routes open to able and ambitious working-class boys. The most common was via the design office, a route barred to women. Designers undertook a long training at evening classes at the Macclesfield School of Art, and were considered as 'staff' rather than shop floor workers. There was a steady input from their ranks into management, from which some took the step of establishing their own firms. It was also possible, though less common, for a man to move from foreman to senior management. (20) The only women in senior management, however, came from families of silk manufacturers, such as Madge Dunkerley at Joseph Dunkerley & Son and Margaret Brown at A.W. Hewetson.

The silk industry, in other words, did not offer women workers a career and status, any more than it offered them high rates of pay. Its beneficial effects upon women cannot be found in material recompenses. Any sense of benefit must be sought in non-quantifiable, immaterial rewards. Such rewards, as has been shown, do not include job satisfaction for the majority of women silk workers. They must be still more intangible, perhaps moral, even spiritual. This is to return to the idea of refinement, of the 'ladylike' qualities of the silk workers. Such concepts are difficult to define, but an attempt may be made by considering the conditions in which the women worked.

The Morning Chronicle correspondent has already been quoted as to the conditions in the silk mills and the "propriety with which the women are able to dress as a result". Certainly the mills were usually kept clean and at a reasonable temperature. John Wright, a Macclesfield silk worker and bitter critic of many aspects of the factory system, nevertheless testified to the Royal Commission on Child Labour in 1838 that, "They are swept every day and whitewashed once a year...I don't know exactly the temperature, but it is very agreeable". As silk is usually thrown rather than spun, there is not the fluff generated which can affect the health as well as the appearance of cotton workers. (When "waste" or broken silk is spun, there is evidence that fluff is created, but this was only ever a minor part of the Macclesfield industry.) Women in the Macclesfield silk mills were therefore better able to preserve a smart appearance than their equivalents in the hot and dusty cotton factories.

There is photographic evidence from around 1900 that some women silk workers at least were smartly dressed in the mills. It is probable, however, that the differences between silk and other women factory workers disappeared during the 1920s and '30s with the general rise in working-class living standards, and, more particularly, the proliferation of smarter cheap clothing following the introduction of rayon. As one contemporary observer wrote: "Every type of woven and knitted garment is being made from rayon...It enables the working girl to wear clothes of a type and quality which previously only the rich could afford." (21) Ironically, most of the rayon was processed in silk mills, and by the end of the 1930s the British silk industry had effectively become the silk and rayon industry.

Other properties of silk may have affected the appearance of the workers. Silk demands careful handling if the delicate fibres are not to be damaged. One weaver remembered:

> Everything had to be clean, and you couldn't have rough hands. If you had rough hands you caught the silk. I had a pot of grease - from Hadfield's - under the loom, and I was always putting it on. I've still got soft hands...feel...and I do all my own housework. (22)

During the slump of the early 1920s unemployed silk workers were, like women throughout the country, directed into domestic service. Macclesfield Trades Council wrote to the Ministry of Labour to complain that,

> The position of a resident domestic servant was offered to the following classes of women, and on refusal to accept all the benefits were suspended...women whose hands it would have ruined for the delicate processes in which they are engaged in their own trade... (23)

Most women wore overalls to work, and this generally seems to have been expected of them. Another requirement was the wearing of stockings. One woman who worked for Brocklehurst-Whiston Amalgamation, the largest firm in Macclesfield, said, "we all had to wear stockings to work. We could get them cheap, seconds, which is why we could wear silk. But as long as we wore stockings of some kind it was all right. Why? Because it would have been bad for trade if we didn't." (24) This may perhaps be a concrete example of the 'refining tendencies' of silk in action. Women silk workers were expected to identify with the products of their labour, financially as well as emotionally.

Outside observers certainly made a connection between the quality of the fabric and the quality of the workers. The Rev. Sturdee attempted a direct correlation between materials and manners: "Mill girls differ according to the raw materials on which they are engaged,...from the refinement of the silk hands you descend, via cotton and other goods, until you get to the roughest type, engaged in rope yarning." The workers were thus identified with the fabric. Silk was a cloth worn by ladies, and so it must be made by ladylike women. Silk was beautiful, exotic and reserved for an elite, so it could not be made by ordinary factory girls. (25)

Yet the image of gentility hid the reality of women's lives. Observers who only saw elegant ladies ignored the sheer hard work (of both mill workers and shop assistants) and the extra burden carried by many married women employees. Interestingly, it took a female observer to link the quality of the product with the effort of the workers. In 1914 an anonymous correspondent for The Common Cause, a women's suffrage journal, wrote:

> The factory work done by women in this town is surely eminently 'women's work'. There is nothing necessarily heavy or disagreeable about the unhurried fashioning of a beautiful fabric...(However) the women of Macclesfield pay, and heavily, for their industrial opportunities...Without hesitation one must pronounce the lives of the women to be frightfully hard, for 'women's work' is not all done within factory hours. For the woman worker this is a town of many opportunites...yet the married woman here is faced with this problem, and has to solve it: she must either keep house on a wage varying from 18s. to 24s. a week, or she must work to make it more. (26)

Her impression was corroborated by another woman who visited Macclesfield at the same time. Margery Lane, reporting for the Women's Industrial Council inquiry into married women's work (1908-14), found that:

> When there are only one or two children in the family it is possible by the strictest economy to keep house on £1 or 18/- a week, but nothing is left over. If the husband's wages fall beneath this sum, as they often do, or if the number of children increases without a corresponding rise in the income, the mothers go out to work. (27)

Lane did not comment upon the suitability of silk for women, or of its effect upon them, other than that: "It is possible for a woman to continue working at the mill after marriage without any very visible harm to herself or her family. Not improbably the work is less trying than the care of several young children." She recognised the strain of the double burden: "The uninitiated can only marvel how the women contrive to keep their children and houses so well on so small an income and with so little time left from outside work. If these are fair specimens of the type produced by factory life, it must be a nursery of the domestic virtues."

Both Lane and The Common Cause reporter were impressed by the numbers of married women within the silk industry. The local Medical Officer of Health, Dr. J.H. Marsh, went so far as to speak of the "town depending for its trade upon married women's work". (28) While this is probably an exaggeration, married women certainly formed a significant part of the workforce. In 1901, 33.2 per cent of the married and widowed women in Macclesfield were in employment, compared with 9.6 per cent nationally. By 1911 the proportion had risen to 34.1 per cent, compared with a national fall to 8.7 per cent. (29) In Macclesfield, then, married women were three to four times more likely to go out to work than women throughout the country. Lane remarked that, "The married women workers of Leek and Macclesfield are, as a rule, engaged in various branches of the silk trade," and indeed it is difficult to see how such numbers could otherwise be accounted for.

Married women's work seems to have been a constant factor in the town's industry, from the early days of button-making onwards. Spink calculated that in 1851, 27 per cent of all women workers were married, and that 32.5 per cent were married or widowed. However, she did not find it possible to distinguish between women working at home and those in the mills. At this date there was still a considerable domestic weaving industry, and the Morning Chronicle correspondent remarked complacently that:

> Very few married women work in the silk mills - the quantity of labour to be performed at home being so considerable, that a natural and generally understood arrangement comes almost imperceptibly into force, and tends to keep within their own dwellings those whose absence from them would be most undesirable and domestically unprofitable.

It is of course possible that the numbers of married women silk workers at this period may actually be greater than that obtained from the census, since domestic duties may have taken precedence over part-time involvement in garret weaving, at least in the eyes of an enumerator.

By the end of the nineteenth century power looms outnumbered hand looms, and the majority of the remaining handloom weavers were working in the mills. There was thus little work in silk available for married women at home, and the great majority of those described as 'in employment' in 1901 and 1911 would be factory workers. The Common Cause correspondent began her first article: " 'This is a town of women you know,' I was told...Nearly every woman, married and single, who belongs to the working class in this town goes out of her home to earn wages." (30) This is of course an exaggeration. However, it comes closer to the truth than the image of London shop assistants, an image which ignores the hard physical effort required of all mill workers and the particular burden imposed upon a substantial fraction of the female workforce.

What did the women workers think about themselves? Their oral testimonies record their pride in their work and their dislike of many of their working conditions. They complained about low wages

Women in the Macclesfield Silk Industry

and old dark mills, and described the burden of housework, the pleasure of friendship, the respect given to considerate or knowledgeable employers, and the resentment of petty rules and factory discipline. They speak of themselves as hard-working, cooperative with one another, and fond of a brief opportunity for entertainment. They do not, however, mention gentility or refinement.

Other sources of evidence for what the women thought of themselves are almost non-existent. They did not leave diaries or autobiographies, nor write to the local newspaper. One significant factor, however, is their union activity. The Macclesfield silk workers, apart from the male handloom weavers, were late to organise. The first union that women could join was the Macclesfield Power Loom Silk Weavers' Association, founded in 1903, which later became the National Silk Workers' Association (N.S.W.A.). (31) By the interwar years most silk workers were members of either the N.S.W.A. or the Leek-based Amalgamated Society of Textile Workers and Kindred Trades. Most of the unions' activities were routine, covering minor shop disputes and wage negotiations, and the officers and most of the executives were male. The one big dispute of the interwar years, though, involved large numbers of women.

This was the lock-out at Neckwear Ltd., a making-up firm whose management attempted to introduce a wage cut in October 1930. The great majority of the 800-strong workforce, mostly young women, refused to accept it. The dispute continued for five months, during which time the N.S.W.A. officials tried to negotiate. Eventually a compromise was reached, amending the lowered rates though not fully restoring them. While the officials negotiated, the workers held noisy demonstrations and mass pickets, which appear to have been successful in stemming a gradual trickle back to work. The <u>Macclesfield Courier & Herald</u> reported that:

> Crowds of anything up to 500 have derided them (returning workers) each evening. Two of the workers decided to join the attacking force and on Tuesday evening left off work again. On several occasions the Chief Constable had attempted to pacify the crowd, who booed and catcalled him into silence. Skirmishes are also taking place on the rim of the 'battle zone', and detachments of demonstrators have followed the staff and semi-staff home and broken windows. (32)

There is no suggestion that these demonstrations were organised by the union leaders. One, leading from behind, commented that though he was: "Sorry there has been disturbances...We admire the girls for the splendid fight they have made on a question of high principle which is usually only associated with strong-minded men." (33)

There seems to have been considerable public sympathy in the town for the Neckwear workers. It is noticeable how the women were prepared to act in defence of their rights as workers and to take whatever actions seemed to them to be necessary, while

199

leaving the conduct of the negotiations to the union leaders, in whom they seem to have had full confidence.

The mass pickets outside the Neckwear factory in 1930 appear in strong contrast to the imagery of the shop assistants of thirty years before or the milliners' apprentices of 1849. Yet as we have seen, the view of women silk workers as smart young ladies was ever only partially correct, at best; a substantial proportion were married women with heavy domestic responsibilities as well as long hours of paid work. It is noticeable that those who commented upon the appearance or refinement of the women were all men. Two were visitors to the town while the third was a Macclesfield manufacturer; all three were concerned with images of the women mill workers. In contrast, the two women observers looked at the material conditions of the women's lives and were interested in their unpaid as well as their paid work; they made no comments at all about their appearance. While the women writers tended to play down the contribution of girls and single women (Lane was explicitly only concerned with married women) the men ignored the question of women's domestic labour. Their concentration upon the image of the luxury fabric and a correspondence with the kind of women who made it mask the hard work, low pay and unrewarded skill that were an integral part of women's experience of the silk industry.

A similar correlation between the images of the product and of the worker can be found in other industries in which women were employed. Coal, for instance, is hard, heavy and dirty. These are not generally considered feminine characteristics, and so all work in the coal industry was judged unsuitable for women. Much of the debate around the pit-brow lasses' work centred around their unfeminine appearance, especially the wearing of trousers. (34) To take an example closer to the silk industry, cotton was a cheap fabric, largely used for clothing poor people. The makers of such a proletarian article were themselves proletarians, without any of the glamour of an exotic fabric to raise their status.

The same correlation can be found in the service industries. Much domestic service involved hard physical effort and contact with dirt, lifting heavy weights, scrubbing floors and cleaning grates. Yet domestic service was thought pre-eminently suitable work for women, since it was performed in the home, albeit someone else's, and the home was women's traditional sphere. The prostitutes who serviced the Victorian army and navy were seen as particularly low, a class apart, yet it has been demonstrated that many were young women who went in and out of prostitution according to the possibilities of other employment and their domestic circumstances. (35) A modern example is the view of nurses as 'angels'; long hours and low pay can be ignored in the concentration on the high moral nature of their occupation. In other words, perceptions of women's work are closely bound up with values attached to the industry they are employed in, values which may have little to do with the actual work performed.

Women in the Macclesfield Silk Industry

NOTES

1. Much of the material in this article is taken from my thesis, Gender and Class in Industry and the Home. Women Silk Workers in Macclesfield 1919-1939, (M.A., Keele, 1985). I would like to thank the staff of the Macclesfield Silk Museum for the use of their archives, particularly the oral history and photographic collections.
2. E. Sturdee, 'A Town of Silk', in Church and People, Vol. XI, No. viii, October 1899.
3. J. Arnold, in Macclesfield - The Silk Centre of Great Britain, (Macclesfield Borough Council Handbook, 1923).
4. S. Davies, A History of Macclesfield, (Manchester, 1961), p. 45.
5. A.P. Wadsworth & J. de L. Mann, The Cotton Trade and Industrial Lancashire 1600-1780, (Manchester), p. 304.
6. J. Corry, The History of Macclesfield, (London, 1817), p. 66.
7. M. Spink, The Employment of Women in Macclesfield in the 19th Century, (Manchester University Dissertation, 1976).
8. Macclesfield Silk Museum (MSM) Interview 97, woman born 1918, winder.
9. Quoted in A. Davin, 'Women and History', in M. Wandor (ed.), The Body Politic, (London, 1972), p. 220.
10. In J. Ginswick (ed.), Labour and the Poor in England and Wales, (London, 1983).
11. J. Norris, The Last Handloom Weavers, (Macclesfield Silk Museum, 1984).
12. The Silk Book, (The Silk Association, Macclesfield, 1951) gives a good description of technical processes, but does not distinguish between male and female labour. For this I have used a combination of census, photographic and oral evidence.
13. MSM, Interview 33, woman born 1893, weaver.
14. MSM, Interview 73, woman born 1915, weaver.
15. MSM, Interview 62, man born 1906, manager.
16. MSM, Interview 91, woman born 1909, winder.
17. In the Wages Agreement scrapbook of the Macclesfield Silk Trade Employers' Association, now in the possession of the Macclesfield Textile Employers' Association.
18. Broadcast 17 May 1933. Transcript classified in the Macclesfield Silk Museum collection as Interview 113.
19. C. More, Skill and the English Working Class, (London, 1980).
20. See for instance, MSM, Interview 49, man born 1902, manager.
21. A. Hard, The Story of Rayon, (London, 1939), p. 2.
22. MSM, Interview 33.
23. Macclesfield Courier & Herald, 14 May 1921.
24. MSM, Interview 51, woman born 1917, spinner.
25. I am grateful to Christine Woods for this idea.
26. The Common Cause, 10 July 1914. I am grateful to Jill Liddington for this reference.

27. M. Lane, 'Leek and Macclesfield' in C. Black, Married Women's Work, (London, 1915), p. 204.
28. Medical Officer of Health, Report, (H.M.S.O. London, 1916).
29. Macclesfield figures from M.O.H. Report, 1923; figures for England and Wales from D. Gittins, Fair Sex, (London, 1982).
30. The Common Cause, 26. June 1914.
31. Barbara Drake, in Women in Trade Unions, (London, 1920), says that women were not admitted to the N.S.W.A. until 1915, but there is strong evidence against this. See my thesis, Chapter 8.
32. Macclesfield Courier & Herald, 16 Jan. 1931.
33. Ibid., 22 Jan. 1931. His attitude speaks for itself.
34. See, A. John, By the Sweat of their Brow: Women Workers at Victorian Coalmines, (London, 1980).
35. J. & D. Walkowitz, '"We are Not Beasts of the Field": Prostitution and the Poor in Plymouth and Southampton under the Contagious Diseases Act', in M. Hartman and L. Banner (eds.), Clio's Consciousness Raised, (New York, 1974).

Chapter 11

WOMEN AND WORK IN THE LANCASHIRE COTTON INDUSTRY, 1890-1939

Michael Savage

There has always been a certain ambiguity over the implications of large scale female employment in the Lancashire cotton industry for the social position of women in the area. On the one hand the fact that it gave women a prominent role in the formal economy seemed to give women considerable potential for exercising autonomy and control, and asserting their independence from the family and household. Yet on the other hand the fact that the sort of work performed by women was also laborious, demanding, and not as well paid as that of male textile workers, could be interpreted as testimony to the patriarchal character of the labour market in which women remained very much a subordinate group.
The first interpretation was widely believed by contemporaries, who saw the availability of female paid labour as a threat to the fabric of family life and male dominance, but many of their prejudices have been disposed of by Hewitt's seminal work. (1) More recently, feminist historians have also argued that women's role in the formal economy was of major importance in enhancing women's power. One notable example of this was the fact that these working women seem to have practised birth control and family limitation at an earlier period than in other parts of Britain. (2) This also fed through to formal political activism. Liddington and Norris emphasised the role played by Lancashire working women in the women's suffrage campaign of the Edwardian period. They stressed the importance of women's experience of paid labour for their political action: "...women workers in the cotton towns were always in a considerably stronger position to demand the vote than women elsewhere. They were better organised and better paid; they could call upon a tradition...to strengthen their determination." (3)
Yet against this 'optimistic' interpretation stands one which emphasises the degree to which women's position in the formal economy remained consistent with their patriarchal subordination. Joyce emphasises how the sexual division of labour in the cotton industry was based upon family authority with women being confined

to the worst jobs, both in terms of wages and autonomy. In his view the sexual division of labour which emerged after 1850 with men monopolising supervisory and 'skilled' jobs, marked the reassertion of the patriarchal control which had been briefly threatened in the early nineteenth century. (4)   Many trade union historians have pointed to the marginalisation of women within collective organisations, (5) whilst Elizabeth Roberts has also argued that the experience of women in Preston's cotton industry did not make them more politically conscious than women in Barrow, where very few women worked. (6)

To some extent these ambiguities are testimony to a general theoretical uncertainty about the significance of paid work for women's social and political activism. (7)   But I want to argue that in the case of the Lancashire cotton industry there were also real variations in the experience of women between places. In order to understand the social implications of women's employment it is necessary to complement our understanding of the work process and the family with an analysis of the labour market. The point I want to establish is that women's experience of similar sorts of work could be very different depending on how their work fitted into specific forms of recruitment, skill acquisition, and job loss. In some cases these key processes were organised by male supervisors, and in this case women remained more dependent on male authority than in those cases where they exercised somewhat more control over the labour market themselves (sometimes working with sympathetic male relatives).   If we realise the importance of the processes by which people get directed to particular jobs in the labour market we also need to recognise that labour markets have specific spatial parameters. As a result different local labour markets can have different characteristics even if they are dominated by the same industry.   In short women had no single experience of the cotton industry, but rather it depended on the precise town in which they worked and the character of its local labour market. (8)

I.   The Question of Skill

Recently considerable attention has been placed on the 'social construction of skill', notably the way in which certain groups of workers are able to define their work as 'skilled' and hence deserving higher wages regardless of the actual content of their work. In particular, male workers have often succeeded in defining their jobs as more skilled than jobs usually done by women. (9) It is, however, essential to recognise that there is more to skill than its social definition (what Turner calls 'intrinsic skill') and that the extent to which a particular job requires rare skills has major effects on the strategies pursued by employers in order to find adequately trained workers. (10)

In this respect, although female labour in the cotton industry may not have been recognised as skilled, there are grounds for arguing that in fact it was. (11) This lay partly in the problems of textile technology. Much has been made of the fact that the cotton industry was the first mechanised industry, and Joyce has even argued that, with the introduction of the self-acting mule and the power loom, "control over the labour process was lost as the craft, or quasi craft, worker became the modern factory proletarian". (12) Yet what stands out is in fact the limited nature of this wave of mechanisation, which far from removing operative skill or work control actually raised the issues in a new form.

There were three main points here. Firstly, as a form of batch production, cotton had distinct processes of stopping and starting the process (unlike iron and steel production, for instance, which was continuous). In weaving, beams had to be fitted and the finished cut removed from the loom, and in spinning cops of finished yarn had to be 'doffed'. These processes were not mechanised. Around many of them (such as beaming) it was possible for small groups of male workers to reassert their handicraft skills. Even non-craft workers on the shop floor had to co-operate routinely to ensure that doffing, or cut removal, could be carried out as efficiently as possible. (13) This related to a second problem. The machines were not automatic so that they stopped when they malfunctioned. To prevent bad work it was necessary for workers to keep a constant watch over the looms (or the mules), to stop them if wrong, and to re-start them (though in case of serious problems the overlookers could be called in). While the basic process was mechanised the machine itself had to be routinely overlooked by the operatives.

Finally, the machines never equated easily with individual workers, so that one worker worked one machine. In cotton spinning each pair of mules usually required a work team of three. In weaving and carding the problem was the other way around. Here one worker could work more than one machine (four looms and up to fifteen carding machines). This arrangement necessitated continued operative co-operation in order to get work done. In weaving, should any single loom need undue attention due to a breakdown, it was imperative that another operative should watch over the other looms to ensure they were running smoothly. Further, at various times of the day the weaver had to leave her looms to fetch fresh weft, in which case she would rely on her neighbour to keep a watchful eye on her looms. (14) The need for human co-ordination was not done away with. Hence the idea that mechanisation reduced the worker to machine minding, or that their introduction marked the 'real' subsumption of labour by capital, is totally misleading, for in fact employees had to be constantly on the watch to ensure smooth production.

There were, however, important differences between the various processes. In some processes, such as in the cardroom, where the cotton was prepared for spinning, it was no great problem if work was not perfect, since it could always be remedied at a later stage. If the strands of cotton were not separated perfectly by one machine they might still be separated later on by the other carding machines. It was only in spinning itself that the work had to be good enough to produce marketable yarn. The same applied to weaving, for it was the weaving process itself which was critical. If there was a major fault such as a 'smash', entire pieces of cloth could be lost, or great amounts of time (up to half a day) spent repairing them. Even routine faults, such as a 'float' where a piece of fluff was caught up in the weaving, created problems and the cloth had to be 'unwoven' before recommencing work. (15)

There were also major differences, however, according to the type of quality being produced. In much of the low quality production aimed at the mass Far Eastern market, cost, not quality was the major consideration and the employer could ignore problems of bad work. On the quality British, European and American markets fine production was essential, and the need for a skilled workforce much more important. Many fine cloths were woven on Jacquard (or dobby) looms, run by punched cards, and the weavers had to be able to 'read' these cards in order to know how to restart the loom after a stoppage. (16) As a result weavers in fine weaving were likely to look after fewer looms than in the less skilled plain trade: in Blackburn, where the plain trade predominated the average weaver had 3.5 looms in 1886, compared with 3.1 in the fine weaving town of Preston. The skills needed for different forms of weaving were highly specific. In 1927 the Bolton Weavers' Union recalled that "some of us remember the time when a plain weaver would have stood as much chance of obtaining work in a fancy mill as she would have of being made the manager of it". (17)

These points indicate the complexity of the demand for skills within the cotton industry. The point I want to emphasise is that there were marked spatial implications in the demand for skills because of the well known localisation of the cotton industry where particular processes became concentrated in specific towns. There were two aspects to this. On the one hand there were differences between towns specialising in weaving and in spinning. The latter were based around Manchester, especially in Oldham and Bolton. The weaving towns were based in the north of Lancashire, clustering around the major centres of Preston, Blackburn and Burnley. This separation was never entirely clear cut - one third of the county's weaving looms remained in the spinning area (18) - yet had major implications for the sort of work which women in different towns could expect to find. There was, however, an equally significant divide between the western towns (Bolton, Chorley and Preston) specialising in fine, high quality cotton, and the easterly towns (Oldham, Blackburn and Burnley) geared to the coarse trade.

We have seen that the types of skills needed by employers depended on the process involved and the type of quality produced, and these were also highly localised, with specific towns specialising in different mixes. Table 11.1 indicates how the sexual division of labour related to the complex spatial pattern. One major feature which stands out is that it is those towns specialising in high quality production - Preston, Bolton and Chorley - which had the highest proportions of female weavers. It is hence not correct to say that women's work was as skilled as men's: in fact women weavers tended to be employed on more skilled forms of weaving. In the fine weaving town of Preston only 9 per cent of the weaving workforce were adult males, whilst in the plain weaving town of Burnley 22 per cent were. The reasons for this variation are complex, but it owes much to the fact that in the western towns since the late eighteenth century there had been abundant male employment in engineering, mule spinning and coal mining, so that when power loom weaving developed after 1840 the only available labour to draw upon was that of women. The easterly towns, however, developed as specialised weaving towns and hence both men and women became reliant upon employment in the industry. Further, in the same places there was a tradition of wool weaving, where it was not regarded as demeaning for men to be weavers, as was the case in west Lancashire. But of course the irony was that men tended to be most commonly found as weavers where skills were less needed (the most notable exception being Nelson, a fine weaving town but where men were well represented). The fine quality weaving employers had to rely upon a predominantly female labour force.

Table 11.1: Spinning and Weaving Employment in Lancashire, 1901

	%-age of working pop in cotton	%-age of cotton workers in spinning sector 1901	%-age of weavers who are male	%-age of weavers who are males over 25
Oldham	41.7	67.1	7.4	6.0
Bolton	35.4	57.7	13.3	9.2
Preston	40.8	21.7	20.7	10.2
Blackburn	52.1	11.5	30.7	17.0
Burnley	53.2	8.1	39.2	21.9

Source: 1901 Census

II. Patterns of Skill Acquisition in Lancashire Cotton, 1880-1914

Employers could not rely on a casualised, unskilled workforce, and many women were engaged on skilled tasks. There was no uniform set of employer responses to the problem of finding an adequate labour force, however, but different strategies were used. The type of strategy used had a number of implications for the capacities of women to engage in collective action.

One side of the coin was seen most clearly in cardroom employment. Here, there was the creation of an elaborate internal labour market for women. The cardroom's occupations were strongly sex typed, with women performing all the operations except stripping and grinding, and the supervisory tasks. The male strippers and grinders were responsible for cleaning the carding machines and had very little contact with the female workers engaged on the routine operations. There was, however, a variety of these routine occupations.

Despite the fact that the cardroom tended to employ younger women, there was an intensive internal labour market by which girls were steadily promoted up a well defined hierarchy. The (male) carder was responsible for the recruitment and promotion of these workers, and even in the 1930s, seniority rules generally did not apply. Broadly, a girl began at age 14 as an assistant on any of the frames used to separate and prepare the raw cotton. After a while she would be moved to the cards, where she would spend a couple of months wiping (i.e. cleaning) the cards, and then be put in charge of 14 or 15 cards (responsible for feeding raw cotton into the frame and collecting the output). After this she would normally be moved to 'Ribbon and Derbies' (where the cotton from the cards was formed into ribbons) then to combers (where the ribbons were combed to make the fibres parallel), and then onto slubbers, and finally onto intermediate or jack frames. It was normally expected that by the age of 27 the woman could have been promoted to become an intermediate tenter: a twelve year training cycle! (19)

According to one Bolton carder, interviewed by Mass Observation, "each job is learnt from the job just before it in order of progression". Thus, as a card wiper, the worker would learn how to tent cards, and as a card tenter she would be taught how to look after Ribbon and Derby machines. It was very difficult for women, once in the cardroom, to get other jobs in cotton outside it. The Bolton carder noted that many women wanted to transfer to winding but they were rarely allowed to do so. "We in the cardroom look upon each girl as a prospective tenter for a particular machine and endeavour to train her for this position." The only exception was that cardroom workers might be transferred to the blowing room (where the work mainly involved putting bundles of raw cotton into the machine which initially broke it down). A carder stated that "if she is strong and it is known to the manager that she is hard up she goes into the blowing room". (20)

The ability to acquire the necessary skills was hence dependent upon the carder's decisions, notably in allowing women to try different work when the regular worker was off sick. The reasons why this internal labour market developed lay in the fact that although much of the work was not highly skilled, absenteeism created immense problems which could disrupt the progress of the cotton over the various carding machines. By creating a well defined job hierarchy workers were encouraged not to miss work since they would be passed over for promotion should this happen. (21)

The situation was very different in winding and weaving. In winding, girls were trained not by working up a mill hierarchy but by being put under an expert, trained, winder and learning from her. There were usually only two men in the winding room, the overlooker, and the labourer who moved the skips of full cops.

Apart from these there were only fully trained winders and their assistants, and not an elaborate hierarchy as in the cardroom and as a result there "was much more of a winding room spirit". In the weaving sheds there was a similar situation where young weavers were effectively taught by older weavers as their tenters before being put on two looms, and after reaching a certain level of proficiency were promoted up to four looms by either the mill overlooker or manager. (22) As in winding the skill transmission was primarily from shop floor worker to trainee without the active intervention of overlookers or male workers, but unlike winding the overlooker's discretion was of considerable importance in being promoted to work on a full complement of looms, with the necessary assistance. Further, unlike winding there were male weavers.

Very broadly, then, a key distinction was between those occupations where skill transmission was from worker to worker, and those where supervisory workers were more actively involved in the process. This difference was of major importance in affecting the capacities of women to engage in collective action. In the latter case workers remained more dependent on supervisors and were less able to challenge their authority, whilst in the former they had more autonomy to mobilise collectively. The contrasts between the militancy of female workers in the spinning sector and the weaving sector is well known. (23) Women who worked in the preparatory process in the cardroom were the last group of workers to be widely unionised, and were not especially politically active. The winders, however, who wound yarn onto cops for weaving were a small but militant group, and the weavers, the majority of the female textile workforce, were also well unionised and militant, at least in some areas. The winders and weavers also tended to be the most experienced industrial workers. Table 11.2 examines the age profile of these different types of worker.

Table 11.2: Age Profile of Female Cotton Workers, 1911

	under 20	20-24	25-35	over 35	total no.
Cardroom	38.0%	22.0%	22.1%	17.9%	55,448
Winding	26.3%	20.3%	26.6%	26.7%	59,171
Spinning	46.2%	22.9%	19.2%	11.7%	55,448
Weaving	32.8%	19.9%	25.9%	21.4%	190,922

Source: 1911 Census

It can readily be observed that winding in particular had higher proportions of older women, especially compared to women working in spinning, who were mainly ring spinners. The fact that the two earlier processes had younger workers, on the whole, than winding and weaving is further evidence of the greater need for experienced workers at the later stages of production.

So far I have emphasised the broad differences between the occupations. Yet there were also major differences in employer strategy between places, depending partly on the quality produced, and partly on the nature of local social relations. These variations were especially marked in weaving, where there were three distinct types of local labour market in various parts of Lancashire.

On the one hand, Preston was characterised by fine quality weaving, with a predominantly female weaving labour force. The problem of finding an adequately skilled labour force was resolved by the delegation of labour market functions to the male supervisory workforce, notably the overlookers. Employers (and managers) played very little part in recruiting workers but relied upon the male workers to secure an adequately skilled female workforce by their local knowledge of the qualities of specific weavers in their neighbourhoods. Hence, whilst skilled weavers could not be identified by their possession of formal qualifications (such as an apprenticeship), they could be known by the overlookers' personal contacts. Since the wages of overlookers were related to the wages of their weavers, employers could normally rely upon the overlookers doing their best to secure a skilled workforce under them. This system had a number of implications for gender relations in weaving. Overlookers, in their attempts to restrict recruitment to their trade, had a distinct incentive not to employ male weavers (who might be promoted to become overlookers). They hence encouraged the feminisation of weaving in Preston, and in the process helped secure a powerful niche for themselves. Furthermore, some overlookers employed their own family members, possibly in place of more skilled workers, in order to maximise family income. (24)

A very different situation developed in Bolton, where weaving was also fine quality and highly demanding. Key employers were far more active in recruiting labour. To become a weaver at Tootal's (one of the leading local firms) a girl had to put her name down at the office when she was 13, and after she was taken on she relied upon the manager to gain promotion to work on more looms. In Preston, the weaving overlookers had an undifferentiated work role encompassing recruiting, general supervision, and maintenance work on the looms, but in Tootal's (at least by the inter-war years) the overlookers were only loom mechanics, while supervision was hived off to a foreman and supervisor. Instead of relying upon male workers to bring forward their female relatives or contacts the employers used the schools to find labour. One cardroom worker, Hilda, observed that, "they just don't ask you at school, they just send you where there's room". At Daubhill Mills the employers developed a range of 'paternalist' institutions, such as factory schools and canteens by which young workers could be channelled into appropriate jobs. (25)

These differences between Preston and Bolton owed much to the legacy of the 1853-4 Preston lockout, which permanently dissuaded

Preston employers from becoming involved in heavy handed paternalism. Employers in Preston were quick to dissociate themselves from social life, left the church supreme in school provision, and were not generally hostile to trade unions, one employer even subsidising them through the hard times of the Cotton Famine. Bolton, however, along with parts of South East Lancashire such as Ashton, where high quality production was also common, remained one of the main sites of pervasive employer intervention throughout the Victorian period, a process which enabled employers to recruit labour by personal contact through the key agencies of school and church. The 'Bolton model' was widely used in small rural mills, where the absence of alternative employment made the local population much more dependent on the mills, and employers could take a much more active role in recruiting labour, often using the local schools and church. The importance of this was to be fully revealed in the inter-war years when the dependence of village populations on rural mills enabled many employers here to undermine union agreements on wages and conditions, so allowing them constantly to undercut the urban employers where unionisation, and a more diversified labour market prevented employers from controlling the situation. (26)

In Blackburn and (especially) Burnley, weaving was generally less skilled, with Burnley specialising in medium weight grey cloths, and Blackburn in plain dhooties. Whereas in Preston the sexual division of labour in weaving matched the family hierarchy, with the men monopolising the supervisory jobs, in Burnley there were large numbers of male weavers, and a greater reliance on family employment. (27) Here, as in Preston, recruitment was largely by family contacts, but the family took on a less patriarchal pattern because of the general equality between male and female weavers. According to a local union official, it was the 'general rule' for male weavers to marry female weavers, and they were also likely to take their children to the weaving shed as early as possible. In these sheds "women work under similar conditions to the men, run the same number of looms and are paid the same rates...and earn as much", and it was also reported that "a female is as good a weaver as a man, in fact in most cases better." (28) The strength of the weaving family in such areas helped to erode the authority of the overlookers, a process manifested in Nelson in the 1890s when the Weavers' Union succeeded in preventing male overlookers from intimidating women weavers. (29) Outside the workplace, Gittins has shown how the husbands and wives she interviewed in Burnley shared domestic labour when they did identical paid work (not where the wife did a less well paid job). It was these areas also where family limitation was practised ahead of all other urban areas, as women chose to restrict their family size, a prospect more easily achieved where gender relations were more equal since most forms of contraception relied on male compliance. This had the further effect of reducing the supply of labour for the cotton mills, so ensuring that the labour market remained tight. (30)

Women were hence bound up in a variety of local labour

markets. In some cases, such as the cardroom, they were part of a highly complex internal labour market. In winding they were part of an exclusive female occupation of almost craft status. In weaving there was more complexity, with pervasive local differences between those areas where employers remained active in recruiting and training skilled labour, those areas where male supervisory workers occupied a key position, and those where the male and female weavers themselves exercised a considerable degree of shop floor autonomy over skill acquisition and work control.

III. The Development of Trade Unionism in the Cotton Industry

The patterns discussed above had important implications for the growth of trade unionism in the cotton industry. The mule spinning sector was unionised early, and by the 1890s had secured virtually 100 per cent membership throughout the county. The Cardroom Unions however remained much weaker, and were dominated by the male strippers and grinders, who used the Union to secure sectional benefits for themselves, rather than general gains for women cardroom workers. (31) The weaving sector was however subject to more intense local variation in strength, as Table 11.3 shows.

Table 11.3: Union Density in Cotton Weaving Towns, 1891

	no. of weavers in union	no. of weavers in town	union density (%)
Burnley	12,045	12,078	100
Bury	3,525	4,711	75
Blackburn	10,800	17,257	62
Rochdale	2,800	5,087	46
Preston	5,000	12,488	40
Wigan	900	2,238	40
Bolton	3,000	10,363	29
Oldham	3,600	13,375	27

<u>Source:</u> L. Pickard, M.A. Thesis, 1980, University of Warwick

The initial heartlands of the weavers' unions were in those areas where there were high proportions of male weavers. This should not lead us to assume that men are 'naturally' more militant than women, however. Rather, the significant determinant of unionisation was the extent to which recruitment was controlled by the workers themselves rather than by either elite male workers or employers. In Burnley and Blackburn, where recruitment was family based and fathers and mothers could pass on membership to their children recruitment was easier than where the labour market was policed by overlookers, as in Preston, or directly by employers, as in Bolton. In Burnley and Blackburn the weavers could normally insist that trainees (tenters) should join the union. Thus in Blackburn the weavers' union developed a very strong shop floor presence, with a powerful committee of mill representatives (almost equivalent to shop stewards), though in other areas the Union failed to establish work-based organisation and relied on neighbourhood organisation, manifested most notably in the collecting system, where members subscriptions were taken on the doorstep by collectors who canvassed on a commission basis. In many areas only the elite unions were well organised at the point of work, and they often used this against other groups of workers. In Preston, the overlookers used their influence to prevent the unionisation of weavers, fearing that they would lose authority at work should this occur. As late as the 1890s the overlookers claimed that of the 1,000 weavers who were related to themselves only five were members of the Weavers' Union. In Bolton, employers such as the Lees at Daubhill remained strongly anti-union, and had the ability to prevent their formation because of their hold in the labour market until the early years of the century (32)

In all areas the weaving unions were dominated by men, even though there were no formal rules preventing women's full participation in the union. Part of the explanation for male hegemony was because it was difficult for women to attend evening meetings in the context of their continued responsibility for domestic labour in many areas; yet there is also considerable evidence of informal bars against women's participation. In Preston it was said that no woman who wished to stand for union office was dissuaded from doing so. In Bolton, even in the 1930s, Mass Observation reported that "in the Cardroom and the Weavers' Union a caucus of males works to keep women from office, although they form the vast majority of members". (33) The character of unionism differed, however, depending on the proportion of male weavers in the town. Where there were small numbers of male weavers there was a general expectation that they would be promoted to one of the elite male jobs, and hence the union tended to be conciliatory to employers. Where there were too many men for there to be general expectations of future promotion, notably in Burnley, Nelson and Colne, unionism took on a very different, more militant character, concerned with increasing the status of weaving as a permanent, skilled occupation. It was these areas of North East Lancashire which became the centres of militant union activity, extending from the demands for 100 per cent unionisation before the First World War, through the campaigns against the more looms system and against wage cuts in the 1920s and 1930s. (34)

There was one major point of paradox between the policies of the spinning unions and the weaving unions. The Weavers' Amalgamation, whose membership was highly localised, sought to establish a uniform list of wages, to cover all cloths in all areas, whilst the Spinners' Amalgamation, whose membership was fairly uniform across the county, defended local list prices.

Effectively, there were two dominant lists of prices in spinning: the Oldham list which provided for coarse spinning; and the Bolton list which was used for fine spinning, but the minor lists, such as Preston's, remained in use well into the twentieth century. In weaving, however, the Blackburn and Burnley lists were replaced by a Uniform List in 1892, which provided complex formulae for converting all forms of cloth into a certain 'uniform' standard which could then be used to calculate their respective prices. (35) The key point is that the impetus towards the establishment of a Uniform List came from those areas specialising in lesser skilled production, notably Blackburn and Burnley, which also tended to be the areas where men were most likely to be weavers. The important thing about the Uniform List was that though it attempted to allow for variations in quality it tended to benefit workers on less skilled weaving since it increased earnings the greater the number of looms worked and according to speed of production. In a sense the formation of the Uniform List had the effect of putting the brake on the wages earned in the more skilled sectors, which tended to be in those areas where there were fewer male weavers. This explains why Preston employers, specialising in fancy cloth, recognised the list, even though the Union was not strong enough to impose it on them. It was in Burnley, however, producing plain goods, where opposition from employers was most marked.

Table 11.4: Wage Changes in Cotton Weaving, 1886-1906 (1)

	wage rates 1886		% increase 1906		wage differential	
	M	F	M	F	1886	1906 (2)
Burnley	21/7	21/4	+20.1	+18.4	+1.2	+2.6
Blackburn	21/-	16/6	+21.0	+50.0	+28.3	+2.7
Preston	21/11	17/11	+13.3	+28.8	+22.3	+7.6
Bolton	18/10	17/4	+31.9	+29.8	+8.7	+8.8
Oldham	-	19/9	-	+7.6		
Lancashire	20/10	19/11	+20.4	+18.0	+4.6	+6.7

(1) All wages for four loom weavers
(2) % by which male wage exceeds female wage
Source: Wage Census 1886, 1906

Table 11.4 indicates how wages in the weaving centres were affected by the Uniform List. There is clear evidence that it did help erode male differentials which had previously been current in Preston and Blackburn, where men had formerly earned over 20 per cent more than women on the same number of looms. On the other hand, local differentials in favour of Blackburn and Burnley remained, though wages in fine quality Bolton also rose fast.

Certainly, however, differences in skill levels between towns were not reflected in local wage differentials, and there is little evidence that more skilled weavers were more ardent unionists.

The differences between the different weaving centres were also manifest in local politics. Women in North East Lancashire gave major support for the women's suffrage movement, and the trade unions actively involved themselves in suffrage campaigns. In ballots on the question of women's suffrage held in 1903 it was the Eastern towns which were prominent in their support. In Bolton the feminist movement was also well organised, though often dominated by women outside the cotton mills. In Preston, however, the trade unions, still dominated by the exclusive male trades, were unsympathetic to women's issues and many feminists were alienated from the Labour Party as a result. (36)

IV. The Cotton Industry in Depression: the Significance of Gender Dynamics

The First World War was of major significance in affecting the sexual division of labour in several branches of the cotton industry, and also led to the adoption of novel employer strategies. Large numbers of male workers left the industry in the early years of the war, and very few cotton occupations were made exempt from military service. In many areas weaving became an overwhelmingly female occupation at this time, and only in parts of North East Lancashire did large numbers of men remain in the industry. In the spinning sector many badly paid piecers took the opportunity to leave the industry, creating major labour shortages and demands for the employment of women piecers. Yet just as demands for female labour in the cotton industry were increasing many employers also found themselves losing labour to munitions plants, which generally paid better wages than the cotton industry.

Most cotton trade unions fiercely opposed the widespread employment of women and pledged themselves to support the re-introduction of male labour after hostilities ended. The Cotton Factory Times stated that "we claim the solemn obligation to all the men who went away will necessitate those women going out as quickly as possible...we must get the women back in the home as soon as the war is over". (37) In most towns women were used as piecers with union consent, though in Preston the Spinners' Union adamantly refused to allow this. Although women were only to be introduced as low grade workers there was a general assumption that unions would not be able to prevent them being promoted to higher level jobs in time. In the spinning industry as a whole the pre-war sexual division of labour was restored after 1918, and there were few attempts thereafter to employ women as piecers.

The widespread demand for female labour, combined with the absence of elite male workers, forced many employers to develop new means of supplying labour. In Preston, employers increasingly looked to the Labour Exchange for this purpose, by-passing the old reliance on the overlookers' personal contacts. In 1916 the cotton employers agreed to fill all vacancies through the Labour Exchange, and this meant that female labour was now directed into employment through the state rather than via male working class contact. This allowed the privileged position of overlookers to be seriously undermined after 1918 and mill managers became much more central to the recruitment and supervision process. (38)

The use of the Labour Exchange was, however, subject to considerable local variation. After 1918 it was still widely used in Preston and in other parts of North Lancashire, but in Bolton, according to Mass Observation, it was rarely called upon. Many large Bolton firms developed welfare schemes, many directed specifically at female labour and designed to retain workers' loyalty. Employers hence still directly recruited their workforce and employers remained active in the labour market. Thus at Cobden Mill all the labour was from school or family connections and the Labour Exchange was rarely used. Recruitment was directed by a full time welfare supervisor who would interview all applicants and make appropriate recommendations which were always followed. This degree of welfarist intervention was rarely found elsewhere. In North East Lancashire the firms were generally too small to allow it, whilst in Preston the leading firms of Horrocks' and Dewhurst's abandoned comprehensive welfare schemes in the early 1920s as soon as money became tight. (39)

The state was hence far more involved in the workings of the labour market after 1914. The 'Preston model', where male overlookers had directed the recruitment of labour, and the 'Burnley model' of family based recruitment, were both eroded by the creation of a bureaucratised state system of directing workers to jobs. In Burnley by the 1930s less than a third of youngsters found work through family contacts. This erosion of family based employment did, however, facilitate women's collective mobilisation since their male relatives were no longer central to the labour market, hence giving them great autonomy to mobilise. Women's activities in many weaving unions increased considerably in this period, and it became more common for them to become committee members. In Preston wildcat strikes initiated by women became a not infrequent occurrence during the 1930s, and women were actively involved in the major industrial disputes of the 1920s and 1930s, and in the Communist led Minority Movement, which became a powerful force in the Blackburn and Burnley Weavers' Unions. Nonetheless, most unions continued to be male dominated, and some, such as the Darwen Weavers' Union went to the length of instituting a Women's Committee to encourage female participation. (40)

To some extent the employers' problem in finding skilled labour increased in the inter-war years, despite the economic problems the industry faced after the loss of many of its markets abroad. Unemployment reached 22 per cent in 1923, recovered to 9 per cent in 1925, but then climbed to 43 per cent in 1931, falling only slowly to 11 per cent in 1937. Yet much of this unemployment was in the coarse production side. Table 11.5 shows that in 1931 unemployment in Bolton's quality trade was well below the Lancashire average. The main declining markets were in the less skilled trades, where the Far East was increasingly able to produce their own goods. The home and European markets, geared to fine quality production remained more buoyant (at least until 1929), and this encouraged firms to abandon their traditional specialisms in favour of crowding into this fine production, demanding more skilled workers. By the 1930s there were complaints of skill shortages in the weaving trade despite the high level of un-employment.

Table 11.5: Male and Female Unemployment in Lancashire Cotton, 1931

		% men unemployed	% women unemployed
Blackburn	- all workers	25.4	41.6
	- cotton workers	48.4	53.9
Burnley	- all workers	20.0	29.5
	- cotton workers	27.4	36.3
Bolton	- all workers	16.7	12.4
	- cotton workers	14.6	15.4
Oldham	- all workers	24.0	21.0
	- cotton workers	25.9	26.5
Preston	- all workers	17.0	20.9
	- cotton workers	26.1	28.9
Lancashire	- all workers	17.2	16.3
	- cotton workers	24.4	28.4

Source: 1931 Census, which is not an ideal source since it tends to understate unemployment

This shift made employers keen to develop their retailing outlets, in order to gain access to the home market. What capital there was (and there was very little since most had been burnt out in the financial speculation of the 1918-19 period) tended to be diverted from changing technology to improving market access. In Preston, for instance, Horrocks' and Hawkins both developed nationwide chains of stores selling their cotton in this period. As a result there was little attempt seriously to change working practices to deskill workers, and the introduction of the automatic loom, which stopped as soon as there was a fault, hence doing away with the need for constant operative attention, was very tardy. Indeed, the growing emphasis upon fine production, combined with the need of employers to work under tighter margins led to a greater reliance of employers upon the workers' skills. Quality control, based in the warehouse, became more stringent, and weavers were subjected to much stronger supervision, and even fines, from the clothlookers, while more women were employed in the warehouse to improve imperfect cloth. The growing importance of the clothlooking function removed autonomy from the overlooker, hitherto the generally acknowledged centre of authority, and allowed managers, liaising with clothlookers, to become more centrally concerned with supervision. (41)

Firms specialising in coarse production attempted to meet foreign competition by increasing labour intensiveness, basically by forcing workers to work more looms than the customary four, with only limited increases in weavers' wages. This strategy had the advantage of needing negligible capital outlay in new equipment, since it could be carried out on the existing looms, but of dispensing with large amounts of labour. It was estimated that one-third of the labour could be dispensed with while production was kept constant. The demands for the more looms system came first from the Burnley employers, whose 30 inch looms were especially easy to attend. (42)

These strategies had contradictory consequences. On the one hand there was a growing need for skilled weaving labour, both in the fine quality side, and in the plain production where work was effectively being speeded up. At the same time, however, considerable amounts of labour was to be dispensed with, and this raised the possibility that skilled women's labour, hitherto pivotal to weaving production, could be dispensed with, in favour of adult men's employment, at least in those towns where there were enough male weavers to make this viable. There was also to be an increased division of labour in the weaving sheds. As we have seen, in the Victorian period workers had to co-operate with each other to cover workers who were absent on special duties. The more looms system envisaged relieving weavers of many of those odd tasks such as cleaning, oiling, and weft fetching, so reducing the need for shop floor contacts. This also might have reduced the need for experienced workers. (43)

There were indeed sporadic attempts to undermine the position of married women at work from the early 1920s. In 1927 it was reported that at some weaving sheds in Bolton and Leigh it was "the practice in periods of slackness to suspend married women and give preference to the single". (44) Plans to implement the more loom system caused such ideas to gain further currency. The Manchester University survey of the effects of the introduction of more looms envisaged a reduction in the number of women workers from 200 to 74, whilst the number of male workers would actually increase from 104 to 126. The Burnley employers suggested that if married women stopped working "it would probably solve the labour surplus in Burnley". More detailed proposals were that married women without dependants should cease work, whilst single men and women should work alternate weeks, but both men and women with dependants should work full time. Other agreements, however, such as that by the Nelson firm of James Nelson, only made provision not to lay off heads of households, and did not specifically refer to gender. (45)

It is possible to examine whether women were more likely to become unemployed than men using 1931 Census data, though there is the danger that unemployed women would have been more likely not to declare themselves as unemployed cotton workers (see Table 11.5). Despite this, in all the weaving towns, there was a higher proportion of female unemployment than male unemployment. This was caused largely by women's concentration in the vulnerable weaving sector, but there is also some evidence that even within weaving women were more likely to be made unemployed, than men. In Burnley, for instance, in an almost entirely weaving town, 27 per cent of male cotton workers were unemployed compared with 36 per cent of female. In the spinning towns, however, there is little evidence that women suffered more than men, largely because the strength of sex typing in the spinning sector meant that equal proportions of both lost their jobs.

The attempt to introduce the more looms system and intensify work was hence bound up with an attack on the position of women in the labour market and there is clear evidence that men were more likely to be used in the new working arrangements. Nonetheless, it is important to recognise that in the major industrial disputes of the late twenties and early thirties men and women usually did stand firm together, united against the use of the system on the employers' terms. In North East Lancashire the removal of women from the labour force would have reduced family income which would not have been compensated for by the increased wages of the male weaver who was redeployed under the new arrangements, whilst in other areas there were too few men to make this a viable proposition. There were a few places, often small weaving villages, where discrimination against women seems to have been particularly acute and caused some tension between men and women. It was from these areas, such as Great Harwood, Accrington, Rishton and Clayton-le-Moors, that some women, presumably desperate for work, were recruited as strikebreakers in the various disputes of the period. (46)

It may be the case that these tensions between men and women fed through into formal politics in the crucial 1928-32 period, and the Labour Party did extremely badly in Lancashire in the 1931 General Election, even compared with its dismal performance in the rest of the country. However, the more looms scheme was never introduced on a wide scale, only about 15 per cent of looms being worked under the scheme in the late 1930s, and with the expansion of jobs for men, especially in those areas where engineering was strong, tensions over female labour became less intense. Indeed, by the 1930s employers were often short of labour for many processes, and skilled weavers were at a premium. In Bolton there was considerable concern about the labour turnover, and in Preston many of the weaving sheds reported skill shortages by 1937. The continued fall in the birth rate, and the difficulties of older women workers staying in the labour market (state unemployment regulations being a major factor here) compounded the problem. (47)

V. Conclusions

The position of Lancashire working women did change considerably in the early years of this century. The central features of this change did not, however, lie in the changes in the workplace or in changes in family life, but in the changing intersection between the two. Before 1914 the social divisions between home and work were of limited significance. Authority in the workplace was related to authority in the household. Where family structure was relatively egalitarian, as it appears to have been in Burnley, women's contribution to the domestic economy was recognised. On the other hand, where supervisors invoked patriarchal control based on male power within the household (as they did in Preston), women's lot was much worse. In both cases, however, the workplace was not a refuge from the family or neighbourhood environment: it offered little potential for women to mobilise as women (rather than as family or class members), and it is unsurprising that many women desired to move out of paid employment into the home.

This situation was, however, to change in subtle but important ways after 1914, not as a result of major changes in technology or working practices, but primarily because state intervention allowed employers to find good weavers without relying on detailed, individual knowledge of workers gained through non-work contacts, a process aided by a growing professional managerial cadre, and suburbanisation. At one level this gave women greater freedom and autonomy in the workplace. They were more likely to be working in a single sex environment (if they were weavers), and did not owe their jobs to the role of working class men. There is indeed evidence that women did develop a stronger shop floor solidarity than before, especially in the mid-twenties and later thirties. At the same time, however, the decline of the cotton industry led to decreased security in the labour market, and many, particularly older women, left the industry. Furthermore, although women's capacities for collective action increased, they were less likely to be used in distinctly feminist ways. Whilst before 1914 any attempt to mobilise collectively inevitably questioned patterns of patriarchal authority more generally (since these were present in the workplace) after 1914 it was possible to organise purely over work based issues. Hence the feminist movement which developed before 1914 in some parts of Lancashire became more difficult to sustain afterwards. Women's political involvement increased, but usually took place inside existing political parties and structures.

NOTES

1. See for a contemporary view the Interdepartmental Committee on Physical Deterioration, British Sessional Papers 1904, Vol. XXXII, and M. Hewitt, Wives and Mothers in Victorian Industry, (Rockcliff, 1958).

2. D. Gittins, Fair Sex, (London, 1982); A. Maclaren,

'Women's Work and Regulation of Family Size', History Workshop, 4, 1977.

3. J. Liddington and J. Norris, One Hand Tied Behind Us: The Rise of the Women's Suffrage Movement, (London, 1978), p. 63. See also C. Morgan, At the Crossroads: Women and Weaving in the Mid-Nineteenth Century, unpublished paper, 1985.

4. P. Joyce, Work, Society and Politics, (Brighton, 1980), p. 111-15. See also M. Burawoy, The Politics of Production, (London, 1985), pp. 95-9.

5. B. Drake, Women in Trade Unions, (London, 1920); K. Burgess, The Origins of British Industrial Relations, (London, 1975).

6. E. Roberts, A Woman's Place, (London, 1985).

7. See for instance many of the essays in A. John (ed.), Unequal Opportunities: Women's Employment in England, 1800 - 1918, (Oxford, 1986); J. Mark-Lawson, M. Savage and A. Warde, 'Women and local politics: struggles over welfare 1918-1939', in L. Murgatroyd, M. Savage, D. Shapiro, J. Urry, S. Walby and A. Warde, Localities, Class and Gender, (London, 1985); M. Savage, The Dynamics of Working Class Politics: the Labour Movement in Preston 1900-1940, (Cambridge, 1987); more generally, R. Milkman, Women, Work and Protest: a Century of U.S. Women's Labour History, (London, 1985).

8. More generally on the significance of 'localities' see M. Savage, The Dynamics of Working Class Politics; D. Massey, Spatial Divisions of Labour (London, 1984); D. Massey and L. McDowell, 'A Woman's Place', in J. Allen and D. Massey (eds.), Geography Matters!, (Cambridge, 1984).

9. H.A. Turner, Trade Union Growth Structure and Policy, (London, 1962). See the essays in S. Wood (ed.), The Degradation of Work? (London, 1982). For the specific case of women and skill, B. Phillips and B. Taylor, 'Sex and Skill: Notes towards a Feminist Economics', Feminist Review, 6, 1980. For a discussion of this concept in relation to work in the silk and wool industries see Jill Norris, ch. 10 and Deirdre Busfield, ch. 8, section I and II.

10. This aspect of skill has recently been emphasised by C. More, Skill and the English Working Class, 1870-1914, (London, 1980).

11. A number of writers have argued that textile manufacturing required little skill, for instance K. Burgess, op. cit., (1975), p. 237; W. Lazonick, 'Industrial Relations and Technical Change: the Case of the Self Acting Mule', Cambridge Journal of Economics, 1979; Joyce, op. cit..

12. Joyce, op. cit., p. 61.

13. M. Friefeld, 'Technical Change and the Self Acting Mule: a Case Study of Skill and the Sexual Division of Labour', Social History, 11, 3, 1986. See also L.H.C. Tippett, A Portrait of the Lancashire Textile Industry, (London, 1969), esp. p. 74.

14. Tippett, op. cit., pp. 88-89; M. Savage, 'Capitalist and Patriarchal Relations in Preston Cotton Weaving 1890-1940', in L. Murgatroyd, et al., op. cit.

15. Tippett, op. cit., p. 74; see the transcripts of the Bolton Oral History Project, esp. 5, 28a.
16. Bolton Oral History, 28a.
17. Bolton Journal, 13/4/28.
18. D. Farnie, The English Cotton Industry and the World Market, 1815-1896, (Oxford, 1979), p. 307.
19. Bolton Oral History, 34b.
20. Mass Observation Worktown Archive, Box. 33.
21. Tippett, op. cit., p. 84.
22. Mass Observation Worktown Archive.
23. See especially Liddington and Norris, op. cit.; J.L. White, The Limits of Trade Union Militancy, (Westport, 1978).
24. See Savage, 'Capitalist and Patriarchal Relations', and for more detail, M. Savage, The Social Bases of Working Class Politics: the Labour Movement in Preston 1890-1940, (University of Lancaster, Ph.D. thesis, 1984).
25. Bolton Oral History, 5; Mass Observation Archive, Box 32, 33; J. Liddington, Z. Munby, J. Seddon, 'There's no Room at Daubhill for me: an Account of the Daubhill Weavers' Strike, Bolton, 1904-5', unpublished paper.
26. On Preston, H. Dutton and J. King, 'The Limits of Paternalism: the Cotton Tyrants of North Lancashire 1836-1854', Social History, 7, 1982, 59-74.
27. B. Drake, op. cit., p. 119.
28. Royal Commission on Labour, Minutes of Evidence, British Sessional Papers, 1892, Vol. 27, pp. 157, 163, 183-4.
29. A. and L. Fowler, The History of the Nelson Weavers Association (Manchester, 1985). See also J. Lambertz, 'Sexual Harrassment in the Nineteenth Century English Cotton Industry', in History Workshop, 19, 1985.
30. D. Gittins, Fair Sex, (London, 1982); for Bolton see the Mass Observation Archive Box 32; for Preston, E. Roberts, op. cit. and Savage, The Dynamics of Working Class Politics.
31. On the spinning unions, A. Fowler and T. Wyke (eds.), The Barefoot Aristocrats, (Littleborough, 1987); R.F. Dyson, The Development of Collective Bargaining in the Cotton Spinning Industry 1893 - 1914, University of Leeds, Ph.D., 1971; R. Penn, Skilled Workers in the Class Structure, (Cambridge, 1984); on the cardroom, A. Bullen and A. Fowler, The Cardroom Workers' Union (Manchester, 1986); generally, Turner, Trade Union Growth. See also A. Fowler, ch. 6.
32. A. Bullen, op. cit.. For the Preston details, Savage, The Dynamics of Working Class Politics.
33. Elizabeth Roberts' oral history transcripts; Mass Observation Archive Box 33; more generally on women's lack of involvement, B. Hutchins, Women in Modern Industry, (London, 1915), pp. 104-8; B. Drake, op. cit.; J. Bornat, 'Lost Leaders: Women, Trade Unionism and the Case of the General Union of Textile Workers, 1875-1914', in John (ed.), Unequal Opportunities.
34. J. White, The Limits of Trade Union Militancy; A. and L. Fowler, op. cit. See also A. Fowler, ch. 6, section II.
35. E. Hopwood, A History of the Lancashire Cotton Industry

and the Amalgamated Weavers Union: the Lancashire Weavers' Story, (Manchester, 1969); A. Bullen, op. cit..

36. Liddington and Norris, op. cit., p. 158. See also J. Mark-Lawson, M. Savage, A. Warde, 'Gender and Local Politics: Struggles over Welfare 1918-1939', in Murgatroyd, et al., op. cit.

37. Cotton Factory Times, 23/6/1916. Generally, see G. Braybon, Women Workers in the First World War, (London, 1980).

38. For more detail, Savage, 'Capitalist and Patriarchal Relations...', op. cit.

39. Mass Observation Archive Box 33. See also Steve Jones, ch. 4, on mill welfarism in the 1920s and 1930s.

40. Minutes of Blackburn Weavers' Association, passim; Savage, thesis, p. 182-3; J. and S. Jewkes, The Juvenile Labour Market, (London, 1938).

41. M. Savage, Control at Work: North Lancashire Cotton Weaving, 1890-1940, Lancaster Regionalism Group Working Paper 7, 1982.

42. J.H. Riley, The More Looms System and Industrial Relations in the Lancashire Cotton Industry 1928-1935, University of Manchester, M.A. thesis, 1981. For more details on employer strategies in cotton in this period see A. McIvor, ch. 1.

43. Board of Trade Survey of Lancashire, 1934.

44. Bolton Journal, 18/2/27.

45. All these cases from Riley, thesis.

46. Riley notes that many strikebreakers in the 1932 dispute came from Great Harwood, Accrington, Rishton and Clayton le Moors. In three of these places there were very great differentials between the rate of male and female unemployment: in Clayton le Moors 58 per cent for women but only 22 per cent for men, in Great Harwood 54 per cent of women compared to 39 per cent, in Accrington 29 per cent compared to 12 per cent, and even in Rishton 29 per cent compared to 19 per cent. See also A. Bullen, op. cit., p. 53 and C.J. Wrigley, A History of British Industrial Relations, Vol. II, Brighton; esp. p. 108.

47. On Bolton, Mass Observation Archive. On Preston, Savage, Control at Work, op. cit.

SELECT BIBLIOGRAPHY

Bornat, J., 'Lost Leaders: Women, Trade Unionism and the Case of the General Union of Textile Workers, 1875-1914' in John, A.V. (ed.), Unequal Opportunities: Women's Employment in England, 1800-1918, (London, 1986)

Braverman, H., Labor and Monopoly Capital, (London, 1974)

Bullen, A., The Lancashire Weavers' Union, (Rochdale, 1984)

Bullen, A. and Fowler, A., The Cardroom Workers' Union, (Rochdale, 1986)

Burgess, K., The Origins of British Industrial Relations, (London, 1975)

Burrows, H., History of the Rag Trade, (London, 1956)

Busfield, D., 'Tailoring the Millions: Women Workers in the Leeds Clothing Industry, 1880-1914', Textile History, 16, 1986

Busfield, D., 'Sex and Skill in the West Riding: Women's Employment in Yorkshire, 1850-1914', (Ph.D., University of York, 1986)

Butt, J. and Ponting, K. (eds.), Scottish Textile History, (Aberdeen, 1987)

Clapham, J.H., The Woollen and Worsted Industries, (London, 1907)

Clarke, A., The Effects of the Factory System, (London, 1899; Reprint, Littleborough, 1986)

Clegg, H.A., A History of British Trade Unions since 1889, Vol. II, 1911-33, (Oxford, 1985)

Clegg, H.A, Fox, A. and Thompson, A.F., A History of British Trade Unions since 1889, (Oxford, 1964)

Coleman, D.C., Courtaulds, An Economic History, Vol. II, (Oxford, 1969)

Davies, S., A History of Macclesfield, (Manchester 1961)

Drake, B., Women in Trade Unions, (London, 1920)

Dutton, H.I. and King, J.E., Ten Per Cent and No Surrender, (Cambridge, 1981)

Dutton, H.I. and King, J.E., 'The Limits of Paternalism: the Cotton Tyrants of North Lancashire, 1836-54', Social History, 7, 1982

Select Bibliography

Dyson, R.F., 'The Development of Collective Bargaining in the Cotton Spinning Industry, 1893-1914', (Ph.D. thesis, University of Leeds, 1971)

Farnie, D.A., The English Cotton Industry and the World Market, (London, 1979)

Firth, G., 'The Bradford Trade in the Nineteenth Century' in Wright, D.G and Jowitt, J.A., Victorian Bradford, (Bradford, 1982)

Fowler, A., 'Trade Unions and Technical Change: The Automatic Loom Strike, 1908', North West Labour History Society Bulletin, No. 6, 1979-80

Fowler, A. and L., The History of the Nelson Weavers' Association, (Nelson, 1984)

Fowler, A. and Wyke, T. (eds.), The Barefoot Aristocrats, (Littleborough, 1987)

Fraser, W. Hamish, 'The Glasgow Cotton Spinners, 1837' in Butt, J. and Ward, J.T. (eds.), Scottish Themes, (Edinburgh, 1976)

Friefeld, M., 'Technical Change and the Self Acting Mule: A Case Study of Skill and the Sexual Division of Labour', Social History, 11, 1986

Gee, N., Shoddy and Mungo Manufacture, (Manchester, 1950)

Gordon, E., 'Women, Work and Collective Action: Dundee Jute Workers, 1870-1906', Journal of Social History, Fall, 1987

Gospel, H.F. and Littler, C.R. (eds.), Managerial Strategies and Industrial Relations: An Historical and Comparative Study, (London, 1983)

Gray, E.M., The Weavers' Wage, (Manchester, 1936)

Hard, A., The Story of Rayon, (London, 1939)

Heaton, H., The Yorkshire Woollen and Worsted Industries, (Oxford, 1920)

Henderson, H.D., The Cotton Control Board, (Oxford, 1922)

Hopwood, E., The Lancashire Weavers Story, (Manchester, 1969)

Howe, A., The Cotton Masters 1830-60, (Oxford, 1984)

James, J., A History of the Worsted Manufacture in England, (London, 1857)

Jenkins, D.T. and Ponting, K.G., The British Wool Textile Industry 1770-1914, (London, 1982)

Jenkins, J.G. (ed.), The Wool Textile Industry in Great Britain, (London, 1972)

Jewkes, J. and Gray, E.M., Wages and Labour in the Lancashire Cotton Spinning Industry, (Manchester, 1935)

Jones, H., 'Employers' Welfare Schemes and Industrial Relations in Inter-War Britain', Business History, XXV, 1983

Jones, S.G., Workers at Play: A Social and Economic History of Leisure 1918-1939, (London, 1986)

Jones, S.G., 'The Lancashire Cotton Industry and the Development of Paid Holidays in the 1930s', Transactions of the Historic Society of Lancashire and Cheshire, CXXV, 1986

Jowitt, J.A. (ed.), Model Industrial Communities in Mid-Nineteenth Century Yorkshire, (Bradford, 1986)

Jowitt, J.A. and Laybourn, K., 'The Wool Textile Dispute of 1925', Journal of Local Studies, II, 1, 1982

Select Bibliography

Jowitt, J.A. and Taylor, R., Bradford, 1890-1914, (Bradford, 1980)

Joyce, P., Work, Society and Politics: The Culture of the Factory in Later Victorian England, (London, 1980)

Jubb, S., The History of the Shoddy Trade, (Batley, 1860)

Kirby, M.W., 'The Lancashire Cotton Industry in the Inter-War Years: A Study in Organisational Change', Business History, XVI, 2, 1974

Kirk, N., The Growth of Working Class Reformism in Mid-Victorian England, (London, 1985)

Lambertz, J., 'Sexual Harassment in the Nineteenth Century English Cotton Industry', History Workshop, 19, 1985

Lazonick, W., 'Industrial Relations and Technical Change: The Case of the Self Acting Mule', Cambridge Journal of Economics, No. 3, 1979

Lazonick, W., 'Industrial Organisation and Technological Change: The Decline of the British Cotton Industry', Business History Review, LVII, 1983

Lazonick, W., 'The Cotton Industry', in Elbaum, B. and Lazonick, W. (eds.), The Decline of the British Economy, (Oxford, 1986)

Lee, C.H., 'The Cotton Textile Industry', in Church, R. (ed.), The Dynamics of Victorian Business, (London, 1980)

Lewis, J., Women in England, 1870-1950, (Brighton, 1984)

Liddington, J. and Norris, J., One Hand Tied Behind Us, (London, 1978)

Lipson, E., The History of the Woollen and Worsted Industry, (London, 1921)

Longworth J., The Oldham Master Cotton Spinners' Association Ltd., 1866-1966, (Oldham, 1966)

McIvor, A.J., 'Employers' Organisations and Industrial Relations in Lancashire, 1890-1939', (Ph.D. thesis, 1983, Manchester University)

McIvor, A.J., 'Employers' Organisation and Strikebreaking in Britain, 1880-1914', International Review of Social History, XXIX, 1, 1984,

Norris, J., 'Gender and Class in Industry and the Home. Women Silk Workers in Macclesfield, 1919-1939', (M.A. Thesis, Keele, 1985)

Norris, J., The Last Handloom Weavers, (Macclesfield, 1984)

Porter, J.H., 'Cotton and Wool Textiles' in Buxton, N.K. and Aldcroft, D.H. (eds.), British Industry between the Wars, (London, 1979)

Roberts, E., A Woman's Place, (Oxford, 1984)

Sandberg, L.G., Lancashire in Decline, (Columbus, Ohio, 1974)

Savage, M., 'Capitalist and Patriarchal Relations at Work: Preston Cotton Weaving, 1890-1940', ch. 10 in Murgatroyd, L., Savage, M., Shapiro, D., Urry, J., Walby, S. and Warde, A., Localities, Class and Gender, (London, 1985)

Savage, M., The Dynamics of Working Class Politics: The Labour Movement in Preston, 1900-1940, (forthcoming, Cambridge, 1987-8)

Sigsworth, E.M., Black Dyke Mills, (Liverpool, 1958)

Select Bibliography

Sigsworth, E.M. and Blackman, J.M. 'The Woollen and Worsted Industries', in Aldcroft, D.H., The Development of British Industry and Foreign Competition, 1875-1914, (London, 1968)

Turnbull, G., A History of the Calico Printing Industry in Great Britain, (Altrincham, 1951)

Turner, B., The History of the General Union of Textile Workers, (Heckmondwike, 1920)

Turner, B., About Myself, (London, 1930)

Turner, H.A., Trade Union Growth, Structure, and Policy, (London, 1962)

Walker, W., Juteopolis, (Edinburgh, 1979)

Webb, S. and B., A History of British Trade Unionism, (London, 1920)

White, J.L., The Limits of Trade Union Militancy, (Westport, U.S.A., 1978)

Wood, G.H., The History of Wages in the Cotton Trade During the Past Hundred Years, (Manchester, 1910)

Wright, D.G. and Jowitt, J.A., Victorian Bradford, (Bradford, 1982)

Wrigley, C.J., A History of British Industrial Relations, 1875-1914, (Brighton, 1982)

Wrigley, C.J., A History of British Industrial Relations, Vol. II, 1914-1939, (Brighton, 1986)

Zeitlin, J., 'From Labour History to the History of Industrial Relations', Economic History Review, XL, 2, 1987

NOTES ON CONTRIBUTORS

MARIA BOTTOMLEY is a school teacher in Bradford. She graduated with a B.A. in History from Birmingham, where in an undergraduate dissertation she first combined an academic interest in the textile industry in Batley with personal experience through family work in the mills.

ANDREW BULLEN, M.A. (Warwick) has been a lecturer in History at Salford University, U.M.I.S.T., Manchester Polytechnic and Southport College of Technology, and has been employed to research a number of textile history projects, including the history of the cotton spinners' union. He is the author of The Lancashire Weavers' Union (1984), co-author with A. Fowler of The Cardroom Workers' Union (1986) and has a Ph.D. in progress.

DEIRDRE BUSFIELD teaches History part-time at the University of York and has been a Research Assistant in the Department of Economics. Her Ph.D. (York, 1986) examines women's employment and the sexual division of labour in the West Riding before 1914 and she has published in Textile History.

ALAN FOWLER is a Principal Lecturer in Economic History at Manchester Polytechnic. He has published widely on the history of trade unions in cotton textiles and is co-author with L. Fowler of The History of the Nelson Weavers' Association (1984), with A. Bullen of The Cardroom Workers' Union (1986) and co-editor with T. Wyke of The Barefoot Aristocrats (1987).

STEVE JONES, B.A., Ph.D., was a Lecturer in Economic History at Manchester Polytechnic. He has published extensively on labour history and leisure and contributed numerous articles to journals including the Historical Journal, Journal of Contemporary History and the International Review of Social History. He is author of Workers at Play: A Social and Economic History (1986) and The British Labour Movement and Film, 1918-1939 (1987).

Notes on Contributors

TONY JOWITT, B.Sc., M.Phil. is Warden of the Bradford Centre of the Department of Adult and Continuing Education of the University of Leeds. He is the editor of Model Industrial Communities in Mid-Nineteenth Century Yorkshire (1986), co-editor with D.G. Wright of Victorian Bradford (1982) and has published a number of articles on regional history and recent regional economic policy. He is currently writing a book on the comparative history of British and American textile communities.

IRENE MAGRATH is a Tutor-Organiser for the Workers' Educational Association in Cardiff. She has taught Economic History part-time at Hull University and is currently in the final stages of writing up her Ph.D. on the history of employers' organisations in Wool Textiles between 1914 and 1939.

ARTHUR McIVOR is a Lecturer in Economic and Social History at the University of Strathclyde. His Ph.D. (Manchester, 1983) examines the history of employers' organisations and industrial relations in North-West England, 1890-1939. He has contributed to The Dictionary of Business Biography and published articles in the International Review of Social History, Medical History and the Society for the Study of Labour History Bulletin.

JILL NORRIS was a Lecturer in Sociology at the University of Manchester and previously Senior Research Officer at the Silk Museum, Macclesfield. Her M.A. thesis (Keele, 1985) examines the experience of working class women in the home and in employment in Macclesfield between 1919 and 1939. She has published extensively on women's history and is the author of The Last Handloom Weavers (1984) and co-author with Jill Liddington of One Hand Tied Behind Us (1978).

MICHAEL SAVAGE is a Research Fellow in Urban Studies at the University of Sussex. He has written in Capital and Class and is joint editor of Localities, Class and Gender (1985). He has recently revised his Ph.D. (Lancaster, 1984) into a book, The Dynamics of Working Class Politics: The Labour Movement in Preston, 1900-1940, which is being published by Cambridge University Press.

INDEX

Amalgamated Cotton Mills Trust, 67, 71
apprenticeship, see women
arbitration, 55, 58, 60, 119
Ashton, 4, 16, 211
Ashton Brothers, Hyde, 67, 69, 71, 73, 77

bad materials, 114
bad spinning, 13
Batley, xi, xvi, 45, 172-3, 175, 177-81
Batley Reporter, 180
Blackburn, vii, 7, 9, 14, 17, 19, 28-9, 31-2, 35-6, 68, 116, 206, 211-12
blacklegs, 8, 11, 15, 27, 38, 100, 139-40, 147
blacklisting, 15, 85, 98-9
bleachers, see labour, trade unions
Bleachers and Dyers Mutual Indemnity Co., 134-5
Bleachers' Association Ltd, 128
Bolton, ix, 4, 12, 16, 34, 68, 117, 128, 136, 138, 206, 210-12, 215, 219-20
Bolton Journal, 139
Bondfield, Margaret, 116
Bradford, vii, x, xi, 85
  employers in, 44-61, 85-7
  employment, xi
  mills, vii, 86, 90-1

population, viii
trade, 94-5
trade unions, 100
wages, 156
Bradford Dyers' Association Ltd, 46, 91, 99, 128
Bradford Manufacturers' Association, 47-8, 52-7
British Wool Federation, 52-3, 60
Brooklands, 9-11, 13, 18, 117, 133
Burnley, 7, 9, 17, 27-8, 32, 35, 112, 206-7, 211-2, 216

calico printers, 130-1, see also trade unions
Calico Printers' Association, 129, 131-3, 141, 146
cardroom workers, see labour, trade unions, women, work
Chew, Ada Nield, 145
Chorley, x, 12
closed shop, 12-3, 40
collective bargaining
  breakdown, 17-8
  Brooklands, 9-11, 13, 18, 133
  Conciliation Board, 141-2, 147
  Conciliation Committee, 18, 119
  cotton, xiv, 20, 91, 110
  decentralised, 147

Index

employers' associations, 8-11, 91
  implications of, 10-11
  Joint Industrial Council (wool), 50, 52-4, 57, 61, 102
  Midland Hotel Agreement, 15, 18
  Morris Court, 54, 56-7
  origins of, 27-40
  procedure, 9
  suspension, 17-18
  women and, 145
  wool and worsted, 85, 91
Common Cause, 197, 198
competition, 7, 9, 46, 60, 91, 103, 156, 218
cotton,
  decline of, 65, 111
  employment in, viii, ix, xi, 29, 65, 111, 207
  exports, 65, 111
  finishing, 127-48
  geography, ix
  industrial structure, ix, 7, 65-6, 107
  labour costs, 31
  machine capacity, x, 29, 65
  markets, 29, 129, 217
  mills, xi, 29
  product specialisation, ix-x, 2, 34-5
  production, x, xi, 111
  raw cotton, 114-5
  recapitalisation, 15, 65, 111
  sectionalism, 107
  see also collective bargaining, employers, labour, trade unions, wages, welfarism, work
Cotton Control Board, 6, 110, 114, 117, 119
Cotton Employers' Parliamentary Association, 5
Cotton Factory Times, 68, 122, 140, 215
cotton finishing, 127-48
Cotton Industry Act, 121
Cotton Manufacturing Act, 1934, 112, 119-21
cotton spinners, see labour, trade unions
Cotton Spinners' and Manufacturers' Association, see North and North East Cotton Spinners' and Manufacturers' Association
Cotton Spinners' Association, 4
cotton weavers, see labour, trade unions
Cox, J.C., 175, 177, 178

Daubhill Mills, 210, 213
Dewsbury, x, xvi, 45, 90, 172-3, 175, 179-80, 183
disputes, see strikes
Drew, J.H., 90, 97-8, 102, 182
dyers, see labour, trade unions

Economic League, 15
Ellis, Anne, 174, 176-7, 182-3
employers,
  anti-unionism, 27, 37-8, 213
  cohesion, xiv
  competition between, 35, 46
  disunity, xv, 2, 3, 46
  division, 1, 17, 46, 177, 180-1
  finishing, 132
  prerogative to manage, 2
  price control, 128
  Provisional Emergency Cotton Committee, 16-7
  solidarity, xiv, 1-7
  weakness, West Riding, 91-2
employers' associations, xiv, 1-21, 44-61, 132-4
  Blackburn, 14, 36, 39
  Bleachers' Association Ltd, 128
  Bolton, 16
  Bradford, 44, 46-7
  Bradford Manufacturers' Federation, 47-8
  Burnley, 39
  collective bargaining, 91
  controlling competition, 7, 9
  Cotton Employers' Parliamentary Association, 5
  cotton finishing, 131-4

231

Index

cotton, origins of, 2, 27-40
Cotton Printers' Association, 4
disunity, 2, 3, 12, 15-17, 20-1, 46, 51-60
Economic League, 15
Employers' Federation of Bleachers, 140-1, 143, 146
erosion of, 15-17, 57
Federation of British Industries, 50-1
Federation of Master Cotton Spinners' Associations, 4-7, 9, 11, 12, 14-17, 19, 66, 110, 119
heavy wool, 173-6, 178, 180-1
Home Wool Buyers' Association, 47
Joint Consultative Board of Textile Employers, 48
Lancashire Masters' Defence Association, 28, 35-9
local autonomy, 2-5
machine manning, 17, 58
Master Engravers' Association, 131
membership, 2-6, 8, 48-9
non-members, 7-8
North and North East Lancashire Cotton Spinners' and Manufacturers' Association, 2-3, 7, 13, 17, 39-40, 66, 73, 110
objects, 1-2, 47, 60-1
Oldham, 4-6, 33
Preston, 34, 39
price fixing, 46
response to trade unions, 6-7
sectionalism, 61
Shipping Federation, 8
Society of Master Calico Printers, 131-3, 141
strength, 20
structural limitations, 44-61
trade regulation, 2, 4, 16, 46-7, 51, 55, 57-8
United Cotton Manufacturers' Association, 3
weakness, 4, 60-1, 146

wool, xiv, 44-61
Woolcombing Employers' Federation, 47
Woollen and Worsted Trades' Federation, 48
Wool Textile Delegation, 50-1
Worsted Spinners' Federation, 48
Yorkshire Dyers' Committee, 48
see also employers' strategies, strikebreaking
employers' strategies
bleaching and dyeing, 142
Calico Printers' Association, 134
efficiency offensive, 14-20
in Slump, 14-19, 51-61, 64-77, 218-9
profit maximisation, 2
recruiting labour, 210-12
World War One, 215
see also strikebreaking, welfarism
employment
cotton, viii, ix, xi, 29, 65, 111, 207
cotton finishing, 127, 129-30
Scotland (cotton), 128
silk, ix, 188-90
wool, vii, ix, xi
worsted, vii, ix, xi
English Sewing Cotton Company, 67-70, 73-4, 77
engravers, see labour
entrepreneur, xiii, 2, 65
exports, 51, 65, 95, 111

Federation of Master Cotton Spinners' Associations, 4-7, 9, 11, 12, 14-17, 19, 66, 110, 119
Fine Cotton Spinners' and Doublers' Association, 67-8, 70, 73, 75
fining, 15, 114-15

Garnett, James, 38
Gee, Alan, 102, 182
General Strike, 1926, xv, 107,

232

Index

115
Glasgow cotton industry, 158
government intervention, xvi, 13, 19, 47-8, 54, 60, 87, 102, 112, 215-16, 119-21
  failure, 1929, 118
  Ministry of Labour, 60, 121
  Ministry of Munitions, 66

Halifax, vii, x, 45, 85, 100, 156
health, industrial
  see work
heavy wool, x, 48, 59, 171-84
Holt, John, 133
Howarth, William, 16, 75
Huddersfield, x, xi, 45, 93, 100, 156, 162-3, 177, 182
Hunt, H.M., 175, 178-9
Hunter, Graeme, 139-40
Hyde, Robert, 66

Illingworth, Percy Holden, 96
industrial health
  see work
industrial militancy
  and women, 171-84, 199-200
  see strikes
industrial relations, xv, 1, 115, 138-40, 142-3, 148
  origins of system, 27-40
  see collective bargaining
Industrial Revolution, viii, 158
Industrial Welfare Society, 66-7

joiner-minding, 18
Joint Committee of Cotton Trade Organisations, 19
Joint Industrial Council (Wool), 50, 52-3, 57-61, 102
Jowett, Fred, 101
juveniles,
  see labour

Kay, Robert, 142
Keighley, x, 45, 85, 100

labour
  adolescent workers, xv, 85, 90-1

aristocracy, xii, 108
bleachers, xv, 127-8, 130-1, 134-143
blowing room, 208
calico printers, 127-8, 130-1
carder, 208
cardroom, xvi, 109, 207-8
child labour, 109
cotton finishing, 127-48
cotton spinners, xvi, 87, 108, 122-3
craft artisans, xv, 88, 131-4
dyers, xv, 127-8, 130-1, 134-143
engravers, 131
fine spinning, 113
half-timers, 91, 109, 110, 160-1
jobbers, 14
juveniles, 45, 57, 86-7, 108, 132, 135
market, xvi, 137, 14, 203-20
mule spinning, 157-9
overlookers, xvi, 14, 45, 55, 57, 60, 85, 93-4, 102, 155, 158-9, 180, 195, 205, 208-12, 215-6, 218
piecers, 108, 122, 215
recruitment, 207-212
ring spinners, 18
Royal Commission on Labour, 98, 108, 162
sectionalism, 93, 102
shortages, 133
spatial pattern, 206
strippers and grinders, 18, 109, 123, 208
tapers, 14
tenters, 208-9
tuners, 180, 183
twisters, 60
weavers, 209, 211, 213-20
winders, 208
wool and worsted weaving, 45, 86, 98
woolcombers, 60, 93, 95, 99, 163
woolsorters, 87, 93, 155-6, 159, 162
Labour Exchanges, 133, 215-6

233

Index

Leeds, x, 59, 156
Lever Bank Mill, Bolton, 143
Lister, Samuel Cunliffe, 101
lock-outs, 4, 8, 11-12, 27-8, 38, 53
   Annual Report on Strikes and Lock-Outs, 132
   Brooklands, 9, 117
   Calder Vale, 1929, 60
   cotton, 1878, 117
   cotton weaving, 1912, 12
   engineering, 1852, 2
   heavy wool, 1875, 173-84
   more looms, 1930-1, 17
   Neckwear Ltd., silk manufacturers, 1930, 199-200
   Preston, 1853, 27-9, 32, 210-11
   propensity, 15
   Stalybridge, 9
   threat, 139

Macara, Charles, 5, 9, 11, 16
MacArthur, Mary, 145
Macclesfield, ix, xvi, 187-201
Manchester, ix, 12, 31, 35, 117, 128, 206
Mass Observation, 208, 213, 216
Mawdsley, James, 108
mechanisation, vii, 17-8, 86-7, 128, 156, 205
   see also technology, work
Midland Hotel Agreement, 15, 18
model industrial villages, xiv, 96
more looms system, xvi, 17-19, 26, 65, 75, 112-13, 115-16, 121, 123, 218-19
Morning Chronicle, 190, 195, 198
Morris Court, 54, 56-7
mule spinning, 157-9
Musgrave Spinning Co., 70, 73

National Government, 120-1
Nelson, x, 13, 116, 123, 207, 211
North and North East Cotton Spinners' and Manufacturers' Association, 2-3, 7, 13, 17, 39-40, 66, 73, 110

Oldham, viii, ix, xii, 4-5, 6, 13, 16, 34, 68, 116, 123, 206
output, ix, x, 45, 69
overlookers,
   see labour
Owen, Robert, xiii

Padiham, 27-9, 37
paternalism, xii, xiv, 2, 7, 15, 27, 73-4, 85, 96-7, 210-11
patriarchy, xv, xvi, 96, 165-6, 203-4
piecers
   see labour
Preston, x, 7, 9, 17, 27-8, 35, 204, 206, 207, 210-11, 212, 215, 219-20
product markets, 15, 29, 35, 129

recapitalisation, 1919-20, 15, 65, 111-12, 118
Ripley, Hugh, 97

Scottish textiles, xiii, xvii, 158
sexual division of labour,
   cotton, 18, 116, 203-4, 206-7, 211
   cotton finishing, 131, 143-6
   employers and, 162-3
   silk, 191-3
   trade unions and, 161-2
   wool and worsted, 153-66
   World War One, 215
   see also skill, women
Shackleton, H.B., 48, 52, 56, 58
silk, xiii, ix
   decline, 189
   employment in, 188-90
   geography, ix
   industrial development, 188
   trade unionism, 192, 199
   women in, xvi, 187-201
skill,
   acquisition, 204, 207-12
   cotton, 204-7

Index

Crompton's mule and, 157-8
definition, 154, 204-5
de-skilling, 87, 161-2, 217
female exclusion from, 161-2
fine cotton, 206
genuine and socially constructed, 154-5, 159, 162, 164-6, 194-5, 204
heavy wool, 181-2
the jenny and, 157
label, 164-6
mechanisation and, 205
sexual division of labour and, 153-66
shortages, 216-17, 219
silk, 191-4, 200
social destruction of, 159, 194-5
spinning, 156-7
transmission, 208-9
undervaluation, xvi
the water frame and, 157
weaving, 108, 211
women and, xv, 90, 143, 153-66, 204-5, 207-12
working class stratification and, 153
Slater and Co., Bolton, 143
Smalley, Alfred, 142
social control, 72-6
socialisation of cotton, 119
Society of Master Calico Printers, 131-3, 141
speed-up
  see work
Spindles Act, 1936, 121
spinning,
  see labour, skill, work
Stockport, 27-8, 128
strikebreaking, 8, 11-13, 139-40, 219
strike insurance, 5, 11-12, 28
strikes,
  Annual Report on Strikes and Lock-Outs, 132, 139-40
  bleaching, 1907, 140
  bleaching and dyeing, 138-41
  Bradford, 1825, 87
  Bradford dyers, 1880, 100
  Carrbrook Printworks, 139-40
  Colne, 1860-1, 28-9
  cotton, 1878, 7, 12; 1913,
13; 1919, 72-3; 1930-2, 17
Dewsbury, 1870s, 90, 100
engravers, 1913, 131
general strike, 115, 117
Great Harwood, 1858, 27-8
heavy wool, 1875, xvi, 171-84
Hepburn and Co., Bleachworks, Ramsbottom, 1892, 139
leadership by women, 1875, 173-84
Littleborough dyers, 1914, 141
Manningham Mills, Bradford, 100-1
Oldham, 1914-19, 13
Padiham, 1859, 27-9
Stockport, 28-9
Sumner's Mill Hill Bleachworks, Bolton, 1893, 139
United Turkey Red Co., 1911, 144
warp twisters, 90
wave of, 1910-14, 142
wildcat, 216
wool, 1925, 53-5
woolcombers, 99
see also General Strike
strippers and grinders
  see labour
Sturdee, Reverend Edwin, 187, 197
syndicalism, 142

Tattersall, John, 5
technology
  cardroom, 10, 18
  cotton, 65, 70-1, 112-14, 205, 220
  finishing, 130, 133
  weaving, 31
  wool, 95, 157, 173
  see also mechanisation
Textile Mercury, 8, 67, 73
Tootal Broadhurst, 67, 69, 71, 72, 75, 210
trade unions
  Amalgamated Association of Cardroom, Blowing and Ring Room Operatives, 109, 118, 122, 212
  Amalgamated Association of

235

Index

Operative Cotton Spinners, 11, 108, 118, 122, 213-14
Amalgamated Association of Weavers, 108, 112, 122, 213-14
Amalgamated Society of Dyers, 99, 102, 130, 137, 145
Amalgamated Society of Textile Workers and Kindred Trades, 199
Amalgamated Union of Engravers to Calico Printers, 137
Amicable and Brotherly Society of Machine Printers, 132, 137, 145
Blackburn Weavers' Association, 28, 33, 36, 39-40
Bradford and District Machine Woolcombers, 99, 102
Bradford and District Warp Dressers, 93, 99
Bradford Woolsorters' Society, 93, 102
cotton, 107-23, 212-5
cotton finishing, 127-48
cotton weaving, 29, 32, 36-7, 212-14
Dewsbury, Batley and Surrounding Districts Heavy Woollen Weavers' Association, 182
and employers' associations, 6-7
First Amalgamation (weavers), 28, 34, 36-40
fragmentation (finishing), 137-8
General Union of Textile Workers, 89, 93, 98, 99-100, 102, 182-3
general unionism, 99-100
Huddersfield Warpers' Association, 93
independent labour politics and, 87, 100-2
industrial unions, 99, 117, 138
junior management role, 33
Macclesfield Power Loom Silk Weavers' Association, 199
male dominance, xvi, 213
membership, 28, 39, 84-5, 88-9, 99, 102, 108-9, 110, 117, 122, 132-3, 136-9, 142, 212
moderation of, 30
National Association of Unions in Textile Trades, 51, 53, 58, 102
National Federation of Bleachers, Dyers and Kindred Trades, 138
National Silk Workers' Association, 192, 199
National Society of Dyers and Finishers, 137
National Union of Women Workers, 175, 178-9, 182
National Union of Woolsorters, 92, 102
North East Lancashire Power Loom Weavers' Association, 28
Oldham Operative Spinners' Association, 6
Operative Bleachers and Dyers (Bolton Amalgamation), 134-5, 137-8, 139, 140-2, 145
overlookers against, 93
recognition, 9-10, 27, 29, 33, 141-2, 144
retardation in wool, 84-103
rural and urban, 211
Second Amalgamation (weavers), 39-40
sectionalism, 118
silk, 192, 199
South East Lancashire Power Loom Weavers' Association, 29
Twisters and Warp Dressers, 99
United Factory Operatives' Association, 29
weakness, bleaching and dyeing, 136. 138
weakness, silk, 199
weakness, wool and worsted, 84-5, 171
welfarism and, 74-5
women in, xv, 84-5, 89-90,

236

Index

102, 108-9, 145, 156, 161-2, 164, 166, 171-2, 174-5, 178-9, 182-3, 192, 199-200, 204, 209, 212-15
Women's Trade Union League, 145
wool, 45, 51, 59
Woollen Operatives' Union, 178
worsted, 84-103
Yeadon and Guiseley Factory Workers' Union, 99
Yorkshire Federation of Power Loom Overlookers, 102
Yorkshire Warp Twisters, 90
young workers and, 90-1
Turner, Ben, 89, 100, 102, 182

unemployment
  cotton, xi, 120, 122, 216-17
  labour exchanges, 133
  more looms system, 115-16
  pay, 114
  welfarism, 69, 75
  wool, xi, xvi
  worsted, 98
United Cotton Manufacturers' Association, 3
United Turkey Red Company, 128
USA textiles, xi-xii, 19

victimisation, 8, 11, 15, 98-9, 137, 138, 140, 183

wages,
  Blackburn list, 28, 32-4, 38, 117
  blue tariff, 176, 178, 180-1
  bonus-on-production, 52, 60
  Census of, 1886, 1906, 98, 131, 143, 214
  cotton, 108-9, 122
  cotton finishing, 131-3, 136, 141
  differentials, 214-15
  dispute on heavy wool, 173-84
  family wage, 108, 116, 123, 162
  freeze, 1910-15, 12
  interwar erosion of, 122
  low, in worsted, 97-8
  male labourers, 144
  minimum, 141
  monthly pays, 138
  more looms system and, 112
  non-payment for stock, 138-9
  Oldham lists, 7, 9
  overlookers, 210
  piecework, 132-3, 144
  piecework wage lists, 9, 14, 30-4, 110, 213-14
  real wages, 112, 114
  reductions, 12, 14, 52-3, 55-60, 75, 111-12, 115, 120, 123, 139, 173
  silk, 193-5
  skilled male workers, 153
  sliding scale, 9
  South East Lancashire, 34, 38
  standardisation, lack of, 136
  time (bleaching), 136
  undercutting, 31, 113
  undervaluation by sex, xvi, 90
  uniformity, lack of (wool), 85, 91
  uniformity, lack of (cotton finishing), 147-8
  Uniform Wage List, 1892, 9, 12, 14, 19, 38-9, 110, 112, 213-14
  weaving cloth, 211, 213-14
  wool, 52-3, 55-60, 123
  worsted, 90, 91, 93, 95
Wakefield, 59
warpers, 93
weavers
  see labour, trade unions, women, work
welfarism, 64-83
  Blackburn, 68
  Bolton, 68, 216
  class consensus and, 74-5, 77
  cotton, 64-77
  education, 64, 67
  football, 70-1, 75
  health, 64, 67, 69, 75, 77
  Hyde, Robert, 66
  Industrial Welfare Society, 66-7

Index

labour discipline and efficiency, 64, 69, 72, 77
mill recreation, 69-72, 74, 76
Oldham, 68
other companies, 71
paid holidays, 64, 69-70, 74
and paternalism, 73-4
pensions, 64, 67
philanthropic motives, 69, 72, 77
profit sharing, 64, 67
proliferation of, 1920s, 67-8, 76
purpose of, 64, 69
recreational facilities, 64, 67
social control, 72-7
state of trade and, 68-9, 71-2, 76
trade unionism and, 74-5, 76
Whetley Mills, Bradford, 87, 90, 92
Whittle, Edward, 28, 33, 38
women and girls,
apprenticeship, 154-5, 159-60, 161-2, 166, 194, 210
authority and, 159, 165, 195-6, 220
burling, 143-4, 155, 160
cardroom, 205
collective action, 171-84, 209, 216, 220
collective bargaining, 145
cotton, xvi, 108-9, 115, 203-20
cotton finishing, 136, 143-6
discrimination, xvi, 102, 145, 147, 219
domestic service, 200
double burden, 197-200
earnings, 153, 171, 211
education, 161
employers and, 162-3, 165
Executive Committee (heavy wool), 174, 176-7, 179-83
family and, 165, 171, 184
heavy wool, 171-84
identification with product, 196-7
image of, 187-8, 190, 196-8, 200

industrial militancy, 171-84, 199-200, 209
in labour market, 173
long hours, 154
low status, 195-6
machine minding, 191, 193, 205
married, xvi, 90, 102, 116, 162-3, 171, 197-8, 200, 208-10, 218
mending, 143-4, 155-6, 159, 160
militant, 144
mule spinning and, 158-9, 161-2
National Union of Women Workers, 175, 178-9
occupations (silk), 192
oral testimony, 198-9
political activism, 203-4, 215
productivity, 163
ring spinners, 209
routine operations, 208
sewing, 153, 155, 166
silk, 144-5, 187-201
skill and, xv, 90, 143, 153-66, 204-5, 207-212
strength, 157-9
strike leaders 173-84
subordination, xvi, 144, 146, 165, 203
tambouring, 143-4
training, 153-6, 159-60, 166, 193, 208
undervaluation, xvi, 102, 143, 147, 159, 166
unemployment, 218-9
unskilled, 153, 162, 164, 166
wages, low, 143-6, 153, 156-7, 162, 175, 194, 199-200
weavers, 121, 155, 162, 173-4, 208-10
winders, 208-10
Women's Trade Union League, 145
wool spinning, 156-9
worsted, xv, 89-90, 98, 144-5
see also sexual division of labour, trade unions, work

Index

Wood, G.H., 50, 93
Wood, Hannah, 174, 176-7, 179-80, 183-4
wool, viii, ix, xi, xv, 45-6, 51-2, 56, 172
  heavy, 171-84
  see also collective bargaining, employers' associations labour, strikes, trade unions, wages, women
Wool and Allied Textile Employers' Council, 50, 52-5, 57-60
Woollen and Worsted Trades Federation, 48, 50, 56-9
Woolcombers,
  see labour, trade unions
Woolcombing Employers, 47, 52-3, 55, 60
Woolsorters,
  see labour, trade unions
Woolspinners,
  see labour
woolweavers
  see labour, trade unions
work,
  absenteeism, 208
  accidents, 134-5
  batch production, 205
  cardroom, 207-8
  conditions, 95, 134-43, 187-8, 195-6, 199
  control, 212
  craft control over, 131-4
  division of labour, 18, 191, 218
  Factory Inspectorate, 134-5
  favouritism, 141
  heavy wool, 181-3
  hours, 72-3, 110, 112, 115, 131, 134
  industrial health, 15, 131, 134-6, 147, 187, 195-6
  intensification, 14, 18, 108, 115-16, 144
  job hierarchy, 208
  joiner-minding, 18
  manning, 14, 18-19, 65, 94, 97, 112, 154, 206
  nightwork, 133, 141, 163
  overtime, 133-4, 141
  political activism and, 203-4
  processes, 130, 134, 191-3, 205-6
  promotion, 208-10, 213
  rationalisation, xvi, 65, 132-3
  scientific management, 18
  silk, 191-3
  speed-up, 9, 14, 97, 108, 134, 158, 218
  spinning, 136, 205
  stratification, 153-4
  sub-contract, 94
  sweating, 97-8, 121-2
  weaving, 136, 205, 208-9
  winding, 208-9
  women and, 171, 203-20
  see also labour, more looms system, sexual division of labour, wages, women
working class radicalism, 87, 100-2
worsted, xv, 44-6, 51-2, 56, 59, 85-6, 91-5
  see also collective bargaining, employers' associations, labour, trade unions, wages, women
Worsted Acts, 86
Worsted Spinners' Federation, 48, 55, 59

Yorkshire Factory Times, 93, 97, 98, 101, 171

For Product Safety Concerns and Information please contact our EU representative GPSR@taylorandfrancis.com
Taylor & Francis Verlag GmbH, Kaufingerstraße 24, 80331 München, Germany